Donna Musialowski Ashcraft, PhD
Editor

Women's Work
A Survey of Scholarship
By and About Women

Pre-publication
REVIEW

"This book is a helpful addition to the resources available to faculty teaching an introductory women's studies course. Instead of the more common topical approach, this edited book takes a disciplinary approach, that is, it presents a summary of how a variety of disciplines address women's issues and work by women. The breadth of disciplines sampled (from the arts to the sciences) is a strength of this book, as is its student-friendly inclusion of key terms and discussion questions. Faculty interested in how different disciplines deal with women should also welcome this book's cogent summaries of key issues and works."

Susan A. Basow, PhD
Charles A. Dana Professor
and Head of Psychology,
Lafayette College,
Easton, PA

NOTES FOR PROFESSIONAL LIBRARIANS AND LIBRARY USERS

This is an original book title published by Harrington Park Press, an imprint of The Haworth Press, Inc. Unless otherwise noted in specific chapters with attribution, materials in this book have not been previously published elsewhere in any format or language.

CONSERVATION AND PRESERVATION NOTES

All books published by The Haworth Press, Inc. and its imprints are printed on certified ph neutral, acid free book grade paper. This paper meets the minimum requirements of American National Standard for Information Sciences–Permanence of Paper for Printed Material, ANSI Z39.48-1984.

Women's Work
A Survey of Scholarship
By and About Women

HAWORTH Innovations in Feminist Studies
J. Dianne Garner, DSW
Senior Editor

New, Recent, and Forthcoming Titles:

Prisoners of Ritual: An Odyssey into Female Genital Circumcision in Africa by Hanny Lightfoot-Klein

Foundations for a Feminist Restructuring of the Academic Disciplines edited by Michele Paludi and Gertrude A. Steuernagel

Hippocrates' Handmaidens: Women Married to Physicians by Esther Nitzberg

Waiting: A Diary of Loss and Hope in Pregnancy by Ellen Judith Reich

God's Country: A Case Against Theocracy by Sandy Rapp

Women and Aging: Celebrating Ourselves by Ruth Raymond Thone

Women's Conflicts About Eating and Sexuality: The Relationship Between Food and Sex by Rosalyn M. Meadow and Lillie Weiss

A Woman's Odyssey into Africa: Tracks Across a Life by Hanny Lightfoot-Klein

Anorexia Nervosa and Recovery: A Hunger for Meaning by Karen Way

Women Murdered by the Men They Loved by Constance A. Bean

Reproductive Hazards in the Workplace: Mending Jobs, Managing Pregnancies by Regina Kenen

Our Choices: Women's Personal Decisions About Abortion by Sumi Hoshiko

Tending Inner Gardens: The Healing Art of Feminist Psychotherapy by Lesley Irene Shore

The Way of the Woman Writer by Janet Lynn Roseman

Racism in the Lives of Women: Testimony, Theory, and Guides to Anti-Racist Practice by Jeanne Adleman and Gloria Enguídanos

Advocating for Self: Women's Decisions Concerning Contraception by Peggy Matteson

Feminist Visions of Gender Similarities and Differences by Meredith M. Kimball

Experiencing Abortion: A Weaving of Women's Words by Eve Kushner

Menopause, Me and You: The Sound of Women Pausing by Ann M. Voda

Fat—A Fate Worse Than Death?: Women, Weight, and Appearance by Ruth Raymond Thone

Feminist Theories and Feminist Psychotherapies: Origins, Themes, and Variations by Carolyn Zerbe Enns

Celebrating the Lives of Jewish Women: Patterns in a Feminist Sampler edited by Rachel Josefowitz Siegel and Ellen Cole

Women and AIDS: Negotiating Safer Practices, Care, and Representation edited by Nancy L. Roth and Linda K. Fuller

A Menopausal Memoir: Letters from Another Climate by Anne Herrmann

Women in the Antarctic edited by Esther D. Rothblum, Jacqueline S. Weinstock, and Jessica F. Morris

Breasts: The Women's Perspective on an American Obsession by Carolyn Latteier

Lesbian Step Families: An Ethnography of Love by Janet M. Wright

Women, Families, and Feminist Politics: A Global Exploration by Kate Conway-Turner and Suzanne Cherrin

Women's Work: A Survey of Scholarship By and About Women edited by Donna Musialowski Ashcraft

Women's Work
A Survey of Scholarship
By and About Women

Donna Musialowski Ashcraft, PhD
Editor

Harrington Park Press
An Imprint of The Haworth Press, Inc.
New York • London

Published by

Harrington Park Press, an imprint of The Haworth Press, Inc., 10 Alice Street, Binghamton, NY 13904-1580

The Haworth Press, Inc., 10 Alice Street, Binghamton, NY 13904-1580

Cover design by Monica L. Seifert.

The Library of Congress has cataloged the hardcover edition of this book as:

Women's work : a survey of scholarship by and about women / Donna Musialowski Ashcraft, editor.
     p. cm.
Includes bibliographical references and index.
ISBN 0-7890-0233-7 (alk. paper).
    1. Women. 2. Feminist theory. 3. Women's studies. I. Ashcraft, Donna Musialowski.
HQ1206.W884 1998
305.4—dc21   98-6170
                                                           CIP

ISBN: 1-56023-909-3 (pbk.)

Dedicated to:
Paul, Sam, Morgan, and Ryan
with much love

CONTENTS

ABOUT THE EDITOR

Donna Musialowski Ashcraft, PhD, is Associate Professor of Psychology at Clarion University in Clarion, Pennsylvania. Dr. Ashcraft's scholarly work has been printed in numerous books and journals, including *Pornography: Recent Research; Interpretations, and Policy Considerations; Journal of College Student Development;* and *Representative Research in Social Psychology.* A prolific presenter at collegiate workshops and conventions, she is a member of several professional organizations, including the American Psychological Association, the American Association of College Women, and the Society for the Scientific Study of Sex. From 1989 to 1991, Dr. Ashcraft served as a member and secretary of the Board of Directors of Stop Abuse for Everyone (an organization especially for battered women), and in 1991 Clarion University awarded her the Clarion University Arts and Sciences Faculty Research Award.

Contributors

Lisa Cosgrove, PhD, is a clinical psychologist in private practice in Natick, Massachusetts, and a lecturer in the Department of Counseling and School Psychology at the University of Massachusetts in Boston, Massachusetts.

Myrna Foster-Kuehn, PhD, is the Chair of, and a Professor in, the Department of Speech Communication and Theater at Clarion University of Pennsylvania in Clarion, Pennsylvania.

Kathryn Graham, PhD, is a Professor in the Department of English at Clarion University of Pennsylvania in Clarion, Pennsylvania. She is also the Chair of the Women's Studies Advisory Committee at Clarion University.

April Katz, MFA, is an Associate Professor in, and past Chair of, the Art Department at Clarion University of Pennsylvania in Clarion, Pennsylvania.

Evonne Jonas Kruger, PhD, is an Assistant Professor in the Department of Business Studies at The Richard Stockton College of New Jersey in Pomona, New Jersey.

Maureen C. McHugh, PhD, is the past Director of Women's Studies, and a Professor in, the Department of Psychology at Indiana University of Pennsylvania in Indiana, Pennsylvania.

Patricia J. Ould, PhD, is the Coordinator of the Honors Program and Associate Professor in the Department of Sociology at Salem State College in Salem, Massachusetts.

Darlene Richardson, PhD, is the Director of Liberal Studies and a Professor in the Geosciences Department at Indiana University of Pennsylvania in Indiana, Pennsylvania.

Martha Ritter, EdD, is a Professor in the Department of Biology at Clarion University of Pennsylvania in Clarion, Pennsylvania.

Jean P. Rumsey, PhD, is an Associate Professor in the Department of Philosophy at Clarion University of Pennsylvania in Clarion, Pennsylvania.

Derek Shanahan, PhD, is an Assistant Professor in the Department of Geography at Millersville University in Millersville, Pennsylvania.

Esther Skirboll, PhD, is an Associate Professor in the Department of Sociology, Anthropology and Social Work at Slippery Rock University in Slippery Rock, Pennsylvania. She is also the President of the Pennsylvania State System of Higher Education Women's Consortium.

Sylvia Stalker, PhD, is the Chair of, and a Professor in, the Department of Education at Clarion University of Pennsylvania in Clarion, Pennsylvania.

Karen Stewart, PhD, is an Associate Professor in the Department of Business Studies at The Richard Stockton College of New Jersey in Pomona, New Jersey.

Preface

This book began even before the university to which I belong implemented a women's studies program. I had been a member of a women's studies committee who had been working together for years on developing a program in women's studies and on writing a proposal for a minor in this field. Part of the proposal was a matter of also developing two new courses to be included as requirements for our women's studies minor. These two courses included a capstone course and an introductory level course. The latter course we eventually called Survey of Women's Studies. A colleague and I collaborated in the development of the survey course. To do this, we got together over lunch and began to discuss what topics should be included in such a course and the arrangement or groupings of these topics.

As we continued this discussion, I became increasingly aware that my perception of what the course should look like was very different from that of my colleague. She was taking a very topical approach to teaching the course, and indeed, many of these topics were issues that I discussed in my Psychology of Women class. I was uncomfortable with this for two reasons: (1) I did not want the survey course to be redundant with my Psychology of Women course, and (2) I thought that a Survey of Women's Studies class should cover a certain amount of introductory information from many different fields so that when students took more advanced courses in these fields they would know what types of topics would be addressed, and indeed, that the exposure to the introductory study of women in these fields would allow students to decide on an informed basis about whether they wanted to take an advanced course in that particular area of women's studies.

I was further disheartened when I examined many of the popular texts for introductory courses in women's studies. They, too, were topic based. Furthermore, I found that while the topics covered in these texts were important, many important disciplines were not included and, therefore, were most likely not discussed in introductory or survey women's studies courses (e.g., Women in Art, Geography, Religion). I was also becoming increasingly aware of how little we women's studies colleagues really knew about each others' fields—even within the realm of women's studies. And so an idea formed in my mind: that what is needed is a book (a text) that allows women's studies scholars and students to understand women's studies within many disciplines. The culmination of this growing awareness is this text, which discusses women within many academic disciplines.

The chapters address women's issues within each discipline and also discuss work conducted by women within each of the fields included. I have attempted to be as complete as possible in my inclusion of various academic disciplines. However, because of size constraints, I have not been able to include every discipline that addresses women's studies. I do not intend to snub those disciplines, nor do I want to leave the reader with the impression that those disciplines that have not been included are not considered important. They certainly are. However, I have opted to incorporate some of the disciplines that have not traditionally been included in other readings and topically oriented texts. Please also note as well that some of the disciplines that have not been described in a whole chapter are incorporated within other disciplines and other chapters. So although they do not receive as much attention as other disciplines, for the most part, they are not totally excluded either.

Thus, the first chapter is an introduction to women's studies and feminist theories, and the second chapter discusses feminist research methods. Chapter 3 addresses women in the sciences; Chapter 4 discusses the biology of women; and Chapter 5 is a discussion of various health issues relevant to women. Other disciplines included in individual chapters are (in order): psychology, sociology, anthropology, geography, business, education, communication, philosophy, religion, literature, and art.

My intention for this book is twofold. First, I want to present a resource so that we all can become familiar with women's studies in various academic disciplines. Second, I suggest the use of this text as a different (and new) way of teaching introductory women's studies courses. I do not imply that this is a better way of teaching the course, but rather a different way, which some people may feel more comfortable with. Just as there are many "feminisms," I believe that there are also many ways to teach feminist courses, in particular introductory women's studies courses. Thus, I hope that many who have been uncomfortable with some feminist pedagogies become comfortable with this one.

Donna M. Ashcraft

Acknowledgments

This book could not have been completed without the help of several people. I wish to first thank the chapter authors for their time and hard work, especially those who volunteered to write chapters with a very short deadline, including Pat Ould and Evonne Kruger. Special thanks also go to Karen Stewart, who gave me a draft of her chapter even before I had a publisher lined up. Her chapter was instrumental in getting a publisher and she was always willing to help when I ran into a crisis, making the extra effort in helping me network with potential authors.

Thanks also go to Paul Ashcraft, not only for his love and support as I completed this project, but also for his expertise on the computer, without which I never would have been able to finish this text. The amount of time he spent on this book seemed to almost equal mine. Thanks also to Sam and Morgan for their patience as I worked on this project.

Finally, I would like to acknowledge Randy Greenberg and the National Museum for Women in the Arts. She was most helpful in acquiring the artwork for Chapter 16, "Women and Art." The National Museum for Women in the Arts is located in Washington, DC, and is the only major museum in the world dedicated to acknowledging and appreciating the work of female artists. The museum not only exhibits the artistic work of women, past and present, but also houses the largest collection on women artists in their library and research center. Certainly, this museum is instrumental in reclaiming women's place in history and today.

Chapter 1

Introduction to Women's Studies and Feminist Theories

Donna M. Ashcraft

WHAT IS WOMEN'S STUDIES?

Women's studies is the field that studies women (e.g., their place in society, their behavior), that studies the accomplishments of women (e.g., the literature they have written, the art they have created), and that studies the world from a different perspective, using sometimes different methods than those typically used (e.g., see Chapter 2 on feminist research methods). The field of women's studies was initiated primarily because society noticed a lack of acknowledgment, and a devaluing, of the work (academic and otherwise) of women. Likewise, a new way of conducting work, thinking about issues, theories, research, and so on, had begun to be formed. With this different perception of women, the field of women's studies was born.

FEMINISM AND FEMINIST THEORY

Defining *feminism* is very difficult. For now, let us define it as believing that women and men are equal and that women should be awarded the same opportunities as men. However, what "equality" means and what we mean by "awarding the same opportunities to women as to men" varies from one feminist theorist to another. For example, some feminists believe that equality means that men and women are essentially the same, that is, that any sex differences that do exist are minimal and most likely caused by society rather than biological factors. Others believe that men and women are not the same. They believe that there are sex differences. However, while society in general has devalued the characteristics, abilities, and tasks of women, these feminists believe that women should be valued in and of themselves; for example, that nurturance and the raising of children is *at least* as important as being the strong, independent bread-winner of a family.

The issue of equality also includes different perceptions of how equality between men and women should be worked toward and this difference in opinion depends upon a person's adherence to a certain feminist theory. Thus, for some theorists, "awarding the same opportunities to women as to men" means that all women should have the same opportunities as all men; for others, it means that these opportunities should be awarded on a hierarchical level. What this latter view means is that not all women are created equal. Some are better at some things than others; for example, some are more creative or artistic than others. Therefore, not everyone should be given a particular opportunity because they may not have the capability to fulfill the obligations of, say, a particular job. More concretely, an example of this view would be believing that not everyone should be able to go to medical school because not everyone has the ability to understand the material that must be learned in medical school in order to be a competent physician. Finally, there are still others who believe that wealth and opportunities should be equally distributed to all. Thus, it should be evident that there are many feminist viewpoints.

What I mean by the term "feminist theory" then, is a mode of thinking, a set of beliefs that influence our ideas about why women are in a subordinate position to that of men and about how to resolve this inequality.

During the course of this chapter, I will briefly describe the main points of the major feminist theories. I am deeply indebted to Judith Evans (1995) for publishing her text titled *Feminist Theory Today: An Introduction to Second-Wave Feminism*, and for clarifying the major feminist schools of thought. I draw heavily on it. I use her division of feminist theory and so will be discussing five schools of thought: liberal feminism, radical feminism, cultural feminism, socialist feminism, and postmodernism.

Liberal Feminism

Early *liberal* (or moderate) *feminists* believed that there are very few sex differences. Those that do exist are minimal, even irrelevant, and are due to socialization rather than differences in anatomy or some other biological factor. Therefore, because women and men are so similar, women should be treated similarly to men. Because there are no sex differences, society cannot maintain discrimination against women. Striving for equality between men and women is justified because men and women are essentially the same.

The type of equality sought by liberal feminists is *equality of opportunity*, as opposed to what Evans calls *equality of condition*. This means that women should be allowed into the same schools as men. They should be allowed to try for the same jobs, promotions, pay raises, contracts, and so on, as men. Liberal feminists are *not* saying that all women should be awarded the same opportunities. They are *not* saying that all women should share equal wealth. Rather, they believe that within society there is a hierarchy and that opportunities should be given to both men and women at each of those levels of the hierarchy. Liberal feminists believe that if there is equality of opportunity, then a certain type of equality of condition will follow. For example, you are probably well aware that even today, there are still some occupations that employ primarily men and others that employ primarily women (Reskin, 1988). You are probably also aware of the concept of the *glass ceiling* (U.S. Department of Labor, 1991). This is the idea that women are allowed to enter certain occupations and advance through promotions to a certain status within such occupations, but very few women enter the highest level, most likely due to discrimination. As an illustration, note that while there are many women in business and even many women in middle management, very few enter the highest levels of management (e.g., U. S. Department of Labor, 1991). Likewise, although there are many women academicians, significantly fewer women than men reach the level of full professor (Keetz, 1991). Liberal feminists believe that these two phenomena will disappear once equality of opportunity is gained.

Thus, what liberal feminists believe will happen once women have gained equality of opportunity is that there will be equal numbers of men and women at each level of the hierarchy. However, a hierarchy of socio-economic status (SES) will still exist; that is, some women will still have a higher status, income, and so on, compared to other women, and the same would be true for men. It would also follow that some men would have a higher SES compared to some women and vice versa. Note that this is different than what was true at the beginning of the women's movement. At that time, most women were not employed outside the home, and those who were earned significantly less than men employed outside the home, even if they were employed within the same profession (e.g., Bernstein, 1988; Larwood, Szwajkowski, and Rose, 1988). For liberal feminists, then, equality of opportunity would certainly help many women. However, early liberal feminists were criticized for this view for two reasons:

1. This view favored middle-class white women and excluded the experiences of minority women and women of lower SES.
2. Some believed that all women should be equal and that there should be only one level of society.

Also, after women began to enter the traditionally masculine work world, some began to experience dissatisfaction. While these early liberal feminists believed that once they gained the same opportunities as men, they would be happy and equality would be achieved, in actuality this was not true. Many of the women who delayed having children to begin careers either regretted not having children or began to realize that their biological clocks were ticking and some experienced difficulty conceiving due to age-related infertility. Others who had children and who had established careers were exhausted from managing the demands of both and began to realize that they could not "have it all" and do all of it well (e.g., Friedan, 1981).

For these reasons, liberal feminism began to change. Whereas early liberal feminists believed that males and females are essentially the same (equal) because any sex differences that do exist are caused by society as opposed to nature (i.e., biology), second-stage liberal feminists began to question the assumption that males and females *are* essentially the same. Thinking evolved such that these later feminists began discussing the possibility that males and females really are different. If one examines the early liberal feminist position, one can see this possibility; they did suggest that some sex differences may exist. It is just that they dismissed them as irrelevant, "not real," because society produced them as opposed to hormones or reproductive structures or brain differences. Thus, if we accept that even sex differences that are produced by society are "real," then one can see this evolution in thinking.

An example of the type of difference that was discussed was the trait of nurturance. Second-stage liberal feminists began to believe that perhaps women really are more nurturant than men. Beyond this, however, second-stage liberal feminists began to suggest that these differences actually make women superior to men, at least in some ways. So for centuries, women were told that their characteristics (femininity) were inferior to the characteristics of men (masculinity), but now these second-stage feminists said just the opposite. Debates ensued, revolving around the issue of whether such traits as nurturance are actually better than such traits as competitiveness.

These second-stage liberal feminists still believed that these sex differences are learned—for example, that girls are taught to be more nurturant than boys while boys are taught to be more competitive and aggressive than girls. This implies, then, that society encourages girls to aspire to be better human beings than boys. The traditional home atmosphere that has kept women in a subordinate position in society for so long may have actually encouraged their growth toward a preferable concern for humanity. By teaching our daughters to be mothers, we have taught them to be more compassionate toward society in general (e.g., Montague, 1992), to be morally superior. However, whereas the early liberal feminists argued that equality of opportunity should be granted to women because men and women were essentially the same, now second-stage liberal feminists believed that equality between men and women should be granted because women are superior to men in some ways. For example, would not the world be a safer place if women were in the positions of authority (such as the President of the United States) instead of men? Since women are more concerned about other people, wouldn't they be less likely to start a nuclear war?

Doesn't this imply that it is men, not women, who should change? This question also focuses on another difference between early and second-stage liberal feminists: whereas early liberal feminists saw nothing wrong with women trying to become more like men, second-stage liberal feminists suggested that perhaps men should become more like women. Note two assumptions about this thinking:

1. This debate suggests that any differences between the sexes can be minimized or eliminated; therefore it is assumed that masculine and feminine traits are learned rather than innate.
2. There is an assumption that both males and females have the same traits but in differing amounts. These two assumptions underlie the movement toward *androgyny*. In the 1970s Sandra Bem (1974) suggested that masculine and feminine traits were not polar opposites after all; instead they could be thought of as complementary. She further suggested that both males and females could have both masculine and feminine traits in their personalities. When both masculine and feminine qualities were found in high amounts in one person, she or he was said to be androgynous. (For a further discussion see Chapter 5.)

Second-stage liberal feminists suggested that males could become more like females and that females could become more like males. This concept could be included in the occupational realm. For example, while early liberal feminists encouraged women to become breadwinners for families and to enter traditionally masculine occupations, second-stage liberal feminists also suggested that perhaps some males would actually prefer to stay home and raise families. However, others argued that since women were the ones who were morally superior, more nurturant, should not they be the ones to raise our children to also be more compassionate? This latter view, however, relegates women to the status quo, that is, subordination, and so some have suggested wages for childrearing and housework. This view of the superiority of women will be addressed more fully when we discuss cultural feminism.

Notice that even if men and women become more like each other, there will still be some women and some men of higher status than other women and men. Thus, second-stage liberal feminists still believed in the hierarchical structure of society. And this is the key to liberal (or moderate) feminism. Although liberal feminists may vary in their views about whether sex differences should be addressed or minimized and about whether men should become more like women or women like men, they all agree that the way to achieve equality between the sexes is to work for equality of opportunity and to work for women's advancement within the already existing institutions of society.

Radical Feminism

A second theoretical perspective is *radical feminism*. Radical feminists blamed a traditionally masculine society for the oppression of women. Adherents to this view believed that implications of sex and gender were responsible for the oppression of women. Whereas sex is the biological division into male and female, gender includes the cultural assumptions about a person because he or she is biologically a male or a female. Beliefs that biological females have certain types of traits or abilities and that biological males have certain types of traits or abilities simply because of their sex is the concept of gender. Radical feminists believed that the artificial assumptions society made about people because of their biological sex kept women in a subordinate position to men. For example, assumptions that women are emotionally fragile, and that men are emotionally stable would keep women in an inferior position in society. Similarly, these assumptions promoted *patriarchy*, or a society in which men have a higher status than women. This patriarchal society then continued, in tautological fashion, to encourage male dominance over women. Thus, radical feminists believed that patriarchy was the cause of women's oppression.

Some even went so far as to suggest that sexuality (e.g., *compulsory heterosexuality*) was partly responsible for the subordinate position of women in society. Compulsory heterosexuality suggests that a patriarchal society requires people to be heterosexual and that the roles men and women play as heterosexuals do not encourage equality between the sexes. Rich (1993) and Firestone (1993) have described heterosexuality as a political institution that disempowers women. It controls women by patriarchal motherhood and economic exploitation. Men use sex and compulsory heterosexuality to subordinate and control women. Rich (1993) and Firestone

(1993) also suggest that people are forced into marriage by family pressure and economic considerations. And those who resist this pressure are excluded from society, ostracized, and marginalized. (The term *compulsory heterosexuality*, by the way, was derived to emphasize that the lesbian experience was absent from feminist writings.)

An example of this view is that some believe that it was women's ability (and role) to have children that led to their subordination (Firestone, 1993). These feminists believed that a woman's biology, that is, her reproductive abilities, forced women into the traditional roles of motherhood and forced them to behave in traditionally feminine ways (e.g., forced them to be nurturant). Some radical feminists would have liked to "free" women from subordination by implementing great changes in reproductive technology. These changes would allow women to terminate unwanted pregnancies, prevent unwanted pregnancies, and experience painless labor when they did decide to have children, for example. Ultimately these changes would allow women the choice of whether to be mothers or not, and whether to adopt traditional roles or not. Others would encourage women to try alternate arrangements to marriage in order to be freed from patriarchal subordination encouraged by compulsory heterosexuality. Firestone (1993), for example, believes that marriage is oppressive and outmoded, that women do not need it for financial reasons anymore. Thus, she suggests alternatives to marriage that would meet the psychological and emotional needs fulfilled traditionally by marriage. Some possibilities include living together as partners/roommates—either in a sexual (homosexual or heterosexual) or non-sexual sense—or households where a group of adults of varying ages live together and raise their children together, among others.

But while compulsory heterosexuality may exist to a certain extent if one examines the negative attitudes toward homosexuality here in the United States, it is most likely that most people are heterosexual because of primarily biological factors. At least, this is what is implied by the research on the homosexual orientation (e.g., Baily and Pillard, 1991; LeVay, 1991; Holden, 1992).

Another example of how sexuality may result in the unequal status of women is the issue of pornography and whether it results in increases in the rape rate in a society. There has been on ongoing debate about whether seeing pornography makes it more likely that a man would rape a woman. While there is some support for this view (e.g., Malamuth, 1978), it is more likely that it is the depictions of violence that contribute to violence in our society (e.g., Donnerstein and Linz, 1984). Whether those depictions of violence are sexually explicit or not is irrelevant. Beyond this, however, one can see that rape itself can serve to control women and keep them in a subordinate position because even if a woman has not been raped, the fear of such a possible attack influences her behavior. For example, she may not go out at night by herself; she may not visit a bar by herself; she may not enter certain areas of a city by herself.

In sum, radical feminists believed that some forms of sexuality were patriarchal in nature. That type of sexuality, along with other forms of patriarchy, were the reasons for women's unequal status with men. Radical feminists believed that to reach equality, society must eliminate the distinction between the sexes, and beyond that, the distinction of race. For example, the differences in the genitals and the differences in skin color would no longer matter culturally. In order to accomplish this, society itself must be reconstructed. Thus, whereas liberal feminists believed that to achieve equality for women, society must be reformed, radical feminists proposed a revolution. The ultimate outcome of this revolution would be that all people—males and females, blacks and whites—would have the same opportunities. Whereas liberal feminists believed that there would be equality at various levels of society, radical feminists believed that there would only be one level of society. Thus, regardless of individual differences all would be able to achieve. No hierarchy would exist. Allocation of goods would occur according to need.

Eventually, this view faded because of its lack of practicality, although we can still see some of its influence today. For example, we can still see a concern over the issue of whether pornography is degrading and potentially harmful to women, even in other feminist schools of thought.

Cultural Feminism

Cultural feminists believe in a culture of women. Just as there is an African-American culture or Polish-American culture or Native American culture, women have a culture, complete with a universal feminine experience. The schools of thought that we have just discussed (especially liberal feminism) have minimized the sex differences and so have been considered *sameness schools* because men and women have been perceived to be essentially the same and therefore equal. Cultural feminism, however, is considered a *difference school,* that is, it believes that there are vast differences between men and women. But unlike society before the women's movement, which devalued the traits and abilities of women, cultural feminists celebrate women. They do not believe in androgyny; they do not want women to become more like men. They want women to maintain their traits and their roles but they want society to value them just as society values the traits and roles of men. (We have discussed some of the concepts involved with this notion previously.) Whereas in liberal and radical feminism, there have been differences of opinion about whether men should become more like women or women like men, *all* cultural feminists believe in the valuing of feminine qualities. However, cultural feminists do differ in whether they believe that the differences in the sexes are biologically based. Some believe that these feminine qualities that should be valued are biologically based. They are referred to as *essentialists*. Others do not believe that the sex differences are biologically based, but rather are learned from society. These are sometimes referred to as *weak cultural feminists*, although *strong cultural feminists* are not always essentialists. I will continue to distinguish between strong and weak cultural feminists throughout this discussion, as Evans (1995) does, but please keep in mind that these terms do not imply anything about their physical, emotional, or any other kind of strength! Whereas liberal and radical feminists have been concerned with a progression of equality between men and women (although their thoughts about how this should be accomplished are very different), cultural feminists are not concerned with this type of progression. As noted, their main concern involves the valuing of anything feminine. Thus, while cultural feminists may believe that women have been oppressed because of patriarchy, they do not want to overthrow society as do radical feminists and they do not encourage women to become more like men and join men in the traditionally masculine world as liberal feminists do. Rather, they stress that women have been devalued. They illustrate this by noting that even our language refers to women in a derogatory way. For example, the terms *bitch* and *mistress* have negative connotations compared to the comparable masculine terms *dog* and *master*. Cultural feminists would like to reclaim these words and use them again with pride.

Another example of the cultural feminist view is the work and writings of Carol Gilligan (1982). Gilligan tested Lawrence Kohlberg's (e.g., 1966; 1969) theory of moral development on girls. His original work, which allowed him to formulate a theory of moral development, was constructed by studying boys only. When Gilligan tested Kohlberg's theory on girls she found that girls tended to score at a lower level of moral development than boys. In particular, she found that girls tended to score at the level of the third stage of moral development, which is based on beliefs that helping and pleasing others is an important reason to behave ethically. Rather than suggesting that the moral development of girls was limited compared to that of boys, as some did, Gilligan suggested that girls' sense of morality was simply different from that of boys. Girls' morality was based on their relationships with other people, on a sense of caring, whereas boys' morality was based on an abstract sense of justice. Gilligan's work is a prime example of cultural feminism because it illustrates three of the most important concepts of this view. First, it describes a certain type of sex difference. Second, it illustrates how women's characteristics have been devalued, that is, the female sense of morality has been suggested to be inferior. Third, it demonstrates the demand to reclaim what is feminine and think about it in positive instead of negative terms, that is, to think about the female sense of morality as being just as valid as the male sense of morality.

This view is somewhat different from what we mentioned in our discussion of liberal feminism. Some liberal feminists began to emphasize differences more than early liberal feminists and they began to suggest that some of the characteristics of women that were different than those of men may actually be superior. They also suggested that these traits could be used to better society and that perhaps men should strive to become more like women. Strong cultural feminists, however, do not encourage men to be more like women because many are essentialists and so would believe that feminine and masculine characteristics are innate. Likewise, according to Evans (1995), strong cultural feminists are not necessarily concerned about using feminine virtues to improve the world. However, weak cultural feminists do believe that men can also have feminine traits and so cannot really be considered as having an essentialist view. Likewise, weak cultural feminists do believe that these positive feminine traits could be used to improve the world.

Like some radical feminists, cultural feminists encourage men and women to live and work apart from each other as much as society permits because they disapprove of anything masculine. They are *separatists*. This is especially true about strong cultural feminists.

I believe that this separatism probably dissuades some from this view. Another problem with cultural feminism, however, is that it ignores individual differences. It assumes that there is a universal female experience but, in fact, nothing is farther from the truth. My experience as a middle-class, white, academic woman is probably very different from that of a poor, African-American woman who cleans for a living. Finally, we should note that another problem with this view is that people often take it to an extreme. That is, rather than only encouraging the valuing of feminine characteristics, some people begin to discuss feminine characteristics as superior to masculine characteristics. When this happens, similar problems that women experienced by being thought of as inferior result; males begin to be thought of as inferior. Certainly, this will breed resentment among the male population.

In sum, cultural feminists emphasize the differences between the sexes and believe that feminine qualities have been devalued. They are not necessarily concerned with achieving equality between the sexes but rather work to value these traits, roles, and abilities again. Beyond this, they feel that women have some valuable abilities and traits that men do not possess.

Socialist Feminism

Socialist feminism is a combination of some of the other approaches we have discussed. This view probably developed out of radical feminism and *Marxism* (an economic system that promotes production in an industrial society and the elimination of class distinction). It suggests that both capitalism and the implications of sex and gender are responsible for the oppression of women. That is, Marxists criticize capitalism and suggest that another economic system would be better. By eliminating capitalism and patriarchal views, women would no longer be oppressed.

Socialist feminists (like Marxists) are very concerned about the representation of all groups of people. Unlike cultural feminists, socialist feminists do not believe that there is one female experience but rather that there are many, and that these experiences depend upon one's group affiliation. For example, as I mentioned before, an African-American woman's experience may be very different from that of a Caucasian woman. Some of the differences in these experiences exist because some groups govern and others are governed. There are employers and employees, privileged and nonprivileged, rich and poor. There is a hierarchy in a capitalist society (as we discussed in the section on liberal feminism). Oppression stems from this hierarchy. Thus, this structural inequality, this hierarchy, must be eliminated such that all will be able to participate fully in the workforce. And so what socialist feminists want is to eliminate capitalism and the implications of gender in order to produce a society where everyone is of equal status and where equality of condition exists.

Let us examine these ideas more closely. As mentioned, socialist feminists are very concerned with adequate political representation of disadvantaged groups. Women are seen as an oppressed and exploited group. Certainly we can see how this can be true with women earning less than men even in the same professions (e.g., U.S. Department of Labor, 1993) and with evidence of discrimination (e.g., Bernstein, 1988; Larwood, Szwajkowski, and Rose, 1988). This oppression and exploitation stems from patriarchy and capitalism. For example, patriarchy has encouraged discrimination against women. Similarly, because capitalism encourages a hierarchy, this type of economic system increases the likelihood that women will be at a lower status in that hierarchy compared to men. One can see how capitalism and patriarchy support each other. Thus, by eliminating patriarchy and capitalism socialist feminists believe women will no longer be oppressed. But how can this be accomplished? How can all women enter the workforce, just as all men do in a socialist economy?

Marxism tried to eliminate the oppression of women as a group at first by using existing traditional roles. They suggested that women are actually the ones who produce the workforce. Likewise, the work women traditionally did within the home was equivalent to that outside of the home. The problem with this thinking, however, is that it still confined women to the home and made them dependent upon the male wage from work outside the home. Thus, women were still oppressed. The fact was that originally Marx was not concerned with women as an oppressed group. That concern did not surface until later with the writings of Engel (Nielsen, 1990) who suggested that women must also participate in the workforce in mass (just like men) and spend less time on work inside the home, for which they do not receive compensation. (Note that the oppression of women is viewed as stemming from their lack of labor force participation.)

Some socialist countries, such as the former Soviet Union, Cuba, and the People's Republic of China, have attempted to implement these changes. And women do make up a significant portion of these countries' workforces. However, just as in capitalist systems, women's work is still devalued; women are paid less than men, and discrimination of opportunity against women exists (Renzetti and Curran, 1992). Likewise, although women participate in the labor forces of socialist countries in significant numbers, they are also still primarily responsible for taking care of the home and children. For example, in Russia, women made up a large portion of the work force, yet they were primarily members of occupations that are traditionally considered feminine. Likewise, they earned less money than men and did the majority of the cooking, cleaning, and childrearing.

While socialism may have sounded good to some in theory, in practice it has not eliminated the oppression of women. Some socialist feminists may argue that this is because we have not yet eliminated the hierarchy of groups completely. We are still members of groups and form some of our identity from our group membership. If society became impartial then our group membership would not influence our status. Thus, if society eliminated stereotypes about men as a group and women as a group, then the group "men" would no longer have a higher status than the group "women." It is not that socialist feminists want to eliminate groups. It is just that they want the differences in groups to be considered without judgments of certain characteristics, abilities, and so on of one group being better than that of another (Evans, 1995). They want all groups to have equal representation in society, but for this to be accomplished we must eliminate incorrect judgments about certain groups, in this case, women and men. While, again, in theory this makes sense and is admirable, psychologists and others recognize that this is easier said than done.

More recent socialist feminist theories explore the origins of women's oppression and expand Marx's and Engle's limited views on the interrelationship between the economy and the family (e.g., Mitchell, cited in Andersen, 1997).

In sum, socialist feminists blame women's oppression on patriarchy and capitalism. They strive to eliminate this oppression by eliminating patriarchy, that is, eliminating inaccurate beliefs about women and men as groups. They also propose to eliminate capitalism and encourage a socialist economy such that women could participate as fully as men in a productive workforce.

Postmodernism

Postmodernist theory has grown out of the field of literary criticism, which uses the technique of deconstruction to analyze literary works. The basic premise behind the theory is that all knowledge is socially constructed, that what we believe to be true and even our cognitive processes are influenced by a variety of assumptions that we have absorbed from society. Thus, ideas about women and men and their relationships have been influenced by societal factors. And in turn, those societal factors have created assumptions about men and women and what relationships between the sexes should be like. Deconstruction is the process of separating reality from the myths, assumptions, and generalizations that have come from society. Postmodernism is a theory; deconstruction is a technique used within the theoretical framework.

Postmodernists believe that there are many ways of interpreting an experience, of understanding something, and that no single interpretation or understanding is correct. For example, it is possible, as Evans (1995) notes, that some women may not believe that women as a group are oppressed or disadvantaged, whereas other women might believe that this is true. A postmodernist could accept this and not condemn either point of view. It follows then that postmodernists reject all other ideologies (e.g., liberal feminism, radical feminism) because they imply that only one point of view is correct (and also because postmodernists believe that those perspectives have not helped women to become free from oppression). Postmodernists also challenge the idea of women as an undifferentiated or homogeneous group (the cultural feminist view; Evans, 1995). They are wary about generalizations (Andersen, 1997) and instead believe that all women have diverse and unique experiences that create each person's understanding, each person's reality. To postmodernists, there is no actual reality, but rather, each person has her own subjective impression about what her reality is.

As Andersen (1997) notes, postmodernism has become popular with some feminists for three main reasons. First, a common theme among some feminist theories is that gender is socially constructed. For example, liberal feminists have always suggested that sex differences exist only because of socialization. Postmodernists also recognize the influence of society on each individual's assumptions or knowledge base.

Second, postmodernists are not essentialists because essentialism would imply that all men or all women are the same because of their biology. While some feminists are essentialists, many are not, and so those that are not can accept at least this aspect of the theory.

Finally, some feminists have endorsed postmodernism because of its implications for the social construction of language. Feminists have long maintained that the way society uses language is sexist. The male as normative is an example of this; that is, males are the norm; females are a deviation from the norm. Thus, when we use the term *doctor*, we may be referring to a woman, but most likely this term will conjure up an image of a man. However, we use the term "lady doctor" or "woman doctor" to refer to a woman in this profession, which implies that most doctors are men and she is an exception to the rule. Likewise, our use of language constructs our assumptions, in this case about women being doctors. Postmodernists also maintain that our use of language helps to construct our ideas about men and women, and that our use of language is not objective, but rather has been influenced by society's use of language. Note, then, that postmodernists do not believe that anything is objective. Instead, they believe that all understanding or knowledge is subjective.

While postmodernism is useful to feminism in the above-mentioned ways and is also useful in promoting the understanding of diversity, it is problematic in that the theory is very abstract and potentially confusing. For example, if there is no such thing as an objective reality, how do we know whether what we are experiencing is real? Furthermore, how can we share or compare our experiences with others (to promote understanding, etc.) if we all have different experiences and understandings?

In sum, postmodernism emphasizes that our understanding of men, women, and gender is socially constructed and that each person's experience, and therefore, each person's knowledge of men, women and gender, are all unique.

SUMMARY

In sum, although many people are feminists, there are many feminist views. Some of these views vary because of a difference in beliefs about whether there are actually any differences in abilities, personalities, and so on between men and women. Others vary even though they believe in sex differences, because some believe that the differences exist due to biological factors while others suggest that the sex differences are due to societal factors. Still other variations involve differences in opinions about whether masculine traits and roles or feminine traits and roles are "better" or whether masculine and feminine qualities are of equal value. Finally, these theoretical approaches vary because of differences in opinions about how equality should be achieved and about the causes of women's subordination in society.

Note that in our discussions of the various theories, even within one theoretical viewpoint, there are differences of opinion on the various factors mentioned above. This has led some feminist theorists to suggest that rather than discussing broad-based feminist theories, we should address opinions on individual feminist issues (e.g., do sex differences really exist?). This approach certainly would allow feminists to think about individual issues and place less pressure on them to conform to the various opinions of one theoretical perspective when they agree with only one aspect of the theory. The passage of time will allow us to examine this topical approach to feminist theory.

KEY TERMS

liberal feminism	compulsory heterosexuality	strong cultural feminism
equality of opportunity	cultural feminism	separatism
equality of condition	sameness school	socialist feminism
glass ceiling	difference school	Marxism
androgyny	essentialism	postmodernism
radical feminism	weak cultural feminism	deconstruction
patriarchy		

DISCUSSION QUESTIONS

1. What is feminism?
2. Does one have to subscribe to a certain mode of thinking in order to be a feminist?
3. What do feminists believe about women, men, and society?

REFERENCES

Andersen, M. L. (1997). *Thinking about women: Sociological perspectives on sex and gender.* Needham Heights, MA: Allyn & Bacon.

Baily, J. M. and R. Pillard (1991). "A genetic study of male sexual orientation." *Archives of General Psychiatry, 48:* 1089-1096.

Bem, S. L. (1974). "The measurement of psychological androgyny." *Journal of Consulting and Clinical Psychology, 42:* 155-162.

Bernstein, A. (1988, February 29). "So you think you've come a long way, baby?" *Business Week,* pp. 48-51.

Donnerstein, E. and D. Linz (1984, January). "Sexual violence in the media: A warning." *Psychology Today,* pp. 14-15.

Evans, J. (1995). *Feminist theory today: An introduction to second-wave feminism.* London: Sage Publications.

Firestone, S. (1993). "The case for feminist revolution." In *Gender basics: Feminist perspectives on women and men,* A. Minas. Belmont (Ed.). CA: Wadsworth, Inc., pp. 285-290.

Friedan, B. (1981). *The second stage.* New York: Summit Books.

Gilligan, C. (1982). *In a different voice.* Cambridge, MA: Harvard University Press.

Holden, C. (1992, January). "Twin study links genes to homosexuality." *Research News,* p. 33.

Keetz, M. A. (1991). *The status of female faculty in Pennsylvania's state system of higher education: An historical perspective, 1974-1989.* West Chester, PA: West Chester University of Pennsylvania.

Kohlberg, L. (1966). "A cognitive-developmental analysis of children's sex-role concepts and attitudes." In *The development of sex differences,* E. E. Maccoby (Ed.). Stanford, CA: Stanford University Press, pp. 82-173.

Kohlberg, L. (1969). "Stage and sequence: The cognitive-developmental approach to socialization." In *Handbook of socialization theory and research,* D. A. Goslin (Ed.). Chicago: Rand-McNally, pp. 347-480.

Larwood, L., E. Szwajkowski, and S. Rose (1988). "When discrimination makes 'sense': The rational bias theory." In *Women and work: An annual review* (vol. 3), B. A. Gutek, A. H. Stromberg, and L. Larwood (Eds.). Beverly Hills, CA: Sage, pp. 265-288.

LeVay, S. (1991). "A difference in hypothalamic structure between heterosexual and homosexual men." *Science, 253:* 1034-1037.

Malamuth, N. M. (1978, September). *Erotica, aggression, and perceived appropriateness.* Paper presented at the 86th annual convention of the American Psychological Association in Toronto, Ontario, Canada.

Montague, A. (1992). *The natural superiority of women.* New York: Collier Books.

Nielsen, J. M. (1990). *Sex and gender in society: Perspectives on stratification* (Second edition). Prospect Heights, IL: Waveland Press, Inc.

Renzetti, C. M. and D. J. Curran (1992). *Women, men and society* (Second edition). Boston: Allyn & Bacon.

Reskin, B. F. (1988). "Occupational resegregation." In *The American woman 1988-89*, S. Rix (Ed.). New York: Norton, pp. 258-263.

Rich, A. (1993). "Compulsory heterosexuality and lesbian existence." In *Feminist frontiers III*, L. Richardson and V. Taylor (Eds.). New York: McGraw-Hill, Inc, pp. 158-179.

U.S. Department of Labor (1991). *A report on the glass ceiling initiative.* Washington, DC: Government Printing Office.

U.S. Department of Labor (1993). *Facts on working women.* Washington, DC: U.S. Department of Labor, Women's Bureau.

Chapter 2

Research for Women:
Feminist Methods

Maureen C. McHugh
Lisa Cosgrove

. . . I doubt that in our wildest dreams we ever imagined we would have to reinvent both science and theorizing itself to make sense of women's social experience. (Harding, 1986, p. 251)

Research is not a single activity, nor is it a specific set of procedures. Even the scientific method is not *one way* of conducting research, but a set of assumptions about how we can come to "know" about the universe (see Tables 2.1 and 2.2). For some, research means the "discovery of truth," whereas for others it is the creation or production of knowledge, or even the collection and telling of stories. Similarly, feminist research is hard to delineate or even to describe. Feminist research is not a single method or set of procedures, or even a unitary approach to the discovery or creation of knowledge. This chapter is an extended description of the diverse approaches to research taken by feminists.

WHAT IS FEMINIST RESEARCH?

Feminist Research Challenges Sexism

Feminist research is, first of all, nonsexist. Feminist research does not accept societal assumptions about the nature of women, gender, or about the differences between men and women. Traditional research is *sexist* to the extent that it incorporates stereotypic thinking about women or gender. *Sexist bias* also refers to research when theorizing does not have equal relevance to individuals of both sexes, and when greater attention or value is given to the life experiences of one sex. One of the most glaring biases

TABLE 2.1. The Scientific Method: Principles and Assumptions

- The universe is orderly and operates according to general laws. Scientists generate theories about the laws and operations of the universe. A *theory* is an organized system of assumptions and principles that is advanced to explain a specified set of events or phenomena.
- Theories or hypotheses about the universe and its laws are tested by "the scientific method." A *hypothesis* is a statement that attempts to predict or account for an observable phenomenon. The hypothesis specifies the relationship among variables and/or events.
- The scientific method is based on *empiricism,* the belief that we can know the world through experience. Empirical scientific research involves careful, systematic, and repeated observations of the variables and events described in the hypothesis.
- The scientist works toward *objectivity.* Science is best conducted by disinterested individuals, i.e., individuals who do not have an investment in the results confirming or disconfirming the hypothesis.

TABLE 2.2. The Scientific Experiment: Principles and Process

Hypothesis. A prediction about the relationship between the variables is stated (e.g., people are more likely to emit hostile responses when they are hungry than when they are satiated, i.e., full).

Control. The method requires that the experimenter be able to manipulate and/or control the independent variable and extraneous variables (e.g., the experimenter must be able to deprive subjects of food for variable amounts of time and control other factors that might make them hostile).

Measurement. The method requires the reliable and precise measurement of the dependent variable (e.g., the experimenter would need a good way to measure hostility).

Randomization. The method requires that the subjects of the experiment be randomly assigned to experimental conditions. Each subject is equally likely to be placed in each of the conditions. Subjects are assigned to conditions using a type of lottery (e.g., the subjects, i.e., people, would have to be randomly assigned to different levels of food deprivation, such as 4 hours, 8 hours, 12 hours, etc. This is to ensure that all the generally hostile people are not in the same condition).

Repetition. The method requires a large number of observations. Many individuals would have to be observed under each of the conditions (e.g., levels of food deprivation).

Replication. The method must be described in detail to allow other researchers to repeat the methods and observe the same results. The study should be replicated with different types of individuals (e.g., individuals from other countries, individuals of different ages, etc.).

---

in the psychological literature was the failure to include women as subjects of research, and at the same time to describe psychology research as studying human (rather than male) behavior. For example, until the 1970s the psychological literature on achievement motivation really referred to achievement motivation in males; research conducted on males by males resulted in a theory that explained male achievement behaviors. (See Mednick, Tangri, and Hoffman, 1975 for an extended discussion.) The theory and methods for measuring achievement did not work well for females, that is, researchers could not predict the achievement behavior of women using the theory or the instruments. Subsequently, females were seen as being deficient in achievement motivation (as opposed to the more accurate conclusion that the theory and instruments were deficient or limited). This bias in the achievement literature remains today; women continue to be viewed as "fearing success" or as making "luck" attributions for their successes and "ability" attributions for their failures. Research demonstrating the inaccuracy of these conclusions (e.g., Whitley, McHugh, and Frieze, 1986) has not been able to alter these "popular" beliefs about deficiencies in women. Similar problems exist throughout the psychological (and sociological) literature. McHugh, Koeske, and Frieze (1986) provide extensive descriptions of sexist practices within psychology and make recommendations to minimize sexist bias.

The guidelines for nonsexist research in psychology are designed to limit gender bias in research, leading to more *sex-fair* research. Similar analyses and criticisms have been offered for other natural and social sciences. One of the initial and important contributions of feminist researchers is this analysis of the way that hidden (and sometimes blatant) sexist assumptions and beliefs about women, men, and gender underlie existing theory and research. For example, much of the research on aggression uses male-only samples of subjects based on the implicit assumption that aggression is a male behavior. On the other hand, research on child rearing typically uses female-only samples, again based on the assumption that child care is provided by females.

Feminists Support Research by Women

Feminists are not only concerned that research be conducted in a sex-fair way. They are also concerned with women's participation in the production of knowledge. They object to societal arrangements whereby a single dominant group (e.g., men) has access to education and produces knowledge for the society. Such arrangements are seen as stemming from and perpetuating dominant-subordinate relations. When men are the researchers, the professors, the doctors, and the experts, this perpetuates the idea that males are superior. Their "expert" findings and opinions often label women as not as good as men, justifying their dominance in society and in interpersonal relationships with women. For example, the label "dependent" is applied to women who rely on men, but is not applied to men who rely on women to cook, clean, and raise children for them (Kaplan, 1983). Women's allegedly lower abilities in math are used to justify their exclusion from many occupations including science and business, but men's allegedly lower abilities in reading and verbal skills do not prevent them from being lawyers, orators, and literary critics.

Feminists hope that the participation of women in the production and teaching of knowledge will help to change the status of women in the academy and in society. Feminists are concerned that women have access to training and research opportunities, that women receive resources to conduct and publish research, and that women receive proper credit for their research findings. In this sense research conducted by women is endorsed by a feminist agenda.

Women's participation in the sciences, social sciences, and in the academy represents not only the potential for women to increase their individual and collective status, it has important implications for what society will come to know. The entry and increased representation of women in various disciplines has resulted in dramatic changes in the breadth, focus, methods, and findings of each discipline. For example, early women psychologists challenged the boundaries of psychology, exploring new content areas and new approaches to social problems (Rosenberg, 1982), and women researchers have revolutionized primatology. Feminist psychologists have paid special attention to the role that the values, biases, and assumptions of the researcher have in choice of methods and all other aspects of the research process including the selection of topics and questions, and the interpretation and potential uses of the research results.

Feminist Research Is About Women and Gender

A popular and more restricted conception of what constitutes feminist research is that it is *research conducted by, about, and for women*. Others have challenged the simplicity of this approach (Kelly, Burton, and Regan, 1994). For example, feminist research may examine *misogynist* attitudes in men and sexist practices in male institutions like the military. Although not about women, such research would serve a feminist agenda if it indicated how to change policies or other military practices to better integrate women into the military. In some cases feminist research is conducted by men.

Another widely held perspective is that feminist researchers are those that see *gender* as a basic organizing principle that affects all aspects of our lives. Lather (1991) defines feminist research as research that puts gender at the center of one's inquiry. Pugh (1990) states that feminism provides a way of looking at the world and a set of values that will influence how one studies a topic. Feminist researchers are concerned with understanding social relationships and pointing out inequalities and injustices. Feminist research is directed toward understanding women's oppression in order that we might end it (Kelly, Burton, and Regan, 1992). "The overt ideological goal of feminist research in the human sciences is to correct both the *invisibility* and *distortion* of female experience in ways relevant to ending women's unequal social position" (Lather, 1991, p. 72). A feminist perspective involves questioning surface realities and accepted ways of doing things (Pugh, 1990). The distinction of feminist research in relation to other forms of research stems from the questions we have asked and the purpose of our work (Kelly, Burton, and Regan, 1992).

Feminist Research Is for Women

Feminist research is research that works actively *for the benefit and advancement of women* (McHugh, Koeske, and Frieze, 1986). One way that research can work for women is to challenge existing stereotypes of women. This was a common approach of early feminist researchers; their findings challenged stereotypic views of women's abilities and attributes. Some examples of this are Hyde and Linn's (1986) work using meta-analysis and Maccoby and Jacklin's (1974) summary; both works document that widely held beliefs about differences between men and women were not substantiated by research. Another form of research that works *for* women is research demonstrating the prevalence of sexual assault or battering of women (e.g., Koss, 1996). Epidemiological research of this nature is necessary to obtain funding for programs and interventions, and also affects our understanding of the causes of male violence toward women (McHugh, Frieze, and Browne, 1992).

Participatory activist research as a research strategy addresses explicitly the feminist issues of usefulness (to women) and contribution to social change. *Action research* is research conducted in lived contexts with the participation of the community; its agenda is social change. For example, the work of feminist psychologist Brinton Lykes is described in Fine (1992). For over a decade Lykes has been engaged in political activism and research with Gautemalan Indian women, documenting their initial concerns and their changing political consciousness as they resist political oppression. Reinharz (1992) prepared a roster of forms of action research for feminists that includes needs assessment and evaluation research in addition to the participatory action research. For example, research that assesses the impact of mandatory arrest of batterers, or the effectiveness of batterers' groups in eliminating violence (e.g., Gondolf, 1990; 1993) would benefit women, address gender issues, contribute to social policy, and help to provide funding and public support for programs. Similarly, research designed to assess the need for a women's center on campus would be feminist social action research.

Yllo (1988) argues that doing research *for* women, and not just *about* women, involves attending to the entire life of the research project, including how the findings are interpreted and used by others. Signorelli and others have commented on the ways in which feminist research on sex differences has typically been misused against women. Feminist researchers may also have an obligation to ensure that the knowledge gained through their efforts is shared with communities of women and with individuals who work with women. Fine (1992) indicates that this has not typically occurred within feminist psychology; most of the research published is addressed specifically to other psychologists, and may not be accessible to other audiences. An example of feminist research that is made accessible is the work of Leonore Tiefer (1995); she has presented her research on the construction of female sexuality to varied audiences including medical researchers, sexologists, feminists, psychologists, students, and the general public.

Summary

We have explored the ideas that feminist research challenges stereotypic beliefs about women and gender, and seeks greater understanding of the experiences of women, especially their experiences of gender inequities or oppression. Feminist research explores the ways in which our social world is structured around gender. A feminist researcher selects both research topics and research methods that will benefit women. Early on Dale Spender (1978) argued that feminist researchers should also concern themselves with developing new criteria for what counts as knowledge (as opposed to having knowledge about females being added to existing sexist knowledge). However, the questions of whether and how research can be conducted to benefit women are both complex and controversial. This question is explored in some depth in the third section of this chapter.

CHALLENGING TRADITIONAL RESEARCH

Speaking for Ourselves

An important contribution made by feminist researchers is to give voice to women's experiences. Feminist researchers frequently use the term *meta-*

phor to describe women's experiences; *In Another Voice* by Carol Gilligan (1982) is a classic example. This metaphor suggests intimacy, physical proximity, dialogue, and interaction. Auditory metaphors are used by women to describe their epistemological positions, as reported by Belenky and her colleagues (Belenky et al., 1986) in *Women's Ways of Knowing*: speaking up, speaking out, being silenced, not being heard, really listening, feeling deaf and dumb, and saying what you mean.

The voice metaphor can be contrasted with the visual metaphor, which scientists and philosophers most often use to express their sense of mind and knowledge (Keller and Grontkowski, 1983). For example, knowing is equated with seeing and truth is equated with light. Feminists have pointed out that visual metaphors such as seeing with the mind's eye suggest a camera passively recording a static reality. Further, this metaphor promotes the illusion that disengagement and objectification are central to the construction of knowledge. Science, for example, is described as standing at a distance or getting the right angle. Actually science is often described as valuing the impairment of vision, as in the terms blind justice, veil of ignorance, and double blind. Such attempts to blind the seeing knower make it difficult to acknowledge the role the knower plays in the construction of knowledge (Belenky et al., 1986). Feminists have questioned these conceptions of blinding and distancing the researcher from the "object" under study. This perspective, known as social constructionism, is discussed in a subsequent section.

The metaphor of voice can be used to describe the exclusion of women from research and science as silence. Recognizing this exclusion or the silence of women is often the first step in a feminist analysis of science. The exclusion of women from science as both researchers and as research subjects has been extensively documented and analyzed (e.g., Rossitor, 1982; McHugh, Koeske, and Frieze, 1986; Rosser, 1990). Silence of women can also be used as a metaphor to refer to the fact that women's exclusion has been almost universally ignored when scientists draw conclusions from their findings and generalize what they have learned from the study of men to the lives of women (Signorella, Vegega, and Mitchell, 1974; McHugh, Koeske, and Frieze, 1986). This means that the drugs, both over the counter and prescribed, that women routinely take have been tested almost exclusively on male subjects. Even drugs that are prescribed primarily for women were tested on men until this bias was brought to the attention of Congress. This also means that many of our ideas about human behavior are really generalizations based on samples of white, educated, and relatively affluent males. Feminists object to the universalization of the male experience, and to seeing the experiences or behavior of a specific group of women as characteristic of women generally.

One of the most obvious ways to rectify this silence and the androcentrism of traditional analyses is to listen to women. This can be done on several levels. First, feminists have worked to recover and reappreciate the work of women researchers and theorists. Women's research has often been ignored, trivialized, or appropriated without the credit that would have been given a man's. For example, Rosalind Franklin's work on DNA was appropriated by her Nobel prize-winning colleagues (Sayre, 1975).

Second, feminists have encouraged researchers to listen to what women say about their own experiences. In the social sciences this has meant recovering women's letters and diaries. Often the experience women describe differs from the ideology of women developed in the era in which they live (DuBois et al., 1987). In psychology this has meant increasing use of interview methods. Women's experiences become the indicator of reality against which hypotheses are tested. Finally, women have struggled to find their own voices, to become the agents of knowledge, to have an equal say in the design and administration of the institutions where knowledge is produced. Partial and distorted understanding of women and the world are produced in a culture that systematically silences and devalues the voices of women (Harding, 1987).

Revising Research

Early feminist critics of traditional research on women made clear suggestions for the revision of research. For example, we argued that researchers should include women, study topics relevant to women, and be objective rather than misogynistic. Within psychology we argued that the context in which men's and women's behaviors were investigated (i.e., the tasks employed, the stimuli used) should be gender-neutral. The context, task, and/or stimuli should not be more familiar or more comfortable for one sex than the other. Oftentimes the tasks, the situations, and the questions had been created by men to study the behavior of men. A male bias had been introduced into psychological research, perhaps unwittingly.

But as feminists attempted to proceed with a revised research agenda, the questions became more complex, and the answers to research dilemmas became more elusive. What women should be included? Which aspects of women's lives should be studied? Should we study the topics previously studied, employing the traditional paradigms, but now include women? Should we compare women to men? What groups of women were appropriate as comparison groups for men?

For example, if we wanted to understand how women relate to each other, how might we investigate this? Within psychology, a traditional approach to studying hostility and aggression is to measure how much shock research subjects would deliver to a target subject (allegedly to help them learn). Often the target subject had previously aggravated or frustrated the experimental subject. Feminist critics question this approach to research. Should we bring women into the laboratory, manipulate the situation to create anger and hostility toward each other, and then measure the level of shocks women are willing to deliver to each other?

To understand women's relation to other women should we have them compete in an experimental game, in which one person's loss is another person's gain, in the laboratory? This exemplifies the problems with the scientific method as employed by psychologists. Shocks delivered at the request of an experimenter to a stranger who has aggravated us in a laboratory do not seem to be an appropriate measure of the hostility women might feel for other women. If women already experience hostility toward other women, why would we want to create more hostility experimentally? Does women's ability to compete with each other in an experimental game give us a clear understanding of competition between women?

The scientific method puts the experimenter in the position of influencing, deceiving, manipulating, observing, and/or interpreting the subjects. Most research designs, particularly the more highly regarded experimental designs, may have undesirable effects on the subjects. The controlled and artificial research situation may elicit more conventional behavior from participants, may inhibit participants' self-disclosure, and may make the situation "unreal" to the participants. Behavior that is exhibited in an unfamiliar setting and entails little self-involvement and often no prior social relationship with the other participants is probably not representative of "real life" behavior (McHugh, Koeske, and Frieze, 1986).

In the experimental method the experimenter creates and controls the context in which the experimental subject acts. The experimental method creates and/or aggravates a difference in status and control between the knower/experimenter and the known/subject. The inequality between the researcher and the research participants is especially clear and problematic when the experimenter is male and the participants are female. Here the research setting most clearly reflects and reinforces the imposition of male definitions of reality on females.

One alternative for the feminist researcher is to use more collaborative and less manipulative methods such as interviews and surveys. A feminist perspective respects women's view of the world and of their own experiences. Interviews, narratives, and diaries are valued approaches in that they validate rather than challenge women's perspectives on their own lives. Having the woman respondent describe her experiences or perspective in her own words is often seen as more desirable than fixed response, forced choice, or standardized tests. Fixed response and standardized tests, like the experiment, often involve the imposition of the experimenter's view of reality onto the respondent. Data collection techniques and research review procedures that encourage respondents to participate in the formulation of goals and hypotheses represents another feminist approach to the dilemma of researcher control (Graham and Rawlings, 1980; Reinharz, 1981).

In this way, feminists developed critiques of traditional research approaches within all existing disciplines. The introduction of women as researchers, theorists, and as appropriate subjects of research leads eventually to a challenge to the methods and paradigms of each discipline. This view of curriculum and disciplinary transformation has been explicated by McIntosh (1984) and Rosser (1990). Subsequently, in most disciplines feminists have worked to discover, design, and devise alternative approaches and methods. For example, Carol Gilligan (1982) began her work by questioning the exclusion of women from moral development research. In her inquiry into the ways women would address moral dilemmas, she employed interview methods that departed radically from the previous research strategies of Kohlberg (1984) and his colleagues. In Kohlberg's (1984) research, subjects respond to hypothetical moral dilemmas, usually writing their responses on paper and pencil measures. Their responses are then coded as indicating the subject's moral stage; the higher stages in the moral hierarchy represent the questioning of rules and authorities to arrive at an autonomous position. Gilligan (1982) conducted intensive interviews with women who were in the midst of making a real life moral decision—whether to have an abortion. She characterizes mature moral decision making in women as caring about the consequences for those around us. Thus, listening to the voices of women resulted in a challenge to the "male" approach to research, and in the creation of knowledge that profoundly challenged theorizing about women across disciplines.

Objectivity and Subjectivity

The human sciences have made a clear distinction between *objectivity* and *subjectivity*. In traditional science, objectivity is equated with value-free repeatable methods of data collection. Scientific methods are based on a belief in the generalizability of objective data. In contrast, subjectivity is viewed as value laden and unrepeatable, based on private events and focused on the unique experiences of the individual, which cannot be generalized (Koeske, 1978; Sherif, 1979; Wittig, 1985).

The distinction between objectivity and subjectivity provides a rationale for many scientific practices. Various safeguards such as using behavioral (as opposed to self-report) measures, minimizing interaction with the subjects of study, concealing the true nature of the study, and standardizing research procedures are recommended to assure research objectivity. These methods are designed to minimize bias (McHugh, Koeske, and Frieze, 1986).

Feminists have challenged the feasibility, the appropriateness, and the utility of the experimenter being distant, neutral, disinterested, and nondisclosing, and challenge the techniques designed to achieve "objective" data (e.g., Sherif, 1979; Reinharz, 1981; Unger, 1981; Wallston, 1981). Feminist researchers have sometimes demonstrated or voiced a preference for subjective methods of data collection. The feminine and the feminist have sometimes been equated with a subjectivist perspective.

This position reflects the commonly accepted stereotype of women's thinking as emotional, intuitive, and personalized. Keller (1985) discusses the ways in which this perspective has contributed to the devaluation of women's minds and their exclusion from science. This position is inherently dualistic in its equation of feminine with intuition and the equation of masculine with objectivity, science, and the scientific method. Because of this perspective and the high value Western societies have placed on objectivity, rationalism, and science, women and the modes of thought cultivated by women have had relatively little impact on the values and direction of society (Ruddick, 1980).

This antirationalist, antiscience position has been adopted by some feminist theorists. Griffin (1978), for example, equates women with nature, and objects to males' use of science and technology to dominate them. She seeks to replace men's objectivity with women's subjectivity. In reaction to Griffin and others, Rose (1983) fears that feminists are retreating into a total rejection of science as the monolithic enemy. Similarly, Keller (1982) observes that there is a temptation for feminists to abandon their claim for representation in scientific culture, and to invite a return to a purely female subjectivity, leaving rationality and objectivity in the male domain. Feminist criticism of science as a masculine model of knowledge may facilitate the growth of an antipathy to science that rejects all scientific investigation carried out under any conditions at any historical time, or more positively may encourage the development of an alternative science (Rose, 1983). In the next section these varied perspectives on objectivity and the scientific method are seen as the basis for three different approaches to feminist research.

FEMINIST PERSPECTIVES ON METHODS

Is There a Feminist Method?

A feminist perspective respects women's view of the world and of their own experiences. For this reason, feminist methods of research have frequently involved interviews, narratives, and more *qualitative* (than *quantitative*) methods. Lather (1991) characterizes contemporary feminist researchers as generating more interactive and contextualized methods of inquiry. However, today most feminists writing about feminist research (e.g., Stanley and Wise, 1990, 1993) reject the simple identification of feminist research with particular methods (and sexist research with others). In their perspective feminist research involves seeing reality differently—that is, from a feminist consciousness—and involves a unique relationship between the researcher and the respondents. Yllo (1988) similarly refutes the idea that certain methods are inherently feminist or sexist. She argues that it is the goal, the question, and the interpretation of the data that determines whether the inquiry is feminist or not. She has used a range of methods including archival analysis of police records to examine the relationships among gender-based expectations, power, and the battering of women.

The Diversity of Feminist Perspectives

Women who define themselves as feminists, and who have been trained in the same discipline, often have very different views about the role of science and the conduct of research. Some feminists have argued that following the procedures of scientific investigations more carefully can lead to a nonsexist science. This position is referred to as *feminist empiricism*, and is discussed in detail in subsequent sections. For others, the feminist critique suggests that the most fundamental categories of scientific thought are male-biased. In this latter view, referred to as *social constructionism*, science is shaped by sexual politics and plays a role in perpetuating sexual politics. These positions are described in detail in this section.

Many feminist researchers across disciplines are in search of a new paradigm, that is, an accepted set of assumptions and procedures for doing research. Harding (1987) contends that it would be a delusion for feminism to arrive at a new (normalized) science paradigm with conceptual and methodological assumptions that all feminists would accept. Rather she suggests that we embrace the complexities, the diversity, and instabilities encountered in the process of attempting to do feminist research. Similarly, in the guidelines for research in psychology, we encouraged dialectical approaches, dialogue between perspectives, and diversity in research methods (McHugh, Koeske, and Frieze, 1986). Using multiple methods, or having researchers who take different perspectives and/or use different research approaches, is seen as a more constructive and valid approach to feminist research than endorsing a single approach as *the feminist method*. Thus, in this chapter, feminist research is not described as a single method or approach but is explored as encompassing a variety of perspectives and research strategies.

Methods, Methodology, Epistemology

Harding (1987) argues that it is not by looking at research methods that one will be able to identify the distinctive features of feminist research. Feminist researchers use any and all of the methods that traditional *androcentric* researchers use, although they might use those methods differently (e.g., they listen carefully to how women informants think about their lives). Feminists have also introduced innovative methodologies (e.g., the use of phenomenological approaches to understand women's experiences) and have raised epistemological issues (e.g., can women be knowers or agents of knowledge?). Each of these contributions is described here.

In her argument against the idea of a distinctive feminist method of research, Harding (1987) encourages us to understand the distinctions among methods, methodology, and epistemology. These concepts and the connections between them are discussed extensively in this chapter. *Methods* are the concrete techniques for gathering evidence or data such as surveys, interviews, laboratory observations, and so on. *Methodology* is the study of methods; it refers to a philosophical perspective or theory that includes a general approach to how research should proceed. The most central issue, according to Harding (1987) and to Stanley and Wise (1990) is that of epistemology. *Epistemology* is a theory of knowledge; an epistemological position involves answers to questions like: "What can we know?" "Who can be a knower?" and "Which knowledge is valid?" Epistemology is a framework for specifying what constitutes knowledge and how to know it (Stanley and Wise, 1993). "A given epistemological framework specifies not only what knowledge is and how to recognize it, but who are knowers and by what means someone becomes one, and also the means by which competing knowledge claims are adjudicated and some rejected in favor of others" (Stanley and Wise, 1993). According to both Harding (1987) and Stanley and Wise (1990; 1993), epistemology, or the question of what constitutes knowledge, is the most basic issue in defining feminist research. Harding (1991) has outlined three feminist positions in relation to epistemology: *feminist empiricism, feminist standpoint,* and *social constructionism.* Each of these is discussed in depth here.

Feminist Empiricism

Despite the feminist critique of scientific research methods, many feminists employ the procedures of the scientific method to study the questions they want to answer. Some feminists have taken on the project of fighting science with science. For example, Maccoby and Jacklin (1974) reviewed and critiqued existing research on sex differences to challenge stereotypic beliefs regarding sex differences. Their critiques are based on adherence to scientific procedures. They would most likely be seen as *feminist empiricists* by Harding (1987) as would the co-authors of the Guidelines for Nonsexist Research in Psychology (McHugh, Koeske and Frieze, 1986). All research conducted by feminists comparing the attitudes, behaviors, and experiences of women to those of men would be classified as feminist empiricism. Research designed to develop instruments to measure gender role identification, achievement motives, love and liking, and any other psychological construct would be viewed as feminist empiricism. Thus, most of the research reported in mainstream or even feminist journals is empirical in nature. Feminist empiricists espouse the position that by identifying and eliminating masculine bias and through more vigorous adherence to the scientific method, we can get an objective picture free of gender bias.

In the feminist empiricist position, social biases are conceptualized as prejudices that are based on false beliefs and hostile attitudes. These prejudices are seen as affecting all aspects of the scientific method, especially the identification and definition of the problem. Feminist empiricists argue that sexist and androcentric biases can influence existing methodological norms of scientific inquiry (Harding, 1987). The operation of such biases, however, is "bad science." Good science can, according to this perspective, and will most likely lead to liberation.

This perspective leaves intact much of science's understanding of the principles of adequate scientific research as they are taught to students. It challenges the practice of empiricism, not the norms. Feminist empiricists criticize the system, but only in the system's terms, only according to system standards (Belenky et al., 1986). Feminist empiricists think that social values and political agendas can enlarge the scope of the inquiry or can reveal the need for greater care in the conduct of the inquiry, but the logic of explanation and research still conform to standard empiricist rules (Harding, 1987).

Feminist empiricists are attempting to produce a feminist science, one that better reflects the world around us than the incomplete and distorting accounts provided by traditional science. In their view, a feminist science would not replace one set of biases with another but would rather advance the true and gender-neutral objectivity of science.

As explained above, other feminists have come to question the possibility of conducting value-free or objective research. For them, a simple revision of empirical research strategies is recognized as an important, but incomplete, solution to research dilemmas.

Feminist Standpoint Epistemology

Feminist critics have analyzed the ways in which existing knowledge is limited or distorted because it was generated from a masculine or androcentric perspective. Our ideas about achievement motivation, aggression, autonomy, and so on are all based on a tradition of men studying male behaviors. Gilligan (1982), for example, argues that not only are Kohlberg's (1984) conceptions of moral development based on male development, but his use of abstract hypothetical scenarios to measure moral approaches is also the result of a masculine worldview.

Some feminists view bias in the research process as resulting from the accumulated common experiences of men—the dominant group. Scientists are supposed to disengage from shared assumptions about the nature of reality and generate alternative testable conceptualizations of reality (McHugh, Koeske, and Frieze, 1986). Individuals who are not members of the dominant group (e.g., women, and men of color) have an advantage in being able to view reality from an alternative perspective (Mayo, 1982). The idea that women can bring a special perspective to research has been termed the *feminist standpoint* position (Harding, 1987; Stanley and Wise, 1993). In the feminist standpoint perspective, "women's ways of knowing" (Belenky et al., 1986) and women's voices (Gilligan, 1982) are different and potentially superior to men's ways of knowing. Belenky and her colleagues (Belenky et al., 1986) interviewed women concerning how and what they knew; their approach to research both implicitly and explicitly subscribes to feminist standpoint theory.

According to feminist standpoint theory, knowledge based on a feminist standpoint is more complete and less distorted than knowledge gained from traditional social science inquiry. The knowledge gained from traditional research contains implicit assumptions about women, gender, and male superiority, and is used to justify male domination. Feminist research conducted from this perspective attempts to explicate its gender assumptions and makes women's experience the central focus. Rather than justify male domination, the research seeks to understand women's experience of subordination, and transform gender and social relations of domination and subordination.

Like feminist empiricism, the feminist standpoint accepts the existence of a true reality and adopts the basic methods of science as the means for knowing that reality. However, from this perspective feminists are seen as superior knowers as a result of being outsiders. As members of a subordinate group, women can comprehend the reality of the relations of domination and subordination. For example, Rose (1983) envisions a feminist biology that does not attempt to be objective and external to the female biological entity, but attempts to make over biological knowledge in order to overcome women's alienation from our own bodies, our own selves.

Thus, a feminist standpoint is recognized and privileged over a male perspective. Realizing that there is a feminist standpoint distinct from the traditional (male) standpoints raises the possibility of there being more than one alternative standpoint. Stanley and Wise (1990) challenge the contention that there is only a single feminist standpoint. They call for the recognition of the validity of black feminists' and lesbian feminists' (epistemological) standpoints. The recent emergence of queer theory is based on the contention of gay and lesbian scholars that being homosexual or bisexual in a society dominated by heterosexuals gives gays and lesbians a particular perspective on the world (Morton, 1996). Thus, within the feminist community, a lesbian would not share an epistemological standpoint with a heterosexual feminist, that is, would not "know" the world in the same way, and would not ask the same research questions. Similarly, black feminist scholars have been articulating their unique epistemological standpoint, which they call black feminist thought. Patricia Hill Collins (1989) and bell hooks (1984; 1989) are two well-known black feminists who argue persuasively that as black women they do not share the same view of the world as white women or as black men (or, of course, as white men). For example, one might consider how each of these groups of women (white feminists, lesbian feminists, and black feminists) might approach the study of motherhood, sisterhood, or research on male-female relations. If we are not willing to accept men studying men as the basis for understanding women's behavior, then are we willing to accept white women studying white women as the basis for understanding black women, or heterosexual women studying heterosexual women as the basis for understanding lesbians? It is not just that each group has a particular set of experiences, but that race and sexual orientation, like gender, are the basis of domination and subordination in our culture.

The idea is that in addition to gender, one's race, sexual orientation, age, ethnicity, class, region, culture, and level of ability affects how one views the world. If each of these constitute a particular standpoint, then is there a single reality? Can anyone's position or perspective on reality be privileged, that is, viewed as superior? Feminist postmodernists and others have raised questions about both feminist empiricism and the feminist standpoint position. For example, Bleier (1984) suggests that the feminist empiricist perspective implies acceptance of the idea that there exists a body of neutral knowledge; that science can be refined until we have the facts right (Bleier, 1984; Schiebinger, 1987). The realization or comprehension that the traditional approaches to theory and research within the natural and social sciences are based on a particular perspective or set of experiences and that there are a variety of other standpoints thus leads many feminists to the adoption of a social constructivist perspective.

Feminism and Social Construction

Social construction is a theoretical orientation that serves as a foundation for several new approaches to the study of human social behavior. The basic insight of constructionist thought is that all knowledge is constructed and the knower is an intimate part of the known. Social constructionists understand that answers to all questions vary depending on the context and the frame of reference for the question, that is, on your particular standpoint. All knowledge is derived from looking at the world from some perspective or another. People are viewed as having created their own versions of reality; social reality is a "negotiated understanding" of the world.

According to Burr (1995) there are four key assumptions to the social construction position. First, social construction challenges taken-for-granted knowledge. Rejecting positivism, social constructionists do not subscribe to the belief that there can be objective, unbiased observation of the world. Second, our understanding of the world is based on our location in a specific historical and cultural context. This corresponds to the discussion above that region, culture, age, race, religion, and so on affects one's understanding and perspective on the world. Within a culture or society people have, through conversation and discourse, arrived at some mutually agreed-upon beliefs about the world. However, those beliefs may not be the same in another culture. Examining the belief systems of any culture or group can give us insight into that culture, but not into the nature of reality. When investigating other "primitive" cultures we have viewed the knowledge held by that culture as a set of artifacts of that culture, but we have often privileged our own knowledge systems as "true." Third, the production of knowledge is a social process. Our knowledge about the world is constructed in daily interactions between people. Our understanding of the world is shaped by what others around us say, by the news, by popular media, by art and culture, by sermons from the pulpit, through school lessons, by literature, and so on. These sources are referred to as discourses in social construction, and are the "data" that social constructionists research. And fourth, there is a connection between knowledge and social action. Social constructions of knowledge created in a cultural context sustain certain patterns of social action and preclude others. How we decide to act depends on our understanding of the world. How we would work for social justice, for example, would depend on our conception of social justice; social justice is a construct we have developed in the context of our lives. Gender and gender equity are similar constructs.

Social construction developed in a social climate referred to as postmodernism. Postmodernism is an intellectual movement centered in literature, architecture, and art. Postmodernism rejects the tenets of modernism, the intellectual tradition that preceded it. Modernism involved the search for truth (enlightenment). Postmodernists reject the idea that there are truths, or true forms, or underlying structures. Postmodernists also reject the idea that the world can be understood in terms of grand theories (such as those of Marx or Freud) or by one system (such as religion). (For an expanded and accessible explanation of social construction and postmodernism, see Burr, 1995.)

Empirical research is not a viable enterprise given a social constructionist perspective. Having rejected the possibility of underlying structures and denied the existence of a single reality, a feminist researcher cannot engage in the search for truth or discovery. Research conducted within a social construction perspective might instead involve the analysis of interviews or narratives. The interview is seen as a construction or a negotiation of reality between researcher and respondent. Alternatively, the researcher may analyze cultural artifacts and products such as films, ads, textbooks, and texts. The analysis would involve deconstructing the text, examining the assumptions underlying the message and format, and considering what the text does not say as well as what it does say. For example, Fine (1992) interviewed women in high school and analyzed the transcripts of the conversations for indications of how these young women resisted certain cultural messages and institutional and societal roles.

Challenging Dichotomous Thinking

The social construction perspective encourages us to critically examine the assumptions underlying our constructions, concepts, and worldviews. Among other assumptions, we are encouraged to challenge the simplicity and unhelpful nature of dualistic and dichotomous thinking. In the case of feminist research this has meant the critical examination of what is meant by "sex" and "gender." Feminists have explored the ways in which individuals who are outside the traditional sex/gender categories, for example gender blenders (Devor, 1989) and transsexuals (Kessler and McKenna, 1978), experience gender in their daily lives. As a result sex/gender is not seen as a naturally occurring dichotomy, but as socially constructed and limiting categories into which individuals are forced. Sex and gender are both seen as continuous rather than dichotomous variables, and gender is viewed as a dependent rather than an independent variable (Unger, 1989). Gender is a construct negotiated in our interpersonal interactions. It resides not in the individual, but in societal discourses and interactions (Bohan, 1993). Bohan (1993) explains the difference between an essentialist approach, for example, "You are friendly," and a postmodern or social constructionist perspective, such as "This is a friendly interaction." Being friendly is a reference to a social interaction; it is not something inherent in any individual. Similarly, feminist psychologists are coming to view gender not as something you have, but as something you do (West and Zimmerman, 1987). In certain situations men and women are encouraged or trained to act differently from each other. Thus, gender is a role enacted in gendered situations. In other situations that are not gendered, the roles are not enacted. Thus, gender is not inherent in the person but is a learned set of responses called for in certain situations. This is very different from the traditional view that gender is the manifestation of underlying biological differences between men and women, and is distinct from the feminist standpoint perspective that women are distinct and special.

The comparative methods of psychology (e.g., analysis of variance and tests of group means) are explicitly based on the use of dichotomous and other simplistic categorical systems. The comparative analytic strategy may not be the most appropriate or helpful way to include women and other non-dominant groups in psychological research (McHugh, 1993). Comparisons between dominant and subordinate groups will be constructed and interpreted in such as way as to (mis)represent behaviors (resulting from oppression) as reflecting essential attributes of the subordinated groups. Difference is likely to be represented as deficiency (McHugh, Koeske, and Frieze, 1986).

Reflecting on Our Own Values and Assumptions

Another dichotomous perspective underlies the traditional research process and is challenged by feminist social constructionists. The distinction between them (subjects) and us (researchers) has been discussed previously, in terms of traditional androcentric research on women and in terms of objectivity. However, merely being a woman does not resolve the us-them dilemma in feminist research. Although we may sympathize, empathize, or even identify with the research participants, this does not mean that they experience us as one of them. Even relationships (among researchers and respondents) referred to in the literature as partnerships, collaborations, or otherwise egalitarian may be better characterized as ambivalent, guarded, contractual, or even conflicted. Reinharz (1988) recommends that in order to hear the voices of others, we have to "study who we are, and who we are in relation to those we study" (p. 15).

Specifically, in terms of methodological suggestions, this means explicitly incorporating reflexivity in the research design (Holloway, 1989; Lather, 1991; Morawski, 1995). In a commonly used reflective approach, the researcher provides an "intellectual autobiography" (Stanley and Wise, 1993) tracing her interest in, relationship with, and approach to the questions and to the research participants. For example, Ussher (1991) traces her interest in women's madness to her mother's "mental illness," thus eliminating the illusion that she is a detached or disinterested knower. The reflexive stance may involve "reflecting upon, critically examining, and exploring analytically the research process in an attempt to demonstrate the assumptions about gender (and increasingly race, disability and other oppressive) relations which are built into a specific project" (Maynard, 1992, p. 16). Holloway (1989) offers such an extended reflexive stance, one in which she reflects on how she made decisions and interpretations throughout her research on heterosexual relations. Fine (1992) offers multiple examples of reflections on the research process, arguing, for example, that we should demystify the ways in which we select, use, and exploit voices of respondents.

One critique of the social constructivist position is that their language (discourse) makes it difficult to understand (access). Perhaps their ideas are quite challenging as well as their language. Some critics have suggested that social construction discourse creates hierarchies within feminism and gives status to some authors and researchers, without contributing to our understanding of women (Kelly, Burton, and Regan, 1994). Others contend that social construction and a postmodern stance undermines our ability not only to do research, but to effect social change.

CONCLUSIONS

Writing about feminist research is not any easier than conducting it. There are no easy or clear answers to the questions raised. This chapter is based on the premise that there is no single feminist method, nor is there a privileged or correct feminist epistemology. Currently, as in all areas, there are competing claims and persuasive critiques. Feminist research is everything from the critique of androcentric conclusions of traditional research to the conduct of a quantitative study of sex differences to the self-reflective narratives of conducting research with battered women. In my personal opinion, feminist research stems from feminist consciousness and is designed to benefit women. If you trace the references to my own work through the paper you can trace my movement from critic of traditional research through feminist empiricism to social constructionism. I can only urge you to similarly work within contradictions, and work through contradictions in mutual respect (Stanley and Wise, 1993). The multiplicity and diversity of voices within feminist research contributes to the richness, variety, and validity of our understanding of women and gender. Feminists hope that it will also contribute ultimately to social change.

KEY TERMS

sexist	objectivity	androcentric
sexist bias	subjectivity	methods
sex-fair	qualitative methods	methodology
misogynist	quantitative methods	epistemology
gender	feminist empiricism	feminist empiricism
participatory activist research	social constructionism	feminist standpoint
action research	the feminist method	social constructionism

DISCUSSION QUESTIONS

1. What is feminist research? How is it different from traditional research?
2. Is there such a thing as *a* feminist method? Why or why not?
3. What is epistemology? What are the three feminist positions with regard to epistemology? How are they different from each other?

REFERENCES

Belenky, M., B. Clinchy, N. Goldberger, and J. Tarule (1986). *Women's ways of knowing: The development of self, voice and mind.* New York: Basic Books.

Bleier, R. (1984). *Science and gender: A critique of biology and its theories on women.* New York: Pergamon.

Bohan, J. S. (1993). "Regarding gender: Essentialism, constructionism, and feminist psychology," *Psychology of Women Quarterly, 17:* 5-22.

Burr, V. (1995). *An introduction to social construction.* New York: Routledge.

Collins, P. Hill (1989). "The social construction of Black feminist thought," *Signs, 14:* 745-773.

Devor, H. (1989). *Gender blending: Confronting the limits of duality.* Bloomington, IN: Indiana University Press.

DuBois, E., G. Kelly, E. Kennedy, C. Korsmeyer, and L. Robinson (1987). *Feminist scholarship: Kindling in the groves of academe.* Chicago: University of Illinois Press.

Fine, M. (1992). *Disruptive voices: The possibilities of feminist research.* Ann Arbor, MI: University of Michigan Press.

Gilligan, C. (1982). *In another voice: Psychological theory and women's development.* Cambridge, MA: Harvard University Press.

Gondolf, E. W. (1990). An exploratory survey of court-mandated batterer programs. *Response to the Victimization of Women and Children, 13(3),* 7-11.

Gondolf, E. W. (1993). Treating the batterer. In *Batterying and family therapy: A feminist perspective,* M. Hansen and M. Harway (Eds.). Newbury Park, CA: Sage, pp. 105-118.

Graham, D. L. R. and Rawlings, E. I. (1990, June). Teaching an emerging feminist research methodology. Paper presented at the annual meeting of the National Women's Studies Association, Bloomington, IN.

Griffin, S. (1978). *Women and nature: The roaring inside her.* New York: Harper and Row.

Harding, S. (1986). *The science question in feminism.* Bristol, PA: Open University Press.

Harding, S. (1987). "Introduction: Is there a feminist methodology?" In *Feminism and Methodology,* ed. Sandra Harding. Milton Keynes: Open University Press.

Harding, S. (1991). *Whose science, whose knowledge?* Buckingham, UK: Open University Press.

Holloway, W. (1989). *Subjectivity and method in psychology: Gender meaning and science.* London: Sage Publications Ltd.

hooks, b. (1984). *Feminist theory: From margin to center.* Boston: South End Press.

hooks, b. (1989). *Talking back: Thinking feminist, thinking Black.* Boston: South End Press.

Hyde, J. and M. Linn (Eds.) (1986). *The psychology of gender: Advances through meta-analysis.* Baltimore, MD: Johns Hopkins University Press.

Kaplan, M. (1983). "A woman's view of DSM III," *American Psychologist, 38:* 786-792.

Keller, E. F. (1982). "Feminism and science," *Signs, 7:* 589-602.

Keller, E. F. (1985). *Reflection on gender and science.* New Haven, CT: Yale University.

Keller, E. F. and C. R. Grontkowski (1983). "The mind's eye." In *Discovering reality*, S. Harding and M. Hintikka (Eds.). Dordrecht, Holland: Reidel, pp. 207-224.

Kelly, L., S. Burton, and L. Regan (1992). "Researching women's lives or studying women's oppression? Reflections on what constitutes feminist research." In *Researching women's lives from a feminist perspective*, M. Maynard and J. Purvis (Eds.). Basingstoke, Britain: Taylor and Francis, pp. 22-48.

Kessler, S. and W. McKenna (1978). *Gender: An ethnomethodological approach.* Chicago: University of Chicago Press.

Koeske, R. D. (1978, March). "Menstrual cycle research: Challenge or chuckle?" Paper presented in panel "Politics of menstrual cycle research," Association for Women in Psychology, Pittsburgh, PA.

Kohlberg, L. (1984). *The psychology of moral development.* New York: Harper and Row.

Koss, M. (1996). *A women's mental health agenda.* Washington, DC: American Psychological Association.

Lather, P. (1991). *Getting smart: Feminist research and pedagogy with/in the postmodern.* London: Routledge.

Maccoby, E. E. and C. N. Jacklin (1974). *The psychology of sex differences.* Stanford, CA: Stanford University Press.

Maynard, M. (1992). "Methods, practice, and epistemology: The debate about feminism and research." In *Researching women's lives from a feminist perspective*, M. Maynard and J. Purvis (Eds.). Basingstoke, Britian: Taylor and Francis, pp. 10-26.

Mayo, C. (1982). "Training for positive marginality," *Applied Social Psychology Annual, 3:* 57-73.

McHugh, M. C. (1990). "Gender issues in psychotherapy: Victim blame/woman blame." Invited address presented at the annual meeting of the American Psychological Association, Boston.

McHugh, M. C. (1993). "Studying battered women and batterers: Feminist perspectives on methodology." In *Battering and family therapy: A feminist approach*, M. Hansen and M. Harway (Eds.). Newbury Park, CA: Sage, pp. 54-69.

McHugh, M. C., I. Frieze, and I. Browne (1992). "Research on battered women and their assailants." In *Psychology of women: A handbook of issues and theories*, eds. M. Paludi and F. Denmark. Westport, CT: Greenwood.

McHugh, M. C., R. Koeske, and I. Frieze (1986). "Issues to consider in conducting nonsexist psychological research: A guide for researchers," *American Psychologist, 41:* 879-890.

McHugh, M. C. and M. Signorelli (1993, August). "Gendered subjects in psychology." Invited presentation to American Psychological Association.

McIntosh, P. (1984). "Interactive phases of curricular re-vision." In *Toward a balanced curriculum: A sourcebook for initiating gender integration projects*, B. Spanier, A. Bloom, and D. Borovik (Eds.). Cambridge, MA: Schenkman Publishing Co., pp. 25-34.

Mednick, M., S. Tangri, and L. Hoffman, eds. (1975). *Women and achievement: Social and motivational analysis.* Washington, DC: Hemisphere.

Morawski, J. (1995). *Practicing feminism, reconstructing psychology: Notes on a liminal science.* Ann Arbor, MI: University of Michigan Press.

Morton, D. (1996). *The material queer.* Boulder, CO: Westview Press.

Pugh, A. (1990). My statistics and feminism—a true story. In *Feminist praxis: Research, theory, and epistemology in feminist sociology,* L. Stanley (Ed.). New York: Routledge, pp. 103-112.

Reinharz, S. (1981). "Dimensions of the feminist research methodology debate: Impetus, definitions, dilemmas, and stances." Paper presented at the meeting of the American Psychological Association, Los Angeles.

Reinharz, S. (1988). "The concept of voice." Paper presented at meeting of Human Diversity, Perspectives on People context, University of Maryland, College Park, MD.

Reinharz, S. (1992). *Feminist methods in social research.* New York: Oxford University Press.

Rose, H. (1983). Hand, brain, and heart: A feminist epistemology for the natural sciences. *Signs, 9,* 73-90.

Rosenberg, R. (1982). *Beyond separate spheres: Intellectual roots of modern feminism.* New Haven, CT: Yale University Press.

Rosser, S. V. (1990). *Female friendly science: Applying women's studies methods and theories to attract students.* New York: Pergamon.

Rossitor, M. (1982). *Women scientists in America: Struggles and strategies to 1940.* Baltimore: Johns Hopkins Press.

Ruddick, S. (1980). "Maternal Thinking," *Feminist Studies, 6(3):* 343-367.

Sayre, A. (1975). *Rosalind Franklin and DNA.* New York: W.W. Norton.

Schiebinger, L. (1987). The history and philosophy of women in science: A review essay. *Signs, 12,* 305-332.

Sherif, C. W. (1979). "Bias in psychology." In *Feminism and Methodology,* S. Harding (Ed.). Bloomington, IN: Indiana University Press, pp. 37-56.

Spender, D. (1978). Educational research, feminist consciousness, and experiences of sexism. *Women's Studies International Quarterly, 2,* 359.

Stanley, L. and S. Wise (1990). Method, methodology, and epistemology in feminist research processes. In L. Stanley (Ed.) *Feminist praxis: Research, theory, and epistemology in feminist sociology,* pp. 20-60. London: Routledge.

Stanley, L. and S. Wise (1993). *Breaking out again: Feminist ontology and epistemology.* New York: Routledge.

Tiefer, L. (1995). *Sex is not a natural act & other essays.* Boulder, CO: Westview Press.

Unger, R. K. (1981). Sex as a social reality: Field and laboratory research. *Psychology of Women Quarterly, 5,* 645-653.

Ussher, J. (1991). *Women and madness: Misogyny or mental illness?* London: Harvester Wheatsheaf.

Wallston, B. S. (1981). "What are the questions in psychology of women? A feminist approach to research," *Psychology of Women Quarterly, 5:* 597-617.

West, C. and D. H. Zimmerman (1987). "Doing gender," *Gender and Society, 1:* 125-151.

Whitley, B. E., M. C. McHugh, and I. H. Frieze (1986). "Assessing the theoretical models for sex differences in causal attributions for success and failure." In *The psychology of gender: Advances through meta-analysis*, J. S. Hyde and M. C. Linn (Eds.). Baltimore, MD: Johns Hopkins University Press.

Wittig, M. (1985). "Metatheoretical dilemmas in the psychology of gender," *American Psychologist, 40:* 800-811.

Yllo, K. (1988). Political and methodological debates in wife abuse research. In *Feminist perspectives on wife abuse,* K. Yllo and M. Bograd (Eds.). Newbury Park, CA: Sage Publications.

Chapter 3

Women in Science: Rediscovering the Accomplishments of Women

Darlene Richardson

OVERVIEW

As early as the beginning of the fifteenth century, historians and scientists described the contributions of *women scientists*. From the late 1970s throughout the 1980s, and ever increasingly in the 1990s, primarily women authors have rediscovered the often-ignored achievements of women in science (see Fausto-Sterling, 1981; Rossiter, 1982; Keller, 1985; Ogilvie, 1986; Schiebinger, 1987; Alic, 1988; Bonta, 1991; Rosser, 1993; among many others). The discovery or rediscovery of these unheralded accomplishments of women in science indicate that distressingly frequently their contributions were deliberately erased or attributed to male colleagues (see Watson, 1968; Sayre, 1975; and Gribbin, 1985 as examples—again among many). Many people think women have entered science only in the twentieth century and that Marie Curie is the only woman scientist of note. Yet hardly anyone realizes that despite Marie Curie's two Nobel Prizes, she was denied membership in the all-male French Academie des Sciences.

Increasingly, papers presented at various national scientific conferences reflect concerns with *gender issues in science* and *feminist critiques of science* (Rosser, 1996; Bleier, 1986; Harding, 1986, 1991). Women both inside and outside of academia have questioned the lack of women's voices in understanding both the meaning and structure of science and scientific knowledge. Feminist critiques of science have wondered about *objectivity* and *subjectivity* in science and asked what are the sexist and racist flaws in design, collection, and interpretation of data (Bleier, 1984). For example, male experimental animals are used because scientists have argued that female hormones make studying females too complicated.

Further study (see Rosser, 1986) indicates that males have varying amounts of hormones in their systems which fluctuate in both predictable and unpredictable ways. Which sex is easier to study may well be the female because of greater regularity of hormone changes. Others have debated about which scientists are permitted to ask which questions (Hubbard, Henifin, and Fried, 1979; Hrdy, 1981; Haraway, 1991) and who is awarded grants from national scientific organizations. As an example, we know that it is only recently that national scientific organizations declared breast cancer a problem worthy of study and funding. Will studies of menstruation and menopause be considered important? Still other feminist scientists have argued that science represents an *androcentric* (and Western) view of the world, such that hierarchical and unicausal solutions are preferred to interactive and multicausal ones (Spender, 1974; Hubbard, Henifin and Fried, 1982). Although many feminists reject science as it is practiced and view science as a tool used against women (see Fee, 1982), feminist critiques of science have been fundamental in changing science for the betterment of both science and humanity. As examples one can list conducting medical research using female as well as male subjects (Rosser, 1990), broadening the study of primates by studying family life among bonobos, gorillas, and orangutans (Haraway, 1979a, b; Montgomery, 1991), and improving the environment through grassroots national and international efforts frequently led by women.

Many women scientists have come to the study of women in science by answering the same questions: why are there so few women scientists in our textbooks, in our course syllabi, in our history books, and, therefore, in our awareness? Ask anyone to name a woman scientist and Marie Curie is the first, and often the only, answer. Women scientists whose work affects our daily lives are forgotten in our textbooks and unrecognized by many of us—even those of us who are scientists or "scientifically minded." Too few of us are familiar with Ellen Swallow Richards, a nineteenth-century American chemist who worked on improving sanitation in the home and on controlling municipal water quality. Nor do we recognize the name Gladys Hobby even though she developed the antibiotic oxytetracycline. These are scientists whose work affects our daily lives yet whose contributions are frequently overlooked (Gornick, 1983).

Subsidiary questions arise when we rediscover important female historical figures in science. Which scientists are recognized in our textbooks and what are their accomplishments that merit their inclusion? I stress inclusion in textbooks because, as Kuhn (1970) says, textbooks are not only the primary source of authority from which "scientists and laymen take much of their image of creative scientific activity" (p. 136) but they are also the primary "pedagogic vehicles for the perpetuation of normal science" (p. 137). If women scientists are not included in textbooks, then it follows that we assume their contributions are nonexistent or insignificant. Indeed, Kuhn (1970) contends that authoritative sources (such as professors and textbooks) systematically disguise scientific revolutions or challenges to "normal" science.

A final aspect of the "problem" of women in science is where to place women scientists in the *male domain* of science. Ellen Swallow Richards was allowed to teach chemistry in the laboratories at MIT, but she was not allowed to be a member of the faculty. When she worked on water quality, that work was declared not science but "home economics" (Rossiter, 1982). In a similar vein, Beatrix Potter was not permitted to present her work on lichen to a scientific assembly—women were not allowed to present their findings or even attend scientific meetings at that time. Thus, women scientists are a problem—the scientific community and culture wants to use their intelligence, skills, and data, but wants to exclude them from the scientific brotherhood (see Keller, 1977 and Vetter, 1980 as examples).

THE UNDERREPRESENTATION OF WOMEN IN SCIENCE

The American Association of University Women (AAUW, 1992) released a report documenting the operation of *gender bias* at all educational levels. Indications are that these biases are operating in our science classrooms at the college as well as the elementary, middle, junior high and high school levels, and that such bias is a factor in women's avoidance or abandonment of the sciences. This gender bias results in women being underrepresented in the scientific workforce. Other factors at work include the perception (reality?) of science as a male domain, the perception that scientists "devote their lives to science" to the exclusion of family life, socialization patterns (boys do not like smart girls), unequal access to mentoring, equipment, and professors' time in graduate school, and unequal rewards (more women than male scientists are underpaid, under-employed, untenured, and unemployed; Brush, 1991).

Women scientists and engineers composed approximately 13 percent of the *science-engineering workforce* in 1986 (National Science Board, 1989). Within this group, women's representation among the various fields differs greatly and supports gender segregation into fields occupied mainly by one gender or the other. For example, 4 percent of engineers, 25 percent of mathematicians, and 40 percent of psychologists are women. Cultural gender stereotypes and discrimination in academia and the workplace are probably most responsible for these differences in fields, with women underrepresented in engineering, physics, chemistry, and geology; well-represented in health sciences, psychology, and mathematics; and overrepresented in nursing and occupational and physical therapy. From the mid-1980s to the present, the number of American women who earned science and engineering degrees remained consistently low—even at a time when national attention was centered on recruiting women into technical fields (Brush, 1991).

How can we attract more women to major in science, math, and engineering when over 70 percent of the women who start out in these majors do not graduate in those fields (Hewitt and Seymour, 1991)? The *attrition rate* of women majors in science is nearly twice that of science majors as a whole (Vetter, 1981). Women earn 40 percent or more of the undergraduate degrees awarded in this country, and up to the mid-1980s increasing numbers of women went to graduate school in the natural sciences and engineering (Office of Technology Assessment, 1985; National Science Board, 1989). Yet, women currently earn only 16 percent of the doctorates in the physical sciences, 10 percent in computer science, and 7 percent in engineering (Holden, 1989). Thus, women leave their science majors (both undergraduate and graduate) at much higher rates than men, and are, not surprisingly, underrepresented in the science/technology workforce. Yet many of these women are high achievers and talented in science (Hewitt and Seymour, 1991; Tobias, 1990).

SCIENCE AS A MALE DOMAIN

Science has been and continues to be a male domain. Just as pool halls and video arcades have been designed and run as male establishments, so has science. Video games have been designed to appeal to male players. The participant imagines himself to invade space, to be a male superhero, and to fight off Ninja warriors. Similarly, the problems and lab exercises used in the sciences have been developed for and by males. Pithing a frog and calculating a baseball ERA are the scientific equivalent of Space Invaders and the Teenage Mutant Ninja Turtles. If video arcade owners wanted to appeal to a broader audience of people, or were interested specifically in attracting girls and women to their establishments, would they hold seminars to teach women to develop interest in their games, or would they design new games (using the same underlying principles) that appeal to women?

Women and girls have received explicit training to avoid domains that are peopled by males. Girls and women are warned not to go into pool halls or male bars. The cultural message girls repeatedly receive is "Women who ignore or disobey this advice deserve what they get." And what do they get? What happens when women invade or enter male domains? They are ridiculed, discouraged, ignored, devalued, excluded, and harassed. MacKinnon (1978) has argued that levels of *sexual harassment* in the workplace can be tied to sex ratios of male to female employees. Sexual harassment is prevalent in sex-segregated work environments. Sexual harassment may be viewed as one technique used by males to exclude and discourage women from entering male domains, or in male terms, "invading their turf." This perspective explains the experiences reported by women as they progress into higher levels of training in science, technology, and medicine. For example, Evelyn Hammond (professor of the history of science and former physics major) and Bernadine Healey (former director of the National Institutes of Health and surgeon) have spoken publicly regarding the racism and sexism they experienced in graduate school and in the operating theater.

Kuhn (1970) and other historians of science have demonstrated the ways in which the individual scientist is shaped in his/her observations and hypotheses by cultural and intellectual traditions. Aristotle lived in a time when women were considered intellectually inferior to men; he proved that purported inferiority by counting fewer teeth in women than in men (Rosser, 1986). In the early nineteenth century, phrenologists created complicated mathematical relationships to ensure that northern European males had larger cranial capacities than any other group (Gould, 1981). Of course we all know that bigger brains mean better brains! Today we view both Aristotle's counting of teeth and the phrenologist's determination that cranial capacity equals brainpower as absurd and evidence of science poorly done.

Similarly, the assumption that science is a male domain affects both fundamental and supplementary aspects of science. Science from a male viewpoint affects the construction of the *history of science*, such as who should be included in textbooks and why. One example from general astronomy textbooks illustrates my contention that extraordinary women of science are rarely included in textbooks, but quite ordinary male scientists are included, occasionally for mundane contributions (Richardson and Sutton, 1993). Tycho Brahe, whose main claim to fame is preservation of astronomical data collected by others, is mentioned in most general astronomy textbooks. In contrast, Annie Jump Cannon, who synthesized years' worth of observations (her own and others) into the seven spectral classes of stars, was not included in most astronomy textbooks before 1985. In more recent textbooks, she and other women workers in the Harvard College Observatory during the late nineteenth to early twentieth centuries are highlighted as boxed text or "astronomical insights." Her work is important in that spectral classes of stars represent evolutionary sequences.

Anther instance of science developed with a male perspective is found in the study of *primates*, apes, chimpanzees, and orangutans, which are our closest relatives. Looking at primates solely from one point of view may shape the underlying assumptions and perspectives of the scientist studying nature—male primatologists tended to study only male-initiated activities and concluded that the male is the primary decision maker in primate groups. Women primatologists studied all types of interactions among members of a troop and developed a more fully inclusive appreciation of the great diversity of social interactions among primates and the complexity of their social relationships. Male perspectives have also affected models and ways of approaching problems such as (refer to Spender, 1981; Bleier, 1984; Tuana, 1989):

- Theoretical models that use dominance rather than cooperation as the primary theme (e.g., the concept of the dominant gene or master gene in biology)
- Methods of research (e.g., attempts to control and reduce nature)
- The topics and funding priorities (e.g., the failure to use female subjects in drug trials and medical research)
- The interpretation of results (e.g., female brains are less lateralized than male brains, with less lateralization equated to lesser abilities)
- The pedagogies used to teach science (e.g. competition, inaccessible language, use of sexist examples and stereotypes)

In her model of *curriculum transformation*, Sue Rosser (1986) ties the research practices, theories and *pedagogies* of science to the composition of science. In each stage of her five-stage model, the number of women in science and their position in the scientific hierarchy are related to the degree to which we have accepted logical positivism and the contention that science is objective and value-free. Rosser suggests that only when women constituted a critical mass and achieved a few positions of influence in scientific communities did we develop feminist critiques of the subject matter, funding priorities, and pedagogy of science. This corresponds to the observations of scholars in other disciplines that a critical mass of 20 to 30 percent represents a turning point in the experiences of women in the contexts of their occupations and employment.

Rosser (1986) developed her model of curriculum transformation based on the work of Peggy McIntosh (1983), a historian who looked at ways of using women's studies techniques and strategies in the study of history. Rosser, a biologist, modified McIntosh's model for science, and biology specifically. There are five phases, which I have modified in terms of examples, relating the phases to science in general:

- Phase I: women are absent from lectures, textbooks, and all readings, and no one questions their absence from science
- Phase II: exceptional women in science are mentioned (the female Nobel laureates)
- Phase III: women are seen as a "problem" or "issue" in science (frequently heard stereotypical comments: we can't have women in the field, lab, classroom, and so on because we have no bathrooms for them; we cannot educate women as graduate students in science because they get married and leave the profession)
- Phase IV: science is reconceptualized with women in science as a category in itself; the inclusion of women's contributions and perspectives are incorporated in a fully integrated manner. As Rosser (1986) says, "the categories for analysis shift and become racially inclusive, multifaceted, and filled with variety" (p. 9).
- Phase V: science redefined and reconstructed to include us all; science transformed to become "better" science with such underlying ideas as dominance and hierarchy, forced duality, and subjectivity and objectivity viewed as assumptions developed within a particular context and social/cultural milieu. Science would be transformed from a Western, white, middle-to-upper-class, male perspective to one in which all perspectives would be utilized to give the best understanding of our observations and experiments.

WOMEN IN SCIENCE AS AN EXAMPLE OF GENDER INEQUITY

Women's participation (or lack thereof) in science both reflects and perpetuates *gender inequities* in education and in society (McHugh and Richardson, 1994). Girls' and women's avoidance of science and math is a critical factor in economic gender inequality. Women continue to earn seventy cents for every dollar earned by men despite two decades of struggle for economic parity. Some authors (Blaxall and Reagan, 1976; Reskin, 1984) have argued that the two factors most responsible for this economic disparity are gender discrimination and occupational segregation. *Occupational sex segregation* accounts for 35 to 40 percent of the difference in male and female earnings (Reskin, 1984).

Occupational sex segregation at the professional level begins in educational sex stratification. Men and women students are not evenly distributed across majors. Women continue to "choose" classes and majors that will result in lower-paying jobs. Women's avoidance of or disinterest in science and math is an important component of their educational and career choices. Although women earn less than men for every scientific field, women in science and women with science and math backgrounds make more than their sisters without science and math. The amount of math a woman takes is directly correlated with the amount of money she earns. According to the National Research Council (1991) the more math a career requires, the higher the pay and the lower the participation of women.

In addition to these structural equity issues, participation is an equity issue for the individual woman who is interested and/or talented in the sciences and mathematics. Shouldn't she be given the same encouragement, opportunity, and financial support that her brother receives? Shouldn't the examples used in class and on tests relate as closely to her experience as to her brother's?

By reaching more students, we create a better understanding of science by people both within and without science. As more diverse people are attracted to study science, science becomes "better" in that different viewpoints and different areas of interest expand science's horizons. An important case in point is how our understanding of primate behavior was transformed through the participation of women primatologists (see Hrdy, 1984; Haraway, 1991). Women primatologists looked at primates in the field and in the lab and studied all interactions—those between males and females, females and females, males and males, adults and young. Previously, most other observers had concentrated on male-initiated activities among adults. The female primatologists used nongendered language to describe what they observed. A troop made up of one male and females and young may be described as a "harem," or the male may be described as a "stud" for the females—whether we use "harem" or "stud" changes our assumptions about behavior and from whose point of view we are studying those behaviors. The use of nongendered language helped the scientists (and us) move beyond the patriarchal stereotype of the male-dominated troop. More recent studies of bonobos, pygmy chimpanzees, underscore that females lead these groups and sexual activities, not displays of strength, influence most social interactions at all levels.

In a series of articles and books Rosser (1986, 1990) examined the issue of gender bias in both the practice and the teaching of science, and has made a series of concrete suggestions for improving our curriculum. In *Female-Friendly Science* (1990), she explains the relationship of concrete, specific suggestions to theoretical models of women's ways of knowing (Belenky et al., 1986) and to models for curriculum transformation. Rosser contends that incorporating women in science at all levels has revolutionized the nature of science in terms of who asks what questions and which answers are deemed acceptable. Women primatologists (see Hrdy, 1984; Haraway, 1991 as examples) have transformed scientific knowledge.

Rosser's latest book (1996), *Teaching the Majority: Science, Mathematics and Engineering that Attracts Women,* compiles thirteen articles on how to modify the curriculum and pedagogy of the science classroom to reach the majority (including women) of our university students. In summary, these suggestions include: use gender neutral language, use appropriate examples or models, allow students to remain longer in the observation stage of experimentation, provide opportunities for students to cooperate rather than compete, and ensure that all students participate in all activities.

HISTORY OF WOMEN IN SCIENCE

Rossiter (1982), Alic (1988), Schiebinger (1987), and others have listed the women scientists who have contributed to science through the ages. Some of these women were praised, more were disparaged and discouraged, and a few were severely punished for their works. Most of these women documented in history are what I call "extraordinary" scientists rather than "ordinary" scientists. The ordinary scientists comprise most scientific workers, whether male or female. These scientists are not particularly recognized for their contributions to science in their times or later. The extraordinary scientists are the Nobel prize-winning scientists or the like who were often rewarded and acknowledged during their lifetimes or soon thereafter. It is the extraordinary scientist whose accomplishments are heralded in textbooks and imprinted in our consciousness of who are the great scientists (Richardson and Sutton, 1993). Most of us in science realize that science is a collaborative and cooperative endeavor with many people contributing to the development of new ideas or products.

Mary Fairfax Somerville and Mary Elizabeth Horner Lyell can be used as a case history that exemplifies what I mean. Mary Fairfax Somerville (1780-1872) and Mary Elizabeth Horner Lyell (1809-1873) were contemporaries, although their life histories and contributions to science show little in common. One was self-educated despite the efforts of her family, both nuclear and extended, whereas the other was nurtured in an academic environment and encouraged to study. One received many honors in her lifetime for her scientific contributions, while the other was best known as the charming wife of a famous man.

Mary Somerville was educated haphazardly in Scotland, although she came from a relatively well-educated family. After her father, an officer in the British Army, returned to Scotland and discovered his daughter "running wild," he sent her to a girls' school where she was taught to read by memorizing pages of the dictionary (Ogilvie, 1986). Her one-year stay at the school was so dreadful that Mary Somerville complained of her ill treatment for decades. Her parents thought that one year's worth of formal education was sufficient for Mary ("for a girl" was unstated but understood), because already she read too much and sewed too little (Osen, 1974; Alic, 1988).

Mary Somerville discovered algebra while reading a fashion magazine (the equivalent, I expect, of today's *Seventeen*). She taught herself algebra, but kept her efforts from her parents, who thought that learning higher mathematics would drive her mad. Her father knew a woman in an insane asylum who was obsessed with longitude (Alic, 1988). Mary's painting teacher introduced her to geometry when they tackled perspective. Mary memorized Euclid's *Elements of Geometry,* which she had obtained from her younger brother's tutor, because her parents confiscated her books so she would not study so much. At night, Mary mentally reviewed the memorized pages of Euclid's geometry before she slept.

Marriage to Samuel Grieg, a navy captain, and early widowhood left her financially independent. At the age of thirty-three, she was ecstatic that she could buy her own library of math and science books (Osen, 1974). She wanted to immerse herself in the study of math and the natural sciences. After three years of independence, she married a second time. Fortunately, unlike her first husband, Mary's second husband, William Somerville, encouraged her interests in mathematics and science. Mary accompanied him, an army surgeon, on his many trips to Europe. She and her husband knew, corresponded with, and entertained most of the great scientists of Europe.

When she was fifty the Society for the Diffusion of Knowledge asked her to translate, explain, and comment upon Laplace's *Mécanique Céleste.* Her explanation of the mathematics necessary to understand this important work became the preface to *Celestial Mechanism of the Heavens* published in 1831. The preface was published separately from Laplace's work and was used as a college textbook for nearly 100 years. Laplace considered her one of the few who understood his work and said that she was one of only two women who had sufficient mathematical background to understand it—the other was a Mrs. Grieg. Laplace did not know that Mrs. Grieg and Mrs. Somerville were the same person. Mary was denounced by both the House of Commons and the Church of England as a "godless woman" for writing *Celestian Mechanism of the Heavens* (Osen, 1974).

Mary wrote three more treatises that made physical laws familiar and understandable to laypeople, but which were of sufficient depth and authority to be of interest to the scientist. She was well honored within her lifetime, but no one noticed the irony of some of the accolades bestowed upon her. As examples, her bust was placed in the Great Hall of the Royal Society—a place where she, as a woman, could not step. Societies on both sides of the Atlantic that did not permit women as members or even in the audience gave her numerous awards. Praise for her was particularly strong in scientific societies at that time because she was a "womanly woman": wife, mother, and society matron, as well as scientific author.

Mary Somerville regretted her role as society matron, however; she said that she was required by her contemporaries to interrupt her work for visitors even though the visitors were unexpected and unwanted. How she wished, she said, that her work could be accorded the respect a man's work commanded—that she might continue with her writing and studying without interruption (Osen, 1974; Russett, 1989). I found it particularly ironic to read in geologist Charles Lyell's journals that he called upon Mrs. Somerville quite often even though he was unexpected. Lyell had no idea, I am sure, that Mary Somerville regarded his visits as interruptions to her work.

I have worked on unearthing the scientific contributions of Mary Elizabeth Horner Lyell by reading primary material in the forms of letters (both Mary's and Charles's) and journals. Mary Lyell was a conchologist and was responsible, for example, for the collection and study of land snails in the Canary Islands in 1854 (Wilson, 1972). She accompanied her husband, Charles Lyell, one of the foremost nineteenth-century British geologists, on many of his geological excursions, which provided him, as the voyage of the *Beagle* did for Darwin, with many modern analogies and metaphors for the study of fossils and their evolution. She also participated in the discussions on evolution between Lyell and Darwin (Wilson, 1970) and her work on snails on the Canary Islands was analogous to Darwin's work on birds and tortoises on the Galapagos Islands.

Unlike Mary Somerville, Mary Lyell was well educated by tutors. Her father, Leonard Horner, was a professor of geology who taught in both England and Germany. He was determined that his sons and daughters would be educated. Mary's younger sister Katherine, who married Charles's younger brother, was a well-respected botanist. Mary Lyell was fluent in French and German and learned Spanish and Swedish in order to assist her husband with his readings and correspondence with other European geologists. She not only worked with Charles in the field by sketching and painting geological structures and cross-sections, but she packed his clothes, geological equipment, and his geological specimens. She had primary responsibility for the cataloging of fossil, mineral, and rock collections.

Although it is impossible to separate her contributions from those of her husband, I can say with certainty that Charles Lyell could not have accomplished what he did without his wife's scientific support. Charles Lyell said of Mary Somerville that had she been married to another mathematician, "we should never have heard of her work. She would have merged it in her husband's, and passed it off as his" (Alic, 1988, p. 190). Although some geologists may claim that Mary Lyell did not have any original geological thoughts, I find it curious that Mrs. Louis Agassiz wrote Mrs. Charles Lyell about the glacial geology of South America. If the women were not intimately involved in geology and knowledgeable about it, why did not Mrs. Agassiz write Mr. Lyell or Mr. Agassiz write Mr. Lyell? One cannot claim that it was not considered "proper" for women to correspond with men who are not kin, because Mary Lyell had a long and fruitful correspondence with William Prescott.

Other geologists, such as Murchison (see Wilson, 1972), mention the attendance of Mary Lyell at special meetings of the London Geological Society and the interest she demonstrated in those lectures. She clearly had a deep understanding of geology, but her knowledge was not acknowledged by either her contemporaries or later historians of science. She truly represents the ordinary scientist whose contributions have been lost to us. She also represents the woman scientist whose work was subsumed within that of her husband, father, or brother.

Other case histories well worth exploring by students include Ellen Swallow Richards (chemist), Rachel Carson (marine biologist and environmentalist), Beatrix Potter (lichen specialist and children's author), and the contributions of Rosalind Franklin and Barbara McClintock concerning DNA (see Keller, 1983).

CONCLUSIONS

Women scientists have been instrumental in changing our view of scientific, technological, and environmental issues (see Hynes, 1989 as one example). They have persisted in their scientific endeavors despite many obstacles—personal, cultural, and structural. Their contributions have been ignored or, in some cases, deliberately erased. It is our responsibility as scholars, scientists, and feminists to discover these women, to recognize their achievements, and to understand the ways in which feminism has transformed science.

KEY TERMS

women scientists
gender issues
   in science
feminist critiques
   of science
objectivity
subjectivity
androcentric

male domain
gender bias
science-engineering
   workforce
attrition rate
sexual harassment
history of science
primatology

curriculum trans-
   formation
pedagogy
gender inequities
occupational sex
   segregation

DISCUSSION QUESTIONS

1. In order to engage these questions and issues, students should determine the representation of professional women (and minorities) in their particular disciplines. Students may determine that there is a skewed distribution by gender in areas of specialization in a particular discipline; e.g., women psychologists are more common in developmental psychology than in experimental psychology. Class discussion could center on the commonalties in gender disparities in these different disciplines and possible causes.

2. Which science courses did you most enjoy or dislike in elementary school, middle school, high school, and college? Which teaching strategies benefited you and other students most? Which teaching strategies made you disinterested in science? What stereotypes of science and scientists did you and your classmates share?

3. Study the styles of teaching in introductory-level science classrooms. Make note of the classroom dynamics (students' attitudes toward content) and teachers' strategies to engage students in the content and in ways of thinking scientifically. Visit another introductory classroom—one other than a science discipline. Note again classroom dynamics and teaching strategies. Are there any pronounced differences between the two classrooms? What are they? Do these differences appear to be based in how and what we teach in various disciplines? Which teaching styles and strategies appear to you to be more successful, which less successful?

4. Choose a field of science. Describe that science in terms of its attitudes, methods of investigations, and accepted paradigms in the past and present. Are there issues, problems, and concepts in that field that developed because men primarily participated in that science? If that science were dominated by women scientists, what changes would you imagine might take place (e.g., questions asked, topics,

types of experiments, methods of investigation, and so on)? Students might choose to look at a more detailed aspect of a science, such as brain and gender and nature and the environment.

REFERENCES

Alic, M. (1988). *Hypatia's heritage: The history of women's science.* London: Pandora Press.

American Association of University Women (1992). *How schools shortchange girls.* Washington, DC: AAUW.

Belenky, M., B. Clinchy, N. Goldberger, and J. Tarule (1986). *Women's ways of knowing.* NewYork: Basic Books.

Blaxall, M. and B. Reagan (1976). *Women and workplace: The implications of occupational segregation.* Chicago: University of Chicago Press.

Bleier, R. (1984). *Science and gender: A critique of biology and its theories on women.* Elmsford, NY: Pergamon Press.

Bleier, R. (1986). *Feminist approaches to science.* New York: Pergamon Press.

Bonta, M. M. (1991). *Women in the field: America's pioneering women naturalists.* College Station, TX: Texas A&M University Press.

Brush, S. (1991). "Women in science and engineering." *American Scientist, 79:* 404-419.

Fausto-Sterling, A. (1981). "Women and science." *Women's Studies International Quarterly, 4:* 41-50.

Fee, E. (1982). "A feminist critique of scientific objectivity." *Science for the People, 14* (5-8): 30-33.

Gornick, V. (1983). *Women in science: Portraits from a world in transition.* New York: Simon and Schuster.

Gould, S. J. (1981). *The mismeasure of man.* New York: Norton.

Gribbin, J. (1985). *In search of the double helix—Darwin, DNA and beyond.* Aldershots, UK: Wildwood House.

Haraway, D. J. (1978a). "Animal sociology and a natural economy of the body politic, Part I: A political physiology of dominance." *Signs, 4* (Autumn): 21-36.

Haraway, D. J. (1978b). "Animal sociology and a natural economy of the body politic, Part II: The past is the contested zone: Human nature and theories of production and reproduction in primate behavior studies." *Signs, 4* (Autumn): 37-60.

Haraway, D. J. (1991). *Simians, cyborgs, and women: The reinvention of nature.* New York: Routledge.

Harding, S. (1986). *The science question in feminism.* Ithaca, NY: Cornell University Press.

Harding, S. (1991). *Whose science, whose knowledge? Thinking from women's lives.* Ithaca: Cornell University Press.

Hewitt, N. and E. Seymour (1991). *Factors contributing to high attrition rates among science and engineering undergraduate majors.* Boulder, CO: Bureau of Sociological Research, University of Colorado.

Holden, C. (1989). "Wanted: 675,000 future scientists and engineers." *Science, 244:* 1536-1537.

Hrdy, S. (1981). *The woman that never evolved.* Cambridge, MA: Harvard University Press.

Hrdy, S. (1984). "Introduction: Female reproductive strategies." In *Feminist approaches to science,* M. Small (Ed.). Elmsford, NY: Pergamon Press.

Hubbard, R., M. S. Henifin, and B. Fried (Eds.) (1979). *Women look at biology looking at women.* Cambridge, MA: Schenkman.

Hubbard, R., M. S. Henifin, and B. Fried (Eds.) (1982). *Biological woman—The convenient myth.* Cambridge, MA: Schenkman.

Hynes, P. H. (1989). *The recurring silent spring.* New York: Pergamon.

Keller, E. (1977). "The anomaly of a woman in physics." In *Working it out,* S. Ruddick and P. Daniels (Eds.). New York: Pantheon.

Keller, E. F. (1983). *A feeling for the organism: The life and work of Barbara McClintock.* New York: W. H. Freeman and Company.

Keller, E. F. (1985). *Reflections on science and gender.* New Haven, CT: Yale University Press.

Kuhn, T. S. (1970). *The structure of scientific revolutions.* Chicago: The University of Chicago Press.

MacKinnon, C. (1978). *Sexual harassment of working women.* New Haven, CT: Yale University Press.

McHugh, M. C. and D. S. Richardson (1994). "Sex, science and equity: A faculty professional development approach." Paper presented at the International Conference for Women in Higher Education, January, 1994, Orlando, FL.

McIntosh, P. (1983). *Interactive phases of curricular re-vision: A feminist perspective.* Working Paper no. 124, Wellesley College, Center for Research on Women, Wellesley, MA.

Montgomery, S. (1991). *Walking with the great apes: Jane Goodall, Dian Fossey, Birute Galdikas.* Boston, MA: Houghton Mifflin.

National Research Council Committee on Women in Science and Engineering (1991). *Women in science and engineering: Increasing their numbers in the 1990s.* Washington, DC: National Academy Press.

National Science Board (1989). *Science and engineering indications—1989.* Washington, DC: U.S. Government Printing Office.

Office of Technology Assessment (1985). *Demographic trends and the science and engineering workforce—A technical memorandum.* Washington, DC: U.S. Government Printing Office.

Ogilvie, M. B. (1986). *Women in science: Antiquity through the nineteenth century—a biographical dictionary with annotated bibliography.* Boston: MIT Press.

Osen, L. M. (1974). *Women in mathematics.* Cambridge, MA: MIT Press.

Reskin, B. (1984). *Sex segregation in the workplace: Trends, explanations and remedies.* Washington, DC: National Academy Press.

Richardson, D. S. and C. J. Sutton (1993). "Ordinary and extraordinary women in science," *Bulletin of Science, Technology, and Society, 13* (5): 251-254.

Rosser, S. (1986). *Teaching science and health from a feminist perspective.* New York: Pergamon.

Rosser, S. (1990). *Female-friendly science.* New York: Pergamon.

Rosser, S. (1993). "Forum: Feminism and Science." *NWSA Journal, 5* (1): 65-76.

Rosser, S. (Ed.) (1996). *Teaching the majority: Science, mathematics and engineering that attracts women.* New York: Teachers College Press.

Rossiter, M. (1982). *Women scientists in America: Struggles and strategies to 1940.* Baltimore, MD: Johns Hopkins University Press.

Russett, C. E. (1989). *Sexual science: The Victorian construction of womanhood.* Cambridge, MA: Harvard University Press.

Sayre, A. (1975). *Rosalind Franklin and DNA: A vivid view of what it is like to be a gifted woman in an especially male profession.* New York: Norton.

Schiebinger, L. (1987). "The history and philosophy of women in science: A review essay," *Signs, 12:* 305-332.

Spender, D. (1974). *Men's studies modified.* Elmsford, NY: Pergamon.

Tobias, S. (1990). *They're not dumb, they're different: Stalking the second tier.* Tucson, AZ: Research Corporation.

Tuana, N. (Ed.) (1989). *Feminism and science.* Bloomington: Indiana University Press.

Vetter, B. (1980). "Sex discrimination in the halls of science," *Chemical Engineering News,* March: 37-38.

Vetter, B. (1981). "Degree completion by women and minorities in science," *Science,* (213) 212.

Watson, J. (1968). *The double helix.* New York: Atheneum Press.

Wilson, L. (Ed.) (1970). *Sir Charles Lyell's scientific journals on the species question.* New Haven, CT: Yale University Press.

Wilson, L. (1972). *Charles Lyell: The years to 1841, the revolution in geology.* New Haven, CT: Yale University Press.

Chapter 4

The Biology of Women: The Process of Becoming and Being Female

Donna M. Ashcraft

INTRODUCTION

It is vitally important for women to be knowledgeable about their bodies so that they can understand the processes they experience without misconception or fear and so that they can know what types of experiences are typical or normal and which are not. This knowledge is helpful in maintaining one's health. If a woman experiences a symptom that she knows to be atypical and that she cannot explain, she can then seek out the help of a professional to determine its cause and possibly a cure. It is the intention of this chapter, then, to provide information about the biology of women with this purpose in mind. Specifically, we will discuss the sexual anatomy of women, menstruation, and reproduction. We also discuss sexual differentiation, the process by which we become male or female, in order to provide a basis for understanding that women and men may actually be more similar than they are different.

THE ANATOMY OF WOMEN

External Reproductive Anatomy

A woman's basic sexual anatomy can be categorized into two parts: the external anatomy and the internal anatomy (see Figure 4.1). Let us begin by discussing the external anatomy. The region that includes the external reproductive structures of the female is referred to as the *vulva*. Thus, the vulva would consist of such structures as the clitoris and clitoral hood, the vestibule including the vaginal opening, the labia major and minor, and the perineum.

FIGURE 4.1. The External Reproductive Anatomy of Women

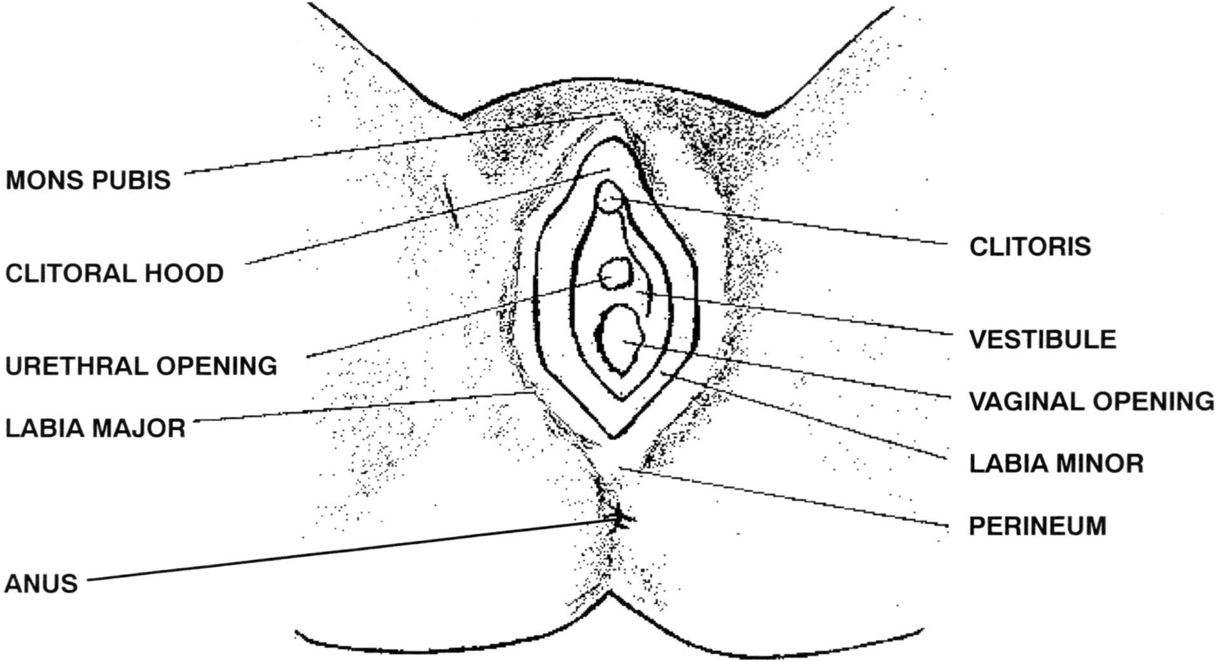

CLITORIS

VESTIBULE

VAGINAL OPENING

LABIA MINOR

PERINEUM

MONS PUBIS

CLITORAL HOOD

URETHRAL OPENING

LABIA MAJOR

ANUS

Artist: Betsy Hetrick.

The *mons pubis* is a layer of fatty tissue covering the pubic bone. Like many of the structures of the vulva, the mons is sensitive to stimulation and pressure on this region can begin to create sexual arousal. Extending down from either side of the mons pubis are the *labia majora* or major lips, and inside the labia majora are the *labia minora* or minor lips. These structures are made of tissue, blood vessels, and many nerve endings, so stimulation to them can also produce sexual arousal. In fact, during sexual arousal they can swell and deepen in color because of the number of blood vessels they contain. This is due to *vasocongestion,* which is an accumulation of blood in the blood vessels in an area of the body which produces a swelling or erection. Thus, because there is an increase in the volume of blood especially in the labia minor, they tend to increase in size and become a darker color during sexual arousal. (Vasocongestion, by the way, is also the mechanism that produces the erection of the penis in males. Essentially, there is more blood flow into than out of the penis and so it becomes thicker and longer, erect.) The labia minor also change position during sexual arousal. They open up, exposing the *vestibule,* which is the area inside the labia minora that contains the vaginal opening, the urethral opening, and the tissue connecting them. This tissue contains many nerve endings (and so is sensitive to stimulation) as well as oil-producing glands that lubricate this entire area, especially the vaginal entrance, thus making intercourse comfortable.

The labia minora meet at the *clitoral hood* in the front part of the vulva, which is located just below the mons pubis. The clitoral hood is a layer that covers the *clitoris*. The clitoris itself is the only structure (on males or females) whose only function is to produce sexual pleasure. It is made of many nerve endings and so stimulation to the clitoris produces sexual arousal. This sexual stimulation can cause the clitoris to swell in size (due to vasocongestion) and eventually retract underneath the clitoral hood so that it can no longer be seen. This is probably because the clitoris is so sensitive. Direct stimulation can cause some women some discomfort, which may explain why the clitoris retracts.

There are many types of stimulation that can produce sexual arousal: visual stimuli and erotic fantasies, as well as direct physical stimulation to the genital region. But whether we are talking about such behaviors as masturbation or vaginal intercourse, it is probably clitoral stimulation that is producing the sexual arousal. There has been debate over whether women experience more than one kind of *orgasm* (sexual peak), which began many years ago during Sigmund Freud's time. Freud (1963) believed that women could have two types of orgasm: a clitoral orgasm and a vaginal orgasm. A clitoral orgasm was one that stemmed from stimulation of the clitoris, that is, masturbation. A vaginal orgasm is an orgasm that stems from stimulation of the vagina, that is, sexual intercourse. He thought that the vaginal orgasm was a sign of mature sexual functioning. Thus, while it was acceptable that children had clitoral orgasms, once women were sexually mature, they had vaginal orgasms because they no longer needed to masturbate and could find sexual pleasure in intercourse. This implied that some women who were unable to achieve orgasm during intercourse were sexually immature. The problem with this thinking is that both vaginal intercourse and masturbation of the clitoris produce stimulation of the clitoris itself. This is because when sexual intercourse occurs, as the penis is inserted into the vagina and thrusting begins, the thrusting moves the labia minora, which is connected to the clitoral hood. The clitoral hood rests on top of the clitoris, so it moves against the clitoris itself, thus stimulating it. What this means, then, is that many women who are unable to achieve orgasm during intercourse may be having difficulty because they are not receiving enough stimulation to the clitoris. Thus Freud's belief in two types of female orgasm is not supported. In fact, Masters and Johnson (1966) have found that physiologically there is only one type of orgasm, that is, whether the stimulation comes from masturbation or vaginal intercourse, the same changes in the body occur during sexual arousal and orgasm. I should note, however, that recently, this debate has resurfaced and I will discuss this more fully when we discuss the Grafenberg (G) Spot.

The last area of the vulva to be described is the *perineum*. This is the area that extends down from the vaginal opening toward the anus. It too is sensitive to sexual stimulation. It is the area where an *episiotomy* is performed. An episiotomy is an incision that is made in the perineum during the later stages of childbirth in order to make a larger opening through which the baby can pass during delivery. The episiotomy has been a fairly routine procedure for a number of years since the medical establishment took over the process of childbirth. However, recently, physicians have been criticized for routinely carrying out this procedure because it is not always necessary and because some methods can be used to reduce the probability of needing this incision (e.g., The Boston Women's Health Collective, 1992). In fact, although this procedure is rather routine here in the United States, it is not in European countries. Doctors' primary purpose in carrying out the procedure is to produce a straight incision, which would be easier to sew up than a tear in the perineum which might occur otherwise. However, not all women tear and procedures such as warm compresses on the perineum and massaging it make this region more flexible, thus reducing the likelihood of tearing or needing the episiotomy.

The last external structures I would like to discuss are the female *breasts*. They consist primarily of fatty tissue and mammary (or milk) glands. The reason that women's breast sizes vary is because of the amount of fatty tissue within the breast itself, which is at least partially inherited. The larger the breast, the more fatty tissue it contains. Although many women express concern over their breast size and their ability to nurse children, there is no correlation. So while many women are afraid that their breasts are too small to produce enough milk for a baby, this is not true because what determines the amount of milk produced is not fatty tissue but the amount of mammary glands a woman has. Most women have approximately the same amount of mammary glands. What this means, then, is that women with smaller breasts can produce just as much (or more) milk as women with larger breasts.

Internal Reproductive Anatomy

Let us begin our discussion of the internal reproductive anatomy (see Figure 4.2) with the *vagina* and work up to the other internal structures. The vagina can be described as an elastic tube approximately three to five inches

FIGURE 4.2. The Internal Reproductive Anatomy of Women

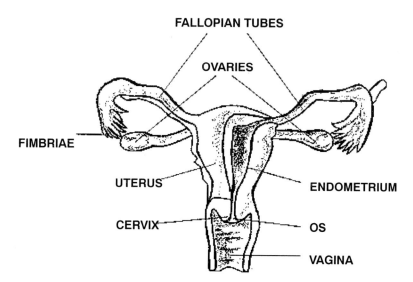

Artist: Betsy Hetrick.

long. It is described as elastic because it can accommodate different size penises, as well as the birth of a child. In its unaroused state the sides of the vagina rest together, as does an uninflated balloon, but during sexual arousal the walls open up, thus allowing for sexual intercourse, if that is the wanted sexual activity. The vaginal walls themselves contain many blood vessels and oil-producing glands. Sexual stimulation causes vasocongestion in the vaginal walls, which produces vaginal lubrication through a sweating response. Essentially, because there is an increase in the volume of blood in the vaginal walls, lubrication is squeezed out of the oil-producing glands.

The vagina also has a large number of nerve endings, but only in the outer (or bottom) one-third section. The inner two-thirds contain very few nerve endings and so are not very susceptible to stimulation. The myth, then, that suggests that women like to engage in intercourse with men who have large penises because larger penises produce more stimulation is not true, at least from a physiological standpoint. Psychologically, this may be a preference, although studies do not support this (Fisher, Branscombe, and Lemery, 1983). Also, although the vagina is somewhat elastic, it is limited in length—thus, only a certain length of penis can enter. Conveniently, the average erect penis is six to six and one-half inches; the average vagina in the aroused state is about five inches.

About one-third to one-half of the way up the front part of the vagina, just below the bladder neck, is another structure called the *Grafenberg* or *G spot*. This structure is different from any of the other structures we discuss because it is an area of soft tissue rather than an actual structure one can point to. This area has become well known because stimulation to it can cause sexual arousal and an intense orgasm (Perry and Whipple, 1982). This orgasm can be accompanied by female ejaculation. While most of us know that (most) men ejaculate when they experience orgasm, many of us are not aware that some women experience ejaculation as well. This lack of education has been unfortunate for some, in that some women who ejaculate think that they are leaking urine rather than ejaculating because the ejaculate is released from the urethra. But lab tests have shown that the content of the ejaculate is very different from that of urine. In fact, it seems to be similar to the fluid that is released from the male prostate gland (Belzer, Whipple, and Moger, 1984). This has led some to believe that this area of soft tissue may be the remnant of what would have developed into the prostate gland if a woman had become male instead of female during prenatal development. (We all start out with the same reproductive structures; they develop differently when we become male or female. See the section on sexual differentiation.)

If we continue to make our way up the vagina, the next structure we encounter is the *cervix* or bottom part of the uterus. This is the area from which a few cells are scraped during the *Pap smear* in order to test for cervical cancer. The cervix has an opening called the *os*, which allows for the passage of sperm to the uterus and the release of the menstrual flow. It is also the opening that widens (dilates) during labor to allow for passage of the baby from the uterus to the vaginal canal.

The *uterus* is a pear-shaped, muscular structure, about three inches wide and five inches in length in women who have not had children. It is where the *endometrium* (uterine lining) forms. It is this uterine lining that is released during menstruation and in which the fertilized egg embeds itself to create pregnancy.

Extending out from the uterus on either side are the *fallopian tubes* (or oviducts), where fertilization occurs. Extending from the fallopian tubes are fingerlike projections called *fimbriae*. The purpose of the fimbriae is to move and create a current that will sweep the egg (released by the ovary into the body cavity) into the fallopian tube. If an egg is to be fertilized it will do so in the outer one-third of the fallopian tube because if it has gone much farther than this, it is probably more than twenty-four hours old and has begun to degenerate. Thus, when you hear that a woman can only get pregnant one day out of the month (menstrual cycle), this is technically true. The problem with this thinking is that sperm live inside a female's body for forty-eight hours on average, but there have been reports of sperm living for as long as five days (Overstreet, 1986). Thus, theoretically, a woman can have intercourse five days before she releases an egg (*ovulation*) and the egg may still become fertilized. This is one of the reasons that the natural family planning method of contraception is not very effective.

Finally, the last internal reproductive structures to be discussed are the *ovaries*. These are almond-shaped glands that basically serve two functions: to produce female hormones and to house and release the eggs. The ovaries produce female hormones such as estrogen and progesterone. They are both important in the maintenance of the menstrual cycle; estrogen is also important in the secondary sex characteristics of females, such as breast development and the more rounded contours of a woman's body.

A female is born with all the eggs that she will ever have. During a menstrual cycle (approximately a month) one egg (occasionally more) is released into the body, where, as mentioned before, it will be swept up into the fallopian tube for possible fertilization. This process continues throughout a woman's reproductive years. Thus, when a woman releases an egg when she is thirty-eight years old, the egg is thirty-eight years old.

This is different from the sperm production of men *(spermatogenesis)*, in which sperm is continually being produced from adolescence onward. As a woman gets older, she releases fewer and fewer eggs until, at the time of menopause, she ceases releasing eggs altogether. This is why women have more trouble with infertility as they get older. The age of the eggs is also another reason for the increased numbers of birth defects that occur when an older (past 35 years) woman gets pregnant.

MENSTRUATION

Although most women experience menstruation during their reproductive years, most know relatively little about the process and many have misunderstandings about it. It is therefore, important to clarify this biological event so that women not only understand their own bodies, but also so that they can make informed decisions about how to deal with certain associated events.

The Menstrual Cycle

The *menstrual cycle* is the reproductive cycle of the female. It begins at adolescence with *menarche* or the first menstrual period and continues until a woman reaches *menopause* or the cessation of the menstrual cycle. Menarche begins when certain physiological requirements are met (e.g., enough fatty tissue on the body and adequate pelvic bone structure; Golub, 1985). Menopause is reached when there is a disruption in the hormonal feedback loops that maintain the cycle which began with menarche.

The menstrual cycle can be divided up into three phases: the follicular phase, the ovulatory phase, and the luteal phase. The follicular phase lasts about thirteen days in a twenty-eight-day cycle; ovulation only lasts one day; and the luteal phase lasts about fourteen days in a twenty-eight-day cycle. Keep in mind, however, that women's cycles vary in length and regularity.

The cycle is influenced by a series of hormonal feedback loops, that is, certain levels of one type of hormone influence the levels of another hormone and also influence other physiological changes. In the follicular phase there is a relationship between levels of estrogen and *follicle-stimulating hormone* (FSH), which represents one of these feedback loops. Notice in Table 4.1 that low levels of estrogen cause an increase in the production of FSH, and when FSH levels increase, estrogen levels increase. Finally, these higher levels of estrogen cause a decrease in the levels of FSH.

TABLE 4.1. Physiological and Hormonal Changes of the Menstrual Cycle

---

Follicular Phase (about 13 days):

    1. Low levels of progesterone and estrogen
- menstruation
- increased FSH

    2. Increased FSH
- increased estrogen
- follicle matures

    3. Increased estrogen
- decreased FSH
- increased LH
- endometrium forms

Ovulatory Phase (1 day):

    4. Increased LH
- ovulation
- increased progesterone

Luteal Phase (about 14 days):

    5. Increased progesterone
- decreased LH
- uterus secretes nourishing substances
- increased blood supply to the uterus

    6. Decreased LH
- decreased progesterone
- decreased estrogen
- corpus luteum degenerates

    7. Return to the follicular phase

Notice also that there is a relationship between the levels of progesterone and *lutenizing hormone* (LH). As LH levels increase, progesterone levels increase; as progesterone levels increase, LH levels decrease. And finally, as LH levels decrease there is also a decrease in the levels of progesterone.

Other events are occurring during the various phases of the menstrual cycle, which are outlined in Table 4.1. Menstruation occurs at the beginning of the *follicular phase* and is caused by lower levels of both progesterone and estrogen. It is important to note that the beginning of menstruation is the beginning of the menstrual cycle, especially if one is using natural family planning methods of contraception. Some women mistakenly believe that the beginning of the menstrual cycle is the first day after menstruation ends. This is incorrect and can negatively influence the effectiveness rate of some natural family planning methods. If, for example, a woman is using the calendar method of birth control, which means that she is estimating the day of ovulation by a counting method, her count is off by a little less than a week. This means that she is probably engaging in intercourse when she is most fertile, rather than least fertile.

As noted, the lower levels of estrogen also cause a subsequent increase in the production of FSH. This increase in FSH not only increases the level of estrogen but also causes the follicle to mature (hence the name follicle-stimulating hormone). The *follicle* is a spherical arrangement of cells that surround the egg. When the egg is released from ovulation the follicle bursts, releasing the egg.

The noted increase in the levels of estrogen now cause the levels of FSH to decrease and the levels of LH to increase. It is at this point that the endometrium forms again. Notice that the endometrium is forming at the end of the follicular phase of the menstrual cycle but before ovulation. This is because the lining of the uterus has already been released at the beginning of the follicular phase and now must be reformed in preparation for possible pregnancy, which would occur at the time of ovulation.

Ovulation occurs because of the influence of LH. The follicle has been ripening and it, along with the egg, has been moving to the surface of the ovary. At ovulation the follicle bursts, releasing the egg into the body cavity, where it will be swept up into the fallopian tubes by the current produced by the fimbriae.

This increase in LH, as noted, also influences an increase in the level of progesterone, which marks the beginning of the *luteal phase*. The increased levels of progesterone, in turn, cause a decrease in the levels of LH, and also cause the uterus to secrete nourishing substances, as well as increase the blood supply to the uterus. These two latter effects occur in preparation for possible pregnancy. A fertilized egg that is implanting into the uterus will need nourishment; the increased blood supply is preparation for the formation of the placenta (discussed below), which allows the fetus and mother to exchange substances.

Finally, lower levels of LH are followed by decreases in both progesterone and estrogen. (Notice that estrogen has remained high throughout the menstrual cycle once it has increased in the follicular phase.) The *corpus luteum*, which is the burst follicle, also degenerates. Once the follicle bursts it is a yellowish mass. The term corpus luteum literally translates to yellow body or yellow mass.

Notice also that lower levels of progesterone and estrogen will again cause menstruation to occur, and so there is a return to the follicular phase. The menstrual cycle begins again.

Menstrual Disorders

Although most women do not have trouble with their menstrual cycles, some do. Three types of menstrual disorders are most common: amenorrhea, dysmenorrhea, and premenstrual syndrome (PMS).

Amenorrhea is the absence of menstruation. There are two basic kinds: primary and secondary. Primary amenorrhea means that a female has never menstruated. She has reached the age of puberty (or passed it) and has not experienced menarche. This can be due to any number of physical reasons, such as hormonal problems. Secondary amenorrhea is an interruption in the menstrual cycle. A woman has experienced menstruation in the past but at present is not menstruating at the usual time. This also is caused by a number of factors. The most obvious would be pregnancy. When a woman gets pregnant she typically stops menstruating because the lining that is shed during menstruation is being used by the fertilized egg. Athletes and women who are anorexic also sometimes experience secondary amenorrhea. While we are not certain about why this occurs, it is most likely due to these women's bodies having too little fat. Athletes are muscular and have a lot of lean tissue but not fatty tissue on their bodies. Likewise, anorexics do not have much fat on their bodies because they are literally starving themselves. It is thought by some that a certain amount of fat on a woman's body is necessary for menarche and menstruation. This may be necessary because a woman's body is designed to have children. Her body stores extra fat in order to nourish the baby should she become pregnant and not receive enough nourishment (Golub, 1985). This is also probably one of the reasons why women have trouble losing that last five or ten pounds and why it is more difficult for women to lose weight than for men.

Dysmenorrhea is painful menstruation. Again, there are two types: primary and secondary. Primary dysmenorrhea is painful menstruation due to an overproduction of prostaglandins. *Prostaglandins* are hormones that cause the contraction of the uterus. It is currently thought that these are the same hormones that cause contractions during labor. When there is an overproduction of them the uterus will contract frequently and severely, thus eventually depriving the uterus of oxygen. It is this oxygen deprivation that causes pain (cramps). It is the same when we exercise our muscles. (Recall that the uterus is a muscular organ.) When we exercise a certain muscle group, we are continuously contracting and relaxing those muscles. Eventually, they become deprived of oxygen and start to hurt. This is why we may feel a burning sensation and muscle pain during workouts.

The best way to eliminate primary dysmenorrhea is to take aspirin (not another type of pain reliever). While this seems like a common-sense thing to do, there is a physical basis for it. Not only does the aspirin relieve pain, but it decreases prostaglandin production, thereby eliminating the source of the problem. This is why women who are in labor are told not to take aspirin. If they do, they decrease prostaglandin production and therefore increase the length of labor.

Secondary dysmenorrhea is painful menstruation due to any other reason than the overproduction of prostaglandins. These reasons can include infections of the pelvic region or a displaced intrauterine (IUD) device, among others.

The most controversial menstrual disorder is *PMS*. It is controversial because even though the general public believes it exists and that there is a physiological reason for it, professionals argue over whether there is actually such a disorder. Some of the problem stems from the lack of a clear definition. Many researchers define PMS in vastly different ways. Definitions vary in what symptoms are included and what time frame should be considered. For example, some researchers include so many symptoms in their PMS symptom checklists that it is virtually impossible for anyone to have no symptoms, and therefore all women have PMS (Tavris, 1991). Other researchers include many fewer symptoms. Likewise, some researchers believe that PMS can occur as much as two weeks before menstruation (which is typically the time of ovulation) while others include only a few days before menstruation.

Let us define PMS as the set of symptoms that occur before each menstrual period and that are severe enough to interfere with some aspect of life. These symptoms can be behavioral (e.g., crying spells), physiological (e.g., binge eating, cravings), or psychological (e.g., depression) in nature. But notice that the symptoms must occur before every menstrual period and must be fairly severe. This definition allows for the possibility that PMS exists but does not imply that every woman has this experience. Too often women experience symptoms and misattribute them to their menstrual cycles when menstruation or PMS have nothing to do with them. Consider, for example, that men also occasionally have cravings for certain types of food (e.g., a big steak) but that they do not blame these cravings on their testosterone levels.

For those women who do have severe symptoms before every menstrual period, hormonal factors may be implicated. But the evidence for this at this time is scarce, rather than abundant as the general population believes. In fact, some symptoms such as the physical ones can be explained in other ways. For example, cravings for high-calorie foods and binge eating may be partially determined by nutritional deficits, especially considering that so many women diet frequently, and by the increased metabolism that accompanies menstruation.

In any case, much more research is needed to determine whether PMS exists and if it does, what its causes are. (For more discussion on PMS see Chapter 6, "Psychology of Women.")

Menopause

Menopause is the cessation or ending of the menstrual cycle. As a woman gets older, her body starts to become less responsive to the hormones that maintain the menstrual cycle. This, in turn, causes the body to produce these hormones in a smaller amount, until eventually the menstrual cycle cannot be maintained and it stops. This decreased sensitivity to hormones actually begins in the later twenties and early thirties, but a woman typically does not notice these changes until she reaches menopause around the age of fifty. The only change a younger woman might notice is a decrease in fertility. This is because as a woman gets older, her ovaries become less responsive to FSH, which means that she will be releasing fewer and fewer eggs. This is why older women have more fertility problems than younger women.

But as a woman grows older and her menstrual cycle begins to cease, she may experience a number of physical symptoms which can cause some discomfort and which are due to the smaller amounts of hormones, especially estrogen, being produced by her body. Keep in mind, however, that what symptoms women experience and how severe they are vary from woman to woman. Because of size constraints we will only discuss a few of the more common symptoms.

One of the symptoms that many women experience is the *hot flash* or hot flush. This is a feeling of warmth that occurs fairly suddenly, causes perspiration, and then dissipates, sometimes leaving the woman feeling chilled because of the sweating. It is thought that this is due to the lower amount of estrogen in the body.

A second physical change that women experience occurs in the vagina. The vagina tends to become shorter and narrower, as well as less elastic. It also tends to produce less lubrication during sexual arousal. These changes can cause some discomfort during sexual intercourse, but this can be minimized by using an artificial lubricant such as KY Jelly.

Women can also experience osteoporosis. *Osteoporosis* is porous and brittle bones. This is thought to occur in older women because estrogen appears to be important in the absorption of calcium, which makes bones strong. But since estrogen is now produced in smaller amounts, calcium is not absorbed as readily, thereby negatively affecting the bones. The chance of osteoporosis can be decreased, however, if women make sure that their intake of calcium is sufficient prior to menopause. Bones stop growing in length sometime during the teen years, yet they can continue to be made denser even through the thirties by having an adequate supply of calcium (The Boston Women's Health Collective, 1992). Calcium, of course, is found in dairy products and other foods such as broccoli.

Finally, women who have reached menopause are also at greater risk for heart disease. It is thought that this is also due to decreased estrogen. There is a negative correlation between estrogen levels and heart disease. As estrogen decreases, the risk of heart disease increases (The Boston Women's Health Collective, 1992). Certainly, though, this risk can also be reduced by healthy habits such as eating right and exercising even prior to menopause.

SEXUAL DIFFERENTIATION

Many people believe that males and females are very different. Certainly the anatomy of the female is quite different from that of the male. But it may surprise you to find out that males and females actually start out looking essentially the same, including their genitals. The differences we find in males and females occur because of a process known as *sexual differentiation*. This is the process through which we become male or female (see Table 4.2).

TABLE 4.2. Stages of Sexual Differentiation

Stages	Females		Males
1. Chromosomal	XX	or	XY
2. Gonadal	ovaries	or	testes
3. Hormonal	estrogen and progesterone	or	androgens
4. Internal Organs	uterus, fallopian tubes, etc.	or	prostate, seminal vesicles, etc.
5. External Organs	vulva	or	penis and scrotum

Chromosomal Sex

This process consists of a number of stages, the first of which is the *chromosomal stage*. All cells, except the reproductive cells (i.e., the sperm and the egg) contain forty-six chromosomes. (Chromosomes contain genetic material that guides the development of a cell.) The sperm and the egg, however, contain half the usual amount of chromosomes, twenty-three. There are two types of chromosomes: *autosomes* and *sex chromosomes*. All cells except the reproductive cells contain forty-four (or twenty-two pairs of) autosomes. These guide the nonsexual development of the fetus. They determine such physical characteristics as hair and eye color. The sperm and the egg have only twenty-two of these autosomes. There are two sex chromosomes in all cells except the reproductive cells. These will help guide the sexual development of a fetus. There are two types of sex chromosomes: an X and a Y. The egg will only have one sex chromosome, an X. The sperm will only have one sex chromosome as well, but it can have an X or a Y.

Thus, when the egg (containing twenty-two autosomes and an X sex chromosome) is fertilized by (or combines with) a sperm (containing twenty-two autosomes and an X or Y sex chromosome), the combined cell contains the forty-four autosomes (twenty-two pairs) and two sex chromosomes (the XX combination for a female, or the XY combination for a male) (see Table 4.3).

At this stage of development, one cannot tell this difference between a male or female unless a chromosomal analysis is completed. Males and females start out looking the same—as a single cell.

Even at this early stage of development errors can occur. While most of us have forty-six chromosomes (including two sex chromosomes) in all our cells except the reproductive cells, some of us have more or less than this amount. We will only be concerned about chromosomal errors that involve the sex chromosomes.

One chromosomal error is called *Turner's syndrome*. This occurs when there is an atypical egg that has twenty-two autosomes but no sex chromosome. This egg is fertilized by an X-bearing sperm. The result is a cell

TABLE 4.3. Fertilization of Egg by Sperm Resulting in Forty-Six Chromosomes

egg	=	22 autosomes	+	X sex chromosome
sperm	=	22 autosomes	+	X or Y sex chromosome
		44 autosomes	+	XX or XY combination

with forty-five instead of forty-six chromosomes (forty-four autosomes and one sex chromosome). This type of person is typically labeled a female because her external genitals develop normally. But her internal reproductive structures, including the ovaries, do not develop. This means that these females are sterile, unable to have children.

Notice what this implies. Female genitals develop even though the female genetic pattern is incomplete. This is because the basic fetus is female. It will begin to develop automatically into a female unless something is added to it (e.g., a Y chromosome or androgens). As you will see in the following discussion, when a Y chromosome is present or when androgens are present, masculinization of the fetus occurs.

While we can discuss individuals who have only one sex chromosome which is an X, you will never hear of someone who has only one sex chromosome which is a Y. This is because at least one X chromosome is needed to survive. Hypothetically, if an atypical egg without an X chromosome were fertilized by a Y-bearing sperm, it would probably be spontaneously aborted (miscarried). Most likely this is because the X chromosome is much larger than the Y chromosome, and therefore contains more genetic material.

Another type of error involving the sex chromosomes is *Klinefelter's syndrome*, where probably an atypical egg with two Xs is fertilized by a Y-bearing sperm, resulting in an individual with forty-four autosomes and three sex chromosomes (XXY), for a total of forty-seven instead of forty-six. Notice that this person has both the female (XX) and male (XY) chromosomal pattern. Which characteristics will develop? Because of the Y chromosome, male characteristics begin to develop, but the extra X impedes this development. Thus, this type of male is typically born with undersized testes and an undersized penis, making him sterile.

The last type of chromosomal error to be mentioned is the XYY syndrome, sometimes called the *supermale syndrome*. In this case, a normal egg is fertilized by an atypical sperm carrying two instead of one Y chromosome. Again, the result is forty-seven chromosomes instead of forty-six, including forty-four autosomes and three sex chromosomes. This type of male has normal male internal and external reproductive structures. But they also have a number of other distinguishing characteristics. They tend to be unusually tall and masculine in appearance. They also tend to have trouble with acne and are somewhat less intelligent than the XY male.

This type of hormonal error received a lot of attention a number of years ago. It was thought that this type of male was more aggressive and violent than the typical XY male because there were more of these men in prison for violent crimes than the proportion in the general population.

However, there are other explanations for this disproportionate volume. Since these males are very distinctive in appearance, they may be more likely to be picked out of a lineup. Likewise, because they are somewhat less intelligent than the normal male, they may be more likely to be caught by police. In other words, they may not be more likely to commit violent crimes, but they may be more likely to be caught when they do commit them (e.g., Unger, 1979).

Gonadal Sex

The second stage of sexual differentiation is *gonadal sex*. *Gonads* are organs that house the future reproductive cells. This would be the testes in males and the ovaries in females. Both of these structures develop from the same *undifferentiated gonad*, that is, a structure that can develop into either the testes or ovary. Thus, the undifferentiated gonad is said to be *bipotential*, having two potential ways to develop. This undifferentiated gonad can be thought of as having two sections, an inner portion, the *medulla*, and an outer portion, the *cortex*. If the Y chromosome is present, the medulla develops into the testes; if the Y chromosome is not present, the cortex develops into the ovary. Ocassionally, errors occur at this stage of development and some are born as *hermaphrodites*, meaning that they are born with both ovarian and testicular tissue. But even in this second stage, one cannot see differences between males and females without the assistance of lab tests.

Hormonal Sex

Once the gonads are developed, they begin to produce hormones that contribute to the further development of the reproductive organs of a male or female. The testes produce androgens such as testosterone and the ovaries produce estrogen and progesterone. If normal amounts of hormones are present and affect the fetus in the typical way, the rest of the internal reproductive structures and the genitals develop. But until the genitals develop somewhat fully, one cannot see differences between males and females because, again, the male and female look the same both internally and externally until these undifferentiated structures develop.

Unfortunately, there can be errors at this hormonal stage of development, but they are better explained after one understands how the internal and external reproductive structures normally develop.

Internal Reproductive Structures

The internal reproductive structures of both males and females (see Figure 4.3) look identical until they begin to differentiate into male and

FIGURE 4.3. The Sexual Differentiation of the Internal Reproductive Organs

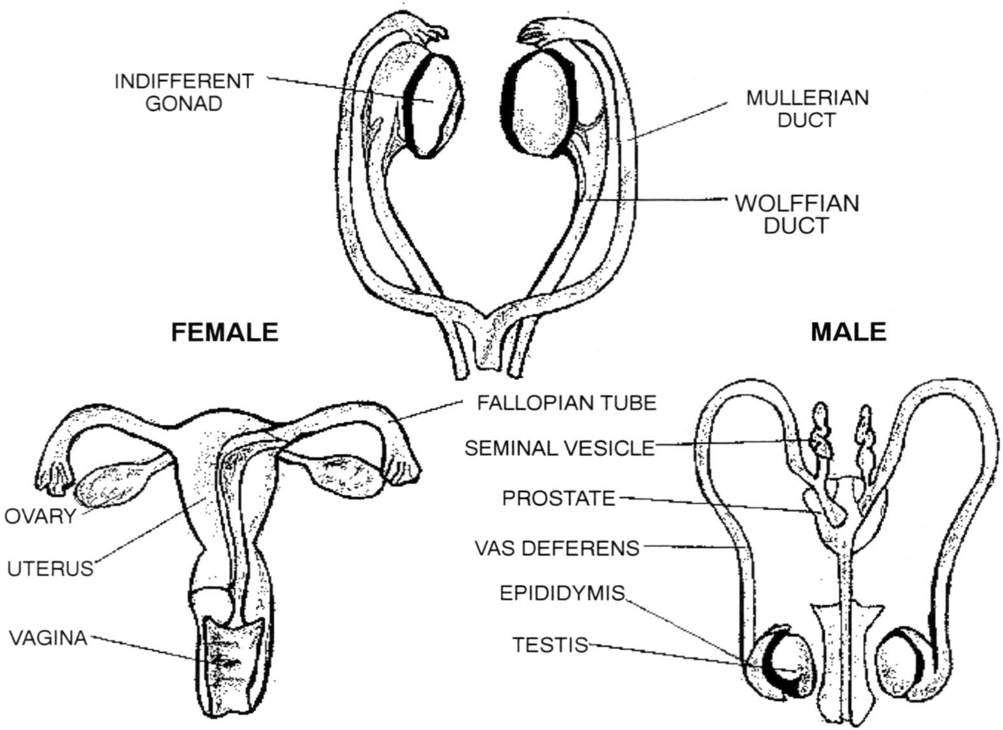

MULLERIAN DUCT

WOLFFIAN DUCT

INDIFFERENT GONAD

MALE

FALLOPIAN TUBE

SEMINAL VESICLE

PROSTATE

VAS DEFERENS

EPIDIDYMIS

TESTIS

FEMALE

OVARY

UTERUS

VAGINA

Artist: Betsy Hetrick.

female structures due to the influence of hormones. Both males and females have wolffian ducts and mullerian ducts. These two sets of ducts are what will develop into the rest of the male and female internal reproductive structures. The *wolffian duct* develops into the internal male reproductive structures and the *mullerian duct* develops into the internal female reproductive structures. If the Y chromosome is present and testosterone is present in normal amounts, and if the testosterone affects the fetus in the usual way, the rest of the male reproductive structures develop; that is, the wolffian duct will develop into such structures as the prostate gland, seminal vesicles, and vas deferens. And the mullerian duct will degenerate. For females, if there is no Y chromosome or testosterone present, the mullerian duct will develop into the internal female reproductive structures such as the upper vagina, uterus, fallopian tubes, and fimbrae. The wolffian duct will degenerate.

External Reproductive Structures

Originally, the external reproductive structures of the male and female also look alike until they begin to differentiate into male and female structures (see Figure 4.4). Undifferentiated structures that develop into different male and female structures are said to be *homologous*. For example, the *labioscrotal swelling* is said to be homologous because it can develop into either the labia of females or the scrotum of males. The *genital tubercle* is said to be homologous because it will develop into either the penis or the clitoris. Thus, at this stage of sexual differentiation, hormones and other factors cause the homologous organs of the fetus to develop either into male or female structures.

Hormonal errors can create problems in the development of either the internal or external reproductive structures and produce ambiguous sex characteristics. Often these characteristics may include internal structures that do not match the external reproductive structures. That is, someone may have internal reproductive structures that are female in characteristic, but their genitals more resemble those of a male, or vice versa. This is called *pseudohermaphroditism*. Three types of hormonal errors that produce pseudohermaphroditism are adrenogenital syndrome, androgen insensitivity, and DHT deficiency.

Adrenogenital syndrome occurs in an XX female who has been exposed to larger than normal amounts of androgens while still in the uterus. This excessive hormonal exposure can occur for two reasons: (1) the fetus's own adrenal glands may malfunction, thus producing large amounts of testosterone to which the baby is exposed; or (2) some drugs have been found to increase levels of testosterone. For example, some medications

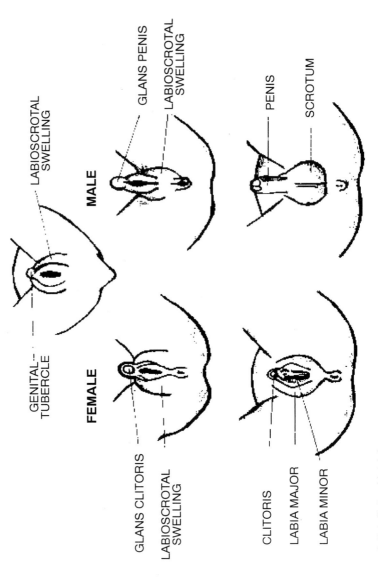

FIGURE 4.4. The Sexual Differentiation of the External Reproductive Organs

GENITAL TUBERCLE

LABIOSCROTAL SWELLING

MALE

GLANS PENIS

LABIOSCROTAL SWELLING

PENIS

SCROTUM

FEMALE

GLANS CLITORIS

LABIOSCROTAL SWELLING

CLITORIS

LABIA MAJOR

LABIA MINOR

Artist: Betsy Hetrick.

that women took in the 1950s to reduce the possibility of miscarriage had this unfortunate result. When the abnormal hormonal exposure results from the malfunctioning of the fetus's adrenal glands, the disorder is called either adrenogenital syndrome or *congenital adrenal hyperplasia*. People with this disorder are also labeled as *fetally androgenized* females regardless of the cause.

The result of this hormonal error is that the genitals become masculinized. For example, the clitoris becomes enlarged and so resembles a penis. The internal reproductive structures, however, are feminine.

Androgen insensitivity syndrome occurs in XY males whose cells, because of a genetic defect, are insensitive to androgens. These males are normal in chromosomal structure, have testes, and their testes produce testosterone. But because of this genetic defect their cells do not respond to testosterone even though it is present in normal amounts. Their bodies develop as though testosterone is not present. Thus, although they have testes, the other internal male reproductive structures do not develop (and neither do the female structures). Their external reproductive structures are more feminine than masculine in appearance.

Finally, *DHT deficiency* is a hormonal error similar to androgen insensitivity syndrome. Males with this deficiency are also normal in chromosomal structure; they are XY. They have developed testes and the testes produce testosterone, but again, because of a genetic defect, they cannot change testosterone into a substance known as dihydrotestosterone (DHT). DHT is needed to complete the development of the male reproductive structures. These males, then, have normal male internal reproductive structures, but their genitals resemble those of a female. Because their testes have not descended into the scrotum (usually this happens during the seventh month of pregnancy), it resembles the labia of the female. Likewise, the penis is undersized and so resembles a clitoris. These males are typically labeled as girls at birth. Interestingly, though, their development into males continues at the time of puberty, when large amounts of testosterone are produced. This testosterone causes the "clitoris" to grow to penis size and causes the testes to finally descend. At puberty, then these "females" become males.

In sum, sexual differentiation is the process by which we become male or female in terms of our reproductive structures. We start out looking essentially the same, but through a series of stages we gradually differentiate into females and males. Occassionally, errors occur at these stages of development that can cause ambiguous sex characteristics. These errors should influence our assumptions about what we consider to be female or male.

REPRODUCTION

Most women, although not all, decide to have children at sometime during their life. It is important, then, to be educated about this process in order to make intelligent, informed decisions about behavior that affect not only a woman's health, but also her child's.

Conception

Pregnancy, of course, begins with the female engaging in sexual intercourse with a fertile male at approximately the time of ovulation. You recall that ovulation occurs at the middle of the menstrual cycle, on about day fourteen of a twenty-eight-day cycle, and that the egg is released into the body cavity where it is swept up into the fallopian tube by the current produced by the fimbriae. The male ejaculates into the female's vagina and the sperm begin their journey through the woman's reproductive structures in order to reach the egg and fertilize it. Even though millions of sperm begin this journey, only about fifty will eventually reach and surround the egg. This is due to a number of reasons: some try to fertilize cells that are not eggs; some lose their sense of direction and swim toward the opening of the vagina, rather than the uterus; others are defective; and still others go up the wrong fallopian tube. As the successful sperm travel, they will pass through the vagina, through the os in the cervix, up the uterus and finally into the fallopian tube where the egg is traveling in the opposite direction.

The egg is surrounded by a jellylike protective layer called the *zona pellucida*. For the sperm to fertilize the egg, it must first dissolve the zona pellucida. It does so through the help of an enzyme, *hyaluronidase*. One can think about the sperm as having several parts: a tail, body, and head. The head contains hyaluronidase and an enzyme inhibitor. As the sperm travel through the female's body and as the sperm bump against the egg, trying to enter it, the enzyme inhibitor wears off, exposing the hyaluronidase, which then can be deposited onto the zona pellucida. The hyaluronidase dissolves the zona pellucida, which allows the sperm to finally enter the egg. Only one sperm may penetrate the egg. Once a sperm has entered the egg, the egg undergoes an immediate change so that no other sperm may enter.

Once the sperm has entered the egg, it too changes. Its tail falls off and the body bursts, releasing the genetic material contained in the chromosomes. It is this process that we discussed in the previous section on sexual differentiation. The egg and the sperm both have twenty-three chromosomes. When the sperm bursts open inside the egg the chromosomes combine for a total of forty-six.

As fertilization is occurring, the fertilized egg is continuing to travel down the fallopian tube to reach the uterus. As the egg is traveling, it is beginning to divide. One cell becomes two; two become four; four become eight; and so on until it becomes a mass of cells called the *blastocyst*. The blastocyst will reach the uterus in approximately one week and will take approximately another week to embed in the uterine wall. This begins the pregnancy.

Pregnancy

Symptoms of Pregnancy

Pregnancy can be divided up into three *trimesters* of approximately three months each. It is during the first trimester that a woman experiences symptoms that may indicate to her that she is pregnant. For example, it is typical to experience such symptoms as fatigue. Fatigue is typical in pregnancy (and not necessarily during just the first trimester) because pregnancy is a stress on the body.

Morning sickness (nausea and sometimes vomiting) occurs in many women during early pregnancy, although the intensity with which they experience it varies. Some women have no trouble at all with nausea; others go to the other extreme and experience vomiting throughout the entire pregnancy, not just the first trimester. While we do not know for certain why morning sickness occurs, a variety of factors are implicated. It may be due to low blood sugar. Because the embryo is growing and developing so rapidly, it may be using up the mother's supply of glucose. The effect is the same when a nonpregnant person is extremely hungry and begins to feel sick because of it. Likewise, it is suggested that the hormones of pregnancy make digestion less effective, producing nausea. In either case, it is suggested that women combat these feelings of nausea by trying to eat foods such as crackers when they begin to feel sick or to eat several small meals throughout the day instead of three large meals. These behaviors can help keep blood sugar steady and coat the stomach with food.

Women may also experience breast tenderness during the first trimester (and beyond) because even at this early date, the breasts are undergoing changes in preparation for possible breastfeeding after the baby is born.

Some people believe that pregnant women experience other symptoms such as food cravings and mood swings. Further, many believe that these may be due to hormonal changes. This may or may not be true. Food cravings may occur because the woman is deficient in a certain vitamin or mineral that is contained in the type of food wanted. Notice, however, that food cravings do not occur only in pregnant women. Don't both men and women experience a craving for a certain type of food occasionally? Likewise, mood swings (if they exist) may not be due to hormone changes either. They may due to fatigue and other symptoms of pregnancy that cause discomfort. Aren't most people a little irritable when they have the flu? Now consider how a woman feels who has been throwing up periodically for six weeks. In fact, pregnancy may be a scapegoat for negative emotions. When I was pregnant with my first child, I was exercising with a friend to an aerobics tape. The aerobic instructors on tape tend to irritate me and I made a derogatory comment about this particular instructor. My friend responded with a comment about how my hormones were really raging. The fact is that my hormones were not raging. I really disliked the aerobics instructor even before I had gotten pregnant!

First Trimester

Many other changes occur during this first trimester. The placenta and the umbilical cord develop at the beginning of this period. These are both essential to the survival of the fetus. The *placenta* is a disk-shaped organ that forms on the wall of the uterus through which the mother and fetus exchange substances such as oxygen and nutrients. The *umbilical cord* consists of blood vessels that connect the fetus to the placenta and therefore the mother. The exchange of substances occurs in the following way. One can think of the placenta as consisting of an inner section and an outer section. The mother's blood circulates in the outer section and the fetus's blood circulates in the inner section. These blood supplies do not mix because they are separated by a *semipermeable membrane.* A semipermeable membrane is one through which some substances can pass but not others. In this case, oxygen and nutrients can pass through the semipermeable membrane but not blood. The fetus's blood leaves its body and travels through the umbilical cord to the inner section of the placenta. In the meantime, the mother's blood is circulating in the outer section of the placenta. While the blood supplies are in the placenta, substances in the blood pass through the semipermeable membrane. Oxygen and nutrients pass from the mother's blood through the membrane into the fetus's blood and waste products from the fetus's blood pass through the membrane into the mother's blood, where it will be filtered by her system. The blood supplies then continue to circulate either through the mother or fetus.

This process is the reason why it is so important that a woman is careful about what she ingests during pregnancy. Most of what enters her blood supply will also enter that of the fetus. This not only includes nutrients from food, but also medications, illegal drugs, and substances contained in tobacco. These substances can harm the fetus, especially during the first trimester when all the systems are beginning to develop.

The *amniotic sac* also forms early in this trimester. It contains amniotic fluid and surrounds the fetus. Essentially the fetus is floating in a bag of water. This sac and fluid seem to serve two purposes: to keep the baby at a fairly constant temperature and to protect and cushion the baby from bumps and jars.

Fetal development is rapid and by the end of the third month what started out as a single cell now takes on human features. All the systems of the body that allow us to function begin to develop during this time: the circulatory system, nervous system, digestive system, reproductive system, and so on.

Second Trimester

The fetal development that began during the first trimester continues during the second trimester. The circulatory, nervous, digestive, etc. systems continue to develop. The fetus also increases in size and during this trimester becomes large enough so that the mother can feel its movements. This is called *quickening*.

The mother also experiences other changes. Typically, the second trimester is considered the most comfortable by women, both psychologically and physically. Physically, the morning sickness usually ends by the end of the fourth month of pregnancy and the fetus is not large enough to cause the woman other physical discomforts. Likewise, psychologically, the mother has gotten over the initial reactions of pregnancy and has not yet typically begun to think about the possible discomfort of labor.

By the end of the second trimester the breasts are ready for nursing and they may secrete small amounts of *colostrum*, even at this early stage. Colostrum is a thin, yellowish fluid that is high in protein and which the breasts produce and release prior to milk production. When a woman decides to nurse her baby, what the baby is initially drinking is colostrum, not milk, at least for a few days. This colostrum is very nutritious and easy for the baby to digest. It also contains some of the mother's immunities and so can help to keep the baby healthy.

Third Trimester

During the third trimester the development of the fetus is completed and the woman's body prepares itself for childbirth. About two to four weeks before birth the baby usually turns into a position ready for birth.

This means that the head is lowered into the woman's pelvic region. This makes some women more comfortable and is sometimes called *lightening*.

In the meantime, throughout this trimester the uterus is also busy in preparation for childbirth. It is during this trimester that a woman experiences *Braxton-Hicks contractions*. These are contractions of the uterus that are not part of labor. Some of these contractions are so mild that the mother does not notice them; others are so strong that they are mistaken for labor contractions (*false labor*). It is thought that they occur in order to strengthen the uterus for real labor contractions. The uterus is a muscular organ. Just as we contract and relax our muscles during exercise to make them stronger, so too is the uterus contracting and relaxing to become stronger to withstand the labor process.

Labor and Childbirth

There are a few signs which indicate that labor is about to begin. In some women there is the appearance of the *bloody show*, which is a spot of bloody mucus released from the cervix. It is thought that this mucus plug helps to keep bacteria out of the uterus, thus protecting the unborn fetus from infection.

In about ten percent of women, the amniotic sac breaks, releasing the amniotic fluid. Labor typically begins within twenty-four hours of the break, and many physicians prefer that the baby is actually born within twenty-four hours. Babies born after this time stand an increased chance of infection.

The labor process is divided up into three stages: first-stage labor, second-stage labor, and third-stage labor. Dilation and effacement occur during first stage labor. *Dilation* is the opening of the cervical os; *effacement* is the thinning of the cervical walls. This first stage of labor is further divided into three substages: early, late, and transition. What substage a woman is in depends upon how far dilated she is. A woman is in *early first-stage labor* if the cervix is dilated from zero to two inches. This is the easiest of the stages and she is fairly comfortable at this point in the process, with contractions being not too severe, occurring on average every fifteen to twenty minutes. She is in *late first-stage labor* when she is dilated from two to three inches. Contractions gradually become more severe and closer together at this stage. The *transition stage* is the most difficult, with dilation of the cervix going from three to four inches. It is during this stage that most women report discomfort.

The length of this stage varies from woman to woman. For some it only lasts two hours; for others it lasts twenty-four hours. On average this stage lasts twelve hours for women who have not yet had children and eight hours for those who have given birth previously.

The *second stage of labor* is the delivery of the baby. This stage can last anywhere from a few minutes to a few hours. With the mother pushing, typically the baby's head gradually moves down through the os and into the vaginal canal. *Crowning* occurs when one can see the baby's head in the vaginal opening. It is at this point that the episiotomy is conducted if there is to be one. Once the baby is delivered the umbilical cord is tied off and cut.

The *third stage of labor* is the delivery of the afterbirth. The *afterbirth* is the placenta and the rest of the fetal membranes. The uterus continues to contract in order to loosen the placenta and with additional pushes from the mother, the placenta and rest of the afterbirth passes out of the uterus and vaginal canal. This stage can take anywhere from a few minutes to an hour.

Prepared childbirth (sometimes called natural childbirth) can sometimes help a woman through this intensive process. The idea behind prepared childbirth is that fear creates tension and that tension can cause an increase in the perception of pain. The fear is that associated with the unknown—not knowing what to expect during labor and childbirth. By educating women about labor and childbirth, fear of the unknown is reduced, which can decrease the perception of pain. This is why women go to childbirth classes during the third trimester. These childbirth classes also teach relaxation techniques and other types of exercises. These techniques (such as breathing techniques) are used during labor to take the mind off of the labor contractions. Occupying the mind helps to reduce the perception of pain. Likewise, these techniques can give women a sense of control over the labor and childbirth process, which is primarily controlled by the medical establishment.

Keep in mind that the process just described is typical but that complications such as breech birth (the baby is in an atypical position) can occur. In some cases a *cesarean* or *C section* is needed. In this process an incision is made in the woman's abdomen and uterus and the baby along with the fetal membranes are manually removed by the physician. The incision is then sewn back up. While some women believe that this may be preferable to the long hours of labor, the C section is major surgery and has the risks involved in that type of procedure. Likewise, recovery from this type of birth takes longer than from vaginal childbirth.

The medical establishment has also been criticized for performing too many cesarean sections. Their numbers have increased to such an extent that 25 percent of all births are C sections, and the number of C section births in the United States is much higher than that in Europe (The Boston Women's Health Collective, 1992).

SUMMARY

In sum, knowledge of biology is useful in dispelling myths, especially those associated with human sexuality, and is useful in helping a woman maintain her health. This chapter has explained many concepts that can be useful in this regard, including the functions and placement of the female reproductive organs; the process involved in menstruation, as well as various menstrual disorders and menopause; and the processes involved in conception, pregnancy, and childbirth. Sexual differentiation was also discussed in an attempt to demonstrate the biological similarities between men and women.

KEY TERMS

vulva	luteal phase	androgen insensitivity
mons pubis	corpus luteum	syndrome
labia majora	amenorrhea	DHT deficiency
labia minora	dysmenorrhea	zona pellucida
vasocongestion	PMS	hyaluronidase
vestibule	menopause	blastocyst
clitoral hood	hot flash	trimester
clitoris	osteoporosis	morning sickness
orgasm	sexual differentiation	placenta
perineum	chromosomal stage	umbilical cord
episiotomy	autosomes	semipermeable mem-
breasts	sex chromosomes	brane
vagina	Turner's syndrome	amniotic sac
Grafenberg (G) spot	Klinefelter's syndrome	quickening
cervix	supermale syndrome	colostrum
Pap smear	gonadal sex	lightening
os	gonads	Braxton-Hicks contrac-
uterus	undifferentiated gonad	tions
endometrium	bipotential	false labor
fallopian tubes	medulla	bloody show
fimbrae	cortex	dilation
ovulation	hermaphrodites	effacement
ovaries	wolffian duct	early first-stage labor
spermatogenesis	mullerian duct	late first-stage labor
menstrual cycle	homologous	transition stage
menarche	labioscrotal swelling	second stage of labor
menopause	genital tubercle	crowning
follicle-stimulating	pseudohermaphroditism	third stage of labor
hormone	adrenogenital syndrome	afterbirth
lutenizing hormone	congenital adrenal	prepared childbirth
follicular phase	hyperplasia	cesarean (C) section
follicle	fetally androgenized	

DISCUSSION QUESTIONS

1. Trace the path of the egg from the time of ovulation until it implants in the uterus or is sloughed off after degeneration. Name the structures it passes by and describe their functions.
2. Describe the hormonal feedback loops and physiological changes that occur during the menstrual cycle. What are some of the types of disorders associated with menstruation? What are some symptoms associated with menopause?
3. What is sexual differentiation? What are the stages of this process? What types of error can occur in each of these stages?
4. Describe the process of conception. What happens during the nine months of pregnancy? What are the stages of labor?

REFERENCES

Belzer, E. G., B. Whipple, and W. Moger (1994). "On female ejaculation," *The Journal of Sex Research, 20:* 403-406.

The Boston Women's Health Collective (1992). *The New Our Bodies, Ourselves.* New York: Simon & Schuster.

Fisher, W. A., N. R. Branscombe, and C. R. Lemery (1983). "The bigger the better? Arousal and attributional responses to erotic stimuli that depict different-size penises," *The Journal of Sex Research, 19:* 377-396.

Freud, S. (1963). *Three essays on the theory of sexuality.* (U. Strachey, ed. and trans.) New York: Basic Books (originally published 1905).

Golub, S. (1985). "Menarche: The beginning of menstrual life." In *Psychology of Women: Selected Readings,* Juanita H. Williams (Ed.). New York: W. W. Norton, pp. 95-109.

Masters, W. H. and V. E. Johnson (1966). *Human sexual response.* Boston: Little, Brown.

Overstreet, J. W. (1986). "Human sperm function: Acquisition in the male and expression in the female." In *Male reproductive dysfunction*, R. J. Santen and R. S. Swerdloff (Eds.). New York: Marcel Dekker, pp. 29-47.

Perry, J. D. and B. Whipple (1982). "Multiple components of female orgasm." In *Circumvaginal musculature and sexual function*, B. Graber (Ed.). New York: Karger, pp. 101-114.

Tavris, C. (1991, November). The myth of PMS. *Redbook, 178(1):* 36,38,40-41.

Unger, R. (1979). *Female and male.* New York: Harper and Row.

Chapter 5

Women's Health: Identifying Women's Health Issues and Concerns

Martha Ritter

WOMEN'S HEALTH DEFINED

Everyone attempting to critically analyze women's health issues must start from a common idea of what "health" means. According to a 1978 edition of *Webster's Dictionary,* health is ". . . physical and mental well-being; freedom from disease, etc." (Guralnik, 1978, p. 345). The Allegheny University MCP Hahnemann School of Medicine (1996) has compiled an expanded version of this definition by stating that "Women's Health is devoted to the maintenance of women's wellness and disease prevention over the life span. It includes treatment and prevention of the diseases, disorders, and conditions that are unique to, more prevalent among, or more serious in women or for which there are different risk factors or interventions for women than for men. It recognizes a multidisciplinary approach, acknowledges gender differences, and respects and includes the values and knowledge of women" (p. 3). This chapter will only briefly discuss a few of the women's health issues with which society is dealing in the 1990s, such as women and societal images, reproductive rights and health, and feminist perspectives in medical ethics. These discussions will not only acknowledge and define some very real health concerns, but should also serve to provide appropriate questions that need to be satisfactorily answered if society is to define a healthy woman, and if all women are to make informed and responsible decisions about their personal health.

WOMEN AND SOCIETAL IMAGES

One of the most elusive and least-defined aspects of women's health is what society perceives as a healthy woman. If the popular press is any judge of a healthy woman, a woman is to be forever young and tan; be blessed with hair any color but white or silver all her life; be wrinkle- and

91

blemish-free; be born beautiful, which means she is white skinned with her monthly menstrual period and contraceptive use under control; and to be physically active with no aches or pains or hint of perspiration or odor. If a person were to actually take the time to consider the popular health topics presented by the press, they might question which articles and advertisements are truly health issues versus which are truly cosmetic issues that have been camouflaged as health issues. Hair color, white (versus clean) teeth, a certain breath odor, and amount and smell of perspiration are not health issues. They are simply cosmetic characteristics of an individual that have been advertised as indicators of good health. But even in legitimate health care centers, real health issues, even today, may be defined by a system that is still male dominated. Concerns about reproductive rights and health, dietary guidelines, the signs and symptoms of menopause, surgical interventions, hormonal and drug therapies, and mental health therapies are still guided by the whims and biases of a select few who seem to have been granted power to dictate a woman's health status (Sloane, 1985; Coward, 1985; Munhall, 1995).

Wrinkles

One exception to this list of what may not be health concerns is the issue of facial wrinkles. Now that science has produced creams and injections that eliminate some wrinkles, at least for a limited time, the public is told that wrinkles are an important part of the aging process that needs to be eliminated (in support of the myth of the fountain of youth). An advertisement that appeared in *Good Housekeeping* offered a prescription cream "*proven* to diminish fine lines and wrinkles. *Proven* to give skin a smoother texture and rosier glow when used as part of a comprehensive skin care and sun avoidance program and when skin care and sun avoidance programs alone are not enough." Also included in large print in this advertisement was the statement that may actually lead the wrinkle issue into the realm of a true health problem. "RENOVA is a dermal irritant, and the results of continued irritation for greater than 48 weeks are not known. In some patients treated with RENOVA for longer than 48 weeks, there is evidence of atypical changes in the skin. The significance of these findings is unknown. Safety and effectiveness of RENOVA in individuals over 50 or in those with moderately or heavily pigmented skin have not been established" (Dermatological Division of Ortho Pharmaceutical Corporation, 1996, pp. 42-44).

What does this warning mean? White-skinned people under the age of fifty can probably use this drug for less than forty-eight weeks and they will show signs of smoother, rosy skin (due to the dermal irritation qualities of the cream?) with diminished fine lines and wrinkles. But other evidence has already shown a high correlation of cellular growth evolving into cancerous-type growth when cells are exposed to continual irritation. In other words, irritating the skin, as this product does, may eventually lead to cancer. In fact, the fine print on the page following the advertisement discusses the implication of continued use of the cream after forty-eight weeks and when the skin shows atypical changes. It discusses animal research on this product, which specifically focused on *carcinogenesis* (cancer causing), *mutagenesis* (causes cellular mutations in development), *impairment of fertility* (difficulty in becoming pregnant), *teratogenic* effects (abnormally formed fetus, monstrosity), and *fetotoxicity* (can kill the fetus). Results have shown all these *aberrations* to occur in some of the animal studies, but studies have not been conducted on humans. Nor was a time frame given for the length of the animal experiments. The teratogenic effects and fetotoxicity seem to be relevant enough that the fine print warns women who are pregnant or who are attempting to become pregnant not to use the cream. (However, the advertisements are geared toward women of reproductive age.) So, while the normal process of aging includes various degrees of wrinkling, which is not a health problem, some of the drugs humans use to avoid wrinkling may be a threat to health.

Several other questions arise that add to the multitude of dimensions involved in women's health issues. There is evidence that pressure from drug companies on doctors to promote company products does exist.

Advertising this cream as a prescription drug does not necessarily mean it is any safer or better to use than an over-the-counter antiwrinkle formula. People understand that the United States does have a Federal Food and Drug Administration that monitors many of the products we use. But many people are not aware that the intricacies of the research guidelines are less stringent and sometimes nonexistent for *topical drugs* and cosmetic products. Most people are too trusting about the research regimen that goes on for many of our "health" products. As many complaints as people voice about our medical industry, we still let the industry blindly lead us with products that are questionable as to effectiveness and safety. Once again, people need to remember that simply because science and technology can enable us to do certain things and create certain products, it does not mean, at least in this case, that those products should necessarily be used.

Furthermore, the original advertisement twice states that this drug has been *proven* to result in the desired effects. The public has for too long been misinformed by the science industry that scientists prove physical phenomena. Science, or scientists, do not prove anything. Science can only provide evidence for a high correlation of cause and effect through a multitude of tests and collected data. According to this advertisement, most evidence indicates that the use of this drug closely correlates with the resulting desired skin qualities for most people, but nothing is proven. The public is not given the data or evidence to support the purported desired results, or even undesired results. We must trust the word of the company. The public, and science, is infatuated with the word "proof" and the power it relays to the "prover," so our society will most likely continue in the misuse of this word on scientific matters. This is an excellent example of the lack of medical research ethics.

This product has been tested on other animal species but not on *Homo sapiens* (the human species). The initial event, wrinkling, is defined by humans as a problem, but it is only a problem for humans. Why do we then test the product, which could possibly be dangerous or deadly, on other species for which wrinkling is not a problem? Is it ethical to threaten the lives of other organisms for a superficial situation that humans have created as a problem?

Society insinuates that facial wrinkling is mostly a concern for the cosmetic appearance of the female. But why do females allow society to define a natural phenomenon of our aging process as a problem? If indeed there is a higher population of women than men, at least in the United States, it is time for the women to take on the full responsibility of educating themselves and members of the male gender, define what are and are not health issues versus cosmetic issues, and give better guidelines for what kinds of research topics our millions of dollars could be used. If women do not choose to clarify such issues they have no right to expect that men will take the initiative. It is foolish to believe otherwise.

Plastic Surgery

A trip to the periodical section of the local library or bookstore offers one a generous smorgasbord of magazines, journals, and periodicals that address a multitude of issues focused on women's health. One is introduced to the fine art of avoiding any signs of aging, be the sign facial wrinkling, age spots on the skin, graying hair, decreasing bone mass, arthritis, loss of bladder control, facial hair growth, or running low on energy (Doress, Siegal, and The Midlife and Older Women Book Project, 1987, p. 37). Unfortunately, we have gained equality with our male counterparts, who have for years warned of the health impacts of stress from our careers, and there are articles on this also. All females, from the most anorexic to the extremely obese, have weight problems, which ruin not only a woman's personal feeling about herself, but also any chances a woman may have of being a perfect sexual partner for anyone or having a chance at the perfect job, and thousands of articles are available on losing or gaining weight in the "right places." These articles imply that good health is expendable in our North American society as women torture and punish their bodies to achieve "that certain look." As many wise people have observed through the years of expanded mass media, the populations with the best access to mass media are also the populations most easily brainwashed, for better or for worse.

The tragedy of this situation is that much of this kind of trash "education" comes from magazines printed especially for women. Women trust these sources to be filled with information to help them better educate themselves about their everyday life activities and the physical body. While many articles are filled with valid advice, paid advertisements within the same magazines once again focus on the issues women still adopt as problems, which they alone can resolve if they just buy and use the correct magic potion.

For example, following the 1983 American Society of Plastic and Reconstructive Surgeons campaign on "practice enhancement," the oversupply of cosmetic doctors flooded the media with "educational" information about body sculpturing. Surgical procedures were touted as safe, effective, and affordable. Even though the perfect body still had not been defined nor any goals or objectives set that clarified how body sculpting might make a woman more perfect, more "a woman," the advertisements went on. The enlarged-breast fetish was building, though by this time women were said to want the implants because of their own inner motivations rather than to please men. In the process, the educational information defined small breasts as a deformity, even a disease, which leads to a woman's total lack of well-being. Physicians were even kind enough to offer financing plans to the consumers who wanted to avoid this mental health hazard and anguish. These same good doctors also continued with numerous speaking engagements to men's associations, where they educated men about the benefits of body sculpting for women (Faludi, 1991).

All this went on without mention of chronic aftereffects, which many women then suffered as real health concerns, such as *hemorrhages* (bleeding), facial nerve damage, scarring, anesthesia complications, *edema* (accumulation of fluid in an area of the body), *fat embolisms* (obstruction in a blood vessel), or even death. Publicity, not breakthroughs in medical technology, had made all the difference in the number of women asking for these "treatments."

Cosmetic, or plastic surgery, was as dangerous as ever. Doctors changing their specialties to plastic surgery due to the lure of bigger profits actually made the procedures more risky than usual, if they were not trained for that work. But the women who chose to pursue the fantasy of the perfect body were not also supplied with the medical reports detailing the follow-up corrective surgeries due to botched jobs the first time on the operating table. For breast implants alone, 20 percent of the patients had to return for further surgery to take care of the chronic pain, infection, blood clots, or implant ruptures that followed the initial surgery. Though the FDA eventually became aware through its own investigations that at least 50 percent of the implant cases were failures—that is, patients experienced chronic symptoms—it chose to stop further monitoring rather than take action because consulting doctors could not decide what constituted "failure" (Faludi, 1991, p. 219). Even after all the health problems and lawsuits directed toward the Dow Corning Corporation and the Bristol-Myers Squibb Company, a television documentary follow-up report in 1995 about the history of breast implants pitted female surgeons against female patients to summarily dismiss the entire matter as another example of female hysteria and ignorance of true medical matters. Women were made to look out of control and foolish for making what, in retrospect, was an egotistical decision and for complaining about the follow-up health problems, which the patients may not have documented from day one of occurrence.

Body Weight

Each generation of both the male and female gender continue to be carefully taught about how we can view our bodies, how we refer to and talk about our bodies, and who has the responsibility to know the most about our bodies and determine the routines needed to theoretically maintain healthy bodies. Industry continues to aggravate women's low self-esteem and high anxiety about a "feminine" appearance. Surveys conducted by the Kinsey Institute confirm that women in the United States have more negative feelings about their bodies than women in any other culture studied (Faludi, 1991, p. 212).

As the search for the woman who is perfect in body and spirit continues, we must not forget the significance of body weight as a criterion. From the personal advertisements in newspapers, where males are searching for the female whose height is proportional to her weight, to the women who suffer terrible guilt and discrimination because of their larger-than-media-prescribed silhouette, weight and diet are a national obsession in North America. The amazing factor, both at the medical and societal levels, is that no one has an ultimate definition of too thin, just-right, or obesity. The definition mostly depends on which dietary conference one attends or to which literature (which focuses most often on one specific aspect of body weight) a person chooses to give attention. For most women in general, just as "fashion dictates the shape of my girls" (mannequins) as proudly proclaimed by Robert Fills (Faludi, 1991, p. 200), fashion also dictates what shape women's bodies should be from year to year. No wonder women become depressed as they are told to change their body shape from year to year as easily as they change their wardrobes! The pressure against being fat in the United States has actually produced a major fear of extra pounds in many women. Vivian Mayer has said, "Fear of fat keeps women preoccupied, robs us of our pride and energy, keeps us from taking up space" (The Boston Women's Health Book Collective, 1984, p. 8) and goes on to state that "mass starvation of women is the modern American culture's equivalent of foot-binding, lip-stretching and other forms of female mutilation."

In fact, one study of teenagers aged twelve to eighteen found that 26 percent of the twelve-year-olds and 49 percent of the eighteen-year-olds considered themselves overweight. In actuality, only 4 percent of those participating in the studies were found to be overweight according to the standard weight tables (Davies and Furnham, 1986).

Consider also the almost-white paste makeup look, which mimics the mute Chinese concubine, during the early and mid-1990s, and women are almost back in their place from the Victorian era. This was the time in which women were warned that a quest for higher education and professional careers would make them physically unattractive. Thus, women of that era were encouraged to adopt an aura of fragility, which was helped along by ingesting near-toxic potions that induced a chalky look to the skin and nearly eliminated the appetite. The very feminine heroines in the Disney stories of Cinderella, Sleeping Beauty, Snow White, Beauty and the Beast, and so on, all share the same pallor of skin and slenderness verging on frailty and helplessness. These characters are the images our female and male children learn to accept as the most desirable women. Is this the message we really want our very young children to incorporate into their everyday view of life and the women who figure in it?

Consider as well the semireligious cult of Barbie and the rite of handing her legacy on to our new generations of young women and men. Barbie is society's representation of the perfect sexual image without the need to consider physical or mental well-being and health. From bound feet forever poised on their toes to achieve the look of the sensual calf, to the too-narrow hips that will always pose a life threat with each child she will never conceive or bear, to the painfully thin waist that has either been achieved through the means of the diseases of anorexia and bulimia, surgical tummy tucking, or distortion after years of wearing a corset, to the surgically enhanced overly large breasts which will lead to painful back and shoulder problems as she ages, to the pursed-lip pout of the forever-child look which completes the sexual fantasies of some people, the physical Barbie is the culmination of the pain and torture women are encouraged to put their bodies through to achieve the perfect image.

But the Barbie cult goes dangerously beyond these surface ideals of the modern United States female. She is also the symbol of an economic system that is purposefully disdainful of the female gender, people of color, and the slaves of poverty. What Mattel does not tell us in the glamour and noise of Barbie marketing is the story of how each Barbie doll is made in the sweatshops of the developing countries of Thailand and Southeast Asia and the *maquiladoras* of Mexico. In the effort to achieve the greatest economic gain, companies such as Mattel do not provide the inside story of how their consumer goods are produced. Within the toy-making factories a nightmare of poorly paid female employees is revealed as these people are exposed to horrible toxic chemicals and dangerous physical environments on a daily basis. Women and children develop and suffer from chronic respiratory infections due to the fabric dust and chemical solvents filling their lungs (Foek, 1997, pp. 9-13). They also suffer pains in their hands, necks, and shoulders; others experience nausea and dizziness; still others suffer from hair and memory loss, shortness of breath, and infections in and around the throat. Once the women become too ill to work, they are fired and replaced by the next economically desperate set of "slaves."

Allowing the myth of the perfect body weight to continue to have so much control over women's everyday lives seems to be a paradox when more information is also available about the negative aspects of giving in to pressure about body weight. For instance, we are now aware of the hormonal and reproductive repercussions of the starvation diets used by our star athletes, models, and beauty pageant queens. We know that magazine photographs of models are routinely altered to hide skin discolorations or "inappropriate" shapes or bulges. We know that genetics still play a major role in determining each of our unique characteristics in the form of body size, shape, chemistry, and metabolism. We also know that our formal and informal education process on nutrition is inadequate and cannot compete with the glamour and pizzazz that goes into advertising from food service chains about fun or romantic foods. Somehow, what we take into our bodies has become a popular cultural event rather than simply restoring the elemental needs of our *cellular metabolism*.

Tragically, we also know of the mortal dangers faced by women suffering with *anorexia nervosa*, bulimia, or both. Anorexia nervosa is a disorder in which (mostly) women literally starve themselves—sometimes to death. It includes a severe fear of becoming fat and is accompanied by a large weight loss—at least 25 percent of original weight (Strober, 1986). People with this disorder tend to have a distorted body image (Garfinkel and Kaplan, 1986). They may weigh only seventy or eighty pounds and still believe that they are fat. When anorexics look at other individuals with anorexia, they may see someone who looks emaciated, but when they look at themselves they see fat people.

This is a particularly dangerous disease because of its medical consequences. Medical conditions that result from anorexia include heart complications such as *arrhythmia* (irregular heartbeat) and heart failure, as well as kidney and gastrointestinal disorders (Mitchell, 1986a). Some die from the disorder. Approximately 5 percent of anorexics die from anorexia and its complications (Szmukler and Russel, 1986).

It is unclear why anorexia develops, but many believe that society's emphasis on thinness causes these women and girls to start to diet (e.g., Garner, Garfinkle, and Olmsted, 1983). Dieting then becomes extreme. Others believe that physiological factors are involved (see Strober, 1986) in this disorder, but this raises a "chicken and egg" question. Did the extreme dieting cause the atypical physiological processes or did atypical physical processes result in extreme dieting?

Bulimia is characterized by binging and purging. Bulimics eat large amounts of food (typically high-calorie, low-nutrition foods) and then often follow the binge by forcing themselves to vomit or taking excessive laxatives (Boskind-White and White, 1986).

This eating disorder can also have extreme negative medical repercussions including intestinal and kidney problems as well as throat and dental problems, due to stomach acid being vomited so frequently (Mitchell, 1986b).

Again society's emphasis on thinness is implicated as a factor in this disorder. It is thought that bulimics start to diet but become discouraged by not losing weight or become so hungry from strict dieting that they give it up and binge on high-calorie foods. This binge makes them feel like they must get rid of the food they have just eaten by throwing up or through the use of laxatives. These processes then give them a sense of control (Agras and Kirkley, 1986).

Should a woman choose to defect from the dietary image defined and marketed by our popular food industries, she will find the change challenging. Too many women still play along with the ploy of the industry to spend too much money on miracle diet schemes. What too few people learn before starting diet plans are the basic elements of healthful eating habits. As a person starts a diet with a drastic drop in calories, one's cellular metabolism also goes down drastically as the cells strive to conserve energy stored in the body. This means that it becomes increasingly difficult to lose weight, especially if physical exercise is not a regular part of the diet regimen. It is common for people to skip from one diet to another as the previous one just "doesn't work" anymore. In response for the next diet, the body prepares itself metabolically for the cyclic drop in calories and becomes ever more conservative in its use of energy sources. This kind of extreme cycle usually results in most of these dieters regaining their original weight within one to five years, and they often end up heavier than ever.

Our bodies have evolved to be metabolically successful for survival. We cannot avoid metabolic cycles without severe health repercussions, and it is a shame that our educational and advertising institutions avoid a practical education in body functioning. If people never understand why their bodies do not respond to dieting as advertised, they will continue to inappropriately nourish themselves, experience poor health, and sustain a poor self-image of their bodies.

Diet pills are another trick of the socioeconomic game to make women what they are not. Granted, some people with intrinsic metabolic dysfunctions may need these chemicals to help stabilize their metabolisms. But the pills have been peddled to people who continue to be insecure about body image. Many pills contain chemicals that act as chemical *analogs* of *amphetamines*. This means their chemical structure is so similar to that of amphetamines that they will bind to receptors in the brain instead of amphetamines, turning off cellular signals for the need for more nutrients, and thus cutting off hunger signals. Depending on the kind of diet pill and its chemical ingredients, undesirable side effects may include dizziness, headaches, high blood pressure, anxiety, and insomnia. Women who are at higher risk for developing serious health problems are those with the preexisting conditions of high blood pressure, diabetes, heart, kidney, or thyroid problems, or who are taking antidepressant medicines (Dobkin and Sippy, 1995). Some of the diet pills that came out in the mid-1990s are especially suspect for causing major health problems to the population taking them. These pills are especially attractive, though, in that they result in immediate weight reduction and do not need an accompanying exercise regimen to be effective. Thus, a woman never has to be responsible for her general overall health; the pill will just deal with the poundage all on its own. The tragedy of this dietary breakthrough is that these pills were created for women with real weight problems that were endangering their health in other ways. Both patients and drug companies have pressured doctors to prescribe these pills to women who do not have weight problems, who are too irresponsible or undereducated to choose more appropriate ways to manage their weight, or can afford to give in to social pressures that continue to convince them that they are imperfect. North American lifestyles call for quick fixes, and this is just another product to fit the bill.

Exercise also was never so popular as a way to gain and maintain a desired weight and figure until ingenious people developed exercise machines and gadgets for home use, gyms became places to pick up potential partners, and the clothing industry came up with the costumes to make people look just right for each particular physical activity. Gone are the days when physical workouts are just a routine of lifestyle—now they are part of a courtship dance and consumer ambush. Exercise in moderation is good and appropriate for most anyone's general health; the extremes are simply that, extreme.

NUTRITION

The hysteria that develops as women become trapped in dietary binges and false images can come to a halt if a woman chooses to take back control of her own person and exercise some power in making appropriate eating decisions. Taking a proactive approach to one's nutritional health is much easier said than done admittedly, given the flashing and hypnotic hoopla from the world-powerful, tradition-laden food industry, the endless "scientific" theories of certified and self-created dietary doctors and mentors, the beauty industry, the food and exercise gurus, fasting rites for cleansing the body as part of a religious ritual, and our trusted peers and lovers who have fallen for the myths and discover that death through starvation for themselves and others may be easier than achieving false images. A relatively simple change in attitude toward eating may be adopted to help us focus on the changes that need to be made to make a lifestyle more comfortable and attainable: focus on feeling well rather than hopelessly attempt to maintain an "ideal" weight. Keep in mind that taking in good nutrients gives our cells the ability to replace themselves with new healthy cells, and produce correctly functioning chemicals such as hormones to keep body systems aligned. It keeps the cells themselves functioning properly so we can avoid such concerns as obesity, clogged arteries and heart disease, anorexia, tooth and gum decay, intestinal problems, allergies, migraines, cancer, infertility, and *osteoporosis* (porous and brittle bones). Hunger is simply cellular messages signaling receivers in our brain that they need a replenishment of certain molecules to continue normal functioning.

Bookstore and library shelves are lined with books recommending the "perfect" diet for a healthy and beautiful body. Most authors will offer at least some appropriate advice that will be beneficial in determining how and what a person should eat. A review of the literature is always a wise way to educate oneself; just avoid the extremes in any dietary method that could do damage to your body. At this point, research into the cellular metabolism of food indicates that our diets must contain the vitamins A (retinol), B1 (thiamine), B2 (riboflavin), B3 (niacin), B6 (pyridoxine), folic acid, B12 (cobalamin), C (ascorbic acid), D (cholecalciferol and ergocalciferol), E (tocopherol), and K. The minerals one's cells need include calcium, zinc, copper, chromium, and iron. The food building blocks needed are carbohydrates, proteins, fats, water, and fiber. Most nutrition books will summarize the function of these molecules in the body and list the sources of foods that supply the particular nutrients. Avoid the vitamin and supplement ads which lead one to believe that all dietary requirements may be satisfied through pills, powder, and liquids. The body is best able to absorb and use nutrients when they are taken as part of real food. Absorption is further enhanced if the nutrients are taken in through eating fruits, vegetables, and grains because of the fiber in those foods. Fiber helps stimulate intestinal muscles and enhances the growth of some intestinal bacteria, all of which helps regulate the absorption of nutrients for cellular use.

Again, shorting oneself on any of these nutrients through food deprivation only slows down cellular metabolism and forces the body to start breaking down muscle tissue to obtain them. Loss of muscle means decreased ability to burn fat because the muscles can do less work. And finally, if the cells themselves cannot build properly functioning new cells, it means people leave themselves wide open to disease because the immune cells (T and B cells) are not able to protect against bacterial and viral infections. If there is a lack of either of these cells or if they are unable to function normally, disease-causing bacterial cells or viral particles will not be recognized by our bodies as foreign. The chemicals normally produced by our cells to help defend against foreign particles will not be able to break them down and disable them to prevent them from causing disease.

Providing nutrients for our body cells is not a popularity or speed-eating contest as media advertising would have us believe. Fast-food chains such as McDonald's, Burger King, and Rax have made eating a cultist process of accumulating as many cheap toys as possible. Each child must have each character or toy from the latest movie, must have the representative token for each season of the year, and must eat fatty, over-salted, under-flavored junk in record time before the cold congeals the fat. Congealed fat is gross and the kids certainly do not want to see that forming on their food. Adults are encouraged to be seen at the "right" eateries to confirm their hipness and obvious ability to stay young and enjoy garish spectacles and lots of noise. Teenagers see eating at certain places as a popularity contest, even though they work under some of the nation's most shameful conditions if employed at some of the most popular food chains.

Prepackaged, overpriced, frozen entrees are now advertised as convenient for the busy person on the run and full of all the nutrients needed for people who do not have time to eat multiple kinds of food to achieve a balanced amount and diversity of nutrients. As our foods become more and more processed, more nutrient value is lost and more chemical fillers, with questionable safety, are added. For example, the skin and insides of a baked potato contain 50 percent of the U.S. RDA for vitamin C. If that same potato were dehydrated and flaked, or packaged as frozen mashed potatoes, it would contain only about 20 percent of the U.S. RDA for vitamin C. If that potato were further freeze-dried, reconstituted, molded, fried in oil, salted, and flavored as a Pringle-type chip, the vitamin C content would lower to 10 percent (Rome, cited in The Boston Women's Health Collective, 1984, p. 26). And the more processed our foods the lower the fiber content, so the less able our bodies to absorb any available nutrients.

Some people have chosen to implement a bit more power through their diets by changing to foods at the bottom of the food chain, plants. By cutting meat from their diets they not only are taking charge of determining how they can eat a balanced diet with different sources of foods, but also adopting a greater voice on the political and economic fronts. Our Western agriculture has evolved to a megabusiness that is dependent on an import and export industry which is fossil fuel, water, soil, and pesticide intensive. Of the shrinking surpluses of grains the U.S. has traditionally produced, over 60 percent goes into feeding livestock (Lappe, 1982).

Cattle especially are extremely poor converters of plant energy into meat protein. This means that rather than feeding more people cheaper food from the base of the food chain, the food industry is highly dependent on producing expensive meat, which is rapidly degrading the planet and decreasing the number of plant and animal species living on Earth. A major outcry has arisen as more rain forests are converted into pastures or grain fields and as more of the U.S. western grasslands are converted into deserts by improper agricultural practices. Some estimates indicate that if

U.S. citizens were to drop their meat consumption by a mere 10 percent, the result would free enough land and resources to grow more than 12 million tons of grain for the 40 to 60 million humans who die each year from starvation (Robbins, 1992).

However people choose to meet their nutritional needs each day, the following are suggestions to help one stick with thoughtful decisions for change:

- Write a list of foods needed before going to the grocery. Stick to the list and pass up glitzy junk food.
- Do not shop while hungry.
- Buy fresh foods whenever possible. They have the highest nutrient value.
- Learn to listen to your body again. Eat when you are hungry only. Do not worry about the tradition of three major meals a day. If smaller quantities of healthy food throughout the day better satisfy your hunger needs, use them.
- Be sure to research nutritional needs thoroughly so any changes in your diet are wise and healthy decisions.
- Improve your overall health and help mold your body silhouette by choosing a moderate exercise routine that is enjoyable and easy to maintain. You are not competing with Jane Fonda on the theory of no pain, no gain!
- If you have difficulty in taking in enough calories, try eating small amounts of nutritious foods more frequently throughout the day. Healthy foods can be high in calories too, such as peanut butter, puddings, and whole-grain cookies. Try new recipes that use herbs and spices to make foods more appealing and flavorful. Meet with friends to eat and talk.
- Keep a written account of your daily food intake and exercise. This will help you sustain a dietary plan that meets your body's needs and lifestyle.
- Be realistic in setting goals during the change process. It takes a while for body cells to adjust and lead to changes in your body proportions.
- Be creative and diverse in choosing foods to eat and where you eat them. Enjoy the process of maintaining a nutritious diet and healthy body.
- Eat foods you like; nutrition is not met through bran alone!
- Volunteer to work at a food co-op to learn about other foods and recipes and gain more information on meeting nutrient needs, and lower the costs of buying food.

- If your community does not a have a food co-op, be the spark that starts organizing one. Arrange with local farmers to buy foods from them rather than from other marketers. Create a local market for their products.
- Grow your own foods if possible, using environmentally friendly techniques. Participate in or start a community garden in your neighborhood. Work with young people to educate them about nutrition and gardening techniques.
- Volunteer to work in a community food kitchen so you can have a voice in the preparation of nutritionally balanced meals for others.

SMOKING

A flagrant example of how the women's liberation movement has been twisted to physically abuse and potentially mortally wound women, especially those in their teens and twenties, is the purposeful and ruthless smoking campaign by the tobacco industry. This campaign has not only specifically targeted young women, but also female and male groups of minority populations whose numbers are especially high in urban environments. Joe Camel, a creation of the R. J. Reynolds Tobacco Company, was a siren who enticed the young to join the "in crowd," offering temptations of posters, neon signs, leather jackets, and flip flop sandals for those people who could "win" them by collecting coupons from Camel cigarette packs. Some of those winners of goods had to buy up to 600 packs of Camels. How does a young person obtain that kind of money in the first place? What a price to pay for so little reward. Is it not interesting that people are willing to pay companies to advertise labeled goods in the form of clothing or some kind of gadget? This free and ubiquitous form of advertising must help the company budget to a major extent or else the company would not work so hard to recruit such salespeople.

One should question any voice that comes from tobacco companies as their ethics have become a matter of intense debate. In 1964, the tobacco industry created a voluntary code which stated that "cigarette companies will not advertise in publications that are directed primarily toward persons under twenty-one years of age." The code theoretically stands firm today (American Heart Association, 1996). However, the sponsorship of community-based events such as festivals and annual fairs, national ballet tours, fashion shows, tennis tournaments, and Congressional Fellowships on Women and Public Policy surely is not done to mainly attract older populations. Also, when the tobacco companies agreed to put health warnings on each packet of cigarettes, this simply freed them from any liability to dying smokers. Their reasoning was that each smoker is smoking under informed consent because of that labeling and thus the company is not responsible for that decision (Kaul, 1997). Should a person believe that the tobacco industry truly cares about the health and welfare of anyone? As detestable as tobacco company ethics are, it is the responsibility of each individual to decide whether to smoke, given the obvious health risks and high cost of an addictive (drug induced) habit.

Smoking cigarettes is not only dangerous to one's health, it can directly kill people through the progressive development of *atherosclerosis* (formation of plaque in the arteries which causes a blockage), *cardiovascular disease*, several types of cancer, and *chronic obstructive pulmonary disease* (frequent infections of the lungs and pulmonary system, and difficulty breathing typically involving asthma, emphysema, and chronic bronchitis). Smoking is one of the major causes of coronary heart disease (heart attacks) in both women and men. It produces a greater relative risk in persons who are under the age of fifty than in people who are over fifty years old. This is due to the physiological effects of smoking. Carbon monoxide, which is released by burning cigarettes, decreases the amount of oxygen available to the heart. The heart, like all other body organs, needs oxygen to function.

Likewise, tar, which is also in tobacco smoke, is a *carcinogen* (produces cancer). Carcinogens disrupt the normal activity of cells in the mouth, throat, and lungs, thereby increasing the likelihood of abnormal cellular growth, which is characteristic of cancer.

Three thousand young people begin smoking each day, according to data collected by the Federal Office on Smoking or Health. "Economist Dr. Kenneth Warner estimates that the tobacco industry would need to recruit 5,000 new young smokers every day just to keep constant the total number of smokers (due to the number of people who quit or die from tobacco-related illness each year)." The World Health Organization states that if our youth worldwide continue to smoke at their present pace, over 200 million of "today's children and teenagers will be killed by tobacco during the second quarter of the next century" (American Heart Association, 1996, pp. 1-2). Pretty impressive figures! But the creative, highly paid minds of the tobacco industry are certainly up to the challenge of gathering new smoking recruits. One of the most recent schemes focused on the urban minority youth of Philadelphia through the lure of Uptown cigarettes. Once again, a mythical image of being "cool" was created to give youth a new sense of identity. Luckily, the Association of the Coalition on Smoking and Health helped spearhead a successful community campaign to oppose the marketing of these cigarettes in Philadelphia. The

R. J. Reynolds Tobacco Company eventually withdrew the product in response to the strong pressure against them.

But still, enticements to smoke continue to be mainly targeted toward minority groups. "Black-owned and black-oriented magazines receive proportionately more revenues from cigarette advertising" than do white-oriented magazines. Additionally, these same magazines more commonly advertise for stronger mentholated brands of cigarettes. "Billboards advertising tobacco products are placed in African-American communities four to five times more often than in white communities." Hispanic communities are also targeted for intensive advertising campaigns, mainly because the statistics of the tobacco industry indicate that "Hispanics tend to be much more 'brand-loyal' than their non-Hispanic white counterparts." No wonder that Reed Tuckson, the former District of Columbia Health Commissioner, defined the tobacco industry's marketing practices as "the subjugation of people of color through disease" (American Heart Association, 1996, p. 2).

Society was well aware of how important and valuable the young female population was to the tobacco industry as everyone became aware of how liberated women were who smoked Virginia Slims. As the advertising slogan said, "You've come a long way, baby," but maybe in reality only as far as the Marlboro Man, who died at his end of the oxygen tank tube. Cigarettes designed for women now come in beautiful watercolor and pastel packaging, with a variety of perfumed scents and exotic flavors. The R. J. Reynolds Company came to the forefront of gimmicks once again in 1990 with the introduction of the Dakota marketing plan. These cigarettes were targeted toward unfeminine females who were eighteen to twenty-four years old, who had no education beyond high school, and who watched soap operas and attended tractor pulls. Talk about another case of passively accepting another stereotype! A 1990 Interagency Committee on Smoking and Health meeting said the Dakota campaign was a "deliberate focus on young women of low socioeconomic status who are at high risk of pregnancy." This same targeted population of women is also the one in which "smoking rates have declined the least and who are more likely than other women to continue to smoke during pregnancy" (American Heart Association, 1996, pp. 2-3).

Over 145,000 women die every year from smoking-related diseases. Lung cancer is the leading cause of cancer death among women today, an increase of almost 400 percent from twenty years ago. For the first time in history, more girls are using cigarettes for the first time than boys. Women using oral contraceptives who smoke are ten times more likely to suffer coronary heart disease than women who do not smoke. "Cigarette smoking in women is also causally associated with cancers of the urinary tract, larynx, oral cavity, esophagus, kidney, pancreas and uterus. Women who smoke are also at greater risk for death from chronic obstructive lung disease, and are more likely than nonsmokers to suffer from chronic bronchitis, emphysema, chronic sinusitis, peptic ulcer disease, and severe hypertension. Smoking has also been linked with decreased fertility in women and with early menopause" (The Boston Women's Health Book Collective, 1984, pp. 37-38).

CONTRACEPTION

All young people are aware of reproductive and contraceptive issues to varying extents. But when the hormones are fresh, one's peers are sending mixed messages, and awareness of the greater issues involved are sketchy, reproduction too often becomes a reality. In the global context, since the 1960s the majority of people want smaller families not only due to economic influences and women's wish for healthier lives, but also because of other life opportunities opening to both men and women. Many countries have readily responded to this evolution in family structure and made educational opportunities and medical facilities more available to more people, even the rural poor. During the 1994 United Nations International Conference on Population and Development in Cairo, 200 governments from around the world agreed that all population policies and programs must be first and foremost responsive to meeting the needs and desires of individuals and families in their quest to limit family size. This is done with a focus on the centrality of women in the family and in society, giving women and girls a chance to fully participate in the life of their communities and nations. This conference affirmed that women have the right to control the number and timing of their pregnancies (Ellertson, 1996). The United States had played a major role in this planning process (Turnbull, 1996). However, in 1995 the U. S. Congress cut funding for these home and overseas programs by one third and appropriated funds months late and in trickling amounts.

In the United States, family planning clinics are especially important to low-income women and some teenage girls. Before such clinics were available, the rate of unwanted children for such women was almost twice that of women who could afford traditional medical care. By 1965, the U.S. Congress saw these family planning clinics as integral components in the "War on Poverty" in their mission to expand economic development, alleviate poverty, avoid welfare dependency, and improve the health of women and children. Each year, these clinics' publicly funded contraceptive services help women avoid 1.3 million unintended pregnancies, which would result in 534,000 births, 632,000 abortions, and 165,000 miscarriages. In the absence of publicly funded contraceptive services, an additional 386,000 teenagers would become pregnant each year. Of these, 155,000 would give birth, increasing the number of teen births by one-quarter. A total of 183,000 teenagers would have abortions, increasing teen abortions by 58 percent. Likewise, without publicly funded contraceptive services, an additional 356,000 women who have never been married would give birth each year, increasing total out-of-wedlock births by one-quarter. Of the 534,000 more women who would give birth, 338,000 would be eligible for Medicaid-covered pregnancy-related care; eight in ten would not have been eligible if they had not become pregnant. The federal and state governments together spend $412 million to provide family planning. However, in the absence of publicly funded contraceptive services, they would spend $1.2 billion through Medicaid to cover the costs associated with the additional births and abortions that would occur. Therefore, for every dollar spent to provide publicly funded contraceptive services, the public saves an average of $3.00 in Medicaid costs for pregnancy-related and newborn care (Forrest and Samara, 1996).

Most of these family planning clinics also offer ten methods of contraception, giving females viable options and counseling for the methods they and their partners are comfortable using and will be most likely to use regularly. All the agencies provide Pap tests, breast and pelvic exams, blood pressure measurements, prenatal, postpartum, and well-baby care, immunizations, and food programs for women, infants, and children. They can also test for sexually transmitted diseases upon the request of the client. These are especially important for the low-income population.

At this point, there exists a general decline in fertility and contraceptives are available in a large percentage of the world, yet most women who have sexual intercourse still experience at least one unplanned birth. Why are unwanted children still being conceived and born? Research suggests a number of factors are involved. For example, male partners sometimes want more children than women do and will not cooperate with contraceptive attempts. No contraceptive is 100 percent effective. Accidents do happen. Likewise, in some countries where large families have been a tradition due to high mortality rates, some couples are still adjusting, somewhat insecurely and inefficiently, to the idea that their children will survive to adulthood. Family pressures can still make long-held beliefs about multiple conceptions difficult to surrender. Additionally, due to distribution problems in some areas, contraceptives are not always regularly available. Choices of methods may also be severely limited and may be unacceptable or unaffordable. Some methods such as the pill may actually endanger a woman's health. Some people are also not taught how to use contraceptives most effectively. Some methods may fail because the couple is not consistent in using a particular device. This may be because the partners cannot agree on a method they both like or because of fear of possible side effects on health. Even if conception is unplanned and unwanted, some women will still choose to give birth either because safe and legal abortion services may not be available or because abortion is not an acceptable option for their value system (Alan Guttmacher Institute, 1995; Ezeh, Seroussi, and Raggers, 1996).

In the social groups of some teenagers, having a child can be a form of rite of passage into adulthood or is mistakenly thought to be a way to gain love from another person. Care responsibilities are not an issue with this mind-set. Teenage pregnancy and out-of-wedlock childbearing are central issues in women's health debates and in the debate over welfare reform. Teenage pregnancies are rising, but three-quarters of the unintended pregnancies and abortions occur in women who are twenty and older. Seventy percent of teenage births occur with unwed mothers, but the greater percentage of out-of-wedlock births occur in the population of older women. Only 5 percent of mothers on welfare are teenagers and only 1 percent are younger than eighteen years. A large proportion of women who begin having children while teenagers tend to end up on welfare and receive assistance for long periods of time. These kinds of facts clearly indicate that ensuring teenagers access to family planning clinics is essential to help women avoid or escape poverty and welfare. Family planning clinics are cost-effective ways to reduce unplanned childbearing and its consequences. Current approaches to welfare reform ignore the realities of an effective education and health care system and instead are focused on disincentives to birth through punitive measures. Such a system of discouraging teenage childbearing is based on the assumption that poor, unmarried teenagers deliberately get pregnant and have babies so they can collect welfare benefits, and that ending such benefits will be enough incentive to stop out-of-wedlock births. Neither assumption is valid according to survey results of women's attitudes toward teenage out-of-wedlock births. Marriage often is simply not an option (Forrest and Samara, 1996). Poor young women no more desire the responsibility and expense of babies than do rich young women who also have intercourse and unplanned pregnancies and can afford to have "quiet" abortions.

What kinds of contraceptives are currently available through family planning clinics? Hormonal methods, which work primarily by preventing ovulation, include *Depo-Provera* (a hormonal injection), *Norplant* (a hormonal implant), postcoital hormonal pills (emergency contraception), and oral contraceptives. Blockade methods block the passage of sperm to the uterus and fallopian tube, thereby preventing fertilization. They include such methods as the male and female condom, diaphragm, and cervical cap. Other methods include spermicides, which kill sperm before they can reach and fertilize the egg, training in periodic abstinence, and intrauterine devices. More permanent methods include tubal ligation and vasectomy. These all carry their own unique risks and side effects and none are 100 percent effective.

Many people are unaware of the availability or even existence of effective *postcoital contraception* in the United States. This means of contraception has been available for thirty years but has been very underutilized simply because people do not know it exists. Estimates determine that 50 percent of undesired pregnancies could be prevented if this form of contraceptive were used (Creinin, 1997). What exactly is emergency contraception? It is a birth control method intended for use after unprotected intercourse. Depending on the method used, it may be effectively used two to seven days after intercourse. It is often inappropriately referred to as the morning-after pill, but this is misleading in that intercourse does not only occur at night. Likewise, it can be used effectively more than twelve hours after intercourse and not all postcoital methods involve taking a pill. If more women were educated about the use of emergency contraception, of the 3.5 million unintended pregnancies in the U.S. each year, which result in about 1.5 million abortions, these kinds of contraceptives could potentially decrease abortions to fewer than 800,000 per year. Many of the approximately 200,000 women who die as a result of unsafe abortions each year around the world could be saved from these mortal procedures. "In the U.S., no contraceptives are specifically marketed and packaged for emergency use" (Ellertson, 1996, p. 2). But doctors can prescribe oral contraceptives such as Lo/Ovral, Nordette, and Levlen, which contain appropriate hormones.

Other new contraceptives on the horizon include those listed in Table 5.1. However, these new forms of contraceptive may be slow coming to the market because of many obstacles to research and development, including present negative public attitudes toward birth control and political pressure to abandon U.S. marketing plans. The high cost and limited availability of liability insurance may also be a deterrent to their production, as may be the limited availability of insurance coverage for contraceptives, despite their cost-reducing benefits. Likewise, men tend to be uncomfortable with the idea that their hormones will be manipulated when traditionally only women have undergone such therapies. Low sperm counts have been an emotional threat to masculinity since the technology to measure them was

TABLE 5.1. Future Contraceptive Methods According to Shelton (1996)

- Hormone-releasing vaginal rings that can be inserted and removed by the user.

- Hormone-releasing intrauterine devices that remain effective for five years.

- Microbicides, with and without spermicides, that prevent the spread of STDs: one example—a polyurethane-foam vaginal sponge.

- Long-acting spermicidal suppositories; improved existing spermicides.

- Lower-dose oral contraceptives that use various hormone combinations, with reduced side effects.

- Transdermal patches that can be applied and removed by the user, providing sustained hormone release with a lower risk of gastrointestinal side effects.

- Menses-including hormones, used to block implantation or terminate early pregnancies.

- Variations of the cervical cap, including one with a one-way valve permitting passage of cervical secretions.

- A single implant that could be used by lactating women; a dual implant system for men that suppresses sperm production.

- Antifertility vaccines that suppress sperm production and provide continuous yet reversible contraception.

- No-scalpel vasectomy in which a closure device is used to block the spermatic duct.

---

developed. Fears of impotence are very real. Males may also experience discomfort about weekly injections of hormones and accompanying side effects. Other obstacles include high development costs; medical research is expensive and time consuming. It also has a poor profit potential. Furthermore, drug company executives perceive that the public is already well-served by existing contraceptives. Finally, the National Institutes of Health have implemented a ban on federal dollars spent on research involving the creation of human embryos for research purposes. This type of research is necessary for some of the possible newer contraceptive technologies to be developed (Service, 1994a, 1994b; Shelton, 1996).

SUMMARY

The dynamic evolution of women's health is under continued redefinition. Women have a long way to go to understand and effectively and proactively deal with the complexity of their health status. It is imperative that we take the issue from its present status of individually constructed weaknesses and failures of one's own imperfect body to the perspective that poor health is a component of normal life which is not a result of a personal imperfection. Women need to better support each other in educating ourselves about our anatomy, our bodily functions, and the chemical reactions that occur from foreign agents entering our bodies from the surrounding environment. We need to implement an energy and passion as we have never done before to take the role of decision makers, be it taking on the role of medical doctor, informed citizen, political representative, or economic analyst to guide our way to better health. We need to stop accepting the role of the victim. It is also appropriate to ask ourselves and our daughters questions that can provide a more confident sense of identity.

KEY TERMS

carcinogenesis	edema	atherosclerosis
mutagenesis	fat embolisms	cardiovascular disease
impairment of fertility	cellular metabolism	chronic obstructive
teratogenic	anorexia nervosa	pulmonary disease
fetotoxicity	arrhythmia	carcinogen
aberrations	bulimia	Depo-Provera
topical drug	analog	Norplant
homo sapiens	amphetamines	postcoital contraception
hemorrhage	osteoporosis	

DISCUSSION QUESTIONS

1. Describe how you might raise your own child in a gender-free fashion. Visit a toy store or the infant and children's sections of a department store. Note and list any gender themes or messages that are apparent in these departments. List any fantasy themes depicted in the fashions that dictate what a female should wear or look like. List gender-neutral items offered for sale. Describe how toys are made and used that may direct a child's image of her or his mental or physical skills.

2. A woman's health may be defined functionally by her social position. Explain how her social position and function may differ according to her race, socioeconomic class, and age. How will these situations then impact the status and maintenance of her health? Is this stratification appropriate?

3. Some people contend that women aid their own oppression in their health status by internalizing cultural messages, beliefs, and values about gender, and thus participate in their own erasure. Explain why you may agree or disagree with this statement. In the examples you use to defend your stance, indicate how this may have affected women in the past and how it may still be apparent at present.

4. Research instances of the feminine ideal and body image across cultures and throughout history. Describe the differences in dress, behavior, educational status, health status, and social roles that are found for "ideal" women from different societies throughout history. Compare these images of femininity to the ideal models in the United States today. Summarize the conclusions you draw about the concept of femininity.

5. Compare and contrast advertisements aimed at a male audience with those that target a female audience. Organize your observations according to the types of products, lifestyles, or body images that are being sold. Note the differences you find in the images used, the feelings conveyed, and the messages implicit in each.

6. Record your personal experience with the way advertising packages and sells sex, beauty, wealth, and a desirable lifestyle. Do these advertising images play a major role in how you make consumer choices? List the last five items you bought. Now, compose a wish list of items you would like to obtain. To what extent is either list influenced by promises of "the good life" or "the look" that these specific products offer? Describe how these products are linked to gender or messages about women's and men's lifestyles and physical images.

REFERENCES

Agras, W. S. and B. G. Kirkley (1986). "Bulimia: Theories of etiology." In *Handbook of eating disorders: Physiology, psychology and treatment of obesity, anorexia, and bulimia*, K. D. Brownell and J. P Foreyt (Eds.). New York: Basic Books, pp. 367-378.

Alan Guttmacher Institute (1995). *Hopes and realities: Closing the gap between women's aspirations and their reproductive experiences*. New York: Author.

Allegheny University MCP Hahnemann School of Medicine (1996). Brochure on the Women's Health Education Program. Philadelphia, PA.

American Heart Association\ (1996). Information brochure: "Home, health, and family: Heart and stroke A-Z guide: Tobacco industries targeting of youth, minorities and women." Dallas, TX: Author.

Boskind-White, M. and W. C. White, Jr. (1986). "Bulimarexia: A historical-sociocultural perspective." In *Handbook of eating disorders: Physiology, psychology and treatment of obesity, anorexia, and bulimia,* K. D. Brownell and J. P Foreyt (Eds.). New York: Basic Books, pp. 353- 367.

The Boston Women's Health Book Collective (1984). *The new our bodies, ourselves.* New York: Simon and Schuster, Inc.

Coward, R. (1985). "The body beautiful." In *Gender images! Reading for composition,* M. Schawn and C. Flanagan (Eds.). (1992) Boston: Houghton Mifflin Co.

Creinin, M. D. (1997). "Emergency contraception: More than a morning after pill." In *Medscape Women's Health.* Magee-Women's Hospital, Pittsburgh, PA.

Davies, E. and A. Furnham (1986). "The dieting and body shape concerns of adolescent girls." *British Journal of Medical Psychology, 59:* 279-287.

Dermatological Division of Ortho Pharmaceutical Corporation (1996). "Renova," *Good Housekeeping, 223(1)* July: 42-43.

Dobkin, R. and S. Sippy (1995). *The college woman's handbook.* New York: Workman Publishing.

Doress, P. B., D. L. Siegal, and The Midlife and Older Women Book Project (1987). *Ourselves growing older.* New York: Simon and Schuster.

Ellertson, B. (1996). "History and efficacy of emergency contraception: Beyond Coca-Cola," *Family Planning Perspectives, 28(2)* March/April, pp. 44-48.

Ezeh, A. C., M. Seroussi, and H. Raggers (1996). "Men's fertility, contraceptive use, and reproductive preferences." In *Demographic and Health Surveys Comparative Study No. 18.* Calverton, MD: Macro International.

Faludi, S. (1991). *Backlash: The undeclared war against American women.* New York: Crown Publishers, Inc.

Foek, A. (1997). "Sweat-shop Barbie: Exploitation of third world labor," *The Humanist,* January/February, 9-13.

Forrest, J. D. and R. Samara (1996). "Impact of publicly funded contraceptive services on unintended pregnancies and implication for medical expenditures," *Family Planning Perspectives, 28(5),* pp. 188-195.

Garfinkel, P. E. and A. S. Kaplan (1986). "Anorexia nervosa: Diagnostic conceptualizations." In *Handbook of eating disorders: Physiology, psychology and treatment of obesity, anorexia, and bulimia,* K. D. Brownell and J. P Foreyt (Eds.). New York: Basic Books, pp. 266-282.

Garner, D. M., P. E. Garfinkel, and M. P. Olmsted (1983). "An overview of sociocultural factors in the development of anorexia nervosa." In *Anorexia nervosa: Recent developments in research,* P. L. Darby, P. E. Garfinkel, D. M. Garner, and D. V. Coscina (Eds.). New York : Alan R. Liss, pp. 65-82.

Guralnik, D. B. (Ed.) (1978). *Webster's New World Dictionary of the American Language.* New York: Avenel Books.

Kaul, D. (1997). "Tobacco deal smells too bad to be any good," *Tribune-Review,* June 29, Pittsburgh, PA, p. 1.

Lappe, F. M. (1982). *Diet for a small planet.* New York: Ballantine Books.

Mitchell, J. E. (1986a). "Anorexia nervosa: Medical and physiological aspects." In *Handbook of eating disorders: Physiology, psychology and treatment of obesity, anorexia, and bulimia,* K. D. Brownell and J. P. Foreyt (Eds.). New York: Basic Books, pp. 247-265.

Mitchell, J. E. (1986b). "Bulimia: Medical and physiological aspects." In *Handbook of eating disorders: Physiology, psychology and treatment of obesity, anorexia, and bulimia*, K. D. Brownell and J. P Foreyt (Eds.). New York: Basic Books, pp. 379-388.

Munhall, P. L. (Ed.) (1995). *Women's experience, volume II*. New York: National League for Nursing Press.

Robbins, J. (1992). *May all be fed: Diet for a new world*. New York: Avon Books.

Service, R. R. (1994a). "Barriers hold back new contraceptive strategies," *Science, 266:*5190.

Service, R. R. (1994b). "Contraceptive methods go back to the basics," *Science, 266:*5190.

Shelton, D. L. (1996). "10M report urges stepped-up contraceptive research," *American Medical News, 39:*23.

Sloane, E. (1985). *Biology of women*. New York: John Wiley and Sons.

Strober, M. (1986). "Anorexia nervosa: History and psychological concepts." In *Handbook of eating disorders: Physiology, psychology and treatment of obesity, anorexia, and bulimia*, K. D. Brownell and J. P Foreyt (Eds.). New York: Basic Books, pp. 231-246.

Szmukler, G. I. and G. F. M. Russell (1986). "Outcome and prognosis of anorexia nervosa." In *Handbook of eating disorders: Physiology, psychology and treatment of obesity, anorexia, and bulimia*, K. D. Brownell and J. P Foreyt (Eds.). New York: Basic Books, pp. 283-300.

Turnbull, W. R. (1996). "Endangered: U.S. aid for family planning overseas," *Issues in Brief,* November, p. 1. Alan Guttmacher Institute.

Chapter 6

Psychology of Women: Theories of Sex Differences and Sex Role Development

Donna M. Ashcraft

WHAT IS PSYCHOLOGY?

Before we begin to study the psychology of women, it is important to understand what psychology is and is not. The popular media is full of false images of psychology and psychologists. Most depictions of psychologists, for example, are caricatures of *clinical psychologists*. These are psychologists who study and try to change abnormal behavior. An example of this depiction can be found on the past popular television series, *Cheers*. Two of the characters, Lillith and Frasier, were portrayed as clinicians, and, in particular, as psychoanalists. Not all psychologists are clinical psychologists, though, and those that are do not all adhere to the psychoanalytic (Freudian) viewpoint demonstrated in the media depictions of clinical psychologists. In fact, that viewpoint is in the minority. As we shall see in this chapter, psychologists and others who study women's behavior are quite varied in their opinions of why women behave in the way that they do. Other psychologists study normal behavior, and not just the behavior of humans, but that of animals as well. What is psychology then?

Psychology is the scientific study of behavior. Psychologists use the scientific method to determine why people behave in the way that they do. The *scientific method* is a group of research strategies that allow one to form objective conclusions. It is the same method that chemists or biologists use in their research. Thus, psychologists use research to study behavior, in this case, women's behavior. The goals of psychology, and therefore psychological research, are to observe, understand, predict, and control behavior. When we observe behavior we can form hypotheses about why people behave in the way that they do and this can lead to research testing those hypotheses. Research will then give us some insight or understanding as to what factors influence or create certain types of

117

behavior. By knowing what variables cause behavior, we can then predict and control. Various therapies, for example, try to change behavior by manipulating certain variables.

Behavior can be divided into two basic categories: seen and unseen. Thus, although the general public tends to believe that if you understand psychology you will understand how people think or how to manipulate them, that really is not true. Psychologists certainly study how people think and how to change people's behavior, but it also studies observable, everyday behavior.

Although the psychology of women includes many different topics, this chapter will mainly discuss whether any sex differences exist and, if they do exist, what some possible reasons for their existence are.

SEX DIFFERENCES AND SIMILARITIES

For years, and even to a certain extent today, people believed that males and females were very different—polar opposites. Many believe that women naturally cry easily and are naturally gentle; men are thought to be naturally competitive and aggressive (Ruble, 1983). Are men and women really that different?

In 1974, Maccoby and Jacklin conducted a landmark study of sex differences in abilities and personality variables. The type of study they conducted is called a meta-analysis. This is when a researcher or research team seeks out all the studies that can be found on a particular topic and combines the studies statistically and reanalyzes them as a whole. Essentially, what they found was that sex differences only seemed to exist in four areas of behavior: verbal abilities, spatial abilities, math abilities, and aggression. It should be noted that even though these differences were found to exist, the differences themselves were very small. They accounted for only 1 to 5 percent of the variance among individuals. What this means is that only 1 to 5 percent of a person's score on a math test or verbal abilities test, for instance, could be accounted for by the sex of the person taking the test. The other 95 to 99 percent of the person's score could be determined by other factors. For example, the other 95 to 99 percent of a person's math score could be determined by such factors as the number of math courses taken or study habits. Some more recent research has even called into question the existence of some of these sex differences. For example, Hyde and Linn (1988) found that there were no sex differences in verbal ability.

More current research also examines the circumstances under which sex differences are most likely to be found (e.g., Eagly and Karau, 1991; Eagly and Wood, 1991). For example, they are more likely to be found when behavior is self-reported than when behavior is observed by an outsider. This implies that people believe they act in sex-typed ways more than they actually do. Sex differences are also more likely to be found when the behavior being assessed is performed when others are present. Most likely, when others are present, people assume that the others will approve of sex-typed behaviors and so they automatically engage in those types of behavior. A third recent finding is that if the behavior being assessed for sex differences requires gender-related skills, sex differences are more likely to be found. For example, if one is studying whether males or females are more helpful and if the method for assessing this behavior is observation of how many males and females help a motorist stranded with car trouble, it is likely that sex differences will be found. In a study using the methodology just described, one might find, for instance, that men are more likely to stop and help than females. But this does not mean that males are more helpful than females. Females may be less likely to stop and help because they are less likely than males to know much about cars, or because of concerns for their safety, or because they are more likely to be caring for children who may be in the car with them. Thus, it is very important to critically assess studies that demonstrate sex differences.

Although true sex differences are difficult to find when one closely examines the research literature, there are many studies that do document these differences. Why? One of the reasons is that sex differences are over-represented in research publications. Studies that demonstrate sex differences are more likely to be published than those that demonstrate similarities. Thus, you will find many examples of sex differences in the literature even if the differences are only statistically significant, not practically significant. A *statistically significant difference* means that the difference between groups is unlikely to have occurred by chance. But the difference may be very small and so lacks *practical significance*. For example, males may score, on average, 74 out of 100 points on a math test; females on average may score 72.8 points on the same math test. The difference may be statistically significant and so the researchers can state that males did better than females on a math test, but in actuality, the difference is only 1.2 points. It is not a difference worth noting. Thus, practical significance is not found.

GENDER ROLES

Gender roles or sex roles are essentially behaviors that encourage people to act in a way which is thought by society to be acceptable for a male or a female. Thus, males act in a masculine way (competitive, aggressive, etc.) and females act in a feminine way (gentle, emotional, etc.).

Bem (1974), however, believes that there are more than two gender roles. She believes that there are four: masculine, feminine, androgynous, and undifferentiated. According to Bem, to be considered *masculine* a person must score high on masculine traits and behaviors and low in feminine traits and behaviors. For example, a masculine person might be very competitive and not very emotional. A person with a *feminine* sex role is one who has a lot of feminine traits and behaviors in his/her personality and not many masculine ones. Thus, a feminine person may be very good at the traditional feminine role of cooking and not very good at the traditional masculine role of fixing a car. An *androgynous* individual is one who is high in both masculine and feminine traits and behaviors. For example, an androgynous person might be both nurturant and competitive. Finally, the *undifferentiated sex role* implies that a person is not very masculine and not very feminine at all. Instead, their personality consists of characteristics that cannot be sex typed. For example, an undifferentiated person might be described as happy.

A couple of points should be noted. First, a male or a female can be categorized into any of these gender roles. Thus, a female can have a masculine (or any other) sex role and a male can have a feminine (or any other) sex role. Second, sex role is a concept independent from sexual orientation. This implies that one cannot determine whether an individual is homosexual or heterosexual from whether they act in a masculine or feminine way. A masculine female or a feminine male are not necessarily homosexual. Finally, these gender roles reflect personality and behavior, not appearance. One can, for example, determine the biological sex of an androgynous individual quite easily (usually) even though her/his behavior can be either masculine or feminine.

It should also be noted that gender roles may vary across ethnic groups. For example, de Leon (1993) found that blacks had more flexible family and gender roles than whites and Puerto Ricans. Likewise, she found that black women were the most masculine and white women were the least masculine among women. Puerto Rican men were found to be the most feminine among men.

There is debate over which sex role is the best model for mental health. With the emergence of the concept of androgyny, some clinicians and others began to believe that androgyny should be encouraged in all individuals because it represented an escape from traditional sex roles. It also seemed to allow for a greater range of behavior because the androgynous individual was acting neither *just* masculine nor *just* feminine, but was acting in both ways, as was appropriate in individual situations. However, more recently the androgynous gender role model for mental health has come under criticism. Some say that androgyny places too much stress on individuals (e.g., Bem, 1981): now they must be good at *both* masculine and feminine behaviors. For example, an androgynous person might have to be good at both baking bread and remodeling houses. In addition, some of the ideas of masculinity and femininity are contradictory and so it could be difficult to act in both ways. For instance, it would be difficult to be both competitive and shy. Finally, although androgyny was seen as a departure from traditional roles, encouraging all people to be androgynous (in order to be mentally healthy) is still dictating behavior to people. In response to these criticisms, there has been a movement toward *gender role transcendence* (Rebecca, Hefner, and Oleshansky, 1976). Gender role transcendence essentially means allowing both men and women to act in ways that they find meaningful for themselves—allowing people to develop their own strengths and personalities, regardless of biological sex and societal expectations. Gender role transcendence would allow a woman, for example, to be traditionally feminine (or masculine, etc.) or to develop any other meaningful approach to life.

THEORIES OF SEX DIFFERENCES AND SEX ROLES

Although many differences between men and women do not exist, many people still assume that there are extensive differences between the sexes. They also continue to behave in ways encouraged by traditional sex roles. Many have formed theories as to why sex differences and sex roles exist. The theories can be divided in two basic categories: biological and environmental. *Biological theories* suggest that sex differences are innate, that is, they occur naturally. *Environmental theories* suggest that sex differences that do exist are due to outside forces and experiences such as socialization factors. Let us examine these categories of theories more closely by discussing some specific examples of theories in these categories and the research that supports or does not support them.

Biological Theories

Hormones

Some theorists believe that the differences in hormones in men's and women's bodies account for differences in behavior. As most people know, men have larger amounts of androgens, like testosterone, in their bodies than women, and women have larger amounts of estrogens and progesterones in their bodies than men. Consider, for example, how we assume that women's emotional states vary along with hormonal changes in the menstrual cycle. Dobson (1995), for example, states, "estrogen levels account for much . . . optimism" (p. 34) during the second week of the menstrual cycle and that estrogen levels fall before menstruation, causing premenstrual tension—"a bleak phase of the month" (p. 35). Consider also how we (and researchers) assume that the higher levels of aggressiveness in males is due to their higher levels of testosterone.

Beyond this, hormones have been suggested to affect sexual orientation, aggressiveness, dominance behavior, and intelligence, as well as other sex-typed behaviors (Bleier, 1984).

Many (some theorists and the general public alike) believe that hormones affect or cause behavior, but when one looks closely at the research on this assumption, one finds surprisingly little support for this idea. Tavris (1991), for example, attempts to debunk the premenstrual syndrome (PMS) myth by noting that the "belief" in PMS may make it more likely that women notice symptoms and attribute them to PMS. In fact, she notes a study which found that men check off as many "PMS" symptoms on a checklist as long as it is not labeled a PMS Symptom Checklist.

Likewise, although many assume that testosterone increases aggressiveness in men, research shows that aggressiveness may, in actuality, increase testosterone levels (Kilmartin, 1994). [See also Bleier (1984) for a complete critique on biological explanations of gender roles and Ramey (1976) for information on the hormonal cycles of men.]

Brain Lateralization

Some theorists believe that sex roles or sex differences can be accounted for by differences in the brain, that during prenatal development males' and females' brains become differentiated or lateralized such that when they are born babies have either a male brain or a female brain (Bleier, 1984; Christen, 1995). Presumably, this occurs because of the influence of hormones as the fetus is developing. The two areas of the brain most likely to be affected in this way are the hypothalamus and the cerebral hemispheres.

The *hypothalamus* is an area of the brain that is important in regulating basic biological needs such as hunger, thirst, temperature control, and hormone development. It is located in the forebrain, which is one of the largest and most complex regions of the brain. It has been suggested that the hypothalamus, important in the control of hormone secretions, must be differentiated among males and females because, as mentioned, females secrete more progesterones and estrogens than males, whereas males secrete more androgens. Also, although there is some debate on this, many believe that males and females secrete hormones in different fashions: males secrete them steadily; females secrete them in a cyclic fashion. Thus, during prenatal development the male fetus secretes testosterone and this desensitizes the cells in the hypothalamus to estrogen. This results in the male secreting hormones in a steady fashion. The female fetus, on the other hand, does not secrete as much testosterone as the male fetus and this sensitizes the cells in the hypothalamus to estrogen. This sensitization results in hormones being released in a cyclic fashion, that is, the menstrual cycle (Bleier, 1984; Tavris and Wade, 1984).

Some evidence exists for this brain lateralization theory in that females have menstrual cycles and males do not and in that females release different hormones than males and this is under at least partial control of the brain, yet it should be noted that we have always *assumed* that males do not have a cycle similar to that of females. Research, however, has not documented this and so the possibility still exists. Indeed, testosterone levels in the male do fluctuate (Tavris, 1991). Furthermore, the lateralization of the hypothalamus does not explain sex roles and differences in the behavior of men and women. Our discussion of the lateralization of the cerebral hemispheres will elucidate this explanation.

If one looks down directly upon the brain through the skull one will see the *cerebral cortex*. It will be evident that that part of the brain is divided in half; the two halves are called the cerebral hemispheres. The cerebral hemispheres are responsible (but not solely) for controlling a number of behaviors including verbal, spatial, and math abilities. The right cerebral hemisphere is responsible for math and spatial abilities; the left cerebral hemisphere is responsible for language or verbal abilities. Thus, theorists who adhere to this explanation of gender differences would suggest that males have greater math and spatial abilities because they are right cerebral hemisphere dominant, that is, their right cerebral hemisphere plays a bigger role in their brain functioning than their left cerebral hemisphere and therefore influences their behavior more. Likewise, they would suggest that females have greater verbal abilities because they are left cerebral hemisphere dominant. You can see that those who believe this theory believe that sex differences in abilities are innate or biologically determined. Is there evidence for this theory?

If one studies the cerebral hemispheres of rats, one will find that the left cerebral hemisphere in female rats is thicker than the right; and in male rats the right cerebral hemisphere is thicker (Diamond, Johnson, and Ehlert, 1979). Thus, there is some evidence that supports this explanation, but one must view this evidence cautiously. How many rats do you know that have good math or verbal abilities? One must always be cautious in generalizing from research findings in other animals to humans.

Sociobiology

Sociobiology is the last biological theory of gender roles and differences we will discuss. *Sociobiology* is the application of evolutionary biology to the social behaviors of animals such as humans. Sociobiologists believe that animals, including humans, are driven to pass on their genes. The social behaviors that they engage in help them to pass on their genes and help the survival of the species. It follows, then, that the social behaviors we engage in are of evolutionary benefit. Just as Darwin suggested that the strongest members of the species will survive because of natural selection (thereby increasing chances of survival for the species), sociobiologists believe that behaviors that we engage in today have survived or developed because they help the species to survive.

Sociobiologists believe that the sex roles that exist today do so because they benefit the species. One area of sex roles is, of course, the roles that men and women play when they are dating and selecting mates. Sociobiologists would suggest that the methods humans use to select their sexual partners are similar to those used by other animals (e.g., Buss, 1994; Layng, 1995). For example, humans tend to prefer others who are physically attractive. This behavior is thought to be of evolutionary benefit because sociobiologists believe that physical attractiveness is a sign of health (e.g, clear skin, shiny hair). We want our mates to be healthy because that means that our children are more likely to be born healthy, thereby ensuring the passage of our genes.

Likewise, the behaviors we engage in during our dates also helps us to chose a "healthy" partner with which to pass on our genes. An example of this would be going out dancing on a date. The physical activity of dancing will help us to determine the physical fitness level (and therefore health) of our date. This is an idea similar to the idea that other species engage in elaborate mating rituals requiring great physical prowess to demonstrate their acceptability (in terms of health) to a potential mate.

The custom of males paying for dates (although this is changing) is also explained by sociobiologists as being of evolutionary benefit to the species. Females are assessing whether their dates will be good providers. This is important to them because females, of course, are the ones who get pregnant, carry the baby to term, and give birth. These biological roles will render the female incapacitated to a certain extent for a certain amount of time. They, therefore, will need assistance in providing for themselves and their children. Thus, the importance of the male as a good provider becomes evident.

Related to this notion is the stereotype that men are more interested in a variety of sexual partners whereas women are more concerned with marriage and a single sexual partner. This, again, ties in with the idea of being driven to pass on our genes. Women are concerned with choosing a good provider as a sexual partner to pass on their genes. This is because of the investment of time in the process of pregnancy, childbirth, and child rearing, mentioned above. Women know that the children they give birth to are their own, with some of their own genes. But men can never be quite sure of the paternity of "their" children. Men can never be quite sure that their sexual partner has not been cheating on them. Therefore, to ensure that he passes on his genes, a man tries to engage in sex with as many females as possible so that at least one of them will get pregnant with his child and so carry on his genes. Thus, women's tendency to favor monogamy and men's tendency to favor multiple sexual partners is explained by sociobiologists as being of benefit to the species.

Although at first glance sociobiologists seem to logically explain sex roles as being due to biological drives, there are a number of problems with the theory. First, although the theory suggests that we engage in sexual intercourse to pass on our genes, our behavior does not seem to indicate this. There is a high abortion rate (Costa, Jessor, and Donovan, 1987) and many couples use contraception faithfully (Ashcraft, Schlueter, and Thornton, 1996). Second, there are problems with the assumption that physical attractiveness is an indicator of health. We are all aware of any number of diseases that do not affect the physical attractiveness of an individual at all or for a long period of time. Acquired Immune Deficiency Syndrome (AIDS) is one of these examples. Someone can test positive for the AIDS virus and not develop symptoms (or the disease) for years. Likewise, different societies have different standards for physical attractiveness. A third problem with the theory is that most of the evidence for the theory comes from animal models. We have already mentioned that we must be careful in generalizing from other animals to humans. Just because there may be parallel behavior does not mean that the animals and humans are engaging in them for the same reasons. In fact, just because we *see* a parallel in behavior does not mean that one actually exists. Fourth, the theory ignores the fact that humans are cognitive creatures. Even if we are driven by instincts, our ability to think and reason will affect our behavior, not just our biological urges. Furthermore, in many cultures mates are not chosen by dating but are chosen by relatives, as in arranged marriages. There are other problems with the theory as well. Can you think of some more?

Environmental Theories

Behaviorism

In simplest form, *behaviorism* (also called *operant conditioning*) suggests that our behavior is determined by rewards and punishments. We all know this on some level. When we reward a behavior it is more likely to occur. When we punish a behavior it is less likely to occur. We use this mechanism to train pets. If you are training your dog to shake paws you reward your dog with a treat or a pat or praise when s/he shakes at your command. Likewise, one can use punishment when trying to discourage certain kinds of behavior. If you want to discourage your cat from getting on top of the table, you could squirt your cat with a little bit of water whenever s/he gets on top of the table. Humans are also affected by rewards and punishments and neither the rewards nor the punishments need be concrete. We are affected by praise, love, and rejection as much as we are affected by money, food, and physical pain.

Behaviorists would suggest that we learn our gender roles because certain behaviors and ways of thinking have either been rewarded or punished. Furthermore, the sex differences in abilities or roles that do exist, do so because different behaviors have been rewarded and punished in females than in males. For example, if we look at it from the traditional point of view, females are more nurturant than males because they have been rewarded (perhaps praised) for that behavior, probably starting when they were very young, and males were either not rewarded for this behavior or were punished for it.

There is some evidence that males and females are rewarded and punished differently even in childhood. For example, the American Association of University Women (AAUW) (1992) reported that girls receive significantly less attention and encouragement from their teachers than boys. To illustrate this point the AAUW noted that boys tend to call out more answers to questions than girls and that when girls did so, they were more likely than boys to be told to raise their hands. Because attention and encouragement can be thought of as rewards or reinforcers, one can see that boys and girls are rewarded differently in school. In this particular example the differential rewards result in girls developing less confidence and self-esteem than boys. The AAUW also reports that African-American girls have even fewer interactions with teachers than Caucasian girls despite the fact that they attempted to initiate interactions more frequently.

There is a problem with the theory, however. Like sociobiology and the other biologically based theories of gender roles, behaviorism does not take into consideration the fact that we do not only respond to our environment (or biological drives); we interpret and think about our environment. Thus, true behaviorists do not see men and women as thinking human beings. It should be noted though, that behaviorism has become more cognitively oriented since it was first conceived.

Classical Conditioning

Classical conditioning (also called Pavlovian conditioning) suggests that we learn by associating a neutral stimulus with an unconditioned stimulus, thereby allowing the neutral stimulus to be responded to in the same way as the unconditioned stimulus. Let us define some terms to clarify this learning theory. A *stimulus* is something that evokes a reaction or response. An *unconditioned stimulus* (UCS) is one that naturally evokes some reaction, an *unconditioned response* (UCR). For example, when a puff of air is blown into your eye, your eye automatically blinks. The puff of air is the unconditioned stimulus; the eye blink is the unconditioned response. A *neutral stimulus* (NS) does not evoke a response on its own. But when one pairs the NS with the UCS repeatedly, the NS will eventually evoke the same response as the UCS. When it does so, the NS is called the *conditioned stimulus* (CS) and the UCR is called the *conditioned response* (CR). Going back to our example, if a noise like a tone was repeatedly made before the puff of air was blown into the eye, eventually the tone itself would evoke the eye blink. The tone before it is paired with the puff of air is a NS; when it evokes the blinking response, it is a CS. Likewise, when only the puff of air causes the eye blink, the blink is a UCR; but when the tone causes the blink, it is a CR.

Some believe that we learn attitudes through this classical conditioning technique. It follows then, that we might be able to learn gender roles and gender role attitudes through this same process. As you can see in Figure 6.1, ideas of masculinity and femininity may develop through this mechanism.

There is, of course, the problem with this theory of not viewing the human organism as a thinking being. However, there is evidence that this mechanism does occur.

Social Learning Theory

Social learning theorists or modeling theorists believe that we learn behavior through the observation and imitation of another's behavior. In

FIGURE 6.1. How Classical Conditioning Affects Sex Role Development

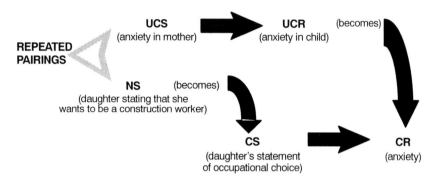

A daughter tells her mother that she would like to become a construction worker when she grows up. Although the mother does not make any negative statements about this occupational choice, the child senses her mother's anxiety about it. This causes anxiety in the child. With repeated pairings, the daughter's occupational choice will eventually evoke negative emotions on its own.

other words, we watch someone's behavior and then we engage in that behavior. Relatedly, we can observe the consequences of someone's behavior and this will affect whether or not we will display the behavior we have just learned. Notice the distinction between learning and performance. Just because someone learns a behavior does not mean that they will display that behavior unless it is the appropriate time to do so. Thus, learning theorists believe that we learn our sex roles by observing other people of the same sex. Daughters learn their sex-appropriate behavior by watching and imitating their mothers, older sisters, aunts, mother's female friends, and so on. Sons learn their sex-appropriate behavior by watching their fathers, older brothers, uncles, father's male friends, and so forth. The model (or person displaying the behavior) does not have to be real. He or she can be symbolic. *Symbolic models* are characters in books, movies, television programs, etc. that display behavior which others emulate. For example, a child who ties a towel around her/his neck like a cape and jumps off a chair may be imitating the behavior of Superman or Wonder Woman. Another may try to be like Barbie by dressing like her. It is important to note, then, that the media is a very important influence on a child's gender role development according to this theory.

Unfortunately, when one examines the content of newspaper comics, movies, books, and television programs, one finds that the characters are very sex-typed even today. For example, an analysis of Sunday comics in both 1974 and 1984 (Brabant and Mooney, 1986) found that males were depicted more than females, and that when females were depicted, the domestic role was the most likely to be shown. More specifically, women were shown in the home 69 percent of the time in 1974 and 72 percent of the time in 1984. The comparable percentages for men were 32 percent for 1974 and 33 percent for 1984.

Similarly, an analysis of television commercials from 1971 to 1985 (Lovdal, 1989) found that men were more visible than women. Approximately 91 percent of commercials in 1985 were narrated by men; 9 percent by women. When women were narrators they usually did not speak to the television viewer in general, but rather spoke to pets, babies, and female dieters. This indicates that females are seen as less authoritative; they cannot influence the audience in general. These suggestions, in turn, will be learned by the television viewer. Likewise, the absence of female models is troublesome.

While these studies may seem dated, more recent research shows the same findings in the 1990s. One study found that illustrations in award-winning children's books typically depict females in the traditional domestic role and that this has not changed from 1937 to 1989 (Crabb and Bielawski, 1994). Another study found that stories in *Seventeen* and *'Teen* magazines typically are about conflicts with boys and show that the female main character needs assistance in solving her problems (Peirce, 1993).

Although there is a trend away from stereotyping in the media, it mostly involves a change in the male role, not the female role. Men are more likely to be shown in successful marriages (Manes and Melnyk, 1974), but women are very unlikely to be shown as both employed and married (Weigel and Loomis, 1981). Of course, this implies that a female cannot do both and thus affects viewers.

There is some evidence to support this theory that suggests that our children and young people are learning traditional roles from the media. Studies show that people who watch a lot of television are more sex typed than those who watch less television (e.g., Lull, Mulac, and Rosen, 1983). However, because this is correlational research, we do not know whether the television viewing is influencing sex-role learning or if people who are sex-typed are simply more likely to watch television.

There are some problems with the theory, however. One problem is the assumption that children learn their sex roles from members of the same sex. Research indicates that this is not always true (Maccoby and Jacklin, 1974).

Psychoanalytic Theory

Freud's *psychoanalytic theory* also explains gender role development but does so by means of identification with the parent of the same sex.

Freud's theory of psychosexual development suggests that we go through five stages. At each stage our *libido* (or life force) is focused on a different part of the body. It is during the third stage, the *phallic stage*, when the libido is focused on the genitals, that sex role development occurs. During this stage boys experience Oedipus complex and girls experience the Electra complex. Both boys and girls are attached emotionally to their mothers. During the *Oedipus complex*, however, a boy develops an unconscious sexual attraction to his mother. He is afraid that his father will find out about this attraction and punish him for it by castrating him. *Castration anxiety* develops. In an effort to decrease this anxiety, boys *identify* or become as much like their fathers as possible. In the unconscious mind, if a boy becomes as much like his father as possible, he becomes the father. Since the father will not harm himself, i.e., castrate himself, the boy does not have to fear castration any longer. At the same time, boys receive from their mothers the love that they have been desiring because the mother loves the father and the boy unconsciously "becomes" the father. It is the identification with the father that creates the male sex role.

The development of the female sex role is slightly more complicated. Although girls love their mothers, according to Freud, they have to reject the mother as the love object and become (unconsciously) attracted to their fathers. This occurs because during this *Electra complex* girls find out that boys have penises and girls do not. They believe that they had one at some time and desire one. They develop *penis envy*. Girls believe that it was their mothers who deprived them of their penises through castration. This causes them to reject their mothers as love objects and adopt their fathers as the love object instead. The girls then proceed to identify with their mothers (or become as much like them as possible) in order to gain the fathers' love. Again, identification is what causes gender role development.

Support for this theory is limited because it is so difficult to test. How does one test for the presence of penis envy or castration anxiety, especially because they occur unconsciously? There are additional problems besides the inability to test hypotheses derived from this theory, however. A basic assumption of the theory is that the male is superior. The penis is viewed as superior to the female anatomy; otherwise penis envy would not be thought to develop. Furthermore, Freud thought that women were less developed morally than men because they did not experience castration anxiety. Other problems in the basic assumptions of the theory include the lack of an explanation of why a little girl would believe that she once had a penis and that her mother cut it off. Why cut it off and why was it her mother who did so? Likewise, even if a little boy was afraid that his father would punish him for being attracted to his mother, why is castration the punishment of choice? The theory also does not account for gender role development in single-parent households. Can you see other problems with the theory?

Cognitive-Developmental Theory

The *cognitive-developmental theory*, more than any of the others we have discussed, views the individual as a cognitive being. According to this theory, a child must pass through a number of milestones in cognitive development before she or he can learn the appropriate gender role. Once a child learns his/her sex, s/he must learn gender constancy. *Gender constancy* is the realization that one will always be a member of the sex that one is at the present time. A little boy who wants to grow up to be a mommy has not yet learned gender constancy. After children learn gender constancy they will then group all males and all females together. Children will then observe their sex group for similarities and draw conclusions about the way they should behave from these similarities. For example, a little girl may know that she is female and that she will always be female. She may also know that Mother, Aunt Sarah, Mom's friend Kathy, and Mom's other friend, Sandy, are all females. She notices that they all are married and stay home to raise their children. She then decides that that is the way females are supposed to act and she behaves in accordance. She plays with dolls and becomes interested in marriage and motherhood roles.

A little boy knows that he is male and will always be male. He also knows that he fits into the same category as Dad, Uncle Joe, Uncle Jim, and Dad's friend Tom. He notices that they all work outside the home and on weekends do yard work such as mowing the grass. The little boy decides that this is the way males are supposed to act and he behaves in accordance. He plays with toy yard tools and becomes interested in occupational and career roles.

Conclusions About the Theories

We have discussed several theories of gender role and sex differences. Which is correct? That is a difficult question to answer. As you can see, most of the theories have some support and most have some problems. Chances are that the environment plays more of a role than biology because of the cross-cultural differences that exist in sex roles (although it is important to not rule out biological influences). Margaret Mead (1963) studied a number of tribal societies and found differences in the gender roles among them. For example, in one society, the *Arapesh*, both males and females displayed behaviors that we, in the United States, attribute primarily to females. They were kind, gentle, and both sexes were involved in child rearing. In another society, the *Mundugumor*, both males and females displayed behaviors that we tend to attribute primarily to males. They were competitive and aggressive. In still another society, the *Tchambuli*, sex roles opposite to those in the United States were found. The males had what we call feminine traits and the females had what we call masculine traits, that is, the males were nurturant and the females were competitive. These types of research findings indicate that the environment or learning, more so than biology, are important in the development of gender roles because there is no reason to believe that the biology of these societies is different from our own. Thus, only learning can account for the differences in gender roles. It is important to note, however, that biology can predispose us to act in a certain way but the environment can change that behavior. It is also important to note that if we do learn our gender roles, we probably do so in a variety of ways, not just one. Thus, many of the theories discussed may be accurate.

KEY TERMS

clinical psychologists	hypothalamus	libido
psychology	cerebral cortex	phallic stage
scientific method	sociobiology	Oedipus complex
statistically significant difference	behaviorism	castration anxiety
	operant conditioning	identify
practical significance	classical conditioning	Electra complex
gender roles	stimulus	penis envy
masculine	unconditioned stimulus	cognitive-developmental theory
feminine	unconditioned response	
androgynous	neutral stimulus	gender constancy
undifferentiated sex role	conditioned stimulus	Arapesh
gender role transcendence	conditioned response	Mundugumor
	social learning theory	Tchambuli
biological theories	symbolic models	
environmental theories	psychoanalytic theory	

DISCUSSION QUESTIONS

1. What are the goals of psychology? Explain each of them.
2. Do you think any sex differences exist? If so, in what areas? Why?
3. If you think that some sex differences exist, what theory do you think best explains them? Why?

REFERENCES

American Association of University Women (1992). *How schools shortchange girls.* Washington, DC: American Association of University Women Educational Foundation.

Ashcraft, D. M., D. Schlueter, and G. Thornton (1996). "College women's contraceptive use, sexual health, and disease prevention from 1976 to 1993." Paper presented at the annual meeting of the Pennsylvania State System of Higher Education in Edinboro, PA.

Bem, S. L. (1974). "The measurement of psychological androgyny," *Journal of Consulting and Clinical Psychology, 42:* 155-162.

Bem, S. L. (1981). "Gender schema theory: A cognitive account of sex typing," *Psychological Review, 88:* 354-364.

Bleier, K. (1984). *Science and gender: A critique of biology and its theories on women.* New York: Pergamon.

Brabant, L. H. and L. Mooney (1986). "Sex role stereotyping in the Sunday comics: Ten years later," *Sex Roles, 14:* 141-148.

Buss, D. M. (1994). "The strategies of human mating," *American Scientist, 82* (May-June): 238-249.

Christen, Y. (1995). "Brain structure explains male/female differences." In *Male/female roles: Opposing viewpoints,* J. S. Petrikin (Ed.). San Diego, CA: Greenhaven Press, pp. 48-56.

Costa, F., R. Jessor, and J. E. Donovan (1987). "Psychosocial correlates and antecedents of abortion: An exploratory study," *Population and Environment, 9:* 3-23.

Crabb, P. B. and D. Bielawski (1994). "The social representation of material culture and gender in children's books," *Sex Roles, 30:* 69-79.

de Leon, B. (1993). "Sex role identity among college students: A cross-cultural analysis," *Hispanic Journal of Behavioral Sciences, 15:* 476-489.

Diamond, M., R. Johnson, and J. Ehlert (1979). "Comparison of cortical thickness in male and female rats: Normal and gonadectomized young and adult," *Behavioral and Neural Biology, 26:* 485-491.

Dobson, J. C. (1995). "Biology determines gender roles." In *Male/female roles: Opposing viewpoints,* J. S. Petrikin (Ed.). San Diego, CA: Greenhaven Press, pp. 32-39.

Eagly, A. H. and S. J. Karau (1991). "Gender and the emergence of leaders: A meta-analysis," *Journal of Social and Personality Psychology, 60:* 685-710.

Eagly, A. H. and W. Wood (1991). "Explaining sex differences in social behavior. A meta-analytic perspective," *Personality and Social Psychology Bulletin, 17:* 306-315.

Hyde, J. S. and M. C. Linn (1988). "Gender differences in verbal ability: A meta-analysis," *Psychological Bulletin, 104:* 53-69.

Kilmartin, C. T. (1994). *The masculine self.* New York: Macmillan Publishing Company.

Layng, A. (1995). "Evolution explains traditional gender roles." In *Male/female roles: Opposing viewpoints*, J. S. Petrikin (Ed.). San Diego, CA: Greenhaven Press, pp.17-23.

Lovdal, L. T. (1989). "Sex role messages in television commercials: An update," *Sex Roles, 21:* 715-724.

Lull, J., A. Mulac, and S. L. Rosen (1983). "Feminism as a predictor of mass media use," *Sex Roles, 9:* 165-177.

Maccoby, E. E. and C. N. Jacklin (1974). *The psychology of sex differences.* Stanford, CA: Stanford University Press.

Manes, A. L. and P. Melnyk (1974). "Televised models of female achievement," *Journal of Applied Social Psychology, 4:* 365-374.

Mead, M. (1963). *Sex and temperament in three primitive societies.* New York: Morrow.

Peirce, K. (1993). "Socialization of teenage girls through teen-magazine fiction: The making of a new woman or old lady?" *Sex Roles, 29:* 59-68.

Ramey, E. (1976). "Men's cycles (They have them too you know)." In *Beyond sex role stereotypes: Readings toward a psychology of androgyny*, A. G. Kaplan and J. P. Bean (Eds.). Boston: Little, Brown and Co., pp. 137-142.

Rebecca, M., R. Hefner, and B. Oleshansky (1976). "A model of sex role transcendence." In *Beyond sex role stereotypes: Readings toward a psychology of androgyny*, A. G. Kaplan and J. P. Bean (Eds.). Boston: Little, Brown and Co., pp. 90-97.

Ruble, T. L. (1983). "Sex stereotypes: Issues of change in the 1970s," *Sex Roles, 9:* 397-402.

Tavris, C. (1991). The myth of PMS. *Redbook, 178(1)* (November): 36, 38, 40-41.

Tavris, C. and C. Wade (1984). *The longest war: Sex differences in perspective* (Second Edition). San Diego, CA: Jovanovich, Inc.

Weigel, R. H. and J. W. Loomis (1981). "Televised models of female achievement revisited: Some progress," *Journal of Applied Social Psychology, 11:* 58-63.

Chapter 7

Women and Sociology: How the Structure of Society Affects Women

Patricia J. Ould

SOCIOLOGY DEFINED

What Is Sociology?

Sociology is the study of the structure of society and how that structure affects interactions among individuals, groups, and organizations. Through the study of social structure and *social interaction* within a particular social context, trends become apparent. These trends, or social patterns, are the behaviors and attitudes that individuals, groups, or organizations have in common during particular social circumstances and time periods.

What Do Sociologists Study?

Sociologists are interested in understanding how societies are structured, and the impact social structure has on social interactions and social patterns. A society's structure is apparent in the relationships among its major social institutions: politics, law, economy, kinship, religion, education, medicine, technology, and the military. How individuals, groups, and organizations negotiate the social structure is also of interest.

Individual characteristics that affect social interaction and one's ability to negotiate the social structure, one's social status or position, are important components of sociological study. Individuals have certain *ascribed characteristics*, assigned usually on the basis of hereditary or biological factors, which determine their social status. Gender, race, and age are among these. Other characteristics, *achieved characteristics*, are the result of individual accomplishment, success, and choice: education, religion, marital status, and occupation. There is some disagreement over the categorization of social class and sexual orientation. Some sociologists consider them ascribed characteristics and others consider them achieved. Sociologists also study social change to explore when social change occurs, what the catalysts of social change are, and what effects social change has on social life and on the social structure of a society.

But these are broad concepts and ideas that often seem intangible. For example, it is difficult to imagine or to describe a study of the effect of the economy on kinship. To understand these concepts sociologists have focused on everyday phenomena. Solomon Asch (1952) studied how others could influence people's perceptions. Stanley Milgram (1974) studied how one's actions could be influenced by an authority figure. Judith Lorber (1993) studied how our gender identity is constructed through the socialization process. Some sociologists have studied deviant behavior in an effort to understand why certain behaviors are considered socially unacceptable, socially prohibited, or punishable. McLorg and Taub (1987) studied the deviant identities of anorexics and bulimics. Other sociologists have studied social movements, a specific type of collective social action that is sustained over time and is focused on bringing about or resisting social change. Bullard and Wright (1992) studied the involvement of African-American communities in grassroots environmental movements. Luker (1984) and Rosenblatt (1992) studied the abortion rights movement as a social movement and its impact on society.

Contemporary Sociological Perspectives

In studying social phenomena sociologists subscribe to different world-views or perspectives. These broad overarching ways of viewing society are called *paradigms* or perspectives. Sociologists use three major paradigms: *structural functionalism, conflict theory,* and *symbolic interactionism.*

Structural Functionalism

Structural functionalism is known also as functionalism or functional analysis. The central tenet of a functionalist approach is that society is a functionally integrated whole made up of parts that influence each other and are mutually dependent. These functionally integrated parts are the major social institutions. Each institution has a functional requisite, a function or role it plays in the perpetuation of society, which it fulfills by meeting certain societal needs. When a society is in balance, when each institution fulfills its function, a normative consensus exists with a set of agreed-upon values, customs, and expected behavior among the members of the society. The society then is in stasis; it is functioning normally or is in equilibrium. If the institutions are out of balance, if one or more institution is not fulfilling its functional requisite, or if there is no normative consensus, then the society is in a state of disequilibrium or dysfunction.

In this perspective women are viewed in terms of their role in society and the function that role performs. The difficulty is how society is defined and the definition of women's roles within society. Society is defined as a patriarchal structure reflecting traditional male-female stereotypes. Generally women's roles are defined within the family, in a very traditional sense, as wives and mothers. In this context, women's roles are viewed as contributing to the stability of society, and are considered functional. When women step outside their traditional roles, when women are "working mothers" or "career women," their roles are viewed as contributing to social change, and are considered dysfunctional.

Talcott Parsons (1951) and Robert Merton (1957) developed this paradigm. The works of Auguste Comte, considered to be the first sociologist, Herbert Spencer, and Emile Durkheim influenced the development of structural functionalism.

Conflict Theory

Conflict theorists view society as composed of groups in competition for control of scarce resources. Conflict theory focuses on the power relations among those groups, with an understanding that power can and does shift from group to group over time, and that those in power attempt to enforce conformity with their views and norms in order that their group interests will be met. Social change, therefore, plays an important role in conflict theory. Change results when power shifts from one group to another.

C. Wright Mills and others developed the conflict perspective. Karl Marx, whose theory of society viewed history in terms of class struggle, influenced their work. Marx theorized that in each society a small group, the bourgeoisie, controlled the means of production and exploited the labor of those who were not owners of production, the workers or proletariat. Marx's theory was based on the economic substructure of a society; that the means of production, society's economic substructure, was the foundation on which all other social institutions, the superstructure of a society, were based. Marx believed that the capitalist system would change when the proletariat developed class consciousness and revolted against the bourgeoisie to seize control of the means of production.

Contemporary conflict theorists C. Wright Mills and Ralf Dahrendorf focused on inequality in U.S. society in developing conflict theory. They observed the unequal distribution of wealth and power among the population that resulted in social conflict. Because they saw conflict as a source of social change, it was not viewed as negative on a societal level. It was viewed negatively, however, on an individual level. Inequities in wealth and power caused most people to suffer while the few with wealth and power benefited tremendously. Those in power, who Mills (1956) called "the power elite," were able to use their greater resources to maintain and advance their positions.

In the conflict perspective society is viewed as being composed of competing interest groups. Because gender groups can represent competing interests, it is possible to analyze the current position of women in society, and how it has changed over time. This type of analysis views changes in women's position in society as the result of conflict. "The focus in conflict theory is on the economics, specifically the competition for scarce resources among groups and its influence on all other social relationships. . . . In conflict theory, we assume that women's position in society is derived from unequal distributions of wealth and power" (Ollenburger and Moore, 1992, p. 14).

Symbolic Interactionism

Herbert Blumer, Charles Horten Cooley, George Herbert Mead, and William I. Thomas developed symbolic interactionism. This paradigm takes a microlevel approach to society. Symbolic interactionists view social interaction as the shared understanding of symbols within a society. Without these symbols, or the shared understanding they produce, individuals would be unable to communicate or form or define relationships beyond a basic animal level. Symbols allow people to work together, to plan for the future, and to create objects. They are the basis of social life. Blumer (1969), who first coined the term symbolic interactionism, theorized that an individual's actions resulted from his or her interpretation of daily events, which he or she learns through interaction with others. Individuals do not recreate meanings on a daily basis. They learn the meanings that have been assigned to certain symbols; they are socialized. Using these shared symbols we construct social reality. Symbolic interactionists are interested in understanding the interaction processes involved in the development of shared symbols and the social construction of reality.

The self also is a symbol; it is based on our idea of who we are as gleaned from our social interactions. It is a changing symbol because it is influenced by our interpretation of others' ideas of who we are. The notion of the looking-glass self, developed by Cooley (1902), suggests that our self-concept develops through our understanding of how others see us. That is, our sense of self is the reflection of ourselves we see in others. If we consistently receive messages that we are viewed negatively by others, we develop a negative self-concept. If the messages we receive are positive, our self-concept will be positive.

Applying the Major Paradigms

Theories about specific social phenomena are developed within each paradigm. Specific theories are based on the major tenets of the paradigm, but focus on a certain aspect of society or some specific social phenomena. For example, sociologists studying deviance from a structural functionalist perspective might argue that a society's definition of deviant behavior is behavior that threatens the social order or status quo. The argument that allowing women to have reproductive freedom threatens the family could be considered a functional analysis of the issue. Part of the functional requisite of the institution of the family is the perpetuation of the society through bearing and raising children. Because bearing children is defined as the functional requisite of women, allowing women to have reproductive freedom, the right to choose when to bear children and the number of births, is viewed as a threat to the functional requisite of the family.

Conflict theorists would argue that the ruling class or bourgeoisie defines as deviant that behavior which threatens their class interests. Having the ability to define deviance maintains the bourgeoisie's ability to exercise power and authority in society. Conflict theorists would argue that a patriarchal structure, one that by definition favors male interests, makes it difficult for women to exercise their reproductive freedom. Allowing women to have the freedom to choose when and how many children to bear threatens the patriarchal structure because it creates the condition under which women can control their own reproduction without the input of men. It places women in a position of power over the perpetuation of the society. Not allowing women to exercise reproductive freedom allows the patriarchy to maintain a measure of control over the perpetuation of the society.

Symbolic interactionists view deviance as the result of labeling; when an individual is repeatedly labeled deviant she or he begins to define him/herself as deviant and to behave in accordance with the label. Symbolic interactionists would argue that when a woman who terminates her pregnancy is defined as a "baby killer," lacking maternal instinct, and sinful, she may feel her decision was wrong and behave in ways that suggest that she feels selfish and guilty, that she is not fulfilling her potential as a woman, and that she is somehow abnormal when compared with other women.

These applications of theory to women's lives may seem awkward or like they miss the point. This is the difficulty encountered when we try to apply theories that do not reflect women's experiences and lives. "There is an inherent flaw in using these historical views of women. These theories are based on male experience, patriarchal structure, and a masculine paradigm. Women are 'fitted' into a theoretical model which developed without women's experiences as a framework or validation point" (Ollenburger and Moore, 1992, p. 14).

FEMINIST SOCIOLOGY

Classical theory in sociology was developed primarily by European men during the eighteenth and nineteenth centuries and therefore was based on ideas and issues of interest to men during that time. Few women were engaged in such enterprises, and those who were involved were largely ignored by early sociologists. Among those women whose work was ignored were social activist Jane Addams, founder of Hull House; Mary Wollstonecraft, author of *The Rights of Women*, an answer to Thomas Paine's *The Rights of Man*; and social theorist Charlotte Perkins Gilman, whose work raised questions about the impact of the legal system on the lives of women, who, by their status as women, were considered the property of their fathers or husbands, and had no legal standing, and no economic or political rights in society. During the 1960s and 1970s, as a result of the Women's Movement, the growing number of women in academia began questioning the content of their disciplines, and the lack of focus on, or interest in, the lives and experiences of women, or the impact of gender on society.

As feminist theorists began to study the effect of gender on social life, they also began to study and test the classical sociological theories. Often they found the theories to be biased because they had not considered the impact of gender; for example, definitions of "work" that do not include unpaid work and overlook the economic impact of housework. Also they found that most classical theory had overlooked aspects of society that did not represent men's everyday reality, such as the family and other aspects of private life.

Not all social theory was considered biased or distorted. Feminist sociologists have found that conflict theory, because it focuses on the power differential among groups in society, can be adapted to study the oppression of women. Feminist sociologists, however, have a different view of the source of social inequality than conflict theorists do. In addition to social inequality or oppression resulting from socioeconomic differences, feminist sociologists also consider sexism, racism, classism, heterosexism, ageism, and ableism as bases of oppression.

Feminist theorists not only challenged sociological theory, they also looked carefully at the research methods used in social research. When sociologists debated over the viability and feasibility of objective or value-free research, feminist sociologists took the position that not only was value-free research impossible, many believed it was not desirable. Feminist sociologists agreed with others in the field who felt that it was not possible for researchers to remain detached from their subjects. They believed that a researcher's assumptions, beliefs, biases, and interpretations, especially those based on their gender, race, social class, age, and sexual orientation, would affect their objectivity. Thus they argued that value-free sociology was a myth.

Feminist sociologists favor adopting a model of self-disclosure in research. Through this model, researchers acknowledge any assumptions, biases, and beliefs, especially those based on their gender, race, social class, age, and sexual orientation, that underlie the research. Through self-disclosure the researcher can develop a relationship with those they are studying, allowing for a dialogue between the research participants and the researcher. Researchers thus do not present themselves as experts, but recognize that they are learners, and that research participants are experts with much to teach. In addition to conducting research to expand the knowledge base, feminist sociological research goals include consciousness-raising and the empowerment of the oppressed. These goals are similar to those of conflict theorists who argue that praxis, the interaction between social theory and social activism, should be the goal of social science research.

SOCIAL MOVEMENTS AND SOCIAL CHANGE: THE WOMEN'S MOVEMENT

A *social movement* is the collective action of a group designed to inhibit or prevent social change or to encourage or bring about change. Sociologists study social movements in order to understand collective action: what makes people act collectively; how do people organize; why do some social movements accomplish their goals, while others do not? We also study social movements to learn about social change. The Women's Movement is an excellent example of a social movement. It began as a grassroots movement and attracted women from every social status. The Women's Movement began with specific goals, achieved some of those goals, and remained actively involved in issues affecting women's lives, and developed new goals. Now in its third wave, it has a quality that few social movements possess, longevity.

The First Wave: Women's Suffrage

The major focus of the first wave of the Women's Movement in the United States was women's *suffrage*: securing for women the right to vote. The women who were the most well-known organizers of this movement, Susan B. Anthony, Elizabeth Cady Stanton, Lucy Stone, Lucretia Mott, Harriet Beecher Stowe, Isabella Beecher Hooker, Julia Ward Howe, and Antoinette Brown Blackwell, worked for women's rights for more than seventy years. The beginning of the first wave was marked by the Seneca Falls Convention of 1848, and the passing of the nineteenth amendment to the U.S. Constitution in 1920 represented its end.

At the start of the first wave, married women in America had no legal rights in marriage; they were treated as the property of their husbands, and had no legal rights regarding their children. Married women could not own property, earn money, make contracts, sue, or be sued. They had to rely on their husbands for money, and if they tried to leave the marriage they could be forcibly returned to their husbands, and until the late 1800s, legally could be beaten by them. The term "rule of thumb" refers to the diameter of the stick a husband could use to beat his wife: it could be no bigger around than his thumb (Dobash and Dobash, 1979).

All women were prohibited from attending college. Women could work, but they were restricted in the type of jobs they could hold: teaching, nursing, sewing, housework, and factory work. Of course, they were not paid the same rate that a man in the same job was paid. Single or widowed women could own property, and they were required to pay taxes on their property. Yet women had no legal right to vote. In this respect, women were subject to the same conditions the American colonists faced before they revolted against the British Crown. The American Revolution was fought, in part, because colonists were taxed by Britain but had no representation in the government levying the tax. They had no vote.

The Women's Movement, begun at the Seneca Falls Convention in 1848, was focused on bringing about social change: improving the status of women and securing their right to vote. The Declaration of Sentiments and Resolutions delivered at the Seneca Falls Convention stated that "all men *and women* are created equal." The goal of the women's rights movement was to secure women's rights by winning the right to vote for women.

The first federal proposals for woman suffrage were presented to Congress in 1868. The first time a formal amendment was submitted was January 1878. It is worth noting that at the time it was called the Sixteenth Amendment. More than four decades later, when the amendment was finally passed; it was the Nineteenth Amendment. Not a word of the original proposal had been changed. (Sherr, 1995, p. xxiv)

To achieve their goals, women began organizing by holding conventions to spread their message to other women. Movement leaders traveled throughout the country speaking to women's groups to encourage them to actively pursue women's suffrage. They demonstrated at government offices and held vigils outside the White House and at governors' mansions in some states. They were the first group to demonstrate at the homes of those they wished to influence or whose actions they wished to target. Then it was considered ill mannered to bring a demonstration to someone's home; now it is common practice. In many ways these women changed the nature of protests and the norms for protest behavior. They were arrested for their actions on some occasions and were considered to be deviants by many.

Many of the women who began the first wave of the women's movement did not live to see their goal of suffrage accomplished. The work did not end, although the level of participation declined, and the movement entered a period that has been referred to as the "barren years" (Klein, 1984). In the years between 1920 and the start of the second wave, some women did continue to fight for issues of importance to women: social welfare legislation, access to higher education for women, and labor movement issues, particularly in the textile industry and factories with high percentages of women workers. Organizations developed during the fight for women's suffrage, such as the National Woman's Party, remained viable and led the way, even though the number of activists had dwindled.

The Second Wave: Women's Equality

A number of events precipitated the start of the second wave of the women's movement. In 1957, "the National Manpower Council (NMC) at Columbia University published its study *Womanpower*, a comprehensive look at the experience of women in the labor force, their employment needs, and the implications of both for education, training, and public policy" (Carabillo, Meuli, and Csida, 1993, p. 2). The NMC called for the Department of Labor to establish a committee to review state and federal law that affected the employment of women. The committee was never established. Women were not faring well in the world of work. Robert Smuts's book, *Women and Work in America,* published in 1959, drew attention to the lack of any substantive change in women's work outside the home since the late 1800s.

Following his election, President John F. Kennedy was pressured to establish a President's Commission on the Status of Women. In 1962, the commission was created and Eleanor Roosevelt was appointed as its chair. Many of the issues identified in the final report of the commission showed the limitations women faced in their career options and their roles in the home. These were precisely the issues Betty Friedan identified in her book, *The Feminine Mystique,* published in 1963. Friedan used these issues to argue for a woman's right to pursue a career and an identity as something other than wife and mother. Women heard a rallying cry in Friedan's words and the second wave of the women's movement was born.

Friedan played another role in organizing women to fight for their rights. She was a founding member and the first president of an organization vital to the movement, the National Organization for Women (NOW). Friedan and others had been working to push the government to take some action on the recommendations of the commission. In particular, they were frustrated in their efforts to get the Equal Employment Opportunity Commission to take its role seriously in the interpretation and enforcement of antidiscrimination laws for women. In response to their frustration with the inaction of the government, NOW was founded in 1966 and was formally incorporated in Washington, DC, in 1967. Because NOW helped galvanize women into action, it played a significant role in directing and supporting the women's movement and keeping the movement focused on its goals.

The second wave took up some of the goals the first wave had not accomplished. NOW's Statement of Purpose summed up those goals: "The purpose of NOW is to take action to bring women into full participation in the mainstream of American society now, exercising all the privileges and responsibilities thereof in truly equal partnership with men" (Carabillo, Meuli, and Csida, 1993, pp. 24-25). Women marched by the thousands, held rallies and demonstrations, signed petitions, organized letter-writing campaigns, litigated against violations of antidiscrimination laws, and did whatever they believed was necessary to make their cause known. The second wave, which lasted more than twenty years, accomplished many of its goals as a result of women's efforts.

During the second wave, women's participation in education and in the labor force increased, especially women's participation in professional occupations. Women's studies courses and degree programs were established at universities and colleges across the country, and more and more women began entering occupations that previously had been traditionally male. The Supreme Court prohibited sex-segregated employment advertising. Women won equal credit opportunity; they could no longer be refused credit based on gender or marital status.

One of the most difficult and significant issues of the second wave was abortion rights. With the *Roe v. Wade* decision in 1973, a woman's right to choose was made legal and states that previously had not allowed the prescription of contraceptives routinely available to all women, regardless of marital status, began changing their laws. *Roe v. Wade* has been threatened a number of times since it was handed down, and although attempts to restrict funding for abortion and to restrict access based on age have been successful, the decision has not been overturned. Abortion rights was a difficult issue because women within the movement did not agree about a woman's right to choose. Some women felt that fighting for abortion rights would jeopardize the movement's ability to secure other rights due to the lack of unity within the movement and because of the strength of the opposition to abortion.

Feminists in the second wave also became activists on the issues of battered wives, sexual harassment, rape, and sexual assault. In response to the victimization of women and their treatment by the legal system, women began organizing to debunk the commonly accepted myths about battering and about rape. They also worked to have legislation enacted against sexual harassment, reform rape laws, and strengthen laws against battering. Rape crisis centers and battered women's shelters were started to provide services and support for victims, to provide community outreach education programs, and to lobby for legislators to enact legislation and reform existing laws. The results of this activism will be discussed in detail in the section on violence against women.

Perhaps the most important goal of the second wave was to ratify the Equal Rights Amendment (ERA). The ERA was passed by Congress in 1972, and sent to the states for ratification. "By 1978, 35 states had ratified it and the votes of only three more were needed; Congress extended the ratification deadline to 1982. Those three votes could not be had and the amendment failed" (Farganis, 1996, p. 55). The battle to ratify the ERA was a difficult one. In some states the opposition was fierce.

> Literature describing lesbian love-making was distributed in the Kentucky House by opponents of the Equal Rights Amendment, outraging some legislators and bringing demands for an investigation. Carol Maddox, a member of Stop ERA, said she had assembled the material in booklet form and had it distributed to support her

argument that passage of the ERA would encourage lesbians to advertise their sexual preferences, which she said were immoral. (Carabillo, Meuli, and Csida, 1993, p. 81)

Following the defeat of the ERA, participation in the Women's Movement seemed to wane, although women still maintained activist roles and continued to fight for their rights. The well-organized factions of the New Right, especially fundamentalist religious groups, began antifeminist, anti-abortion campaigns and called for a return to the traditional "family values" of the 1950s. Groups touting a "father knows best" view of how the world should be have played a significant role in political campaigns since 1984. The backlash against women has been well documented by Susan Faludi (1991) and others. The Women's Movement has had to take a defensive rather than an offensive position in the fight for women's rights. Rather than breaking new ground and fighting new battles, women seem to be fighting to hold their ground, to keep the rights they earned from being overturned.

The Third Wave: Women's Future

The emergence of the third wave of the Women's Movement has not been firmly established by a specific event, yet young women are writing and talking about a third wave. As yet the focus of this phase of the movement is not clear. Young women at the forefront of the third wave are writing about feminism, exploring its boundaries, identifying the many different forms of feminism, and discussing the difficulty of living up to feminist ideals. Younger feminists also are aware of the problems that beset the first and second waves of the movement. One major problem was that the movement did not represent the interests of all women. In particular, women of color and working class and poor women did not feel the movement reflected their views and the reality of their lives. The second wave also experienced discord over issues related to sexuality and sexual orientation. The feminists representing the third wave were raised in a world where feminism was not a new idea, and they struggle to make it fit their experiences and their lives.

By bringing their considerable intellectual power and commitment to social change to bear on their own life experiences, [the contributors to this book], and many other young women and men who are not represented here, push our notions of what is good and bad, correct and incorrect behavior and ideology for a feminist. By broadening our view of who and what constitutes "the feminist community," these thinkers stake out an inclusive terrain from which to actively seek the goals of societal equality and individual freedom they all share. At the same time they continue to build upon a feminist legacy that challenges the status quo, finds common ground while honoring difference, and develops the self-esteem and confidence it takes to live and theorize one's own life. (Walker, 1995, pp. xxxiv-xxxv)

Perhaps the women of the third wave will represent the views and interests of women of all classes, races, sexual orientations, and beliefs.

What is the future for the Women's Movement? What will be the defining issue of the third wave? Does the identification of a third wave by younger feminists make it so? When we consider the infancy periods of the first and second waves of the movement, each began with a period of struggle as the women in the movement fought to establish their identity, an identity that would resonate with other women, and help define the focus of the movement. The first wave grew out of the Abolitionist Movement, as women began to recognize the limitations they faced without the vote. The second wave grew out of the civil rights and antiwar movements when women felt their roles in those movements were limited because of their gender. It began when women sought to expand their role beyond that of homemaker and mother, when they recognized that their role in society had remained relatively unchanged since the turn of the century.

In both instances women were stepping out of their traditional social roles, upsetting the balance of society, changing patriarchal rules. Is it not surprising that they began by seeking to define themselves, or rather to redefine themselves? These women sought to recreate themselves in a new social role, a new identity, born of their past and creating for women a future. Perhaps these self-identified third wave feminists, who are struggling with their feminist identities, are at the start of the process of defining the next era of the future for women. The defining event of the third wave will come; whether they are fully aware of it or not, the next wave of feminists are preparing for it already.

VIOLENCE AGAINST WOMEN

Violence against women was an issue targeted by the Women's Movement.

During the first decade of the second wave, feminists exposed three systemic forms of violence that are used to reinforce women's subordinate position in society: sexual harassment, rape and battery. Through consciousness raising, women discovered that these forms of violence were widespread and highly under reported because women felt ashamed when attacked and, usually, blamed themselves. (Kahn, 1995, p. 367)

Sexual harassment, sexual assault, rape, and domestic violence are viewed by some as sexual terrorism because they are ways of subordinating women. Women's fear of these crimes, especially fear of rape, affects the way women live their day-to-day lives. Fear makes women feel that they need to be ever vigilant, cautious, and aware. Because women are terrorized by the fear of rape, they alter where, when, and how they travel around their own communities. How often have you admonished a woman for walking alone to her car after dark, or felt nervous when someone walked behind you down a street at night, or felt afraid to go someplace by yourself? These fears are commonplace among women, part of their day-to-day consciousness. The conclusion therefore is drawn that women are victims of sexual terrorism.

As a result of feminist activism, the societal response to *sexual harassment*, *sexual assault*, *rape*, and *domestic violence* changed. Rape crisis centers, shelters for battered women, and hotlines were developed. Laws relating to each of these issues changed to benefit women, and the legal system's response also changed.

Sociologists study violence against women as a social problem, and as a form of criminally deviant behavior. The change in societal reactions to violence against women is one measure of the positive social change brought about by the Women's Movement.

Sexual Harassment, Sexual Assault, and Rape

Definitions

Language plays an important role in every culture. How concepts are defined can affect social behavior. The history of defining criminal sexual behavior exemplifies the status of women in society.

> Reactions to rape in a society provide a theoretical "window" into underlying assumptions about the sexes and gender relations. . . . Deviance and crime are not objective properties of behavior but definitions constructed through social interaction, in the case of rape these constructions tell us something about the way society perceives women, men, and the proper role of each. (LaFree, 1989, p. 13)

Sexual harassment, sexual assault, and rape may seem to be vastly different behaviors. In fact, they are not all that different. Each is representative of negative attitudes toward women and the differences among sexual harassment, sexual assault, and rape are not differences in kind but differences in the degree of negative attitudes toward women. We can view these terms on a continuum ranging from relatively minor behaviors that denigrate women such as disparaging jokes or remarks, to serious behaviors that represent physical harm such as aggravated rape, or rape-murder.

The term sexual harassment was coined by feminists in 1976 (MacKinnon, 1979). In 1981, the Supreme Court ruled that this type of behavior was a prohibited form of sex discrimination. Issues of sexual harassment achieved prominent media attention in 1991 during the Senate confirmation hearings to appoint Clarence Thomas to the Supreme Court when Anita Hill, a former employee of Thomas, came forward with accusations of sexual harassment. Hill was regarded with suspicion because she had not complained sooner, and not surprisingly, Thomas was confirmed and now sits on the U.S. Supreme Court. Women continue to face negative reactions when they report sexual harassment, but women continue to win cases in court. Supreme Court decisions have upheld and strengthened laws against sexual harassment.

The Equal Employment Opportunity Commission defines sexual harassment as all unwelcome sexual attention that affects an employee's job conditions or creates a "hostile" working environment (Adler, 1991). Sexual harassment occurs most frequently in the workplace, but also can occur in schools, on playgrounds, in classrooms, and in public places. It typically is verbal behavior consisting of jokes, unwanted sexual innuendo, or pressure to be sexually intimate. It also can involve display of sexually suggestive or explicit materials in common work areas, which contributes to a hostile environment.

Sexual assault and rape each involve physical contact. Rape occurs when someone is forced to have sexual intercourse (vaginal, oral, or anal) against her will and without her consent. Sexual assault is any unwanted sexual touching excluding sexual intercourse. Although these definitions may seem straightforward, the application of the laws against rape and sexual assault show that they are not clear in practice. In cases of acquaintance rape, or date rape, when the victim and rapist are known to each other, it becomes more difficult to establish that what occurred was rape and not consensual sex.

The difficulty in acquaintance rape cases lies in two issues: force and consent. These phrases mean that the victim must prove that she did not consent and that force was used. Estrich argues that part of the problem may be that most often "a criminal law that reflects male views and male standards imposes its judgement on men who have injured other men" (Estrich, 1987, p. 60). Thus definitions and interpretations of force and consent reflect male views and experiences. When women do not behave as men would expect them to behave, their behavior becomes suspect. A second issue is that the standards for resistance and for lack of consent place more emphasis on the behavior of the victim than on the behavior of the defendant. Victims must establish that they resisted the offender, and that they were forceful in their resistance. It is no longer required that a victim physically resist. However, they must establish that they made it clear to the defendant that they wanted him to stop what he was doing. In cases of acquaintance rape, if the victim has been on a date with the offender, the myth persists that a woman would lie and claim a rape occurred to protect her reputation.

Early definitions of rape reflect that women were considered the property of men. "Rape entered the law through the back door, as it were, as a property crime of man against man. Woman, of course, was viewed as the property" (Brownmiller, 1975, p. 8). In addition, although the behaviors we now identify as sexual assault and sexual harassment existed, they were not defined as criminal behaviors. Indeed, the terms sexual assault and sexual harassment did not exist. In the latter part of the twentieth century, through the efforts of feminist activists, sexual assault and sexual harassment were identified and defined as criminal. Legal definitions of rape underwent significant changes, and the rules of procedure for rape also changed. In the last fifteen years, most states removed the marital exemption for rape; husbands now can be charged and convicted for raping their wives.

The Statistics

The Uniform Crime Report estimates that one in three women will be raped in her lifetime, and according to the FBI's "crime clock" one woman is raped every five minutes in the United States (Federal Bureau of Investigation, 1993). These are daunting statistics, made even more discouraging by the fact that rape is the most underreported of all crimes. It is estimated that only 16 percent, approximately one out of every six rapes, are reported to the police (National Victim Center, 1992). Of those rape cases reported to the police, few will result in arrest and conviction, and the average convicted rapist will spend less than one year in prison or jail (U.S. Senate, Committee on the Judiciary, 1993).

Society's Response

The social responses to sexual harassment, sexual assault, and rape reflect the status of women in society. These crimes have been defined as women's issues, and are viewed as women's responsibility. Although sexual harassment and sexual assault primarily affect women because women are more likely than men to be victimized, they also affect the lives of the families and friends of victims.

Myths about rape continue to be pervasive in our society. Probably the most commonly accepted myth is that women are at greatest risk of being raped by a stranger. The image of the stranger who jumps out of the bushes at night is the image that most people have about rape. In fact, women are at greatest risk of being raped by someone they know. Myths based on victim precipitation theories, the idea that women increase their risk of being victimized by their behavior, also are common. The following statements are examples of victim precipitation myths: Women who dress seductively are at greater risk of being raped. Women who go to a bar alone, or walk down a dark street at night are at greater risk. If a woman goes to a man's room or home she is asking for sex and should not be surprised if she is raped.

Myths based on rapists' motivations to rape also are common. Images of rapists as sex starved, unable to control their sexual urges, mentally ill, normal men driven to it by the way women dress or behave, and the idea that a man has to pressure a woman to have sex are rape myths based on rapists' motivations.

Most of these myths blame the victim. They are based on the idea that women are responsible for being raped and may account for women feeling ashamed, embarrassed, and responsible when they are raped. Certainly they are reasons women are reluctant to report rape to the police, or to tell even those closest to them that they have been raped. Many victims are afraid they will not be believed, or even worse, that they will be admonished for causing the rape.

Feminist activists have worked to debunk rape myths through the creation of rape crisis centers that conduct public education and outreach programs. Rape crisis centers also maintain hotlines and provide support for victims. Other changes include changes in rape and sexual assault laws, and changes in the treatment of rape and sexual assault victims by medical personnel, police, and other legal system personnel. Rape crisis centers typically do community outreach to educate about rape and sexual assault in the schools, at community groups, and in police departments. Through the activism of these groups many medical professionals, police, district attorneys, and other legal professionals receive specialized training on working with survivors of rape and sexual assault, and the handling of rape cases.

Compared to men, women are more fearful of being a victim of crime even though their victimization rates are much lower than men's (Riger and Gordon, 1988; Ortega and Myles, 1987). Women do not have a generalized fear of crime. They are fearful of the types of crime for which they are at a greater risk: rape, sexual assault, and other crimes that are committed almost exclusively on women. Women experience fear of rape or sexual assault as part of their day-to-day lives.

> Female fear is the result of the interaction of social, sexual, and psychological forces. Perhaps its strongest component is ultimately the fear of death. . . . Another aspect of female fear is even more common. Women across the country do not feel safe out alone in their neighborhoods at night, especially if they live in large cities. . . . Race, marital status, and age are all related to women's sense of safety. . . . Within each of these demographic categories, however, women are twice as likely as men to feel very unsafe. (Gordon and Riger, 1991, pp. 8-9)

Unfortunately women tend to be most fearful that a stranger will rape them, when in fact, their risk of rape is much higher from someone they know. The U.S. Department of Justice, Bureau of Justice Statistics (1994) reported that at least 55 percent of rapes are acquaintance rapes. Also, more than 47 percent of rapes occur at or in the victim's home, or the home of one of the victim's friends, relatives, or neighbors (U.S. Department of Justice, Bureau of Justice Statistics, 1993).

Although women seem to be more fearful of stranger rape, the consequences of being raped by someone a woman knows are more difficult to survive. In addition to feelings of helplessness at being unable to protect themselves from being violated in the most intimate way, victims of acquaintance rape also must survive the loss of trust that accompanies being harmed by someone they know.

Some women have responded to their fear by organizing Take Back the Night rallies. A Take Back the Night rally usually is held in a public outdoor location. Women march en masse through an area carrying signs, candles, and so on, and congregate afterward to hear activists talk about rape prevention. The first such rallies were organized in the late 1970s. The purpose of the rally is to make women feel safe on the street at night, to draw attention to women's fear of crime, and to publicize the crimes committed against women. Other women have encouraged women to take "model mugging" courses or self-defense courses. "Model mugging" courses were designed to teach women how to react to being attacked.

In the last two decades, as a result of the efforts of feminists, great strides have been made in changing societal reaction to sexual harassment, sexual assault, and rape. People are more aware of the pervasiveness of these crimes. They are less likely to stigmatize victims, and are more willing to openly discuss these types of victimization. Yet misperceptions and myths about these phenomena, their victims, and perpetrators persist.

The Legal System's Response

In the discussion above of the statistics on sexual harassment, sexual assault, and rape, the underreporting of rape was noted as a difficulty in defining the scope of the problem. One reason that rape has been under reported is the way victims have been treated by the legal system. For many years women's experiences in reporting and prosecuting rape cases were viewed as *secondary victimization*. Especially in cases of acquaintance rape, women were viewed suspiciously when they reported a rape. This reaction was not surprising given the content and interpretation of the laws against rape. The law itself held rape victims to a different standard than all other victims. Robbery victims never had to demonstrate their lack of consent nor were required to resist being robbed. When someone reported a robbery the victim was believed unless some evidence appeared to raise questions about their veracity.

Rape laws and the treatment of rape victims have changed dramatically in the last two decades. During the 1970s, reform of existing rape laws became a major focus of the feminist agenda. Reforms included enactment of *rape shield laws* and revision of existing rape laws to expand definitions of who can be raped, what constitutes rape, and what makes rape criminal. Rape shield laws limit admissibility of the prior sexual history of a victim of rape as evidence. Only in very rare cases can a victim's prior sexual history be offered as evidence that a rape was not committed. Prior to the passage of these laws a victim's prior sexual history was used routinely to suggest the rape victim actually had seduced the rapist.

Two important changes in the definition of who could be raped were the result of reform of rape laws. The laws became gender neutral, including males as potential rape victims; and marital exemptions for rape were removed in forty-three states. Prior to these changes traditional statutes punished a man for the rape of a woman. Making the law gender neutral expanded the definition of who could be raped to include men, a largely invisible group due to homophobic stigma. Gender neutrality is problematic in that it also expanded the definition of who could rape to include women. "Rape . . . is not a gender-neutral crime. The empirical reality is that men rape, not women. . . . Gender neutrality suggests that rape law can be made and enforced without regard to the different ways men and women understand force and consent" (Estrich, 1987, p. 82).

The more important change in the definition of who could be raped was the removal of the marital exemption for rape. A remnant of legal history that made women the property of their husbands, rape law was interpreted so that a woman's consent to marriage was defined as permanent consent to sex at her husband's request. If a wife refused sex to her husband and he forced her to have sex, the marriage contract protected him from being charged with rape. Since 1975, 43 states have revised their laws to allow husbands to be charged with sexual assault or rape under certain conditions.

A second rape law reform focused on what behavior was punishable as rape. The original definition was limited to penetration of the vagina with a penis. Rape now may include oral, anal, or vaginal penetration and any intrusion, however slight, with any part of a person's body or any other object into the genital or anal openings of another person's body. This change significantly broadened the type of behavior that constitutes rape.

In addition to changes in rape laws, the treatment of rape victims by the criminal justice system, and in particular by police, has changed dramatically. Police departments have created special units that handle rape and sexual assault cases. The officers who work in these units, and most patrol officers, undergo special training on the treatment of rape victims. This training has sensitized most police officers to the situation of the rape victim and resulted in the development of police procedures that try to minimize further traumatization of the victim. Many police departments also have working relationships with local rape crisis centers, and call on the services of rape crisis counselor/advocates to provide support for rape victims during the investigation and any court appearances.

A female police sergeant who taught police academy courses on rape and sexual assault described to me a tool she used to convey what rape victims experienced to the mostly male police officers in her class. Just before the last break in the three-day workshop, she would tell the class that they would begin the last section of the course by choosing two or three class members to describe in detail their last sexual encounter. She left it up to the class to decide who would be chosen and how they would be chosen. The class then was given a fifteen-minute break to discuss the "exercise." Of course they returned from the break to express their outrage. The sergeant then would ask, "What do you think you are asking a rape victim to do?" It was a very effective teaching method (Silveira, 1991).

Although there have been improvements in the legal system's response to rape and to rape victims, problems persist. Rape victims who have been assaulted by someone they know continue to be treated as though they are suspect. Many women complain that police or prosecutors do not believe them. The stigma of being raped has not completely disappeared. In particular, juries, whose members do not have the benefit of the training members of the legal system have undergone, are not always provided with enough education or decision guidelines to make decisions not influenced by personal bias. We continue to hear comments of judges who contend that victims of rape are somehow to blame for their victimization either through poor judgment or their dress or behavior. Training for the bench does not automatically include the type of training available to police, district attorneys, and other members of the legal system.

Prevention, Precaution, and Self-Protection

Are sexual harassment, sexual assault, and rape preventable? In reality, it is not possible to absolutely prevent any type of crime, although the common myths of our society would lead us to believe it is both desirable and possible. Preventing crime implies that the behavior of criminals can be controlled. It is not possible to completely control the behavior of anyone who commits a crime, so it is not possible to prevent a harasser from harassing or a potential rapist from committing rape. If we could prevent crime, police departments would function differently and would serve a very different purpose. No one would need to be afraid of being a crime victim, especially women who fear rape. Everyone can take precautions to lower their risk of being a crime victim, but there are no absolutes. Even those who take precautions may be victimized.

Reducing the incidence of sexual harassment requires the commitment of the community, educational institutions, workplaces, or any venue where harassment might occur. In educational institutions or workplaces administrators and employers can institute programs to clearly define what constitutes harassment, and make it clear that harassment will not be tolerated. Responding immediately to charges of harassment sends the message to everyone that harassing behavior is inappropriate and unacceptable. Supporting victims of harassment who choose to file charges is another means of reducing its incidence. Making the commitment to educate people about sexual harassment and instituting procedures to respond to sexual harassment when it occurs will help to reduce its incidence.

There are no personal precautions against sexual harassment that one can take. Most women experience some form of sexual harassment as an annoying, but common occurrence: wolf whistles or other suggestive noises, under-the-breath comments, or comments yelled from a distance. Most women have experienced these behaviors, were annoyed by them, and went on their way without giving them a second thought. No action on the part of the recipient of sexual harassment could prevent these occurrences. Most often it happens unexpectedly. It is not possible to identify public areas or circumstances that are conducive to sexual harassment; it is unpredictable.

Individual strategies for lowering one's risk of being raped are useful, but their usefulness is limited. Rape is a crime that affects more than the individual who was victimized. Rape also affects the friends, family, co-workers, and acquaintances of that individual.

> There must be changes in how people think about rape—how it happens, who is responsible, and what can be done. Those who think about this topic must shift the emphasis from what individuals can do to what groups, organizations, and institutions can do. . . . Individualized issues must be merged into social policies for correcting what is now a collective problem. (Gordon and Riger, 1991, p. 125)

To reduce the risk of rape, we must first acknowledge that it is a societal problem, not solely an individual's problem.

Most precautions that individuals take are precautions against stranger rape. Since the majority of rapes are acquaintance rapes, these strategies have limited usefulness. How does one take precautions against a date? What are the indications that a date might rape? Is a person who suspects all potential dates as capable of rape being overly cautious? Obviously, taking precautions against the most common form of rape is at best problematic. Standard precautions seem inadequate for protection against those we know. These inadequacies show the need for a broader societal approach.

A societal approach to taking precautions against rape involves education, collective awareness, and collective action. Programs to educate the public about what rape is, and to break down the common myths and stereotypes about rape, rapists, and rape victims help to change beliefs about rape and sexual assault and involve the community as a whole in the commitment to prevent rape. The public can be educated through media campaigns, outreach programs to schools, and community outreach. Through education, community awareness about rape is raised. When the community as a whole is aware, a community-based effort to identify potentially dangerous areas in the community and to raise general awareness of opportunities to change attitudes about rape can be undertaken. As awareness is raised, the likelihood that collective action will be taken increases.

Communities can work collectively to identify situations that are conducive to attack and identify strategies to publicize those situations and change them. Collectively policing and responding to media coverage that promotes stereotypes and myths about rape or increases women's fears are activities that communities can undertake. Legislators can be encouraged to take an active role in promoting and funding community education programs and victim assistance programs. Finally, women can be encouraged to learn to protect themselves if they are attacked. Overall these programs will improve conditions in the community and enhance community cohesion by promoting collective action.

Domestic Violence

Spousal abuse was identified by women in the second wave of the women's movement as unacceptable and criminal behavior. Initially, heterosexual, married women were identified as victims of domestic violence. As more people began speaking out on this issue, we learned that lesbians and gay men, unmarried cohabiting couples, and those dating can find themselves in violent relationships with their partners. Anyone in an intimate relationship can experience domestic violence.

At its root domestic violence is about the power differential that may exist in an intimate relationship. Abusers are demonstrating their power over their partners; they become more violent when their power seems less than absolute. The need for absolute power and the need to demonstrate power over a partner are not always present at the start of a relationship. They may develop over time. Very often abusers have traditional views about and expectations of the roles they and their partners play in their relationships. When these role expectations are not fulfilled, violence ensues. "The four main sources of conflict leading to violent attacks are men's possessiveness and jealousy, men's expectations concerning women's domestic work, men's sense of the right to punish 'their' women for perceived wrongdoing, and the importance to men of maintaining their position of authority" (Dobash and Dobash, 1992, p. 4).

More recently the issue of battered heterosexual men has been identified and has created quite a controversy. The controversy about battered husbands centers on the interpretation of the data on battering. Surveys on the incidence of violence in intimate relationships have shown the rate of battering by wives against husbands to be nearly identical to the rate of husband-on-wife battering. One frequently cited study shows a slightly higher rate of battering by wives, 124 assaults per 1,000 couples, than the rate for husbands, 122 assaults per 1,000 couples (Straus, 1993). When these data are placed in context, however, the interpretation changes. The data do not indicate who initiated the violence, making it impossible to determine whether the battering occurred in self-defense.

Research that places violent behavior in intimate relationships in context shows that most often men initiate violence against their spouses, and women respond to defend themselves, their responses involve a narrow range of violent acts, and are not intended to inflict injury. When wives kill their spouses, most often they do so in self-defense (Saunders, 1988). In cases of assault, when the severity of the injury resulting from the assault is considered, Straus's (1993) own data show that the rate of severe assaults by wives against their husbands is much lower than husband-to-wife severe assault, 0.6 per 1,000 for wives compared to 3.7 per 1,000 for husbands. Injury from domestic violence is the leading cause of injury to women in the United States; approximately 4,000 women are killed each year by spouses or lovers (U.S. Department of Justice, Bureau of Justice Statistics, 1994).

Are there gender differences in perceptions of violence? Do men and women have similar views about what constitutes violent behavior? When do men and women perceive their own behavior as violent? Do these perceptions differ? These questions also are relevant to the controversy surrounding husband abuse and mutual battering. Research has not focused on these questions, and they remain unanswered.

Society's Response

Society's reaction to domestic violence, the perpetrators of domestic violence, and their victims has changed in the last twenty to twenty-five years. No longer viewed as a private matter, the prerogative of a husband (see "the rule of thumb" discussed above), or the responsibility of a wife, "in many countries it is now well known that violence in the home is commonplace, that women are its usual victims, and men its usual perpetrators" (Dobash and Dobash, 1992, pp. 1-2). Yet myths about domestic violence persist. The most common myths are that alcohol and drug use causes battering, that battering must not be too bad or the woman would leave, and that women ask for it because they stay with their partners.

Alcohol and drug abuse are commonly thought to be causes of domestic violence. Although related to domestic violence, no causal relationship has been established between substance abuse and battering in the research on causes of domestic violence. Batterers generally are not alcoholics or drug addicts, and not every partner, when under the influence of alcohol or drugs, behaves violently (Gelles, 1993). Being under the influence of alcohol or drugs has been a common rationale or excuse offered by batterers for their behavior. Partners have accepted this excuse because most often a contrite promise that it will never happen again accompanies the justification.

Other myths that persist about domestic violence blame the victim for not leaving the relationship. Reasons why victims stay in violent relationships are grossly misunderstood. Victims of domestic violence do not enjoy being battered. They remain in those relationships due to economic hardship or because they fear their spouses will retaliate if they leave. They also remain because social pressure to maintain a marriage or long-term relationship has convinced them that they are responsible for their situation, and because they have been cut off from the social support network that would help them leave.

Many battered women remain with their batterers because without a home or employment they have nowhere to go. Often these women have children to consider. One common characteristic of domestic abuse is the systematic social isolation of victims by their batterers. These circumstances, coupled with the fear that the batterer will retaliate if they leave, keeps women in these relationships when they would prefer to leave. When victims of domestic abuse take action to end the relationship the violence often escalates. Many women who get restraining orders or leave their abusers are stalked, beaten, raped, sometimes killed, or forced to kill in self-defense.

> In her historical and contemporary study of *Women Who Kill*, Ann Jones cites numerous [cases of women who kill their partners after years of abuse . . . For Jones, "Homicide is a last resort, and it most often occurs when men simply will not quit." . . . Jones notes that many case records show men following, harassing and beating their wives for years before they are themselves killed by the woman who had for so long been their victim. For Jones, it is misdirected to ask "why women stay" and more telling to address "Why don't men let them go?" (Dobash and Dobash, 1992, pp. 8-9)

In an effort to aid women who are victims of domestic violence, the Battered Women's Movement developed as a part of the Women's Movement in the early 1970s. Shelters were established to aid women who wished to leave their abusers, but had nowhere to go. Women were given support, legal advice, assistance in finding employment and a permanent home, and protection from their abusers. The locations of battered women's shelters were kept secret to prevent abusive partners from retaliating against those being sheltered. If a location became known, the woman was moved to another shelter or to a safe house, and the police were notified to protect staff and other shelter occupants.

The Battered Women's Movement also brought the issues of domestic violence into the public eye and worked to educate the public about the realities of violence in intimate relationships. By dispelling the myths about domestic violence the movement sought to gain support for the victims of domestic violence, to force the legal system to respond more harshly and effectively against batterers, and to increase public awareness about the extent and scope of abuse in intimate relationships. This was one of the most important social movements of our time, which sought to change deeply held cultural beliefs and entrenched social and institutional patterns of response, while struggling to move away from supporting male violence and toward its rejection.

The Legal System's Response

Just as there have been changes in the response to and processing of rape and sexual assault cases, so too there have been changes in the legal system's handling of domestic violence cases. Police departments no longer treat domestic violence as a private matter between domestic partners. They are much more proactive in their response to domestic violence calls. Some of these changes are due to civil suits won by women who were seriously injured when police failed to act to protect them. In one Connecticut case, a woman won her suit against a police department that allowed her husband to continue to beat her and cause her permanent neurological damage when the responding officers did not subdue or control the batterer. The police department also was found to be negligent because they did not respond immediately to the woman's call for assistance. In addition, they had failed to enforce a restraining order preventing the assailant from entering the state of Connecticut when the woman first called to inform the police of her husband's violation of the restraining order by his presence in their jurisdiction.

In response to this and other successful liability cases, legislatures have expanded police powers in responding to cases of domestic violence, and police departments have improved their efforts in handling domestic violence cases. Most police departments now have special domestic violence units, and all officers receive specific training in handling domestic violence calls. In many states the restraining order process has been streamlined, making it easier for women to secure a restraining order. Some states even allow police departments the authority to issue emergency restraining orders when court is not in session. This procedure offers immediate protection to victims, and coupled with increased police vigilance in enforcing restraining orders has reduced the likelihood of injury to victims in some cases.

Although the legal system response has improved in the last twenty years, it still is beset with problems. Many victims continue to refuse to cooperate in the prosecution of cases out of fear, or because they believe that the abuser has been chastened by being arrested, and will not harm them again. Although it is still possible to prosecute in these cases, it is more difficult, and many judges and juries are less likely to convict when the victim does not cooperate. Restraining orders are not easily enforced. They require vigilance on the part of both the victim and the police. Many times a restraining order is like a red flag to an abuser, an excuse to escalate the level of violence. Unless a victim has the time or the opportunity to notify the police of the restraining order violation, she may be seriously injured or killed. Part of the improvement in the legal system is the awareness that the violence may escalate, and the education of battered women about the need for increased vigilance when they receive a restraining order.

Prevention, Precaution, and Self-Protection

Preventing domestic violence is no more possible than preventing other forms of violence against women, or any other type of crime. The best that can be done is to reduce the incidence of domestic violence. The societal approach of education, collective awareness, and collective action is necessary to effectively respond to this problem. It is an issue that cuts across class, race, age, sexual orientation, and ethnicity; no social group is free of the potential for domestic violence. Therefore the best response is one that includes all segments of the community. Educating the public, pressuring legislators and policymakers for services for victims and forceful action against perpetrators, and actively working to change perceptions of and attitudes toward domestic violence are the most effective means of reducing its incidence. Engaging the community in a unified response against domestic violence is the most hopeful means of preventing its occurrence. Directing public education programs at identifying the sources of domestic violence, and working to develop intolerance for domestic violence among community members is one response to this issue.

When a community is aware of the issues it can come together to act collectively to create change. Developing community awareness and fostering an atmosphere of activism against domestic violence is not easy. The accomplishments of the Battered Women's Movement demonstrate that it is not impossible. Strong leadership and commitment are critical to its success.

In 1972, the first refuge for battered women [the British term for a shelter] opened in Britain. Others were soon to follow throughout

Britain as well as in Europe, the United States, Canada and Australia as activists travelled within and between countries sharing ideas and providing support for opening new refuges.

The battered-women's movement has now extended throughout much of the world, providing shelter and working for social change. For example, in 1988 Welsh Women's Aid sponsored an international conference with delegates representing over forty countries. (Dobash and Dobash, 1992, p. 12)

The existence of the network of providers of assistance to victims of domestic violence in the United States shows both the scope of the problem and the commitment to responding it. The National Coalition Against Domestic Violence, in its 1991 directory of domestic violence providers, identified over 1,500 programs operating in the United States with shelters housing about 300,000 abused women and their children (Dobash and Dobash, 1992). Unfortunately even with this number of shelters, providers are unable to serve the number of women and children in need of assistance.

Continued international commitment to reducing the incidence of domestic violence and changing expectations of domestic partners was evident at the United Nations Conference on Women in Beijing in 1995. Responding to domestic violence was a major focus of the conference and was reflected in the Internet discussion on the Beijing-95 list,* the documents ratified by the official UN delegates to the conference, and the sentiments expressed by those attending the concurrent NO (nongovernmental organization) conference.

In the United States, commitment to reducing violence against women, including domestic violence, was evident in the enactment of the Violence Against Women Act in 1994. This act increases federal funding for battered women's shelters and a national hotline, mandates harsher penalties for abusers, offers incentives to states with mandatory arrest policies, and imposes federal penalties on abusers who cross state lines in pursuit of a fleeing partner. Although the changes mandated by this act will have an impact on the incidence of domestic violence, activism and education to change attitudes about the status of women in society in general and the role of partners in intimate relationships also are necessary components for creating change.

---

*An e-mail subscription list that allowed subscribers to discuss issues related to the conference. The list was created almost a year before the conference and continues as a place where people can share ideas and report activities and progress or problems related to the resolutions passed by the U.N. delegates.

KEY TERMS

social interaction	social movement
ascribed characteristics	suffrage
achieved characteristics	sexual harassment
paradigm	sexual assault
structural functionalism	rape
conflict theory	domestic violence
symbolic interactionism	secondary victimization
feminist sociology	rape shield laws

DISCUSSION QUESTIONS

1. Use the major sociological perspectives to analyze a social issue affecting women today. How does the theoretical perspective affect your view of the issue? Consider feminist sociologists' model of self-disclosure. How would adopting this model affect your analysis of the issue?
2. Do you agree that the third wave of the women's movement has begun? What are the indications that it has begun? Discuss the potential defining issues of the third wave. What direction do you think the women's movement should pursue as we approach the millennium?
3. Discuss the change in the legal system's response to rape and sexual assault. How have these changes affected the social responses?
4. Domestic violence, rape, sexual assault, and sexual harassment have been called sexual terrorism. Discuss why this characterization is appropriate.

REFERENCES

Adler, Stephen J. (1991). "Lawyers advise concerns to provide precise written policy to employees." *The Wall Street Journal,* October 9, section B, p. 1.

Asch, Solomon (1952). *Social psychology.* Englewood Cliffs, NJ: Prentice-Hall.

Blumer, Herbert (1969). *Symbolic interactionism: Perspective and method.* Englewood Cliffs, NJ: Prentice-Hall.

Brownmiller, Susan (1975). *Against our will: Men, women and rape.* New York: Bantam Books.

Bullard, Robert D. and Beverly H. Wright (1992). *The quest for environmental equity: Mobilizing the environmental movement, 1970-1990.* Philadelphia: Taylor & Francis, pp. 39-49.

Carabillo, Toni, Judith Meuli, and June Bundy Csida (1993). *Feminist chronicles 1953-1993.* Los Angeles: Women's Graphics.

Cooley, Charles Horton (1902). *Human nature and social order.* New York: Charles Scribner's Sons.

Dobash, R. Emerson and Russell P. Dobash (1979). *Violence against wives.* New York: Free Press.

Dobash, R. Emerson and Russell P. Dobash (1992). *Women, violence and social change.* New York: Routledge.

Estrich, Susan (1987). *Real rape.* Cambridge, MA: Harvard University Press.

Faludi, Susan. (1991). *Backlash: The undeclared war against American women.* New York: Anchor Books.

Farganis, Sondra. (1996). *The social reconstruction of the feminine character,* Second edition, Lanham, MD: Rowman & Littlefield Publishers, Inc.

Federal Bureau of Investigation (1993). *Crime in America.* Washington, DC: U.S. Government Printing Office.

Friedan, Betty. (1963). *The feminime mystique.* New York: Dell Publishing Co., Inc.

Gelles, R. J. (1993). "Alcohol and drugs are associated with violence—they are not its cause." In *Current controversies on family violence,* R. J. Gelles and D. R. Loeske (Eds.). Newbury Park, CA: Sage, pp. 186-196.

Gordon, Margaret T. and Stephanie Riger (1991). *The female fear: The social cost of rape.* Chicago: University of Illinois Press.

Kahn, Karen (Ed.) (1995). *Frontline feminism, 1975-1995: Essays from* Sojourner's *first 20 years.* San Francisco: Aunt Lute Books.

Klein, Ethel. (1984). *Gender politics: From consciousness to mass politics.* Cambridge, MA: Harvard University Press.

LaFree, Gary D. (1989). *Rape and criminal justice: The social construction of sexual assault.* Belmont, CA: Wadsworth Publishing Company.

Lorber, Judith. (1993). "Night to his day: The social construction of gender." In *Paradoxes of gender,* J. Lorber (Ed.). New Haven, CT: Yale University Press, pp. 3-27.

Luker, Kristin. (1984). *Abortion and the politics of motherhood.* Berkeley, CA: University of California Press.

MacKinnon, Catherine A. (1976). *Sexual harassment of working women: A case of sex discrimination.* New Haven, CT: Yale University Press.

McLorg, Penelope and Diane E. Taub (1987). "Anorexia nervosa and bulimia: The development of deviant identities," *Deviant Behavior 8(2),* pp. 177-189 Philadelphia: Taylor & Francis.

Merton, Robert (1957). *Social theory and social structure.* New York: Free Press.

Milgram, Stanley (1974). *Obedience to authority.* New York: Harper & Row.

Mills, C. Wright (1956). *The power elite.* New York: Oxford University Press.

National Victim Center (1992). *Rape in America, a report to the nation.* Washington, DC: U.S. Government Printing Office.

Ollenburger, Jane C. and Helen A. Moore (1992). *A sociology of women: The intersection of patriarchy, capitalism & colonization.* Englewood Cliffs, NJ: Prentice-Hall.

Ortega, S. T. and J. L. Myles (1987). "Race and gender effects on fear of crime: An interactive model with age," *Criminology, 25:* 133-152.

Parsons, Talcott (1951). *The social system.* New York: Free Press.

Riger, Stephanie and Margaret T. Gordon (1988). "The impact of crime on urban women." In *Rape and sexual assault II*, Ann W. Burgess (Ed.). New York: Garland Press.

Rosenblatt, Roger. (1992). *Life itself: Abortion in the American mind.* New York: Random House, Inc.

Saunders, D. G. (1988). "Wife abuse, husband abuse, or mutual combat?" In *Feminist perspectives on wife abuse*, K. Yllo and M. Bograd (Eds.). Newbury Park, CA: Sage, pp. 90-103.

Sherr, Lynn. (1995). *Failure is impossible: Susan B. Anthony in her own words.* New York: Random House, Inc.

Silveira, Patricia. (1991). Personal interview.

Smuts, Robert (1959). *Women and work in America.* New York: Columbia University Press.

Straus, M. A. (1993). "Physical assaults by wives: A major social problem." In *Current controversies on family violence*, R. J. Gelles and D. R. Loeske (Eds.). Newbury Park, CA: Sage.

U.S. Department of Justice, Bureau of Justice Statistics (1993). *Criminal victimization in the United States: National crime survey report.* Washington, DC: U.S. Government Printing Office.

U.S. Department of Justice, Bureau of Justice Statistics (1994). *Violence against women.* Washington, DC: U.S. Government Printing Office.

U.S. Senate, Committee on the Judiciary (1993). *The response to rape: Details on the road to equal justice.* Washington, DC: U.S. Government Printing Office.

Walker, Rebecca, ed. (1995). *To be real: Telling the truth and changing the face of feminism.* New York: Anchor Books.

Chapter 8

Women and Anthropology: Including Women in the Evolution and Diversity of Human Society

Esther Skirboll

WHAT IS ANTHROPOLOGY?

The study of *anthropology* is about becoming human through evolution and being human through culture. This is a very large discipline in terms of areas of study; and, although there are numerous subfields and specialties in anthropology, the three largest areas are:

Biological Anthropology

Within this subarea anthropologists study our closest genetic relatives, the other primates, in an attempt to reconstruct early prehuman and human societies with the goal of better understanding the origin of the human family and human social life. We also study the fossils of prehuman ancestors (called *hominids*), which lived up to millions of years ago, in an effort to follow the course of our physical evolution. Biological anthropologists are also interested in modern humans (*Homo sapiens*) in terms of our genetics, diseases, differences, and similarities in adaptations to varied environments, and many other aspects of our biological adaptations.

Archaeology

Archaeologists are anthropologists who study the past of human social groups. We do this by studying items that people made or altered in their lives. These objects, called *artifacts*, were left behind by earlier groups of

people all over the world. Generally artifacts, including remains of architecture, are eventually buried through natural climatological events, or by
being built over by later peoples. Therefore, much of the work in this field
requires digging into the earth and removing the artifacts, bones, and other
important remains useful in the attempt to piece together the human past.

Sociocultural Anthropology

Social/cultural studies, the largest subfield in anthropology, focuses on
human culture within social groups of today and in the recent historical past.

Although anthropologists are interested in urban peoples, we are primarily concerned with social systems that are preindustrial or non-Western
in culture. This includes Native American tribal groups in North, Central
and South America, native peoples of Australia, New Guinea, and the
Pacific Islands, and preindustrial populations of Africa and Asia.

Social anthropology is a *comparative social science*. That is, we examine
individual social systems and compare them with others, but do not decide
that one is better than another. This comparative approach is very helpful
for women's issues because it is through the comparison of women's roles,
duties, obligations, and privileges in many different social groups that we
can begin to say some important things about women in society in general.

ANTHROPOLOGY AND WOMEN'S STUDIES

The earliest anthropologists, in the 1800s, were men who lived in the
industrial Western societies such as England, Scotland, France, and the
United States. In these countries society was driven by men; and when
anthropologists traveled into the field to learn about tribal societies, it was
the men in these societies who were the primary subjects of their study.
Therefore, much early anthropological work simply ignored the women in
the societies studied. Early anthropologists did not deliberately avoid studying women, but they often assumed that women in all societies were confined to the home, were supported economically by men, and were able to
work only within the home on domestic chores that had little recognized
value in the society at large, as was the case in their own countries. Therefore, little was learned about women's roles in non-Western societies.

A few women took an interest in non-Western societies in the 1920s;
some of them, such as Margaret Mead (1928, 1963), became famous for
their work. Although Mead did not confine her study to women, she
included women in her work.

The Importance of the Work of Women Anthropologists Since 1970

The interest of anthropologists in issues pertaining to women's roles, status, and contributions to their societies began in earnest in the 1970s with more women anthropologists working in the field, and has continued since then. The notion that women have always been confined to domestic lives, and are without influence in politics, religion, and the economic and social systems where they live has been drastically changed. The surge of interest by mostly women anthropologists in this topic has produced a large literature (Rosaldo and Lamphere, 1974; Martin and Voorhies, 1975; Reiter, 1975; Schlegel, 1977; Dahlberg, 1981).

By comparing the roles of women in varied kinds of social groups, anthropologists have made important contributions to the understanding of women within human society as a whole. These contributions include:

1. A great increase in the amount of information about women and girls in their own social groups. Since we began asking questions about women's roles and positions in social groups, the results have been a rich and varied literature that continues to grow. We also now have women's voices from within their social systems to enrich our knowledge with their point of view. (See, for example, Deloria, 1988.)

2. The concept of what is "natural" (that is, genetically controlled) versus what society has deemed proper and acceptable for women and men to do and accomplish in life has been greatly altered by studying women in cultures very unlike our own. We now realize that our concept of what appears to be "natural" in our society is in reality largely due to our specific cultural construction of gender roles, and not to "nature." Furthermore, we can show that attitudes toward women in our society are the result of historical, societal, and economic events.

3. A new understanding has been reached regarding the respect and influence that women have in many social systems. Western society has been patriarchal for such a long time that many students and others believe women have never had, and cannot attain, significant social status and respect in society. Anthropologists studying women in diverse contemporary groups have learned that in many of them women are respected for their economic, political, social, and religious roles. Although there is no evidence of a matriarchal society (one in which women hold all or most of the important political and economic positions), in many societies women who take an

important part in religious and political systems are esteemed by themselves and others and feel pride and satisfaction in their place in society outside as well as in the home.

The American Anthropological Association has recognized the importance of the work done by and about women in the discipline, and in 1989 published *Gender and Anthropology: Critical Reviews for Research and Teaching* (Morgan, 1989), an anthology encompassing many areas of research on gender issues in the field.

ANTHROPOLOGY AND THE EVOLUTIONARY VIEWPOINT

Evolution means change through time. This concept is applied to biological change from simple organisms to very complex organisms over time; it also can be applied to social groups that become more complex as they utilize increasingly complicated technology to extract energy from the environment. We are aware, however, that human groups around the world adapt to their environments differently and with different types of technology. In some cases, social changes resulting from new technology occur much faster than in other cases where people remain in a balance with their environments for long periods of time and change very slowly.

Very simple social groups using simple tools (technology) developed before people had domesticated plants and animals, and when they lived in very small groups. Before people became farmers, they foraged in their environment for food and all other resources. There still are groups who live in this way and who are called *foragers* or hunters and gatherers. Through time people's ways of life, technology, and economic systems become more and more complex. Today people live at various levels of technological complexity from very simple farmers using hand tools, to agricultural farmers using mechanized technologies, to industrial workers, to highly complex computer-based workforces in which there is a great deal of job specialization.

The roles and status of women have varied greatly over time within these groups. We will be taking a detailed look at several examples showing the ways in which women's positions vary. However, we must start at the beginning by taking a brief look at biological anthropology.

BIOLOGICAL ANTHROPOLOGY AND WOMEN

In the grand scheme of relationships among species, human beings (*Homo sapiens*) are *primates*, a group of mammals that includes, besides ourselves, apes, monkeys, and prosimians. In particular, the evolution and behavior of apes has been closely studied both in captive groups and in the wild. Apes are of great interest to anthropologists because genetically they are our closest living relatives. Chimpanzees and humans are especially close, sharing a large percentage of genetic traits. Since chimpanzees are very like us genetically, we believe that by studying their behaviors and those of the other higher primates, we may learn more about basic patterns of behavior that may be common to primates. We must remember, however, that we are very different in many ways both genetically and behaviorally from chimpanzees, since the ancestors of humans and of chimpanzees have been separate groups for about five million years. This is a very long time; and we are not exactly like any ape species.

Among the many people studying primate behavior in the wild are several notable women including Jane Goodall, who studies the chimpanzee in Tanzania (Goodall, 1965, 1971, 1979, 1986); Dian Fossey (1981, 1983), who studied the mountain gorilla and gave her life in her efforts to prevent poachers from hunting them into extinction; and Birute Galdikas, who studied the orangutan in Borneo (Galdikas, 1979).

Biological anthropologists also study early hominids by examining their fossil remains in an effort to understand the pace and direction of prehuman and human biological evolution. Many experts have also been interested in the origins of family and group life; and some have suggested possible scenarios for the lifeways of our ancient ancestors.

One hypothesis for the formulation of the early prehuman family is that of Owen Lovejoy (1981). He suggests that there is high infant mortality among chimpanzees because chimp mothers must carry their babies along while finding food for themselves. He supposes that in human societies, in which infants are even more helpless than chimpanzee babies, being unable to grasp their mothers' hair, new survival strategies had to be developed. In such situations, he believes that a cooperative relationship was begun between individual males and females, in which males traveled farther from the home base than females and provided food for females, especially meat, allowing them to remain closer to home with their infants, and thus reducing infant mortality. He further suggests that one male would provide food for one specific female, thus forming a pair bond and originating *monogamy* very early in hominid evolution.

While this hypothesis seems comfortable to many people, there are several problems with it (see Campbell and Loy, 1997). First, there is no evidence to show that infant mortality was lower in early human groups than it was in chimpanzee groups. Second, evidence of modern foraging societies strongly suggests that females do not remain at home to care for infants but instead are very active foragers themselves, providing large proportions of the food eaten daily by the group (Lee, 1993; Estioko-Griffen, 1986). Many foraging peoples are not monogamous, but men may have several wives; and in some such groups, women may have more than one husband. Lovejoy's notion of very ancient family life appears to be based, in part, on the idea that women cannot provide for themselves and their children safely, but benefit from remaining at home to care for their offspring while their mates provide for them in part.

Nancy Tanner (1981) suggests an alternative model for the behavior of early prehuman groups in which nursing hominid mothers, in need of greater nutrition, foraged successfully for themselves and their children. Females who were able to effectively provide for themselves and to share food with young children were more intelligent and resourceful than those who could not do so. Such intelligent females were able to survive long enough to produce more offspring with intelligence like themselves. Tanner suggests that this behavior may have been the origin of sharing in prehuman groups. Males may have shared food also, but she suggests that pivotal human relationships were in the sharing between mothers and children, not mated pairs. While Tanner's hypothesis was published about the same time as that of Lovejoy, it has been less widely repeated in texts of biological anthropology.

Ideas about group and family life in the very distant past are hypothetical, and we must use caution in accepting them. A good way to check the validity of such scenarios is to check them against the behavior of known foraging groups in the present and recent past, and to look at the archaeological record of ancient peoples.

ANTHROPOLOGISTS STUDY WOMEN OF THE PAST THROUGH ARCHAEOLOGY

Archaeologists study remnants of the human past by carefully excavating the artifactual remains of ancient prehuman (hominid) and human social groups. This includes several millions of years of ancient history. The way in which the finds are interpreted often tells us a great deal about the attitudes of the archaeologists themselves. Such interpretations about what ancient cultures were like have often been strongly influenced by male bias.

Students are frequently surprised to learn that the comic strip stereotype of the caveman pulling a woman by the hair to his cave is not based on anything factual. It is often accepted without question that women were completely dominated by men in the distant past. There is no archaeological evidence whatever to support such a generalization of past lifeways.

Since contemporary foraging women make important economic contributions within their societies, are generally not dependent on men for food, and have an important place in the lives of all their people, it must be assumed that women in similar past groups did the same. However, it is only in fairly recent times that archaeologists have begun to question the "caveman" approach and to reassess these interpretations (Gero and Conkey, 1991).

An example of the way women anthropologists have been reassessing archaeological information is in the analysis of ancient sculptures and carvings of women that were made between 20,000-15,000 years ago and during the Upper Paleolithic period in Western Europe. These objects, which depict nude women of various bodily forms, have generally been called Venus figurines. Most interpretations of their purpose have been made by men who thought they represent fertility figures with sexual and reproductive purposes.

In a recent study of the textbooks that refer to these objects, Nelson (1997) lists twelve textbook authors in archaeology and physical anthropology who discuss Venus figurines. Most authors mention sexual aspects of the figures such as breasts and/or buttocks when, in fact, these traits are only present on some of the figurines. Nelson suggests that men are usually assumed to be the artists who made these figures for the pleasure or use of other men. She believes we must reassess these objects, considering other possible explanations for their manufacture and use. It is possible, for example, that women may have made some of them for women's purposes. This reexamination reminds us that we must use caution in the interpretation of archaeological remains.

Recent excavations of Iron Age Russian burial mounds called kurgans have revealed the remains of women buried with bronze daggers and arrowheads, suggesting that in this culture women may have served as warriors (Davis-Kimball, 1997). At one of the burial sites, Davis-Kimball and her associates have found three types of female burials. Some have artifacts such as spindle-whorls, which are associated with female weaving activities; some burials have ritual artifacts such as clay or stone altars, which suggest women active in religious practices; and seven of the burials contain swords, daggers, and arrowheads, suggesting warrior activities. Davis-Kimball points out that when Russian archaeologists excavate similar female burials with weapons, they interpret the weapons as symbolic, intended for use in the afterlife. (When male skeletons are buried with military equipment, the interpretation is generally that they were used by the deceased during life, in a military fashion.) However, Davis-Kimball and her associates found evidence for life on horseback in the bowed legs of one young woman and an arrowpoint in the chest cavity of another, suggesting battle activity.

Little evidence presented in the archaeological literature suggests that women took part in the political life of their societies. However, as the Central American Mayan script is deciphered, we have learned that noble Maya women in prehistoric Mexico not only were revered as ancestors, but also held important political position, even ruling as "true kings" in at least one Maya city (Schele and Freidel, 1990).

In South America when the fifteenth century Inca controlled a powerful state-level society in Peru, there is evidence that Inca women inherited and controlled property and held important positions within their kin groups, which also functioned as work groups contributing to the state political system (Mosley, 1991).

As scholars working in far-flung parts of the world continue to add bits of evidence about women of the past, we are certain to see a new picture taking shape in which women take their place as important players in the reconstructed picture of the past through archaeology.

SOCIAL ANTHROPOLOGY LOOKS AT WOMEN IN SIMPLE SOCIAL SYSTEMS

Social anthropologists interested in the roles of women in contemporary society study foraging and various kinds of farming societies all over the world. In the near future it is likely that foraging groups will be completely absorbed into farming social systems. It is important to examine the roles of women in these groups because these lifeways are likely to portray very basic attitudes about women.

Anthropologists have learned that in all human societies the work of obtaining necessary food, shelter, and other resources is divided among the people in the group. It is usual for labor to be divided based on sex, the *sexual division of labor*, and age of the people in the group. Although there is a great deal of variation among groups in the way labor is divided up, it is very common for women to search for vegetables, fruit, and medicinal plants, and for men to hunt and fish. This is not a hard and fast rule because women do hunt and men do collect vegetable foods in many groups, but this division of labor is a generalization that was probably as true in the distant past as it is now. It is simply more efficient for people to divide labor and then share the results than requiring each person to carry out all the chores necessary for survival individually. Problems arise in interpreting this basic information, however. Meat is generally highly valued by people, and therefore, it was assumed that men who provide the meat have more prestige and power than women whose work was often described as repetitive and boring. However, when studies were made of the labor of women and men and the levels of respect and status they receive in various societies, the results were very different from this over-simplified assumption.

FORAGING SOCIETIES

The Agta are an example of a foraging social group that still exists in the Philippine Islands. Agnes Estioko-Griffin studied the Agta in the Sierra Madre mountains of Luzon (Estioko-Griffin, 1986). Agta live far from modern Philippine towns and cities, but they do obtain cloth and metal objects from outside groups in trade for forest products. Agta also raise some crops such as cassava and rice, but they depend heavily on hunting, fishing, and gathering for food. Both men and women hunt regularly among the Agta, although they do not use the same techniques. Men are solitary hunters, entering the forest at night and killing their prey with bow and arrow. Women frequently hunt with other women or men, using knives and taking hunting dogs with them. Girls frequently learn to hunt from their mothers, and continue hunting with them and their sisters as they mature. They hunt wild pigs and deer in the forest, often tracking them for hours or days, and then carrying the meat home. Women also spearfish and gather wild foods and medicinal herbs. According to Estioko-Griffin, men hunt more frequently and bring in more meat and fish than women do, but women provide a substantial amount of the meat and fish eaten.

Another foraging society that has been intensely studied for many years is the Ju/'hoansi (sometimes known as the !Kung) of South Africa. Most of these people are now confined to reserves where their traditional lifeways have been forcibly altered; but, fortunately, their traditional lives were studied and filmed prior to these changes, and have enriched the anthropological literature greatly. Richard Lee, who worked with the Ju/'hoansi for several decades since the 1950s, studied the relative contribution to the diet made by women as gatherers and men as hunters. He found that men produced 45 percent of the food, and women produced 55 percent. Vegetable food provided primarily by women made up 70 percent of the diet (Lee, 1993). Lee makes this comment about them with regard to the relationship between men and women in marriage and sexuality:

". . . we see a picture of relative equality between the sexes, with no one having the upper hand" (p. 92).

Therefore, in these two brief examples we have evidence for divisions of labor in which women's jobs are far from those thought traditional for them. For further descriptions of foraging societies in which women are clearly important and respected contributors to their groups, see Draper (1975), Turnbull (1961, 1981, 1983), Hoebel (1978), and Berndt (1981).

WOMEN IN SMALL-SCALE FARMING SOCIETIES

With the domestication of wild plants and animals for food after 10000 B.C., groups of people all over the world gradually became farmers. Farmers who generally cultivate crops without fertilizer, irrigation, or the use of the plow and animals for labor are called *horticulturalists*. Horticultural farmers still exist all over the world, especially in tropical areas. They frequently live in villages of several hundred people who often cooperate in family groups for the production and storage of food and other commodities. Horticultural farmers vary widely in the plants and animals they raise, in the way in which labor is apportioned, and in the roles of women and men in their societies. In some horticultural groups men do the farming, and in others this is a job for women. However, there are no groups in which women do not contribute their labor to the society.

Among North American Native horticultural groups, the *Iroquois* of colonial times are well known due to their unique political system, the League of the Iroquois, and for their efficient and prosperous farms and long trade relationships with the British. It was Iroquois women who were the primary farmers, and they who stored and then distributed food resources both to their families and to hunting and raiding parties of men. In discussing the position of women in Iroquois tribes, Reiter maintains that they possessed both economic and political power. The matrons of extended family groups had voting rights in the selection of tribal leaders and representatives to the League. Economically they controlled the distribution of not only farm products, but also the products of the hunts provided by men (Reiter, 1975).

THE EFFECT OF COLONIALISM ON WOMEN'S POSITION IN SOCIETIES

With the spread of Western European powers into Africa, Asia, and the Pacific, native social systems in these areas were changed dramatically.

Western powers such as England, France, and Spain were strongly patriarchal in their structure, and they imposed their ideas of how society was to be run on the native people they encountered. This involved not only conversion to Christianity, but the imposition of male-dominated economic and political systems as well. In some cases, they ignored or overthrew the women in native society who held power in favor of their husbands, brothers, and sons.

An example of this is the case of the Igbo people of Nigeria, a tribal society that has been studied by Van Allen (1976). Among the Igbo, although men held most of the important political positions and controlled the most valuable agricultural products, women owned their own crops and profits made in the marketplace. As wives and mothers, they belonged to kin groups that met to discuss and to influence decisions and actions in which they took an interest. They made rules observed by both men and women, about crops, markets, and other issues, and thus had an important economic and political role in spite of their lesser position in relationship to men. The women were accustomed to receiving respect for their collective decisions, and to being considered as serious contributors to society.

Under British colonial rule, the Igbo land was divided into areas under the administration of individual Igbo men who, in turn, were under the domination of the British. The Igbo who were placed in power by the British frequently misused their positions and ignored the traditional rights of Igbo women. Finally, in 1925, rumors that women were to be taxed alarmed the women, who took part in a mass protest against this. Finally the British, using armed soldiers, put an end to this rebellion and punished the people by confiscating goods and destroying property. The British refused to believe that women had organized the rebellion, and thought instead that men had instigated it. In fact, the British simply ignored the women in the belief that their interests and actions were trivial and could be dismissed. In this way, women lost much of the control they had enjoyed in their society. In this example we can begin to see that under the domination of patriarchal Western rule, many women in tribal societies worldwide have lost the positions and the respect they enjoyed under their traditional lifeways.

A LOOK AT GLOBAL DEVELOPMENT AS IT AFFECTS WOMEN'S LIVES

Many feminist anthropologists are now interested in the effects that global economic development has on women's lives in "underdeveloped" countries. Ester Boserup (1970) noted that European colonial administrators were responsible for the deterioration of the status of women in developing countries. When a new method or technology was introduced to the agricultural system in many African countries, women were ignored, as men were trained to use the new techniques. Furthermore, many African women lost control of agricultural land to which they once had rights.

Safa (1986) studied the effects on women in Southeast Asia, Mexico, and Jamaica of the relocation of jobs requiring unskilled labor from industrialized nations to small underdeveloped nations. Women frequently form the greater part of this labor force. The effects on them of this type of development depend upon many factors including the position of women in the society prior to the arrival of these corporations in the area, and the conditions under which the women work. For a recent summary of the work of women anthropologists on the impact of development on women, see Lockwood (1997).

CONCLUSIONS

We have seen that the subjects of anthropological study reach into the biological and cultural/behavioral aspects of the human condition as well as into the past of human societies. Prior to the entry of women into anthropology, questions asked, data collected, and conclusions drawn about the relationships of women and men in ancient and modern societies were often biased by the assumptions made by researchers. Beginning in the 1970s, and continuing today, the serious study of women in all varieties of social systems has contributed much information previously missing from the ethnographic record. We have become aware not only of the great variety of roles and behaviors thought proper for women in social systems worldwide, but also of the ways in which women themselves feel and what they have to say about their lives.

It is becoming clear that, while women rarely hold the most powerful positions in highly stratified societies, there is a long and rich history of their participation in every aspect of social behavior in simple and complex societies. We now have ample evidence of a balance in the participation of both sexes in social, political, economic, and religious life in a wide range of social systems across time and culture. Such information provides a hopeful and encouraging background for the continuing efforts of women in our own society to achieve such a balance.

KEY TERMS

anthropology	evolution
biological anthropology	foraging/foragers
hominid	primate
Homo sapiens	monogamy
archaeology	sexual division of labor
artifacts	horticulturalists
sociocultural anthropology	Iroquois
comparative social science	

DISCUSSION QUESTIONS

1. How did study of non-Western social systems by men from patriarchal societies affect the way in which the women of these societies were portrayed?
2. How has the interpretation of the place of women in societies of the past been affected through study by women anthropologists?
3. In what way does the comparative approach of anthropology help in constructing a picture of the roles of women in the present and past?
4. In what way has colonization and development of non-Western societies affected women's roles in their own social systems?
5. Many people have believed that it is "natural" for women to remain within the home in order to care for their children. What evidence do we have to suggest that women and men can care for children without remaining within the home?

REFERENCES

Berndt, Catherine H. (1981). "Interpretations and 'facts' in Aboriginal Australia." In *Woman the gatherer*, Frances Dahlberg (Ed.). New Haven, CT: Yale University, pp. 153-203.

Boserup, Ester (1970). *Women's role in economic development.* New York: St. Martin's Press.

Campbell, Bernard G. and James D. Loy (1996). *Humankind emerging.* New York: Harper Collins.

Dahlberg, Frances (Ed.) (1981). *Woman the gatherer.* New Haven, CT: Yale University Press.

Davis-Kimball, Jeannine (1997). "Warrior women of the Eurasian steppes," *Archaeology, 50(1):* 45-48.

Deloria, Ella Cara (1988). *Waterlily.* Lincoln, NE: University of Nebraska Press.

Draper, Patricia (1975). "!Kung women: Contrasts in sexual egalitarianism in foraging and sedentary contexts." In *Toward an anthropology of women*, R. Reiter (Ed.). New York: Monthly Review Press, pp. 77-109.

Estioko-Griffin, Agnes (1986). "Daughters of the forest," *Natural History, 95:* 36-42.

Fossey, Dian (1981). "The imperiled mountain gorilla," *National Geographic, 159(4)*, 501-523.

Fossey, Dian (1983). *Gorillas in the mist.* Boston: Houghton-Mifflin.

Galdikas, Birute M. (1979). "Orangutan adaptation at Tanjung Puting reserve: Mating and ecology." In *The great apes*, D. A. Hamburg and E. R. McCown (Eds.). Menlo Park, CA: The Benjamin/Cummings Publishing Co., pp. 195-233.

Gero, Joan M. and Margaret W. Conkey (Eds.) (1991). *Engendering archaeology: Women and prehistory.* Oxford: Basil Blackwell Ltd.

Goodall, Jane (1965). "Chimpanzees of the Gombe Stream Reserve." In *Primate behavior*, I. DeVore (Ed.). New York: Holt, Rinehart and Winston, Inc., pp. 425-473.

Goodall, Jane (1971). *In the shadow of man.* Boston: Houghton-Mifflin.

Goodall, Jane (1979). "Life and death at Gombe," *National Geographic, 155(5)*, pp. 597-620.

Goodall, Jane (1986). *The chimpanzees of Gombe.* Cambridge, MA: The Bellknap Press of Harvard University Press.

Hoebel, E. Adamson (1978). *The Cheyennes: Indians of the Great Plains.* Fort Worth, TX: Holt, Rinehart and Winston, Inc.

Lee, Richard B. (1993). *The Dobe Ju/'hoansi.* New York: Harcourt Brace College Publishers.

Lockwood, Victoria S. (1997). "The impact of development on women: The interplay of material conditions and gender ideology." In *Gender in cross-cultural perspective*, C. B. Brettell and C. F. Sargent (Eds.). Upper Saddle River, NJ: Simon and Schuster.

Lovejoy, C. Owen (1981). "The origin of man," *Science, 211(4480):* 341-350.

Martin, M. Kay and Barbara Voorhies (1975). *Female of the species.* New York: Columbia University Press.

Mead, Margaret (1928). *Coming of age in Samoa: A study of adolescence and sex in primitive society.* New York: William Morrow.

Mead, Margaret (1963). *Sex and temperament in three primitive societies.* New York: William Morrow.

Morgan, Sandra (1989). *Gender and anthropology: Critical reviews for research and teaching.* Washington, DC: American Anthropological Association.

Mosley, Michael E. (1991). *The Incas and their ancestors: The archaeology of Peru.* New York: Thames and Hudson.

Nelson, Sarah M. (1997). "Diversity of the Upper Paleolithic 'Venus' figurines and archaeological mythology." In *Gender in cross-cultural perspective*, Caroline B. Brettell and Carolyn F. Sargent (Eds.). Upper Saddle River, NJ: Prentice Hall, pp. 67-78.

Reiter, Rayna R. (Ed.) (1975). *Toward an anthropology of women.* New York: Monthly Review Press.

Rosaldo, Michelle Zimbalist and Louise Lamphere (1974). *Woman, culture and society.* Stanford, CA: Stanford University.

Safa, Helen I. (1986). "Runaway shops and female employment: The search for cheap labor." In *Women's work*, Eleanor Leacock and Helen Safa (Eds.). South Hadley, MA: Bergin and Garvey, pp. 58-71.

Schele, Linda, and David Freidel (1990). *A forest of kings: The untold story of the ancient Maya.* New York: William Morrow.

Schlegel, Alice (Ed.) (1977). *Sexual stratification: A cross cultural view.* New York: Columbia University Press.

Tanner, Nancy Makepeace (1981). *On becoming human.* New York: Cambridge University Press.

Turnbull, Colin (1961). *The forest people.* New York: Simon and Schuster.

Turnbull, Colin (1981). "Mbuti womanhood." In *Woman the gatherer*, Francis Dahlberg (Ed.). New Haven, CT: Yale University, pp. 205-219.

Turnbull, Colin (1983). *The Mbuti pygmies: Change and adaptation.* New York: Holt, Rinehart and Winston, Inc.

Van Allen, Judith (1976). "'Aba Riots' or Igbo 'Women's War'? Ideology, stratification, and the invisibility of women." In *Women in Africa: Studies in social and economic change*, Nancy J. Hafkin and Edna G. Bay (Eds.). Stanford, CA: Stanford University Press, pp. 59-83.

Chapter 9

The Geography of Women: The Influence of Capitalism and Gender on the Spatial Organization of Society

Derek Shanahan

INTRODUCTION

With the relative lack of geographic teaching at all academic levels in the United States, it may not seem immediately clear what geography has to do with the systematic study of women's lives. This chapter will therefore attempt to clarify what a geographic perspective on social issues entails today, while drawing out some of the connections between women and the ways in which capitalist society operates. Essentially, a contemporary geographic perspective emphasizes the spatial outcomes of various social processes such as the operation of the economy, racism, and sexism. A closely related idea that guides geographers' research is that the way space is organized can actually help produce and maintain societal rules and ways of living. Literally, the way we organize space in society can make society work in a particular way. Our cultural values are also underpinned by the spatial organization of society. These two fundamental geographic ideas, that social processes have spatial outcomes, and that society works the way it does in part because of the organization of space (and this includes the gendering of space), will guide the discussion presented in this chapter.

An exhaustive account of the geography of women is not possible here of course, so the examples presented will be selective, but hopefully, representative, of the great range of geographic studies of women that have developed over the last twenty years or so. The discussion is divided into three sections. First, there will be a brief introduction to the main concepts and theories used here. Second, the development of capitalism and the changes it brought to industrializing countries will be related to changes in women's lives. Basically, as capitalism developed through various social and economic crises over the last two centuries, men and women were affected differently by these changes. There has been a progressive de-skilling of the production process as capitalists seek to accumulate wealth more efficiently. Capitalism has also become highly mobile while creating a world economy. These changes in the production process led to well-defined spatial, and gender, divisions of labor. In other words, capitalism has produced spatially uneven outcomes within individual countries, and across the globe, with some regions (such as the U.S. South), and some countries (those in the developing world), being used as sources of cheap labor. There has also been a greater and greater separation of the sites of production (workplaces), and social reproduction (the home). As we shall see, these changes provided a powerful impetus for the eventual reorganization of urban space to incorporate suburbs. Domestic labor was also progressively devalued and became associated almost solely with women. Third, we shall turn our attention to the more recent move toward postmodern and postcolonial research. Here the emphasis is placed on representations of women in the landscape, and activity segregation in the uses made of the city by men and women. These examples all highlight the ways in which the organization of space (house design, city planning, etc.) both constrained and enabled women and men differently in their everyday lives.

GENDER, PATRIARCHY, AND GEOGRAPHY

Drawing on research from feminist studies in general (Oakley, 1974, 1981), a concerted attempt was made in the 1970s and 1980s to make women visible in geographic research (for example see Zelinsky, 1973; Tivers, 1978, 1985; Zelinsky, Monk, and Hanson, 1982). Allied with this concern was a growing need to theorize empirical studies of the geography of women. Several key concepts were thus applied to the case studies so produced. The most important of the concepts were *gender* and *patriarchy*, and by the mid-1970s arguably the most important theory applied to research in geography was that with a *Marxist* orientation (Harvey, 1973).

Gender denotes a process whereby people are ascribed particular roles in society by virtue of their biology. It should not be confused with the term "sex," which refers to our actual biological makeup. The gendering process is a culturally specific representation of a person's biology, and it directly affects the quality of life of men and women. Important for this discussion is the idea that just as people are gendered, so too are work roles. This sexual division of labor is often justified by reference to biological and "natural" arguments, and the innate abilities of women. Supposedly women are more naturally able to perform domestic work and child rearing, for example. Such justifications are false. In this regard sexism is much like racism in that each reduces people's abilities and potentials (intellectual, cultural, and political) to their biology. Our biology supposedly dictates the people we can become. While so-called natural laws of human biology have been presented as ultimate justifications for inequality between men and women, in fact, the gender divisions of society are socially constructed. Thus:

> Restraints formerly placed on women's actions (governing every form of behavior from bicycling to voting) have increasingly been shown to have their roots in political and economic relations rather than in the laws of biology. (Jackson, 1989, p. 106)

When we think of certain jobs as typically male or female, such as housework or mining, these perceptions reflect the gendering of work roles, that is, they reflect a social and cultural definition of who should do what, and are not inevitable, natural roles emanating from our biology (Knopp and Lauria, 1987; Haraway, 1991). This gendering occurs for reasons that are economic and political and, in turn, the process of gendering reflects male power in society (patriarchy). Female subordination, passed off as inevitable and natural because of women's biological make-up, is a result of patriarchal ideology.

Patriarchy sanctions the "systematic subordination of women by the exercise of male power legitimized by custom, tradition and myths about women's innate biological capacities" (Cater and Jones, 1992, p.129). And each gendered role that emanates from false patriarchal assumptions about the nature of women usually has its own space; a woman's place is in the home, while a man is often expected to be the breadwinner of the family, working outside of the home. Just as people and work roles are gendered, so too are landscapes. Our cities, rural areas, and even our houses, it is argued, all reflect a spatial organization developed around capitalist patriarchy (Hayden, 1980). Patriarchy has a geography.

A further complexity must be added to this theorization of gender. Differences in class are also reflected in the landscape (McDowell, 1986). Class and gender interact in complex ways (Massey, 1991), and the relationship between capitalism and gender is hotly contested. (See for example Harvey, 1989; Deutsche, 1991; Massey, 1991.) While it has become clear that patriarchy and women's subordination cannot be reduced simply to products of economic determinism, that is, simply as the result of capitalism, it is true, however, that capitalism especially has provided a critically important impetus for the prolonged subordination of women. The effects of class, and more broadly capitalism, on women are usefully shown from a Marxist perspective, although Marxism is only one possible way of approaching this topic.

Marxism is a complicated and ever-evolving theory of societal formation and change, and at the risk of gross oversimplification some rudimentary comments about Marxism must be made. Marxism can be thought of as a comprehensive theory about how the economy functions and how wealth is produced in different historical eras. For our purposes, Marxism can give us some insights into how capitalism produces and distributes (or restricts access to) wealth (Rius, 1976; Marx, 1987). *Capitalism* is seen as an historically specific economic and social system that is infested with internal contradictions, which will eventually cause its downfall as people in the working class become aware of their exploitation, and revolution occurs. An example of one such contradiction is that between the worker and the owner of the means of production (for example, a factory owner). For maximum profit to be made by the owner of a factory, costs must be reduced to a minimum. One of the costs that the owner has great power over is labor costs. The owner attempts to keep wages as low as possible, thus increasing profits. However, the worker attempts to secure higher wages, which will reduce the profits made by the owner. In other words the worker and owner are antagonistic toward each other. An internal contradiction exists. This is not the only contradiction in capitalism but it is important here because it emphasizes the basic motive of the capitalist system, which is to produce as much profit as possible while keeping costs, especially wages, at a minimum. Marx (1987) argued that because of power inequalities in society, workers are exploited by capitalists who refuse to pay them the wages they deserve.

As capitalism attempts to accumulate more and more wealth through changing the production process, it affects men and women differently, and it also affects the spatial organization of our society. As England (1991, p. 136) shows:

> the location of residential areas, work-places, transportation networks, and the overall layout of cities in general reflect a patriarchal capitalist society's expectations of what types of activities take place where, when, and by whom.

That capitalism survives, and revolution has not occurred in many countries, is indicative of the ability of capitalism to reinvent itself in the face of crises. This reinvention is sometimes termed *restructuring*.

Restructuring in the industrialized countries of the world has produced changes in the relative numbers of job types performed. Thus industrialized countries have undergone a large decrease in the number of manufacturing jobs, with a simultaneous rise in unemployment rates. Basic manufacturing work is now often carried out in developing countries where labor costs, among other things, are extremely low by comparison to wage rates in the United States. A recent example of this is the Nike corporation setting up manufacturing plants in Indonesia where wage rates are as low as two dollars a day per person. Manufacturing jobs can easily be moved around the globe by capitalist multinational corporations because such jobs have been de-skilled and require little if any training of the workforce. The de-skilling of jobs has helped industry become more efficient by simplifying and standardizing the way products are made. A good example of this is the automation involved in the car industry. Workers stand along a conveyor belt and repeat the same task again and again. Such automation has allowed products to be made more cheaply, which is an advantage for the consumer, but it has also had some negative effects. One of these negative effects is that capital is now highly mobile and can therefore seek out the cheapest pools of labor throughout the world (Dicken, 1992). This has produced a great decline in the numbers of people employed in traditional manufacturing industries in the United States, for example, and has caused the economic decline of many urban areas here as elsewhere. Because of the mobility of capital there is now a well-defined *spatial division of labor* that is both national and global. At the national level, as we shall see, suburbs in North American cities have also been used in similar ways by capitalism, and women have been directly affected by this process (Massey, 1984).

These basic concepts will now be applied to several examples that seek to show the interconnections among class, gender, capitalism, and the spatial organization of society that underpins, and sometimes actually guides, the constitution of society.

CITY SPACES AND GENDERED WORK ROLES

With the advent of the industrial revolution in the eighteenth century in Britain, long-lasting changes to the social, economic, and geographic structure of Britain occurred. The progressive *enclosure* of common land ensured a growing number of propertyless people. Before land became the exclusive property of a relatively small elite, peasants had certain rights that allowed them to graze on common land and to grow crops. This provided a measure of independence and survival for them. But enclosure of this common land removed those rights. This spatial reorganization of common land by the state restricted access of poorer people to the land and removed a vital means of survival for those people. From a Marxist perspective, the peasantry had lost all control over the ownership of the means of production (the resources and tools used to create wealth in any historical era), and now they only had their labor to sell in order to survive. They became a large, underemployed reserve of labor to fill the factories of the industrial revolution. In this way a new form of spatial organization in society aided in the creation of a cheap labor source for capitalism. This spatial strategy to effect change in British society was clearly acknowledged by some members of the English political elite. Trevelyan (1965) notes a report to the Board of Agriculture in 1794 concerning enclosure of common land in part of rural England in which the spatial strategy of restricting access to the land for the masses is seen to have many advantages for capitalism. Thus:

> . . . when the remaining commons are enclosed, then that "subordination of the lower ranks of society, which in the present time is much wanted, would be hereby considerably secured." (Trevelyan, 1965, p. 154)

The workforce needed for the emerging capitalist economy could only be secured by subordinating the mass of the poor, and this could only be achieved with a radical reorganization of space. A new geography of private property was crucial to capitalist society.

Women played an important role in the early decades of the industrial revolution. Indeed, women and children were seen as more easily exploited than were men, and so they worked in the textile mills and the factories along with men, albeit at lower wages. However, this situation was soon to change as capitalism avoided recurrent crises. An excellent example of capitalism's response to various economic and social crises is afforded by the coal mining industry in Britain. Despite the creation of much wealth and the growth of the British Empire, economic recession was not uncommon throughout the industrial revolution, and in such times unemployment rose. Along with unemployment there was also a growing concern that the family unit was in moral crisis because women worked outside of the home. Partly in order to protect jobs for men, and partly to solve a perceived problem with the reproduction of labor power (Rowbotham, 1973), the Mines Regulation Act of 1842 excluded women and children from paid work in the mines (Jackson, 1989). In other words, state intervention in the form of a new law produced a sexual division of labor in these areas. Women had always performed mining tasks, but as capitalism developed job roles were gendered. Mine work came to be seen as "men's work." The effect of this law was to remove women from the most lucrative jobs in these areas, because little else was available in terms of paid labor in the coal mining regions of Britain (Massey, 1984), and women were progressively restricted to the home and to unpaid, laborious, but necessary, domestic labor.

THE GEOGRAPHY OF CAPITALIST CHANGE

At this point it is worth summarizing the social changes brought about by industrial capitalism. First, work roles were gendered, with women being progressively isolated in unpaid domestic work. This increased women's dependence on men, and even devalued female children to the point where marked rises in fertility occurred in coal mining regions in this period as families sought to produce enough male children to ensure future financial security in the face of the dangers of mining that constantly threatened to prematurely end the husband's ability to work (Friedlander, 1974; Haines, 1977). Male children would provide security against such an eventuality. Women were thus subordinated to the male breadwinner, and such subordination supports the ideology of the nuclear family, because men now had greater power over financial resources. Women's lack of independence forces marriage as an economic necessity in many respects.

Second, a twofold spatial division of labor developed. At the regional level those areas in Britain with coal deposits became entirely dependent upon the coal mining industry for their economic well being. There were (and still are) relatively few other types of jobs that women could turn to for economic survival, and this reinforced women's dependence on men. Other regions of Britain were developed more broadly, and the southeast of England, especially around London, has always been economically superior to the north of Britain (Cater and Jones, 1992). Spatially uneven economic development is an integral part of capitalism. For example, the southern states of the United States are relatively undeveloped compared to other areas of the United States, and so higher unemployment and lower standards of living result. At the local level capitalism encouraged the home to become the exclusive site of unpaid domestic work.

Remembering the brief discussion above about capitalism's need to minimize costs in order to maximize profits, then it is possible to perceive a great benefit to capitalism with such a *spatial* and *gendered division of labor*. Domestic labor essentially ensures the social reproduction of the workforce for tomorrow. Old people are cared for, children are nursed and looked after while they attend school, clothes are washed and food is cooked. All of this labor is unpaid. As Cater and Jones (1992, p. 133) argue, the "reproduction of labor power is a necessity to capital, but a costly one," but with women to provide most of the services of social reproduction for free, then capitalism has succeeded in passing off a huge cost to the family unit. By spatially reorganizing the city, and removing the place where social reproduction occurred from the place where production was carried out, capitalism was better able to make the creation of tomorrow's workforce (which is essentially what the rearing of children amounts to) a private, family matter. And private issues should be paid for by the family concerned. To hire someone to perform all the necessary domestic chores was, and still is, prohibitively expensive for most people. A cheap domestic worker was needed, and this is the role that women were forced to take. What occurred in the coal regions of Britain and, of course, in the rapidly industrializing cities elsewhere, is a particular development of *public* and *private space*. Private space, that of the home and the house, became the preserve of the woman, while man gained almost exclusive rights over the public spaces of paid work in the cities. While arguments were made that it was "natural" for the woman to perform the domestic chores, the actual reality of the situation is that women had little choice. Societal and cultural values reinforced the ideology of the nuclear family, and the notion that women's biology predisposed them to be domestic laborers. The home, as private space, is the geography of this social process.

Distinctions between private and public space, who may use such spaces, and for what purposes, will be returned to in more detail below, but for now we must jump to the twentieth century to analyze how urban spaces developed as capitalism avoided successive social and economic crises. Urban form clearly reflected the private and public spaces of capitalist organization by the end of the nineteenth century. To combat some of the deplorable residential conditions of industrial cities there was a gradual development of housing outside of the urban centers. The ultimate expression of this move toward healthier housing was the suburb. While there were definite benefits for public health from suburban residential development, there were also negative consequences for the lives of women.

England (1991) makes the important argument that suburbs, with their emphasis on family life and owner-occupied housing, explicitly supported the ideal of the nuclear family. This type of family formation, with a male breadwinner and a female restricted largely to domestic labor, was fundamentally different from the precapitalist ideal of marriage as an economic partnership in which women contributed financially to the family (England, 1991; but see also Oakley, 1976). Capitalism produced a gendered division of labor, which was organized spatially. In short, suburbs were, in many respects, a spatial response to economic changes brought about by capitalism and the emerging, socially constructed, idea of the nuclear family. This nuclear family was of course gendered in terms of its activities (work roles, etc.) and was based on a patriarchal ideology.

England (1991) and other authors (McDowell, 1983; Monk, 1992) have also emphasized the role of the state in the creation of suburbs through an explicit support of patriarchal ideology. Thus new towns in the United States of the 1930s were built around the ideal of the suburban housewife and the husband who commuted to work as "normal" and "traditional" (Monk, 1992, p. 130). McDowell (1983) notes that the social construction of the ideal housewife has also supported a lucrative consumer durables industry. (See also Miller, 1983.) Suburban housewives quickly became the focus of a huge industry marketing labor-saving devices for the domestic sphere. There is, however, a more recent finding concerning suburbs and capitalism. With the world recession that has affected so many countries over the past two decades (Dicken, 1992), capitalism has restructured in order to maintain the accumulation of wealth. As male-dominated manufacturing jobs have declined in many industrialized nations, there has been an increase in temporary, part-time, low-wage jobs. Just as capitalism can find and exploit cheap labor sources in developing countries, so can it find and exploit cheap labor sources in developed countries too. The suburbs with their large populations of women have often provided just such a source of labor.

Restriction to the domestic sphere of society has thus produced numerous negative consequences for women. It has long been known that women's restriction to unpaid domestic labor has left them highly isolated and dependent on men (Friedan, 1963). Domestic labor is time consuming. Women generally have fewer financial resources than men, and the time constraints imposed by domestic chores tie them more closely to the home. Historically, the restriction of women from full-time, paid work means that they are less likely to be organized in terms of labor unions, when they do work, than are men, and are economically vulnerable in this respect. Add to this the need to complete domestic labor, such as collecting children from school or cooking food for the evening meal, and it becomes clear that women's time constraints in any single day are considerable. Housewives in Britain in 1985, for example, spent 76 hours per week on domestic chores (Cater and Jones, 1992, p. 116), a figure that is comparable to the United States (Oakley, 1974). Suburbs, with their distance from the city, leave many women *spatially entrapped*. Employment opportunities for women will consequently be much reduced.

Capitalism has taken advantage of this situation by relocating some activities to the suburbs (McDowell, 1983; England, 1991). This has led to the creation of so-called *pink-collar ghettos* with, for example, the movement of clerical jobs to the suburbs of cities in the United States (Nelson, 1986) to take advantage of housewives who can really only work part time, given the time constraints produced by excessive domestic labor demands made upon them. Thus domestic labor, and limited financial resources, heavily restrict women in terms of spatial mobility. Of course, class is also an issue here. A relatively affluent middle-class woman is certainly going to be more mobile than a poorer working-class woman, but generally research indicates that the spatial division of labor in capitalism underpins and maintains the gender division of labor by placing greater restrictions upon women's time and mobility. Indeed, Vaiou (1992, p. 255) showed in a study of women in Helioupolis, Greece that many women were forced to leave paid employment because of "family responsibilities and pressures." Quite simply, the gender division of labor and the contemporary spatial organization of the city greatly disadvantages women. Suburbs are based upon planning principles and zoning laws that separate residential uses from other activities. It is difficult therefore to combine shopping with work and everyday domestic chores such as taking children to daycare (Monk, 1992).

A NONSEXIST CITY

Hayden (1980) has long criticized sexist city and home design. The organization of our cities and homes reflects patriarchal ideology in that architects and planners follow policies that support the ideal of the nuclear family, and therefore assume a home-oriented woman and a male breadwinner. There were, of course, public health issues involved in reducing the slum squalor of the nineteenth-century city but the solution to these housing concerns emphasized a patriarchal view of social life, and thus a gendered division of labor. Hayden (1980) outlined the basic difficulties presented by the geography of the city for a woman who wanted to work outside of the home. The conventional home, whether in the suburb or the city, is organized around the idea that an individual will be available to undertake cooking, cleaning, and child care in an isolated or private manner. Kitchens, bedrooms, and basements all reflect isolated workspaces and a preconceived idea of the important tasks for families to carry out in the seclusion of their homes. Suburbs themselves are notoriously underserviced and often have a dearth of daycare facilities, poor public transportation, and limited laundry and shopping facilities. The situation is exacerbated for single women, or women who have been subject to male violence. Few other housing options exist for these individuals who must accomplish paid work, child care, and all other domestic chores. Poor public transportation exaggerates the distances between school, supermarket, workplace, and home so that it becomes difficult for the single woman to accomplish all the necessary tasks of an average day.

Hayden (1980) therefore defines a nonsexist city. Such a city would employ a vastly different organization of space than the typical capitalist city at present. Patriarchal ideology would be rejected, and planning policies that support a value system designed to foster women's independence would be encouraged. Private housing would not be developed in isolation from the services that could support women in paid employment. Thus, a nonsexist city would, perhaps, be built around communal living arrangements that would help to eradicate the gendered division of labor, and include men in domestic work. Communal living arrangements would include private living space for families but would also include food service facilities, day care facilities, and ease of access to public transportation.

Some experimental living arrangements already exist, and the idea of different types of city planning has surfaced many times over the past 100 years. Typically these "utopian" communities included both communal and private space for living, and they often emphasized the need to reduce the isolation of domestic labor. Currently radical living arrangements exist in many industrialized countries. For example, the Nina West homes in London, England are designed for single women (Monk, 1992). These residences include purpose-built apartment complexes that are close to public transportation and other services such as schools and supermarkets. The apartments themselves have been built with enclosed safe play areas for children, which parents can easily monitor while doing chores. There is a day care facility in the complex and there are also communal laundry facilities. Such organization of space reduces time and mobility constraints on women and gives greater opportunity for women to enter paid employment, and thus increase their independence.

POSTMODERN AND POSTCOLONIAL
GEOGRAPHY OF WOMEN

Postmodern and postcolonial research are relatively new research strategies that seek to deconstruct our more traditional theories about how society works. Specifically, these types of analysis challenge the idea that there is only one, monolithic, scientific method. Scientific method and the idea of the objectivity of the scientist are both modern ideals. *Modernism* claimed that the traditional scientific method was the only way of discovering true knowledge. *Postmodernism* argues that traditional science is only one possible method of producing knowledge, and further, postmodernism criticizes modernist science for silencing alternative knowledge claims and alternative voices. Traditional science has privileged the knowledge claims of a small elite, originally identified as European, white males. By contrast, postmodernist approaches to social scientific research attempt to allow the voices of previously powerless groups to be heard. Closely allied to postmodernism is *postcolonialism* (Blunt and Rose, 1994). Postcolonialism seeks to redress the effects of imperialism, especially on non-Western culture groups (Said, 1979). With the end of empire and the decolonization of much of the world, there has been a growing volume of criticism concerning the effects of past colonial episodes. As with postmodernism there is an emphasis, in postcolonial research, on the representation of multiple voices and multiple ways of knowing. Thus, previously powerless peoples from the developing world, and from within the developed world, have benefited from being made visible in this way. Postcolonialism and postmodernism have been particularly useful in defining aspects of women's experiences that were invisible to traditional scientific and modernist sensibilities (Jameson, 1984; Barnes and Duncan, 1991; Massey, 1991).

Geography has been much influenced by the changes outlined above. In particular there has been great innovation in cultural geography (Jackson, 1989), and there have been some excellent collaborative research volumes between distinct intellectual disciplines (for example, see Bender, 1995). Cultural geography has been revitalized of late as an important subdiscipline of geography, and draws ideas and theories from fields as varied as literary criticism and cultural anthropology. Using such ideas, studies of the geography of women have begun to explore more subtle aspects of the spatiality of women's lives. In essence the following examples all attempt to "read" the urban landscape for implicit and explicit patriarchal cultural values. These cultural ideals dictate who may use certain spaces in the city, and how they may use these spaces. Such *activity segregation* again greatly restricts women's mobility.

City Landscapes and Activity Segregation

. . . there are strong pressures exerted on women to physically restrict themselves to the domestic aspects of cities and urban life. These range from ways of restricting their mobility (from corsets and high heels to jokes about women drivers) to an ideology which encourages women to consider themselves physically frail. (McDowell, 1983, p. 59)

Unequal gender relations in society are reproduced in the geography of everyday life, and never more so than in the structure of cities. Monk (1992) analyzes cities in light of their political and ideological role in social life. City landscapes, through the architecture employed in them, represent many of the deeply held sentiments and values of society. Buildings and monuments celebrate past historical episodes and people of note. However, male figures predominate. Women, when they are portrayed, will very often take on an ideological or spiritual role rather than emphasize the person herself. For example, statues of Queen Victoria in cities such as London and Sydney show her resplendent with all the paraphernalia of monarchy and empire. She is symbolic of British imperialism. And while many men are represented as military heroes, on horse and in the heat of battle, women are just as likely to be represented in erotic form. Thus, a patriarchal representation of women is evident in the city. Male power is even more conspicuous when we consider the ways in which the spaces of the city are permitted to be used.

The archetypical modern man, perhaps, is Baudelaire. His literary evocations of nineteenth-century Paris did much to crystallize in the mind's eye the ideal of the modernist city of industrial capitalism by the turn of the century (Harvey, 1989; Deutsche, 1991; Massey, 1991). Baudelaire's Paris was one of extremes. Great wealth coexisted uneasily with the most desperate poverty. And yet the view of Paris we receive is one of brilliant nightlife, boulevards, cafes, and an affluent population strolling along the boulevards enjoying all the city had to offer. In true modernist fashion this view of the city is presented as the only view, as if the city were seen, and used, in the same way by all who lived there. But this was not the case. Baudelaire's Paris is patriarchal and affluent.

The Parisian strollers enjoyed the public spaces of the city because they could. They had money and power. To be poor or female, or both, was to be restricted in the way in which the public spaces of the city could be used. Indeed, the distinction between public and private space is crucial here (Massey, 1991). The public spaces of cafes, bars, and brothels did indeed include women, but those women were there for the benefit of men. Poor women might work in the cafes or brothels, while wealthier women were secluded in the suburbs. Of course, wealthy women could also enjoy the boulevards and cafes, but only arm in arm with their husbands, so to speak. Baudelaire's literary constructions of his experiences in the city, of all that he took pleasure in seeing and doing, were also often erotic (Deutsche, 1991; Edholm, 1995). Patriarchal power was so great that all unaccompanied women were sexually objectified. To be a single woman in the public spaces of the city was to bring moral suspicion from men. Single women implied sexual availability "because 'respectable' women simply could not wander around the streets and parks alone" (Massey, 1991, p. 47). The cultural mores of the time reinforced a patriarchal ideology that gendered the spaces of the city. Women could not experience the city with the same safety or freedom as men could.

Interestingly, critiques of nineteenth-century masculine views of the city have also come to focus on the art of the time. The great painters of the Parisian salons, for example, produced some of our most enduring images of the city. Thus we have studies depicting the cabaret, the patrons of brothels, and the boulevards, all the spaces that men like Baudelaire frequented and enjoyed. By contrast, women painters of the time did not produce similar images. More likely were images of secluded spaces, of the private sphere of women's activity. Domesticity loomed large in these studies of gardens and flowers (Pollock, 1988).

If art criticism seems a little too abstract to draw many conclusions about everyday social life, then a recent study concerning a poor woman from late nineteenth-century Paris should serve to provide more concrete evidence of the patriarchal nature of urban space. Edholm (1995) has attempted to make visible the life of Suzanne Valadon, a working-class woman of the 1880s in Paris. Edholm compares the everyday experiences of Baudelaire and his Paris to that which Valadon would probably have had. Hers is a view of Paris, and Parisian life, "from below" (Edholm, 1995, p. 139). As we have seen, Baudelaire's Paris is one of extreme mobility and comfort. He walks the boulevards at ease, stopping to inspect cafes and people. Valadon, on the other hand, is poor and is a woman.

At the beginning of the nineteenth century Paris had been the site of much social unrest. Cramped eighteenth-century city design, with narrow streets, had made it easy for the masses of the working classes to barricade streets and control urban territory. By the end of the century Paris had been redesigned. The boulevards were specifically designed to exclude the poor. They were wide and lined with bars and restaurants for the wealthy to enjoy. Aggressive policing kept the presence of the poor to a minimum in these areas. Boulevard life was commodified. It was there for the consumption of the wealthy, particularly male, Parisian. So patriarchal had the boulevards become by the end of the nineteenth century that Paris was known as a center for "sexual consumerism" (Edholm, 1995, p. 156), and working class women were often stereotyped as prostitutes, when in fact it is far from certain that prostitution was inevitably used by working-class women to make ends meet. Poverty was the defining feature of social life for Valadon, as it was for so many in Paris at that time. While middle- and upper-class women were secluded in the suburbs, poorer women lived wherever they could in the squalor of slum life. Houses and homes that the wealthy enjoyed did not exist for the poor, and many of the mundane domestic chores of life were performed publicly on the squalid streets hidden behind the grand boulevards. Life here was insecure and brutal in many ways. Such extreme poverty saw women in particular developing networks of support within small neighborhoods. Only in these relatively small residential areas would someone like Valadon have felt even remotely safe given the prevailing patriarchal organization of the city.

The question posed is whether or not a working-class woman like Valadon could have experienced the city as Baudelaire did. Of course the answer is no. For Valadon to walk the Boulevards as a single woman, especially a working-class woman, would have "signalled non-respectable, and her sexual availability would probably have been assumed" (Edholm, 1995, p. 160). In such a space Valadon would have been subject to open harassment. Thus, Valadon's Paris, as a poor woman in the late nineteenth century, was a place of very restricted mobility. And her class also removed any possibility that she could have enjoyed the services offered by the cafes along the boulevards. Even to stop and look in at the crowds at the cafes would bring unwanted attention and the strong possibility of being seen as a prostitute.

We might ask similar questions of the late twentieth-century city. Valentine (1992) studied the perceptions of fear in the city of groups of working-class, middle-class and upper-class women in Reading, England. When asked which environments, and people, the women feared most, they were in agreement that public spaces and strangers caused them the most fear. Such fear affected their spatial mobility. For example, they would not take a shortcut to their homes if it meant walking through an empty parking lot or a park. While some trepidation over these spaces might be justified, crime statistics in Britain overwhelmingly show that women have a much greater likelihood of being hurt in the home by someone they know. In other words, Valentine's study shows a remarkable mismatch between women's perceptions of unsafe spaces and the reality of male crime against women in Britain. Possible reasons for this disparity come from both the gendered way in which children are brought up, and the sources of information about crime that exist.

Once girls and boys reach the age of eleven years, parents begin to treat them differently with regard to issues of safety in using the city. Girls are encouraged not to stray far from home, and if they do venture away they are only to do this with friends. Parents tend to emphasize the safety of the home to girls, and the security of the male breadwinner. By contrast, boys of the same age are not taught to fear being away from home. Parents perceive boys as being better able to look after themselves in public spaces. Consequently, boys also have an incorrect view of the spaces that are most dangerous to them. Valentine (1992) thus found that young men do not fear certain public spaces and situations, and yet statistics show that young men are actually in the greatest danger in these places. The sources of information about crime also influence the perception women have of unsafe places. Press reports tend to emphasize rape and battery of women in public spaces, especially in parks and parking lots, and suggest that these areas are to be avoided by women. And yet the press does not emphasize to the same degree the alarming domestic abuse against women:

> By disproportionately publicizing attacks committed in public places rather than domestic violence, the media place the dangers women fear into the public environment and link crimes with particular locations such as parks and railways. (Valentine, 1992, p. 26)

Ultimately women are coerced, once again, into the private sphere of the home, and the public spaces of the city are controlled by men. The geography of women's fear thus shows that the city is still a place to be traversed with care, and that its spaces are to be used differently by men and women. City spaces are indeed gendered.

SUMMARY AND CONCLUSION

Women's lives have historically been structured differently than the lives of men. Inequality between men and women arises in a variety of ways. The development of capitalism has reinforced a particular geography of the city in which women's mobility has been severely restricted. The private space of the home, as the site of domestic labor, has become the domain of women. That the distinction between private and public spheres in social life, that is the distinction between the everyday geography of men and women, still remains very much a reality is evidence that patriarchy still guides the way capitalist society operates.

In summary, this discussion has attempted to introduce a variety of empirical examples of the differences between the lives of men and women from a geographic perspective. All social processes produce spatial outcomes. In turn, these spatial divisions in society reinforce and reproduce society's mores and cultural values. We have seen how patriarchy has led to the gendered division of labor, and how this cultural definition of work roles has produced a spatial division of labor in both the home and the city. Patriarchy is served by this geography of the city because women are continuously put at a disadvantage in terms of their ability to compete for paid employment. Continuing disadvantage maintains male power. While it is certain that changing the geography of the city will not eradicate patriarchal bias, new geographies of society can help to reduce the inequalities between men and women.

Capitalism produced spatially uneven economic development within and between countries, and also influenced the nature of patriarchy. Capitalism has certainly produced great wealth, but not everyone shares equally in terms of opportunity. The cities that capitalism spawned embodied the gendered division of labor, and were designed to improve the efficiency of capitalism. A geography of the city still exists that reproduces women's inequality. A gendered division of labor is supported by a spatial division of labor. While women are differentiated along class lines, they are also differentiated by race. Nothing here has been said of the interactions between race and patriarchy, in part because relatively little geographic research has been completed in this respect. However, an excellent introduction to some of these issues is afforded by Jackson (1989) and Spivak (1988). What questions might we ask ourselves about the nature of patriarchy and the geography that supports it?

KEY TERMS

gender	public and private space
patriarchy	spatial entrapment
Marxist	pink-collar ghettos
capitalism	modernism
restructuring	postmodernism
spatial division of labor	postcolonialism
enclosure	activity segregation
gendered division of labor	

DISCUSSION QUESTIONS

1. Marxist approaches to the study of society are but one possible way of studying the effects of capitalism on society. What other theories

exist that might help us understand social inequality? Incidentally, Marxism is very complicated, but a humorous (it is presented in a cartoon format) and very accessible introduction to Marxism is given by Rius (1976).

2. What other aspects of everyday life might exhibit the influence of patriarchy?

3. What issues involving the differences between men and women in society have recently arisen in your local area, or in the United States in general? How do these issues relate to the way men and women use space?

4. How does the media represent crime against, or involving, women? Do these reports confirm research findings from Britain that certain types of crime, and the places in which they occur, are emphasized while other types of crime remain unreported?

5. What government statistics are regularly collected that report on the progress, or lack of progress, for women in the United States?

6. How might the geography of poor women in the United States differ from that of wealthier women?

7. Little has been said about the intersection of race and patriarchy. In what ways might race, gender, and patriarchy interact to produce different geographies of the city for women of different racial backgrounds?

8. In what ways do you feel your own life to be restricted by the geographies produced by patriarchy and the operation of the economy?

9. In what ways can you see the influence of inequality for women built into the historical record of your community? What type of history is told by the monuments erected in your community?

REFERENCES

Barnes, T. J. and J. S. Duncan (Eds.) (1991). *Writing worlds: Discourses, texts and metaphors in the representation of landscape.* London: Routledge.

Bender, B. (Ed.) (1995). *Landscape. Politics and perspectives.* Oxford: Berg Publishers Ltd.

Blunt, A. and G. Rose (Eds.) (1994). *Writing women and space.* New York: Guilford Press.

Cater, J. and T. Jones (1992). *Social geography: An introduction to contemporary issues* (Second ed.). New York: Edward Arnold.

Deutsche, R. (1991). "Boys Town," *Environment and Planning D: Society and Space, 9:* 5-30.

Dicken, P. (1992). *Global shift.* London: Guilford Press.

Edholm, F. (1995). "The view from below: Paris in the 1880s." In *Landscape. Politics and perspectives*, B. Bender (Ed.). Oxford: Berg Publishers Ltd., pp. 139-168.

England, K. V. L. (1991). "Gender relations and the spatial structure of the city," *Geoforum, 22:* 135-147.

Friedan, B. (1963). *The feminine mystique.* New York: Norton.

Friedlander, D. (1974). "Demographic patterns and socio-economic characteristics of the coal-mining population in England and Wales in the nineteenth century," *Economic Development and Cultural Change, 22:* 39-51.

Haines, M. (1977). "Fertility, nuptiality and occupation: A study of coalmining populations and regions in England and Wales in the Mid-Nineteenth Century," *Journal of Interdisciplinary, 8:* 245-280.

Haraway, D. (1991). *Simians, cyborgs, and women: The reinvention of nature.* New York: Routledge.

Harvey, D. (1973). *Social justice and the city.* London: Edward Arnold.

Harvey, D. (1989). *The condition of postmodernity.* Oxford: Basil Blackwell.

Hayden, D. (1980). "What would a non-sexist city be like? Speculations on housing, urban design, and human work," *Signs, 5:* 170-187.

Jackson, P. (1989). *Maps of meaning.* London: Unwin Hyman.

Jameson, F. (1984). "Postmodernism, or the cultural logic of late capitalism," *New Left Review, 164:* 53-92.

Knopp, L. and M. Lauria (1987). "Gender relations as a particular form of social relations," *Antipode, 19:* 48-53.

Marx, K. (1987). *Capital.* New York: International Press.

Massey, D. (1984). *Spatial divisions of labour: Social structures and the geography of production.* London: MacMillan.

Massey, D. (1991). "Flexible sexism," *Environment and Planning D: Society and Space, 9:* 31-57.

McDowell, L. (1983). "Towards an understanding of the gender division of urban space," *Environment and Planning D: Society and Space, 1:* 59-72.

McDowell, L. (1986). "Beyond patriarchy: A class based explanation of women's subordination," *Antipode, 18:* 312-321.

Miller, R. (1983). "The Hoover in the garden: Middle class women and suburbanization, 1850-1920," *Environment and Planning D: Society and Space, 1:* 73-88.

Monk, J. (1992). "Gender in the landscape: Expressions of power and meaning." In *Inventing places: Studies in cultural geography*, K. Anderson and F. Gale (Eds.). Melbourne: Longman Cheshire, pp. 123-138.

Nelson, K. (1986). "Female labor supply characteristics and the suburbanization of low-wage office work." In *Production, work, territory: The geographical anatomy of industrial capitalism*, A. Scott, and M. Storper (Eds.). London: Allen and Unwin, pp. 160-181.

Oakley, A. (1974). *Women's work.* New York: Pantheon Books.

Oakley, A. (1976). *Women's work: The housewife past and present.* New York: Vintage.

Oakley, A. (1981). *Subject women.* London: Martin Robertson Press.

Pollock, G. (1988). *Vision and difference: Femininity, feminism and histories of art.* Andover, U.K.: Routledge.

Rius (1976). *Marx for beginners.* New York: Pantheon Books.

Rowbotham, S. (1973). *Hidden from history: 300 years of women's oppression and the fight against it.* London: Pluto Press.

Said, E. (1979). *Orientalism.* New York: Vintage Books.

Spivak, G. C. (1988). "Can the subaltern speak?" In *Marxism and the interpretation of culture,* C. Nelson and L. Grossberg (Eds.). Urbana: University of Illinois Press, pp. 271-313.

Tivers, J. (1978). "How the other half lives: The geographical study of women," *Area, 10:* 302-306.

Tivers, J. (1985). *Women attached: The daily lives of women with young children.* London: Croom Helm.

Trevelyan, G. M. (1965). *British history in the nineteenth century and after: 1782-1919.* Harmondsworth: Penguin Books.

Vaiou, D. (1992). "Gender divisions in urban space: Beyond the rigidity of dualist classifications," *Antipode, 24:* 247-262.

Valentine, G. (1992). "Images of danger: Women's sources of information about the spatial distribution of male violence," *Area, 24:* 22-29.

Zelinsky, W. (1973). "Women in geography: A brief factual account," *The Professional Geographer, 25:* 151-165.

Zelinsky, W., J. Monk, and S. Hanson (1982). "Women and geography: A review and prospectus," *Progress in Human Geography, 6:* 317-366.

Chapter 10

Women in Business: The Experiences of Women in the U.S. Workforce

Karen Stewart

INTRODUCTION

In 1866 a U.S. senator said that giving a woman the right to vote would put her "in an adversary position to men and convert all the now harmonious elements of society into a state of war, and make every home a hell on earth" (Rosenberg, 1992, p. 55). While this quote specifically provides insight into the deep concern expressed over giving women the right to vote, women have heard similar concerns voiced over the years as they have struggled to earn a legitimate role in the American workplace.

Records from the early 1900s report that just over 21 percent of the workforce were women (Edwards, Laporte, and Livingston, 1991). While women have always worked—either in the home or in family-operated businesses or farms—most American women never received a paycheck for their efforts until World War II, when a shortage of adult male employees enabled women to fill factory jobs important for the war effort (Sitterly and Duke, 1988). In the immediate postwar period most of these women returned to domestic responsibilities. However, some women who discovered the joys and benefits of being employed outside the home stayed in the labor force and became role models for the female workers who would follow. For many years women continued to be considered a reserve workforce. They were used to fill positions during times of national emergency (Rosenberg, 1992). Only in recent decades has this situation changed. Today statistics reveal that women compose 46.1 percent of the workforce (Dobrzynski, 1996). Factors that facilitated women's entry into the labor force in greater numbers include the following (Daily, 1993): (1) technological innovations such as automatic washing machines and dishwashers, which decreased the amount of time needed to do housework, (2) development of better methods of birth control, which resulted in a steady decline and recent leveling off of fertility rates, and (3) medical advances that have reduced the amount of time devoted to caring for sick children. Government regulation of women's rights in the workplace has also been instrumental.

With greater numbers of women employed outside the home, there has been an increased interest in whether places of employment are responsive to the needs of women. Felice Schwartz is the president and founder of a national nonprofit research and advisory organization that works with businesses to effect change for women. As a result of her site visits to companies and discussions with top executives, she has developed a zero-to-five scale that rates firms with regard to their treatment of female employees. This scale, as reported in *Harvard Business Review* (Schwartz, 1992), is summarized in Table 10.1.

The significance of being familiar with this scale is that women can recognize that some firms are more responsive than others to the special issues that affect working women. Lists of firms that have policies favorable to women can typically be found. It behooves women to learn who these companies are and to seriously consider them when seeking employment. This scale also helps companies recognize where they are and gives guidance for improvement.

TABLE 10.1. How Firms Rate in Their Treatment of Women Employees

Rank	Characteristic
0	This firm is not interested in developing women in the workplace. No effort is made to recruit, train, or promote females. Lawsuits may result.
1	This firm does not address the needs of female employees. This firm does track numbers and fill out EEOC forms. The goal is to keep one step ahead of the law.
2	This firm is more responsive to women's needs. There are a few policies regarding unpaid maternity leave, child care, or part-time clerical jobs. However, little thought is given to women's upward mobility or removing obstacles that reduce women's on-the-job productivity.
3	This firm addresses matters such as family and work issues or leadership development on a limited basis.
4	This firm is truly responsive to women's needs. Very few firms are here yet.
5	This represents an ideal, egalitarian environment. This firm has a level playing field for both men and women.

GOVERNMENT RECOGNITION
OF WOMEN'S RIGHTS IN THE WORKPLACE

Over the last four decades a series of key governmental actions opened opportunities for working women. In 1963 the *Equal Pay Act* was passed. This act states that employers must provide equal pay for substantially equal work. The following year, *Title VII of the Civil Rights Act* banned employment discrimination based on race, color, sex, or national origin and created the *Equal Employment Opportunity Commission* (EEOC) to enforce antidiscrimination laws. It is interesting to note that "sex" was added to Title VII with the hope that its inclusion would ensure the defeat of this act. In the early 1960s President Kennedy issued an executive order that required contractors to take affirmative action to recruit, hire, and promote minorities. In a 1967 executive order, President Johnson added to women to the protected groups. Other actions that have significance in this area are summarized in Table 10.2.

TABLE 10.2. Governmental Actions That Have Helped Working Women

Age Discrimination in Employment Act (1967)	Protects workers from forty to seventy years old from discrimination in hiring, firing, and other terms of employment.
Rehabilitation Act (1973)	Bans discrimination against qualified individuals with handicaps who can perform essential job functions with "reasonable accommodation."
Equal Credit Opportunity Act (1974, amended 1976)	Prohibits discrimination against women desiring financial services.
Pregnancy Discrimination Act (1978)	Extended Title VII protection of the Civil Rights Act to pregnant employees.
EEOC (1979)	President Carter unified enforcement of Title VII, the Equal Pay Act, the Age Discrimination Act, and the Rehabilitation Act under the Equal Employment Opportunity Commission (EEOC).
Executive Order by President Reagan (1983)	Required federal agencies to increase by a minimum of 10 percent their goals for hiring minority subcontractors.
U.S. Supreme Court decision (1986)	Upheld a California law that requires employers to grant leave for pregnant workers. This must be done even if leaves are not granted for other health conditions.

A more recent act is the *Civil Rights Act of 1991*. This legislation was designed primarily to overturn several recent Supreme Court decisions that made it more difficult to bring employment discrimination suits (Dworkin, 1993). This law allows persons who have been discriminated against to sue for punitive and compensatory damages along with the usual Title VII damages of back pay plus interest and other lost job benefits. The employee now has the right to sue for such things as emotional pain, suffering, inconvenience, and other nonpecuniary losses (Dworkin, 1993). This act has the effect of making it more meaningful for victims of sexual harassment to pursue claims and therefore, more likely that women will pursue them.

Another significant piece of legislation is the *National Family Leave Act,* which President Clinton signed into law in 1993. This act requires businesses to permit up to twelve weeks of unpaid leave annually. Leave may be taken to care for an elderly parent, a sick child or spouse, or a newborn or adopted baby.

This evolution of government action has helped move society toward greater equality for working women. However, the impact of these laws changes over time as the courts render new interpretations of existing laws.

THE SOCIALIZATION PROCESS AND SEX STEREOTYPING

Catalyst, a nonprofit research and advocacy group for women, took a census of women who are corporate officers and who rank among the top five earners at the nation's largest 500 companies (Dobrzynski, 1996). The census revealed that among the 12,997 corporate officers at those 500 firms, only 1,303 or 10 percent were women. Furthermore, among the 2,430 people holding the title of chairperson, chief executive, vice chairperson, president, chief operating officer, or executive vice president, only fifty-seven or 2.4 percent were women. Until recently the common explanation for the small number of female senior executives has been what Fisher (1992) called the *pipeline argument.* According to this argument women have not yet been in the managerial ranks long enough to allow them to gain the necessary knowledge and experience to rise to top managerial ranks. Females represented 15 percent of all managers in 1968. According to Ann Morrison, coauthor of *Breaking the Glass Ceiling* (Morrison, White, and Van Velsor, 1987), one could expect 15 percent of today's senior managers to be female. These figures are also unexpectedly low given that by 1981, 43 percent of all lower and middle managers were women.

A survey that analyzed the career progress of 1,000 male and female midlevel managers sheds further light on the subject (Segal and Zeltner, 1992). The managers all had comparable educational backgrounds, were career-oriented, and performed similar job functions. The survey showed that over the five-year period examined in the study the women's salary raises lagged 11 percent behind the men's. The women had also received fewer job transfers. The researchers stated the women had done all the same things, yet their progress was less and they earned less. Their overall conclusion was that the women had been discriminated against. The issue then becomes one of trying to explain what factors might help account for women's relatively slow rise in the managerial ranks over the past twenty-five years. There are two schools of thought on this matter (Feur, 1988). The first school believes women have not risen more rapidly in the corporate world due to external barriers. The second school attributes the problem to internal barriers to success.

External barriers mean that women must meet a more stringent set of behavior criteria than men to climb the corporate ladder (Morrison, White, and Van Velsor, 1987). Additional external factors that may impede women's progress include men in power having lower expectations for female employees, the exclusion of women from old-boy networks, women being assigned to powerless positions, and the relative lack of role models and mentors for women (Feur, 1988).

Internal barriers include the biological fact of maternity and typical female socialization (Schwartz, 1989). Traditional economists argue that women make work-related decisions based on their anticipated household and child-rearing responsibilities (Hood and Koberg, 1994). As a result, women are viewed as making an insufficient investment in their work skills and end up in low-pay, low-status positions. While some women do opt to limit their responsibilities in the workplace, the generalizations that a single woman will leave her job when she marries and a married woman will leave when she has a baby are simply no longer true (Buhler, 1991). In many cases a young couple needs two incomes to maintain their standard of living. According to the Families and Work Institute, 48 percent of married women in the workplace bring in half or more of their families' income (*Investor's Business Daily*, 1995). It was further noted that 11 percent of working women bring home more than half their families' income and 4 percent earn all the families' income. Women have also been socialized to the notion that they can have a family *and* a career. Furthermore, the generalization that women place family demands above work demands does not accurately describe women who choose a managerial career. In a study of the nation's highest-ranked female executives, nearly half had never married or were divorced (Baum, 1987). Of those who had married, almost one-third did not have children.

However, it does seem apparent that the way in which men and women have been socialized, and the resulting stereotypes, do play a role in the limited progress women have made in their attempt to climb the corporate ladder. Most parents, either consciously or unconsciously, express certain assumptions when raising their children (Sitterly and Duke, 1988). Qualities such as achievement, independence, self-reliance, and responsibility tend to be reinforced for boys. Adults tend to reinforce the qualities of attractiveness, kindness, lack of selfishness, and good behavior for girls. Sitterly and Duke (1988) state that these assumptions carry over into societal stereotypes that are difficult to overcome.

Stereotypical judgments of women's behavior have created a "catch 22" for women entering business (Sitterly and Duke, 1988). The catch is that when women engage in behavior typically associated with successful male executives (e.g., being demanding), they may be judged on women's stereotypes (i.e., being picky) rather than by objective evaluations of their actions (Sitterly and Duke, 1988).

Other misconceptions that negatively affect women in business follow (Hunsaker and Hunsaker, 1991):

1. *Men are intellectually superior to women*—Research does not support this viewpoint.
2. *Men value achievements and meaningful work more than women*— Work itself satisfies both men and women.
3. *Men are inherently more assertive than women*—Cultural conditioning may cause women to hide negative feelings such as hostility or aggressiveness (Heinen et al., 1975). Since women generally have been socialized to avoid or smooth over hostilities, females may find it more difficult to manage conflict within the organization. But the tendency of females to be more relationship oriented (Alpander and Guttman, 1976) can also be beneficial. An important aspect of the managerial task is building alliances and partnerships with employees, customers, and suppliers. Furthermore, although women may not inherently be as assertive as men, women can learn task roles requiring influence and assertiveness (Heinen et al., 1975).
4. *Women don't work for money*—This generalization is both true and false. Women work for the same reasons as men—for money, security, and self-fulfillment (Sitterly and Duke, 1988). One pervasive myth is that women would not work if they did not need the money. While this is true for some women (and some men as well), it is also true that many people would choose to remain employed as a means

of providing purpose and meaning to their lives. But it also must be recognized that some women are working out of sheer economic necessity. The divorce rate in the United States continues to be high, and the majority (87 percent) of all single-parent households are headed by women (Hunsaker and Hunsaker, 1991). Furthermore, uncertain economic conditions in recent times have impressed upon both women and men the importance of finding and keeping steady employment.

Sex roles and sex role stereotyping have made it especially difficult for women who seek career advancement through foreign job assignments. Women have traditionally been discouraged from applying for job positions in foreign countries (Feltes, Robinson, and Fink, 1993). Reasons include cultural differences that result in women not being accepted as business decision makers and no legal requirement for U.S. firms to consider women for such positions. Of particular interest is a Gallup poll of over 22,000 adults in Asia, Europe, North America, and Latin America. That study found that most women in most of the countries surveyed said they preferred working for a man (Burkins, 1996). Since international assignments are becoming more important for individuals seeking executive positions within a firm, despite the inherent difficulties, it is necessary for women to have opportunities to participate.

GENDER-BASED DISCRIMINATION

Sex role stereotyping entails making judgments about employees based on traditional stereotypes about gender (Kelly, Young, and Clark, 1993). While discrimination by sex is expressly prohibited by Section 703(e) of Title VII of the Civil Rights Act of 1964, exceptions are allowed for *bona fide occupational qualification* (BFOQ) reasonably necessary to the normal operation of that particular business or enterprise.

One case in which the U.S. Supreme Court held that gender was a BFOQ involved a rule adopted by the Alabama Board of Corrections. That rule excluded women from employment in jobs that required close contact with inmates in a maximum security prison for men (*Dothard v. Rawlinson*, 1977). The majority opinion was that women were likely to be victims of sexual assault, which would reduce their ability to maintain order in the prison. Since maintaining order in the prison is a primary job function, gender was ruled to be a BFOQ.

Another case involved a male applicant who sued Pan American World Airlines for rejecting him as a flight attendant. The federal court disallowed the airline's contention that women were superior to men in "providing reassurance to anxious passengers" and in "giving courteous personalized service" (*Diaz v. Pan American World Airways*, 1971). This sex discrimination case would be filed under a claim of disparate treatment. *Disparate treatment* involves conscious or intentional discrimination against an individual on the basis of sex.

Another form of sex discrimination is debated in the courts under the *disparate impact* theory. Under these circumstances an employer is guilty of discrimination in the absence of any intent when the effects are the same as if there had been an intent to discriminate (Boatright, 1997). An illustration of disparate impact discrimination would be a seemingly neutral employment requirement of three years' military experience for the position of police officer (Kelly, Young, and Clark, 1993). This policy would have the impact of excluding most women from consideration. Facially neutral employment tests or qualifications that have a disparate impact have generally been found to be illegal if those tests or requirements are not necessary for job performance.

The Price Waterhouse Case

An interesting case of disparate treatment sex stereotyping occurred in recent years (Kelly, Young, and Clark, 1993). Ann Hopkins was employed as a management consultant by Price Waterhouse. In the spring of 1982 Price Waterhouse was considering eighty-eight candidates for partnership. Ms. Hopkins was the only female among those eighty-eight individuals. At that time the firm had 662 senior partners, seven of whom were female. Ann appeared to be a likely candidate for partnership since she had billed more hours for consulting contracts than any of the other candidates in the fiscal year prior to the partnership nominations.

Comments on Ms. Hopkins' candidacy were submitted by thirty-two partners. Thirteen partners supported her bid, three recommended her candidacy be placed on hold, eight recommended denial of her request, and eight indicated they were unable to express an informed opinion. The final decision was to place Ms. Hopkins's candidacy on a one-year hold. The alleged reasons were poor interpersonal skills and unfeminine behavior. When Ann was informed of this decision by her male supervisor, the supervisor suggested that Ann should walk, talk, and dress more femininely, wear makeup, and have her hair styled. It should also be noted that some of the comments written by senior partners described Ms. Hopkins as macho, suggested she overcompensated for being a woman, and recommended she take a course at a charm school. She was also criticized for her use of profanity (Kelly, Young, and Clark, 1993).

During the following year, Hopkins's position with the senior partners deteriorated and she was not nominated for partnership. She resigned from Price Waterhouse and filed charges of sex discrimination under Title VII in the U.S. District Court for the District of Columbia. The court found in her favor. Three factors combined to produce discrimination: comments by partners based on sex stereotyping, an evaluation process that gave weight to those comments, and problems of stereotyping in the firm's evaluations that the company failed to address (*Hopkins v. Price Waterhouse*, 1985).

The case then went to the U.S. Court of Appeals. That court held this was a *mixed motive case* (*Hopkins v. Price Waterhouse*, 1987). Under these circumstances, there are both legitimate and illegitimate reasons for an employer's decision. The court ruled Price Waterhouse had legitimate concerns regarding Ms. Hopkins's ability to work well with subordinates and coworkers. Illegitimate issues revolved around her alleged "unfeminine" behavior. Since the court found that sex stereotyping contributed to Ms. Hopkins's denial of partnership, the court of appeals ruled in her favor.

Price Waterhouse then appealed the decision to the U.S. Supreme Court. This court held that in disparate treatment cases involving mixed motives the burden of proof could shift from the plaintiff (Ann Hopkins) to the defendant (Price Waterhouse). However, the Supreme Court rejected the clear and convincing standard and instead adopted a preponderance of evidence standard. This had the effect of reducing Price Waterhouse's burden of proof (*Price Waterhouse v. Ann B. Hopkins*, 1989). The case was then remanded to the U.S. District Court for the District of Columbia.

This court applied the rules set forth by the U.S. Supreme Court. To win, Price Waterhouse had to show by a preponderance of the evidence that Ms. Hopkins was denied partnership due to her poor human relations and management skills and not because of impermissible sex stereotyping in the review and evaluation process. Once again, Price Waterhouse lost the case. Ms. Hopkins was awarded back pay in the amount of $371,000 and Price Waterhouse was required to make her a partner (*Price Waterhouse v. Ann B. Hopkins*, 1990). This ruling sends a clear signal that firms may not base employment decisions on illegal forms of sex stereotyping.

Managerial Strategies for Reducing Sex Stereotyping

Given these kinds of lawsuits, it is suggested that employers try to reduce sex stereotyping in the workplace. Strategies for reducing problems that can arise from sex stereotyping in the workplace are shown in Table 10.3 (Kelly, Young, and Clark, 1993). These strategies are especially important now that the 1991 Civil Rights Act permits punitive damages in sex discrimination cases.

TABLE 10.3. Strategies for Reducing Sex Stereotyping

Foster commitment of top management	This group plays a critical role in establishing the corporate culture, and its leadership patterns are followed by other employees.
Adopt gender-neutral terms	Evaluations should be based on important job-related skills. Avoid comments that are gender specific.
Educate the workforce	In-house training sessions may be used to implement this strategy.
Conduct objective employment evaluations	Hiring, performance, and promotion evaluations should be based on job-related criteria.
Review workplace diversity	Try to identify areas where sex stereotyping may be occurring.
Institute family-friendly policies	Allow for job sharing, flextime, work-at-home arrangements, and parental leave. This reduces perceptions that women are less committed to the company than men.
Create a fair working environment	Use gender-neutral terms and constructive discussion.
Document employment decisions	Use gender-neutral reasons to explain why an individual was not hired, promoted, or retained.

WOMEN IN MANAGEMENT

Current perceptions suggest that women wield more power and influence in today's marketplace (Snavely, 1993). There are more women in the workforce; there are more college courses that focus on women's issues; and there are numerous articles and books written about working women. Yet this perception may be more myth than reality. A study found that both men and women continue to expect males to make better leaders (Powell, 1988). Also, when human resources professionals and undergraduate business students were asked to complete an instrument designed to assess their stereotypes about women as managers, the results showed that males in both groups held more unfavorable views about women as managers than did their female counterparts (Owen and Todor, 1993). It appears that discrimination toward female managers will not disappear in the foreseeable future and that companies still need to make concerted efforts through education and training to dispel beliefs that women managers are less capable.

Others have reported that women in managerial ranks face subtle discrimination in the form of stricter and more constraining expectations about appropriate behavior (Morrison, White, and Van Velsor, 1987). Also, women may be passed over for important assignments by men who are simply uncomfortable working with them or who assume women are not free to take on assignments due to family commitments (Owen and Todor, 1993).

WOMAN-TO-WOMAN MENTORING

For women to succeed in the workplace, it is important for them to form the type of mentoring relationships that have enabled men to advance in their chosen careers. *Mentoring* is a process in which individuals who are usually higher-level managers take junior employees under their wing and provide counseling or coaching. Building such supportive relationships, however, is often more difficult for women. Although women are generally known for their nurturing behavior and teamwork, the work environment changes the dynamics of the relationship.

Some of the difficulties that may be encountered follow (Parker and Kram, 1993):

1. *Disconnections between women*—When junior/senior women are paired in a mentoring relationship, the differences in career stages may limit self-disclosure, active listening, and feedback.
2. *Mentors may be seen as surrogate mothers*—Although this role can be both comforting and powerful, the outcome may be less than desired. The junior woman may be overpowered by a mother/mentor and the senior woman may be saddled with a daughter/protégé whose expectations may be impossible for her to fulfill.
3. *Search for self*—This concern is related to generational differences. The senior woman may have made the decision to devote herself to her career. The junior woman may have grown up in an environment in which she was encouraged to "have it all." The junior woman may fear choosing between these two options and also fear being judged for making a choice different from that made by her superior. On the other hand, the senior woman may resent the junior woman's expanded options.
4. *Search for the perfect mentor*—Sometimes the junior woman expects too much from the senior mentor. The junior woman believes the mentor will be empathetic, patient, and readily available. However, the mentor may have worked long and hard to win her coveted place

in the organization. She may feel the junior woman expects and demands preferential treatment and that compliance with those requests would undermine the mentor's legitimate authority.

5. *Tokenism concerns*—Woman-to-woman alliances are still relatively new in the workplace. This results in a very visible mentoring relationship. If the outcome is not successful or if the protégé falls short of expectations, the mentor may face accusations of poor judgment and/or poor coaching. Consequently, senior women may be reluctant to take on such a high-risk endeavor.

As the numbers of senior female managers increase, it is expected that some of the problems identified above will lessen (Parker and Kram, 1993). Mentoring relationships can provide a valuable growth experience for senior managers and can help them demonstrate their leadership abilities.

WOMEN AS ENTREPRENEURS

Women are forming small businesses at twice the rate of men (Goldman, 1994). There are approximately 6.5 million enterprises with fewer than 500 employees and almost one-third of those enterprises are owned or controlled by women. At present, one out of ten American workers is employed by a female-owned company. Reasons for this rapid growth in female-owned enterprises include the downsizing of corporate America, the so-called glass ceiling, which blocks women's entry to top-level positions, a desire to balance work and family, and a desire to accomplish more professionally. This growth in female entrepreneurship is not limited to services and neighborhood retail shops, although females are drawn to these areas due to low start-up costs. Increasing numbers of women are drawn to traditional male bastions such as manufacturing and construction (Goldman, 1994).

Studies that have been conducted over the years indicate that there are no significant differences between male and female entrepreneurs on personality dimensions (Buttner, 1993). Also, male and female entrepreneurs share similar motivations—the need to achieve, the desire for job satisfaction, and professional recognition. The survival rate for these business endeavors is also comparable for both sexes.

The primary gender-based differences for small-business ownership are that women report having to work harder to prove their competence to customers, suppliers, and other resource providers; men choose to operate their own businesses for business-based reasons, whereas women view the decision as a lifestyle choice; and if connections to networks of suppliers, customers, and bankers are important, women may be at a disadvantage since most of these needed advisors are men (Buttner, 1993).

The impact of women entrepreneurs may be greater than it first appears (Goldman, 1994). Women business owners emphasize training, teamwork, reduced hierarchy, and quality more than male entrepreneurs. This female style of management translates into an informal, consensus-building approach that may help businesses become more competitive in a global environment. Another important difference is that female entrepreneurs tend to measure success differently. While they are concerned about profits, they believe their ultimate success rests on the development of their employees and exceeding customer expectations.

SEXUAL HARASSMENT IN THE WORKPLACE

Although many people have heard about sexual harassment in the workplace, men and women alike are often unclear about what constitutes sexual harassment. The Equal Employment Opportunity Commission (1990) defines *sexual harassment* as any unwelcome sexual conduct that is a term or condition of employment or that creates an intimidating, hostile, or offensive work environment. In 1976 sexual harassment was first recognized as an illegal form of sexual discrimination. Sexual harassment usually falls into one of three categories (Harris-Lange, 1992): (1) *verbal*—comments, sexual jokes, or insults; (2) *nonverbal*—suggestive noises or gestures, leering, or offensive pictures; and (3) *physical* —unwanted touching. EEOC guidelines state that sexual harassment occurs when submission to this behavior is explicitly or implicitly a term or condition of employment; submission to or rejection of such conduct is a basis for employment decisions affecting that individual; or the conduct affects an employee's job performance or creates a hostile work environment. While the most common pattern of sexual harassment involves a male superior and a female subordinate, it should be noted that anyone can be victimized in the workplace and the particular circumstances can vary greatly. EEOC guidelines make a distinction between two types of harassment as described in the following sctions.

Quid Pro Quo

This involves a situation in which submission to sexual advances or requests is made a condition of receiving or keeping a job or job benefit (Dworkin, 1993). In this case a supervisor is using his legitimate power to extract sexual favors and the issue is usually more about abuse of that power than it is about sexual relations. The following conditions typify a quid pro quo sexual harassment court case (Dworkin, 1993): (1) the harassment must be committed by an employee who has power or control over a job benefit; (2) that employee must explicitly or implicitly threaten to exercise that power to deny the benefit if the desired behavior does not ensue; (3) because this abuse of power is seen as especially egregious, the behavior need only occur once to hold the employer liable; and (4) the employer is held strictly liable because the employer has empowered the supervisor with control over the job benefit.

Quid pro quo harassment violates Title VII of the Civil Rights Act. This provision states that men and women should not be treated differently in their compensation, terms, conditions, or privileges of employment. A woman who is promised a promotion or threatened with a demotion unless she performs certain sexual favors is being treated differently on the job simply because of her gender.

At first the courts were reluctant to view this type of sexual harassment as a form of sexual discrimination unless the victim had suffered economic loss. However, in 1981 a court held that sexual harassment is illegal even when there is no economic penalty. That court ruled that no woman should be forced to endure the psychological trauma of a sexually intimidating workplace as a condition of employment (*Bundy v. Jackson*, 1981).

Hostile Working Environment

This form of sexual harassment, first recognized by the Supreme Court in 1986, involves conduct on the part of co-workers and others that cause a woman (or man) to be very uncomfortable (Boatright, 1997). Hostile working environment is more pervasive than quid pro quo and is also harder to prove. This situation involves such things as sexual remarks and jokes, staring and suggestive leers, and unwanted sexual touching. This form of harassment rests on the belief that the employer should use its power to control the work environment so employees are not forced to tolerate offensive, intimidating, or abusive conditions in order to earn a living (Dworkin, 1993). The following conditions typify a hostile working environment case (Dworkin, 1993): (1) psychological harm is created by the employer's failure to control the workplace (no loss of job benefit is necessary); (2) the harassing behavior can be done by co-workers or a supervisor; (3) the employer is liable if it knew or should have known about the offensive behavior and failed to use its power to correct or stop it; and (4) the offensive behavior must have occurred with enough frequency to make the work environment hostile.

A survey of federal government employees found that 42 percent of the women who responded claimed that they had been sexually harassed on the job, while 14 percent of men reported similar experiences (*The New York Times,* 1988). But only 5 percent of the victims reported filing a formal complaint. Many victims do not report the problem because of embarrassment or anxiety, fear of reprisals, fear of not being believed, or concern that others will blame them for what happened. Others simply hope that by ignoring the problem it will go away.

It is important for firms to adopt a policy against sexual harassment; to expeditiously and thoroughly investigate complaints; and to take immediate and constructive action (McCalla, 1991). Controlling sexual harassment in the workplace is important for a couple of reasons: the cost of liability settlements can be prohibitive and the cost of lost productivity, absenteeism, turnover, and severance can also be substantial (Lawlor, 1995). Plus, it is the right thing to do.

SUMMARY

Women's roles in the U.S. workforce have evolved considerably over the course of the twentieth century. While great strides have been made in the acceptance of women as equals, we are still far from the egalitarian ideal in which gender would no longer be a relevant factor in employment decisions.

KEY TERMS

Equal Pay Act	National Family Leave	disparate treatment
Title VII of the Civil	Act	disparate impact
Rights Act	pipeline argument	mixed motive case
Equal Employment	external barriers	mentoring
Opportunity	internal barriers	sexual harassment
Commission	bona fide occupational	hostile working
Civil Rights Act of 1991	qualification	environment

DISCUSSION QUESTIONS

1. What was the first time in U.S. history that women entered the work force in significant numbers?

2. Name and describe factors that contributed to the entrance of women into the workplace.
3. Discuss some approaches that could be used to determine where a firm is on Felice Schwartz's 0-5 scale shown in Table 10.1.
4. Name and discuss two legal actions that helped women in the workplace.
5. Explain what is meant by internal and external barriers to women's success in the workplace.
6. What is a bona fide occupational qualification and how does it relate to gender-based employment discrimination?
7. What are the differences between the quid pro quo and hostile working environment types of sexual harassment?

REFERENCES

Alpander, Guvenc, and J. E. Guttman (1976). "Contents and Techniques of Management Development Programs for Women," *Personnel Journal,* (February): 26-79

Baum, Laurie (1987). "Corporate *Women," Business Week, 22* (June): 72.

Boatright, John (1997). *Ethics and the* Conduct of Business. Englewood Cliffs, NJ: Prentice-Hall.

Buhler, Patricia (1991). "Managing in the 90's," *Supervision* (November): 21.

Bundy v. Jackson (1981). 641, F. 2d 934 (D.C. Cir.).

Burkins, G. (1996). "Send her to Congress." *The Wall Street Journal,* March 26, 1(A).

Buttner, E. Holly (1993). "Female entrepreneurs: How far have they come?" *Business Horizons, 36* (March-April): 59-65.

Daily, Catherine (1993). "The (r)evolution of the American woman," *Business Horizons, 36* (March-April): 1-5.

Diaz v. Pan American World Airways (1971). 442, F.2d 385 (5th Cir.).

Dobrzynski, Judith (1996). "Study finds few women in 5 highest company jobs," *The New York Times,* 18 October, D4(L).

Dothard v. Rawlinson (1977). 433 U.S. 321.

Dworkin, Terry (1993). "Harassment in the 1990s," *Business Horizons, 36* (March-April): 52-58.

Edwards, Aubrey, S. B. Laporte, and A. Livingston (1991). "Cultural diversity in today's corporation," *Working Woman* (January): 45-61.

Equal Employment Opportunity Commission (1990). *Policy guidance on current issues of sexual harassment.* Washington, DC: Government Printing Office.

Feltes, Patricia, R. K. Robinson, and R. L. Fink (1993). "American female expatriates and the civil rights act of 1991: Balancing legal and business interests," *Business Horizons, 36* (March-April): 82-86.

Feur, Dale (1988). "How women manage," *Training* (August): 23-31.

Fisher, Anne (1992). "When will women get to the top?" *Fortune,* 21 September, 44.

Goldman, Gigi (1994). "Women entrepreneurs," *Business Week,* 18 April, 104.

Harris-Lange, Janet (1992). "Everybody's problem," *Entrepreneurial Woman* (May): 77-79.

Heinen, J. Stephen, Dorothy McGlauchin, Constance Lageros, and Jean Freeman (1975). "Developing the woman manager," *Personnel Journal, 54* (May): 282-289.

Himelstein, Linda (1997). "Breaking through," *Business Week,* 17 February: 64.

Hood, Jacqueline and C. Koberg (1994). "Patterns of differential assimilation and acculturation for women in business organizations," *Human Relations, 47:* 159-181.

Hopkins v. Price Waterhouse (1985). 618 F. Supp. 1109 (D.C.D.C.)

Hopkins v. Price Waterhouse (1987). 825, F.2d 458, (D.C. Cir.).

Hunsaker, Johanna, and P. Hunsaker (1991). *Strategies and skills for managerial women.* Cincinnati, OH: South-Western.

Investor's Business Daily (1995). "The new breadwinners." November 30.

Kelly, Eileen, A. Young, and L. S. Clark (1993). "Sex stereotyping in the workplace: A manager's guide," *Business Horizons, 36* (March-April): 23-29.

Lawlor, Julia (1995). "Stepping over the line," *Sales and Marketing Management,.* (October): 90-92,94,96,98,101.

McCalla, Robert (1991). "Stopping sexual harassment before it begins," *Management Review, 80* (April): 44-46.

Morrison, Ann, R. White and E. Van Velsor (1987). *Breaking the glass ceiling: Can women reach the top of america's largest corporations?* Reading, PA: Addison-Wesley.

The New York Times (1988). "Wide harassment of women working for US is reported." July 1, B6.

Owen, Crystal and W. D. Todor (1993). "Attitudes toward women as managers: Still the same," *Business Horizons, 36* (March-April): 12-16.

Parker, Victoria and K. Kram (1993). "Women mentoring women: Creating conditions for connection," *Business Horizons, 36* (March-April): 42-51.

Powell, Gary (1988). *Women and men in management.* Newbury Park, CA: Sage.

Price Waterhouse v. Ann B. Hopkins (1989). 109 S.Ct. 1775.

Price Waterhouse v. Ann B. Hopkins (1990). 737 F. Supp. 1202 (D.C.D.C.).

Rosenberg, Rosalind (1992). *Divided lives: American women in the twentieth century.* New York: Hill and Wang.

Schwartz, Felice (1989). "Women as a business imperative," *Harvard Business Review, 70* (March-April): 105-113.

Schwartz, Felice (1992). "Management women and the new facts of life," *Harvard Business Review, 67* (January-February): 65-76.

Segal, A. and W. Zeltner (1992). "Corporate women: How much progress?" *Business Week, 8* (June): 74.

Sitterly, Connie and B. Whitley Duke (1988). *A woman's place: Management.* Englewood Cliffs, NJ: Prentice-Hall.

Snavely, B. Kaye (1993). "Managing conflict over the perceived progress of working women," *Business Horizons, 32* (March-April): 17-22.

Chapter 11

Women and Education:
Women as Students and Teachers,
and in the Curriculum

Sylvia Stalker

INTRODUCTION

Women's place in the field of education is complex and multidimensional. As students, girls and women are often given different opportunities than their male counterparts. They are expected to achieve, or fail, in different academic areas, they are treated differently from their male peers by teachers and administrators, and often they are denied or limited in their access to particular areas of study. Recent work done by educators concerned with the "genderization" of learning has opened exciting and challenging approaches to enabling female students both to achieve in traditional, male-dominated fields and to give value to antipatriarchal, or feminist, ways of learning and knowing. The female student, then, is the first focus of this chapter on women in education.

Second, this chapter addresses women as teachers. Women are often assumed to have an inborn ability to teach, based upon their more private roles of childbearer and nurturer. However, it is the caregiving aspect of teaching that is considered appropriate for women, not the involvement with knowledge nor decision making. Women are thought to work most appropriately with young children, rather than with complex subject matter at higher grade levels. Changes are currently being seen in women's roles in the academic professions, especially in positions of leadership. In addition, feminist pedagogy has developed strategies for using the theory of feminism to change systems that limit all students' development, especially that of girls.

The place of women in the curriculum is the third aspect this chapter addresses. Women have been absent for too long in history textbooks and courses, as authors or subjects in literature, or as researchers and contributors in the sciences, humanities, and arts. The omission or inadequate presentation in traditional curricula of women's accomplishments in all fields of endeavor is a major concern, since it is through curriculum that learning occurs.

This chapter, then, presents recent research and practice in the field of education that contribute to our contemporary understanding of the role women have as learners and professionals, and how women are treated as a subject of study.

GIRLS AND WOMEN AS STUDENTS

> [S]chool success is awarded to the student with an analytical, cognitive learning style, one who is individualistic, independent, competitive, and able to engage in highly abstract, analytical, linear, and logical thinking. (McCormick, 1994, p. 63)

Theresa McCormick (1994), in her book *Creating the Nonsexist Classroom: A Multicultural Approach*, suggests that the values and practices most prevalent in schools today encourage children to develop knowledge and skills that are considered appropriate for males and inappropriate for females. Girls and women students are forced to function in a system that rewards analytical thinking, typically attributed to males in our society, and denies or disregards feelings and intuition as significant factors in learning and knowing. Schools reward independence and competition, qualities that are encouraged and expected in young boys, yet often considered unfit for girls, who we teach to be dependent on others and to work cooperatively with peers.

From infancy and throughout childhood, girls and boys are treated differently from one another and are taught to behave and learn differently. The old nursery rhymes telling us that girls and boys are made of sugar and spice, snips and snails, respectively, may not be as well-known among today's children as they were several generations ago, but they are still a part of our cultural expectation. Girls are sweet, docile, and agreeable, or at least they should be, while boys are expected to be rambunctious and playful.

Many parents and teachers today realize that damage is done to girls and boys, too, when they are limited by expectations and stereotypes. *Title IX of the Education Amendments of 1972* prohibits sex discrimination in education programs receiving federal funds. Since almost all school districts in the United States receive some type of federal funding, compliance with Title IX has necessarily been a concern to school administrators since it became the law.

Issues of gender equity in schools have also been a part of the national discussion on school reform since about the same time as the passage of Title IX. In 1973, Nancy Frazier and Myra Sadker wrote the first major book on the subject, *Sexism in School and Society,* and many other important studies have followed (Orenstein, 1994; Sadker and Sadker, 1995; Wellesley, 1995). The *Women's Educational Equity Act,* passed in 1974, began providing a wealth of resources for educators concerned with sex equity, as it was then named, and hundreds of seminars and workshops were held all over the United States to educate practicing teachers about the constraints of sexism and strategies for overcoming them.

In *Failing at Fairness: How Our Schools Cheat Girls,* Myra and David Sadker (1995) report on their extensive studies of classrooms across the United States over the twenty-five-year period since 1972. The AAUW report *How Schools Shortchange Girls* (Wellesley, 1995), reflects over five years of work and over 1,300 studies, including the work done by the Sadkers. The findings do not indicate a much more positive picture than that of the early 1970s. Girls are still cheated by teachers' behaviors and the school culture in many ways.

Sex Differences in Messages in the Classroom

What are the behaviors and messages that children learn in the classroom? How, specifically, do girls learn to function in schools? For one, girls are taught to be dependent through their interactions with teachers and classmates. Girls ask for help, and receive it, more frequently than boys. Teachers give boys more thorough directions on how to accomplish tasks for themselves than girls. Teachers are less likely to offer explanations and directions to girls. Instead, teachers do it for them (Sadker and Sadker, 1995).

Girls may also learn in the elementary classroom that they are less important than boys. Across all types of coeducational classrooms, with female or male teachers, the AAUW report concludes that males receive more teacher attention than do females (Wellesley, 1995).

Differences in the type and content of teachers' comments to girls and boys reveal another lesson to students. The Sadkers identified four types of teacher comments to students in classrooms they observed: praise, acceptance, remediation, and criticism. Boys in their study received more of each type of comment than girls; the smallest difference between comments to girls and boys was in acceptance. While girls receive an "OK," "all right," or "yes" from teachers, boys much more frequently hear comments that reward their actions and thinking, as well as identify, clarify, or correct their errors (Wellesley, 1995). Girls are intellectually challenged less by teachers, and as they continue through school, their self-confidence diminishes along with their academic achievement (Sadker and Sadker, 1995).

As girls lose self-esteem, the Sadkers report, they begin to underestimate their ability. Girls believe that they must work harder to be adequate at the tasks presented to them. The Sadkers conclude that girls believe that they can also achieve, but that they have to try harder in order to do so.

In Collette Dowling's (1981) book, *The Cinderella Complex: Women's Hidden Fear of Independence*, she describes the process of girls becoming helpless. Girls, she suggests, become dependent precisely because tasks are made too easy for them and because they are overprotected. Girls learn that "good" girls receive help, and that all they have to do to keep the help coming is be "good." Dowling identified passivity and a dependent orientation toward adults as the most stable and predictable of all female character traits across all educational levels.

Sex Differences in Pursuit of Subject Areas

Differences in gender stereotypes not only influence the ways in which children approach learning, they also have an impact on which subject areas students pursue and are able to achieve. Mathematics and the sciences are traditionally seen as more difficult than the humanities. They are also considered "male" subjects. Girls are protected from the intellectual challenges of engaging in these fields by a society that reinforces gender stereotypes. Girls who need help at difficult tasks and who accept stereotyped expectations that certain academic areas are more appropriate for males are less likely to engage and achieve in them. On the other hand, girls who reject traditional gender roles and report that they do not see math as a "male" subject achieve higher in math than their traditional female classmates (Wellesley, 1995). What exactly are the differences in achievement and participation between male and female students? In what academic areas are differences found? Why do they exist?

Verbal abilities have commonly been assumed to be greater in girls than in boys. The AAUW report (Wellesley, 1995) surveyed recent studies that used standardized test scores such as the Scholastic Achievement Test (SAT), the National Assessment of Educational Progress (NAEP), and the National Education Longitudinal Survey (NELS). The AAUW report concludes that differences do exist in verbal abilities, but that they have decreased markedly over the past twenty years. Girls outscore boys on tests of verbal ability, but the difference is insignificant or nonexistent in some studies.

Girls perform better than boys on most reading tests, concludes the AAUW report (Wellesley, 1995), but the differences are very small. In the

NAEP reading tests, boys did less well on items relating to literary passages but as well as girls on expository passages. It is very possible that these differences reflect culturally defined biases. Boys prefer and read more nonfiction than girls, and girls read more fiction than boys (NAEP, cited in Wellesley, 1995).

Mathematics achievement is an area in which gender differences are found, but a significant decline in differences has been found since the mid-1970s (Wellesley, 1995). Gender differences in mathematics achievement are small, but they vary across grade levels and are greater at the higher grades. Girls and boys score about the same in problem-solving ability in elementary and middle school, but by high school, males score higher. Males outscore females on the SAT-Math, as well as the Preliminary Scholastic Aptitude Test (PSAT) (Wellesley, 1995).

In the sciences, boys outperform girls but, unlike mathematics, gender differences in science achievement are not decreasing. In fact, differences between females and males in science achievement may be increasing. The NAEP test results indicate that between 1978 and 1986, gender differences in science achievement increased for nine- and thirteen-year-old students. For seventeen-year-olds, gender differences in science achievement are largest, but they did not shift over this period of time (Wellesley, 1995).

Differences in participation in mathematics and science courses have been reported by the National Science Board of the National Science Foundation and were included in the AAUW report. In mathematics, females and males take the same courses up to calculus, which is taken by 7.6 percent of the boys but only 4.7 percent of the girls (Wellesley, 1995). In the sciences, girls are more likely to take advanced biology and boys are more frequently enrolled in physics and chemistry. Overall, after four years of high school, girls have taken 3.1 science courses compared to 3.3 for boys (National Science Board, cited in Wellesley, 1995).

Sex Differences in Learning Styles

Do female students approach learning and knowing differently? How can girls and women achieve in subjects which they consider difficult and more appropriate for males? How can they achieve in classrooms where they may learn that they are less important and less able?

In their 1986 study, *Women's Ways of Knowing*, Belenky et al. researched these questions and interviewed hundreds of women enrolled in different educational programs. They concluded that women feel alienated in many academic settings and find much of formal education peripheral to their lives. They argue that approaches to learning and teaching need to be more closely aligned with women's development as learners in order for them to succeed.

Belenky and colleagues found that women view and know the world through five different "ways" or stages:

- *Silence.* A position in which women experience themselves as essentially mindless and voiceless, subject to the whims of external authority.
- *Received knowledge.* A perspective from which women conceive of themselves as capable of receiving, even reproducing, knowledge from all-knowing external authorities but not capable of creating knowledge on their own.
- *Subjective knowledge.* A perspective from which truth and knowledge are conceived of as personal, private, and subjectively known or intuited.
- *Procedural knowledge.* A position in which women are invested in learning and applying objective procedures for obtaining and communicating knowledge.
- *Constructed knowledge.* A position in which women view all knowledge as contextual, experience themselves as creators of knowledge, and value both subjective and objective strategies for knowing.

There are dangers in readily accepting differences in learning styles between male and female learners. Differences from the dominant (male) methods of learning can be seen as deficits. The too-easy response to gender differences in learning approaches is to call for remediation of the students (female) rather than to examine the instructor or the curriculum.

One response to differences among male and female learners is an argument that single-sex education would be more beneficial to girls and women than coeducation (Monaco and Gaier, 1992; Caplice, 1994; Simpson, 1996). Supporters of single-sex classes believe that girls and boys have different learning styles; in short, girls learn cooperatively while boys learn competitively. They believe that separating the sexes would raise girls' self-esteem and confidence, enhance their leadership and oral communication skills, boost their standardized text scores, and increase their interest in advanced course work in the traditionally male subjects (Simpson, 1996). Results of a 1992 study by the National Coalition of Girls' Schools support this last conclusion. The study found that 48 percent of seniors at all-girl schools said they would pursue math, science, business, or engineering degrees in college—nearly double the national average for girls (cited in Saltzman, 1996).

Kristin Caplice (1994) analyzed the hidden curriculum through which schools perpetuate the subordination of women in society in building her case for single-sex schools. Students in coeducational classrooms learn that girls are quiet, passive, and not as capable as boys, but when girls are with only other girls, they gain confidence and shed inhibitions. Girls' self-confidence and motivation, typically at a decrease during the adolescent years in coeducational settings, have a greater chance to grow in single-sex settings, and has increased academic achievement.

This writer's experience in a four-year women's college affords me a personal perspective on the issue of single-sex schooling. Although I believe that there are appropriate uses of single-sex education at this moment in history, I could not advocate its use extensively. Educators can learn a great deal from study of single-sex schooling, and for individuals, these experiments may result in both immediate and long-term benefits. However, our society needs individuals who can work with each other. Few individuals do not have to function in a mixed social or work setting, and although the study of single-sex institutions contributes to our knowledge and understanding of learning and teaching, we need to address gender, race, and class inequities present in our public schools and reform existing systems.

WOMEN TEACHERS

This section of the chapter on women and education addresses issues about teachers and their work and the impact of the feminist movement on teachers and teaching, primarily through the development of feminist pedagogy.

Women are approximately 72 percent of the public school teachers in the United States today (Wellesley, 1995), a proportion that is surprisingly close to the 67 percent in 1888 (Rothman, 1978). In the principal's office, however, women are fewer than 30 percent, and in the superintendency, women are fewer than 5 percent (Wellesley, 1995).

During the 1850s, champion of the common school movement Horace Mann promoted hiring women as teachers because they could be paid lower salaries than men (Morian, cited in Grumet, 1988). Catharine Beecher, founder of the Central Committee for Promoting National Education, also justified lower wages for women. In a petition to Congress in 1853 asking for free normal schools for female teachers, Beecher wrote:

> To make education universal, it must be moderate in expense, and women can afford to teach for one half, or even less the salary which men would ask, because the female teacher has only to sustain herself; she does not look forward to the duty of supporting a family,

should she marry; nor has she the ambition to amass a fortune. (Sklar, 1973, p. 182)

Beecher also believed that women were more suited than men to the work of teaching because they were more "benevolent" and more willing to "make sacrifices of personal enjoyment." She saw school as an extension of the domestic culture of the home where women could work "not for money, not for influence, nor for honour, nor for ease, but with the simple, single purpose of doing good" (Hoffman, 1981, p. 10).

Woman's True Profession (Hoffman, 1981) is an important collection of autobiographical writings, essays, and short stories about teaching in the United States between 1830 and 1920. The personal perspectives of the writings provide a significant contribution to a field in which the work of women has been primarily only the object of study. In some cases, teachers' perspectives do not conform to popularly held views of women teachers, such as those of Beecher or Mann. For example, teaching is often considered either an extension or a substitution for mothering. Writings that editor Nancy Hoffman includes in the book reveal that the need for satisfying work and an income were far greater motivators for many women entering teaching. Many women chose teaching instead of marriage, since the roles of wife and teacher were incompatible well into the twentieth century in most states. Many others chose teaching because it provided opportunity to foster social, political, or spiritual change.

Madeleine R. Grumet (1988), in *Bitter Milk: Women and Teaching*, draws upon the fields of curriculum theory and gender studies to examine the work of teachers. She argues that an understanding of the close relationship between the public and private worlds of teachers can inform our understanding of what we teach children and how we do it. As primary caregivers and nurturers in the family, women teach children—often unintentionally—that knowledge evolves in human relationships. As mothers contribute to the future through the processes of biological reproduction and nurturance, teachers contribute through ideological and critical nurturance.

Dorothy Dinnerstein, in *The Mermaid and the Minotaur: Sexual Arrangements and Human Malaise*, argues that as long as women provide the primary parenting of children, both males and females will "seek the paternal order as a refuge from the domination of mother" (cited in Grumet, 1988, p. 25). The female teacher, then, in representing the primary parent in the domestic world and yet the immediate authority figure for children in the public world, is full of contradictions and possibilities for herself as well as for her students.

The predominance of women in teaching and the view that teaching is an extension of parenting and, therefore, most appropriate for women, are factors in the process now identified as the "feminization" of teaching. Michael Apple (1986), in *Teachers and Texts: A Political Economy of Class and Gender Relations in Education*, argues that teaching is currently undergoing a protelarianization caused, in part, by curricula and technology that de-skill teachers' independence and creativity, and by worsening working conditions. He argues that the study of the close relationship between gender and class can help us understand what is happening to teaching and curriculum today, and help us to transform educational systems.

FEMINIST PEDAGOGY

Theories of *feminist pedagogy* have emerged over the past several decades which emphasize the valuing of individuals' contributions to the learning environment, often through strategies of collaboration, reflection, and constructivist learning. At its most basic, feminist pedagogy reflects good teaching that seeks to alter patterns of male dominance in educational systems and enable teachers to provide fair and equitable opportunities for all students.

In 1982, the need for feminist pedagogy was clearly documented in Roberta M. Hall and Bernice Sandler's *The Classroom Climate: A Chilly One for Women?* The writers identified over 30 ways teachers treat female and male students differently. The report inspired self-studies on many campuses and in many schools, as well as a great deal of research at all levels of schooling to study teachers' behaviors and their effects on classroom participation.

In 1996, Lisa A. Silverberg joined Hall and Sandler in authoring a second report, *The Chilly Classroom Climate: A Guide to Improve the Education of Women*. They acknowledge that students come to school with different backgrounds and experiences, and they also incorporate an understanding of the intersections of gender, race, ethnicity, and economic status of students and teachers. The 1996 report recognizes that classrooms are still chilly climates for many students. They point to teachers as the most crucial factor in changing students' participation and academic success.

Based upon the liberatory teaching theory of Paulo Freire and John Dewey's progressive educational theory, feminist pedagogy extends teaching further in addressing questions of gender, race, and class. The theme of two recent issues of *Women's Studies Quarterly* (1987 and 1993), feminist pedagogy is defined in the opening article of the latter as:

> a theory about the teaching/learning process that guides our choice of classroom practices by providing criteria to evaluate specific educational strategies and techniques in terms of the desired course

goals or outcomes. These evaluative criteria include the extent to which a community of learners is empowered to act responsibly toward one another and the subject matter and to apply that learning to social action. (Shrewsbury, 1993, p. 8)

Focusing on the active participation of students and teachers in the learning processes, Shrewsbury goes on to identify feminist pedagogy as teaching/learning that is engaged at several levels: with self, through reflection and analysis; with content; with other learners to confront sexism, racism, classism, homophobia, and other destructive hatreds; and with community, to effect social change.

Central themes of feminist pedagogy are useful to an understanding of the underlying values and classroom strategies used. Shrewsbury identifies three themes: empowerment, community, and leadership (pp. 10-14), which overlap with the five themes named by Sandler, Silverberg, and Hall (1996): neutrality, experience, inclusion, nonhierachical classrooms, and participation (pp. 40-41).

Neutrality

Feminist pedagogy challenges the myth of neutral or value-free education. All education reflects the values of someone, usually the instructor, who selects the content to be learned, the context for teaching, and the teaching methods.

Experience

Feminist pedagogy acknowledges personal experience as an important factor in learning and as an appropriate subject of inquiry. An assumption is that learning is enhanced when students are able to relate content to their own lives.

Inclusion

Feminist pedagogy challenges the politics of all forms of domination: gender, race, class, and ethnicity. Curriculum as well as methods of teaching, should be inclusive.

Nonhierarchical Classrooms

Feminist pedagogy questions the traditionally accepted classroom process of teachers transmitting knowledge to students, usually through lectures, and promotes the view that learning is an interactive process through which students are able to construct knowledge. The "talking head" model of instruction is challenged and is replaced with a model of the instructor as a facilitator with particular knowledge and experience. Two useful images characterize the feminist teacher: one who "seeks authority with, not authority over students" (Culley and Portuges, 1985, p. 15) and the "midwife teacher" who draws knowledge out (Belenky et al., 1986).

Empowering Students—Participation

In addition to active participation in their own learning, feminist pedagogy is an effort to empower students, through learning, with the knowledge and skills needed outside the classroom in order to effect social change. The classroom, then, becomes a community of learners that supports individual development and mutuality.

Collaborative learning, involving small groups of students who share in each other's learning and success, is especially appropriate in a feminist classroom. It encourages girls and women to participate, and it de-emphasizes traditional, individual competition while promoting listening and cooperation.

Nancy Schniedewind (1993), in her article "Teaching Feminist Process in the 1990s," describes feminist process skills that students learn through feminist pedagogy: communicating, developing a democratic group process, cooperating, integrating theory and practice, and networking and organizing. She stresses that students educated in traditional classrooms do not have the opportunity to participate actively and equally in a democratic classroom. For example, she prescribes communication exercises in which students learn to share feelings, differentiate between thoughts and feelings, and give constructive feedback to peers.

Students also learn to resolve conflicts, take on a variety of leadership roles in groups, and to work in groups in which each student's participation is essential to the group's successful completion of its task. In higher education and even in some high schools, feminist pedagogy provides opportunities for students to apply theory and practice through fieldwork. Student teaching, for example, is an opportunity for applying learned theories of education and feminist pedagogy in classrooms. By analyzing and evaluating their teaching, student teachers recreate theory and continue a process that they will use in their lives and careers.

WOMEN AND GIRLS IN THE CURRICULUM

Curriculum can be conceived of in several aspects. In its most limiting sense, curriculum is the guidebook containing instructional content and suggested strategies for its delivery. This is the formal, or intended curriculum. As a nearly static entity, the *formal curriculum* is readily accessible for study. Researchers interested in the portrayal of women and girls in the formal curriculum began examining the pages of textbooks in the 1970s, the same time as the beginnin work done on teachers' treatment of gender differences in the classroom.

Women on Words and Images published a major study, *Dick and Jane as Victims*, in 1975, and reported that the ratio of males and females in elementary school reading books was far from equal. Males outnumbered females as central characters in stories (5:1), as biographical figures (6:1), and as adult characters (3:1).

Illustrations in texts and children's literature were also extensively studied in the 1970s. Typically, researchers found proportions of illustrations of women to men similar to the ratios in text, but stereotypical gender roles and activities were more readily obvious. In one study, researchers found that girls and women watched boys and men do interesting things. Women were portrayed as housewives, teachers, or nurses, while men were portrayed in over 150 different jobs (Weitzman and Rizzo, 1974).

In the 1990s, curriculum is once again the focus of research on gender differences in education. Myra and David Sadker (1995) examined math, language arts, and history textbooks used in the intermediate grades and found ratios of 3:1 and 2:1 of males to females in illustrations. One widely used 1992 social studies textbook, intended for sixth graders, contained not even one adult American woman. The Sadkers suggest that when students do not learn about women through the curriculum, they fill in the gaps with their own stereotypes and distortions, already prevalent in the larger society.

The *null curriculum* is a useful concept for consideration of women's place in the curriculum. When women are excluded from curriculum materials, we can consider their portrayal as an empty set. History books that emphasize military and political leaders, for example, are likely to place women's activities in the null curriculum, as well as the contributions of working class and poor people.

The Sadkers provide a clear example of the null curriculum in the story of Catherine Littlefield Greene. Greene worked with Eli Whitney in developing the cotton gin. A flaw in Whitney's model caused the cotton seeds to clog, but Greene created a successful machine by using brushes to remove them. In addition, Greene sold her estate and paid for the legal battles in order to win the patent for Whitney.

Are publishers and writers solely to blame for the omission of Catherine Littlefield Greene from our common knowledge about the invention of the cotton gin? A richer and more complex context for the story includes consideration of women's roles in the 1780s and the factors present in that society which limited their participation. Women simply did not own property, write books, or register for patents at that time in history. Do our history books tell us these facts? Sexism and racism have denied people opportunities to participate in the economic, political, and intellectual society throughout history. The lessons learned by studying such examples of discrimination are essential ones, many educators would contend. Studying material identified in the null curriculum and making it overt can be considered part of a liberatory curriculum, especially when learners are able to apply their understanding of bias and discrimination to their own lives.

A third concept of curriculum includes not only the intentional, formal learning that takes place in schools, but also the unintended learning that simultaneously occurs as a result of the systems and structures of schooling. This *hidden curriculum* includes the personnel of a school and people's relationships to each other. Are all or most teachers women, and are the administrators men? Who supervises and evaluates whom, and how? Is the custodial staff composed equally of women and men, or primarily of minorities? Who makes major decisions in the schools? Who does not?

Classroom structures that compose the hidden curriculum teach students about the society which schools reflect and reproduce. What is the place of women, men, or minorities within that society? Are all students treated equally in school? Do teachers' behaviors demonstrate that all students are expected to achieve and succeed? Is being in the classroom a pleasant experience for students, or it is threatening, or irrelevant?

Questions of the hidden curriculum are some of the same issues to which feminist pedagogy is addressed. An analysis of the unintended and typically harmful lessons that students learn about themselves and others through the hidden curriculum has led to the development of multicultural and nonsexist teaching strategies to combat and overcome stereotypes, bias, and discrimination. Study of a school's hidden curriculum shares many of the same concerns as a study of the null curriculum: why do bias and discrimination exist to such a great extent, and who benefits and who is harmed by them?

In addition to the exclusion of girls and women in the curriculum (identified in this writing as the null curriculum), other forms of sex bias have been named and studied. Stereotyping of members of both sexes is common in curriculum materials, as is the subordination or degradation of girls and women. Material on women and minorities is often isolated, rather than integrated in curriculum, or it is treated superficially.

James Banks, a leader in the field of multicultural education, has formulated approaches for correcting bias and integrating women and minority groups in the curriculum. He describes four levels of curriculum: (1) the contribution approach, which focuses on heroes, holidays, and discrete cultural elements; (2) the additive approach, in which content and themes are added to the curriculum without changing its structure; (3) the transformation approach, in which the structure is changed to enable students to view concepts, issues, events, and themes in diverse ways; and (4) the social action approach, in which students take action to help solve important social issues (Banks, 1989).

Banks's first two approaches are readily apparent in schools today. For example, February is Black History Month, during which lessons on famous black Americans are taught and bulletin boards display appropriate heroes and events. Similarly, March is Women's History Month. Isolating the study of minorities and women in this manner actually marginalizes them, reinforcing their position in society as outside the mainstream and worthy of only a fraction of the whole curriculum.

Levels three and four, however, reflect curriculum that is pluralistic and liberatory. When students learn to see events and issues from other perspectives, they learn to value both human diversity and commonalities. When students learn about bias and discrimination, for example, their recognition is a primary step toward changing harmful systems and structures.

CONCLUSION

I want to use a student's voice in concluding this chapter because her words connect the three themes I have used: students, teachers, and curriculum. She is African American and was a twelfth-grader in a New York-area urban high school in 1991 when she was interviewed by the Sadkers:

> In twelve years of school, I never studied anything about myself. (Wellesley, 1995, p. 105)

This student did not learn in school about people she considered to represent her ethnicity or culture, her socioeconomic class, or her sex. She considered herself outside the curriculum, and she regarded the formal content as irrelevant to herself. She saw her teachers as different from herself, rather than as people whose work and values she could adopt. We can assume, too, that no teacher was able to provide opportunities for her to want to learn and achieve.

Students, teachers, and curriculum must be different from the example of school failure this student's statement represents. Work done by the researchers and theorists I have included in this chapter contribute to our understanding of women in education and to efforts to help schools change, but progress has not been adequate. A system in which the following statement is heard from every student—"I've learned a lot in school about myself, the world, and my place in it"—exists only in our imaginations.

KEY TERMS

Title IX of the Education Amendments of 1972
Women's Educational Equity Act
feminist pedagogy

formal curriculum
null curriculum
hidden curriculum

DISCUSSION QUESTIONS

1. What are the different behaviors and messages that boys and girls learn in the classroom? How do they learn them?
2. What are the differences in achievement and participation between male and female students? In what academic areas are differences found? Why do they exist?
3. Do female students approach learning and knowing differently than male students? How? Should there be any changes in teaching techniques to accommodate these differences? If so, what?

REFERENCES

Apple, Michael W. (1986). *Teachers and texts: A political economy of class and gender relations in education.* New York: Routledge.

Banks, James (1989). "Integrating the curriculum with ethnic content: Approaches and guidelines." In *Multicultural education: Issues and perspectives,* J. Banks and C. Banks (Eds.). Boston, MA: Allyn and Bacon.

Belenky, Mary Field, Blythe Clinchy, Nancy Goldberger, and Jill Tarule (1986). *Women's ways of knowing: The development of self, voice, and mind.* New York: Basic Books, Inc.

Caplice, Kristin (1994). "The case for public single-sex education," *Harvard Journal of Law and Public Policy, 18 (1):* 1-32.

Culley, Margo and Catherine Portuges (Eds.) (1985). *Gendered subjects: The dynamics of feminist teaching.* Boston: Routledge and Kegan Paul.

Dowling, Collette (1981). *The Cinderella complex: Women's hidden fear of independence.* New York: Summitt Books.

Frazier, Nancy, and Myra Sadker (1973). *Sexism in school and society.* New York: Harper & Row.

Grumet, Madeleine R. (1988). *Bitter milk: Women and teaching.* Amherst: The University of Massachusetts Press.

Hall, Roberta M. and Bernice R. Sandler (1982). *The classroom climate: A chilly one for women?* Washington, DC: Project on the Status and Education of Women, Association of American Colleges.

Hoffman, Nancy (1981). *Woman's true profession: Voices from the history of teaching.* New York: The Feminist Press.

McCormick, Theresa Mickey (1994). *Creating the nonsexist classroom: A multicultural approach.* New York: Teachers College Press.

Monaco, Nanci M. and Eugene L. Gaier (1992). "Single-sex versus coeducational environment and achievement in adolescent females," *Adolescence, 27 (107):* 579.

Orenstein, Peggy (1994). *School girls: Young women, self-esteem, and the confidence gap.* New York: Doubleday.

Rothman, Sheila (1978). *Woman's proper place.* New York: Basic Books.

Sadker, Myra and David Sadker (1995). *Failing at fairness: How our schools cheat girls.* New York: Touchstone.

Saltzman, Amy (1996). "A look at the research: Lots on girls, little on boys," *U.S. News & World Report,* July 8, 52.

Sandler, Bernice R., Lisa A. Silverberg, and Roberta M. Hall (1996). *The chilly classroom climate: A guide to improve the education of women.* Washington, DC: The National Association for Women in Education.

Schniedewind, Nancy (1993). "Teaching feminist process in the 1990s," *Women's Studies Quarterly, 21(3&4)* Fall/Winter: 17-30.

Shrewsbury, Carolyn M. (1993). "What is feminist pedagogy?" *Women's Studies Quarterly,* 21(*3&4*): 8-15.

Simpson, Michael D. (1996). "What's the verdict?" *NEA Today, 15(3):* 25.

Sklar, Kathryn K. (1973). *Catharine Beecher.* New Haven: Yale University Press.

Weitzman, Lenore and Diane Rizzo (1974). *Biased textbooks: A research perspective.* Washington, DC: The Research Center of Sex Roles in Education.

Wellesley(1995). *How schools shortchange girls—The AAUW report: A study of major findings on girls and education.* Wellesley College Center for Research on Women. New York: Marlowe & Company.

Women on Words and Images (1975). *Dick and Jane as victims: Sex stereotyping in children's readers.* Princeton, NJ: Women on Words and Images.

Women's Studies Quarterly (1987). Feminist pedagogy, 15 (*3,4*), Fall/Winter.

Women's Studies Quarterly (1993). Feminist pedagogy: An update, 21 (*3,4*), Fall/ Winter.

Chapter 12

Gender and Communication: The Influence of Gender on Language and Communication

Myrna Foster-Kuehn

The latest buzz on sex differences, the hottest development in the debate on homemaking versus careerism, or the newest take on how to resolve confusion over interpersonal relationships between women and men seems to be waiting on the next headline or talk show lineup. Issues dividing women and men hold a perpetual interest for us. And why not? Our gender and our need to communicate with others are inescapable facts of life. Gender communication is the fabric of our daily lives. But what exactly *is* gender communication?

A simple answer would be that studying gender and communication is learning about how women and men talk differently? But when we take a closer look at that basic idea, things get more complicated. The answer is not as easy as it would seem. Some say that not all communication is gender communication (Ivy and Backlund, 1994), while others believe that communication cannot escape the effects of gender and therefore all communication is "gendered" (Schaef, 1981; Thorne, Kramarae, and Henley, 1983; Spender and Kegan, 1985). Although gender and sex are sometimes used interchangeably, the two concepts have very distinct meanings.

Once you begin learning about gender and communication, it readily becomes apparent that gender is more than simple biological classifications, and communication is more than just talk. This chapter provides an overview of the various approaches to understanding "gender and communication" by examining the definitions of gender and communication, the social construction of gender communication, how the language usage of women and men reflects and shapes our daily interactions, and how anyone can become a more competent communicator.

DEFINING GENDER AND COMMUNICATION

Sex and Gender

Most of us have very little difficulty filling out forms that ask us to indicate our sex. Our choices are naturally simple: male or female. *Sex* is a designation based on biology. We use genetic and biological qualities to define whether a person is female or male. Each of us is labeled at birth based on observable physical evidence, that is, the nature of the genitalia. We assume that, except in very extreme cases, most individuals are clearly one sex or the other and will grow and develop accordingly. Our daily interactions are not as clear-cut, however. How often do parents carefully pick the "right" color baby clothes for their newborn to avoid those awkward social moments? The *Saturday Night Live* television comedy show enjoyed a great spoof on gender identity confusion with their "Pat" character, who kept people guessing whether she was he or he was she.

Fascinating stories about individuals who pass for the opposite sex suggest that outward appearance and display are not necessarily conclusive evidence of sex. It was recently in the news that jazz musician Billy Tipton, who had lived life as a man, was discovered (upon her death February 1, 1997) to be a woman. The secret was well kept. Billy Tipton was married until ten years ago. The couple adopted three sons, who apparently had not learned the truth until after Tipton died at the age of seventy-four. Clearly while genetic codes and biological definitions can be specifically denoted, they cannot be used to accurately ascribe specific behaviors, communication or otherwise.

While sex is a classification based on genetic factors, and not easily subject to change, gender is socially and psychologically constructed. *Gender* refers to the masculine, feminine, or *androgynous* characteristics of individuals. Wood (1997) points out that gender "is neither innate nor necessarily stable. It is acquired through interaction in a social world, and it changes over time" (pp. 25-26). Thorne, Kramarae, and Henley (1983) explain, "Gender is not a unitary, or 'natural' fact, but takes shape in concrete, historically changing social relationships" (p. 16). In other words, gender is learned. Socially endorsed views of masculinity and femininity are taught to individuals through a variety of cultural means.

Communication

We are living in the "communication age." Technology has become so sophisticated that we can easily and quickly access information and people around the world. As the channels for communicating have expanded, so have the meanings of the term *communication*. Back in the 1970s, Dance and Larson (1976) isolated 126 definitions of communication. It is sufficient to suggest that communication is very complex and difficult to define. In very broad terms, communication can be defined such that "(1) humans are thought to be social creatures constantly in search of meaning in a social world, and (2) all human behavior is thought to be communicative in the sense that it may be interpreted as meaningful by others" (Arliss, 1991, p. 10). Wood (1997) provides a much more focused definition for communication as "a dynamic, systemic process in which two levels of meanings are created and reflected in human interaction with symbols" (p. 36). A clear, in-depth grasp of the complexities of communication requires a closer look at the components of these definitions.

Communication Is a Dynamic Process

Both of the above definitions point out that human communication is not static; it is an ongoing, dynamic process of sending and receiving messages for the purposes of shared meaning. The transactional model of communication describes communication as a process that flows back and forth simultaneously, both verbally and nonverbally (DeVito, 1988; Taylor et al., 1989). Wood (1997) points out that "because communication is a process, there are no definite beginnings or endings of communicative interactions" (p. 36). The interactions you engage in, the messages you send and receive, may influence what you think and do later. The influence, or effect, of your communication continues beyond the immediate encounter.

Communication Involves Negotiation of Meanings

Humans are symbol-using creatures (Blumer, 1969; Cassirer, 1978). Symbols are arbitrary, abstract, and ambiguous. Humans choose ways of representing phenomena and use symbols to communicate. Because human communication is symbolic, it requires thought to interpret meanings. And while people may hold similar conceptions of words, they also have unique experiences with them that alter their perceptions. Based on their past and ever-expanding experiences, people strive to anticipate a situation, predict how certain behaviors will lead to certain reactions from others, act accordingly, and reap positive rewards from the situation. When people cannot form adequate expectations and are unable to predict what will happen in situations, they experience uncertainty (Berger and Calabrese, 1975; Berger and Bradac, 1982). One reaction to this discomfort is to communicate to gain information and reduce uncertainty.

The key to effective communication, then, depends on shared meaning—coming as close to common understanding as is humanly possible.

Consider, for example, how different people in different contexts may respond to any of the following words: pig, girl, baby, honey, beautiful, hot, cool, or phony. Watzlawick, Beavin, and Jackson (1967) were a group of clinical psychologists who were among the first to note that *all communication has both a content and relationship level of meaning*. The content level of a message is its literal meaning: Pig—"a young swine of either sex weighing less than 120 pounds" (Stein, 1979). The relationship level of meaning defines each person's identity in relation to each other and reflects how people feel about each other: Pig—a law-enforcement officer. (You guess what feeling would be associated with this meaning!) This level of meaning is the primary source for interpreting the literal message.

Communication Is Systemic

Wood's (1997) definition indicates that all communication is influenced by the *context* in which it takes place: "all communication occurs in particular situations, or systems, that influence what and how we communicate and especially what meanings we attach to messages" (p. 37). Context must be viewed as more than simply the physical space, environment, and locale. The relationships of those involved, how they feel at the moment, the time of day, and other interactions that have preceded or are anticipated, all affect meaning.

Our culture is the largest system affecting communication. Communication and gender are social constructs that influence and are influenced by our daily activities. These broad constructs establish the basis for the various communication contexts we find ourselves in and affect the choices that we make about interacting with others.

THE SOCIAL CONSTRUCTION OF GENDER

Communication and Social Change

Eakins and Eakins (1978) argue that it is "difficult to separate language and society. Language does not so much reflect society as it makes up a part of social process" (p. 21). Communication is a form of behavior, and communication acts are all part of the micro political structure that undergirds the larger political-economic structure of our lives. Henley (1973) states that communication helps establish, maintain, and convey the various signals of control, compliance, defiance, and dependence that influence us and those around us. While it is true that gender is socially created, it is also true that individuals make up society and have an impact on its perspectives.

As with many things, gender clearly varies across cultures and over time within a single culture. Changes do not just happen. They grow out of rhetorical movements that alter cultural understandings of gender and, with that, the rights, privileges, and perceptions of women and men. For this reason, insight into relationships among gender, communication, and culture must be informed by knowledge of how rhetorical movements sculpt social meanings of men and women.

Rhetoric is persuasion. *Rhetorical movements*, therefore, are social actions designed to persuade large groups of people to accept and act upon certain points of view. The objective is to change existing attitudes, private and governmental policies, and law. There have been a number of women's movements in America that have altered the meaning, roles, status, and opportunities of women. More recently, there have been men's movements through which men attempt to redefine masculinity on both personal and social levels.

The study of women's movements in America cannot simply be delegated to one section in an introductory chapter on gender and communication and provide the depth and detail it deserves. Campbell (1989a; 1989b) offers a comprehensive study of early feminist rhetoric. A variety of other texts deal with newer movements (Reuther, 1975; Chase, 1991; Faludi, 1991). Julia Wood (1997) provides an excellent delineation of the rhetorical shaping of gender from its beginnings to today in her text, *Gendered Lives: Communication, Gender, and Culture.* She provides the following summary:

> Contributing to the cultural conversation about gender are rhetorical movements, which aim to change social views and policies regarding men and women. Launched in 1840, the first wave of feminism included two movements, one advocating women's equality with men and one proclaiming women's difference from men. Ironically, arguments developed by the two rather contradictory movements combined to secure many basic rights for women, including the right to vote. During the second wave of feminism, which began around 1960, even more voices joined the chorus attempting to define women's nature, rights, and roles. Ranging from liberal feminist organizations such as NOW, which engages in public communication, lobbying, and organizing to fight against political and material discriminations against women, to cultural feminists such as revalorists and womanists, contemporary voices offer alternative visions of women and femininity.
>
> Men's movements too have been diverse. Many men joined with women feminists to speak in favor of fundamental equality for

women and to free men from oppressive social expectations. Yet other men regard male feminists as traitors who are undermining masculinity itself. Organizations such as Free Men seek to restore ultra-macho ideals of manhood, while the mythopoetic movement encourages men to discover and cultivate a distinctively male mode of feeling and of relating to other men. Against the backdrop of men's and women's movements are two others, which in opposite ways respond to feminist philosophies and efforts at change. The backlash movement is not a coherent, unified rhetorical movement but rather is a melange of messages that aim to stop further feminist efforts and to reverse some of the victories won through women's activism. (p. 108)

Although many women younger than thirty reject the label "feminist" (Wallis, 1989), every person's life has been deeply affected by feminist movements. The inclusion of discussion on social movements, for our purposes in this chapter, is primarily to illustrate the broad basis for a detailed examination of how the language use of women and men is reflected in and shapes our daily interactions.

Language Usage of Women and Men

Naturally, language usage of women and men has changed through the years, roughly paralleling the form and impact of social movements. As seen by efforts across various social movements, reshaping cultural perceptions is inexorably linked to reshaping language usage. Many researchers point to the tremendous impact that language use in general has on the human experience and particularly the role that language plays in determining which thoughts and even which feelings we experience (Arliss, 1991).

Those who have recognized how language serves to limit perceptions and exclude certain populations have variously referred to it as linguistic relativity, determinism, the worldview problem, and the *Sapir-Whorf hypothesis*. Essentially, they have argued that the particular language we speak serves to segment a continuous world—to divide it into parts that we can identify and talk about—and to put it back together according to a given set of rules. In this way, each language system embodies a particular worldview and probably influences not only what its speakers can say, but also what they can think (Arliss, 1991, p. 27).

Gender researcher Dale Spender (1985) describes language as "our means of ordering, classifying and manipulating the world. It is through language that we become members of a human community, that the world becomes comprehensible and meaningful, that we bring into existence the world in which we live" (p. 3). Our use of language enables us to define reality. If you do not have a word for something, can you think about it? Perhaps you can envision a thing without knowing what to call it. But how do you envision abstractions for which there are no physical referents? You contemplate ideas in the form of words. What happens when there are no words for something? Typically, we usually find some way to talk about what we feel or think by stringing several related words together and using qualifiers such as "it was kind of like . . ." The term *sexual harassment* was unheard-of a generation ago. The various acts of sexual harassment were not new phenomena. The growing awareness of the practices we now refer to as sexual harassment required a means by which they could be perceived differently, and identified and addressed as such.

Most people do not spend a great deal of time considering the possibility that their thinking is limited by their language. And researchers and scholars do not agree on the idea of *linguistic determinism*: If language determines thought, if we cannot think without using language, then how did a given language develop in the first place? It is clear, however, that there is an interesting and powerful relationship between thought and language. It is fairly easy to delineate trends in our language system that, at a collective level, define maleness and femaleness in our experience and, in the process, close certain doors to a segment of the population.

LANGUAGE AND SEXISM

There is a large body of research which shows that aspects of language used with regard to the sexes may serve to limit what we can say and possibly what we can think about men and women (Arliss, 1991). In Western society, our language negates women's experience by denying and dismissing women's importance and sometimes their very existence. In so doing, it represents men and their experiences as the norm and women and their ways as deviant. This marginalizes women (Spender, 1984, 1985; Bem, 1993).

English is a patriarchal language that reflects a system rooted in the belief that the male sex is superior. Language and linguistic practices such as the use of the generic male pronoun, man-linked terminology, formal terms of address, and sexual metaphors and labels reflect this belief.

The Generic "He"

The use of the *generic "he"* when the referent of a pronoun is not specifically male or female is the grammatical rule in the English language. Hence, it would be grammatically correct to say, "Each person is entitled to his own opinion," or "Each citizen is entitled to his day in court." The generic "he" is meant to refer to both women and men, and therefore create a perception of inclusiveness. The male generic language (examples are nouns such as businessmen, chairmen, mailmen, and mankind, and the pronoun he to refer to both women and men) purports to include both women and men. Research since the 1970s provides convincing evidence to the contrary. The use of the generic "he" is perceived as a masculine pronoun and conjures up masculine images (Moulton, Robinson, and Elias, 1978; MacKay, 1980; Todd-Mancillas, 1981; Cole, Hill, and Dayley, 1983; Hamilton, 1988). Research shows that masculine generics are perceived as referring predominantly or exclusively to men (Henley, 1989).

Ivy and Backlund (1994) show that besides the fact that generic masculine pronouns are not really generic, other negative consequences of using exclusive language have emerged from research. They summarized research in this area that demonstrates that exclusive pronoun usage does the following:

1. It maintains sex-biased perceptions.
2. It shapes people's attitudes about careers that are "appropriate" for one sex but not the other.
3. It causes some women to believe that certain jobs and roles are not attainable.
4. It contributes to the belief that men deserve higher status in society than women do. (p. 75)

Man-Linked Terminology

Man-linked terminology is an extension of the generic "he" and male generic language. This type of terminology involves the use of words or phrases that include "man" in them as though they should operate as generics. As noted above, male generic language excludes women. The attention that feminist movements have given to the impact of language use has prompted many individuals and corporations to make concerted efforts at avoiding gender-biased language by using alternatives to male generic language. Man-linked terms also include expressions such as "man the phones" or "manned space flight." Tables 12.1 and 12.2 list typical man-linked terms, many common expressions, and possible non-gendered alternatives for them.

Our language is filled with many other expressions that are masculine in derivation, such as master. The female equivalent term for master is mistress. Mistress is not a common part of everyday language. Typically when

TABLE 12.1. Typical Man-Linked Terms and Possible Alternatives

Term	Alternative
chairman	chair, chairperson, moderator
fireman	firefighter
mailman	mail carrier
policeman	police officer
foreman	supervisor
mankind	people, humanity
manpower	workforce, personnel, workers
manhole	sewer access

TABLE 12.2. Common Expressions and Matching Nongendered Alternatives

Expression	Alternative
man about town	worldly person; socialite; jet-setter
man a post	fill a post
man for all seasons	all-around expert; Renaissance person
man the phones	answer the phones
man-made	artificial; handmade; synthetic
manned spaceflight	piloted spaceflight
man-of-war	battleship
man on the street	average person; common person
man overboard	person overboard
man-to-man	person-to-person; one-to-one
man your positions	go to your positions
no-man's-land	limbo; dead zone; void
one-upmanship	going one better; one-up tendency
self-made man	entrepreneur; self-made person
Renaissance man	all-around expert; Renaissance person
modern man	modern people; modern civilization

it is used as a referent it is with the negative connotation of adulterer. It would be common to hear, "He's a master at the game!" Rarely, if ever, is "She's a mistress at the game!" used. Again, master is a masculine term that people use as a generic, when actually it evokes masculine imagery and applies more to men than women. Think about the frequency of expressions such as master a skill, master bedroom, master switch, master plan, mastermind, masterpiece, masterful (Maggio, 1988). The use of these expressions is thoroughly ingrained in our culture—to the point where they seem innocuous. While the impact and implications may be fairly subtle, other language practices are much less so.

Traditional Terms of Address

Traditional terms of address define women on the basis of relationships with others. By attaching the formal term Mr. to a man's surname, regardless of his age or marital status, the speaker or writer can easily signify formality, distance, and respect. In contrast, the linguistic tradition requires dual labels of respect when addressing women: Miss or Mrs. Each term not only denotes respect and distance, but also indicates marital status. The term Miss has also come to connote youth, since it is assumed that only young women are "maidens." Therefore, a woman who retains the title Miss into adulthood is often labeled an "old maid."

The use of the term Ms. to designate a woman without identifying her marital status was born out of the feminist movement of the 1960s. It is a relatively new addition to the language (it was not until 1987 that *The New York Times* would print "Ms." if a woman preferred that title; Stewart, Cooper, and Friedley, 1990) and some still find its use awkward. The extent to which our society defines women by marriage and family is further apparent in the still-prevalent tradition of a wife adopting her husband's name on marrying. Symbolically, she exchanges her individual identity for one based on her relationship to a man. Some small-town newspapers follow a standard format for wedding announcements: Mrs. John Smith, formerly Nancy Jones. . . . New traditions are developing, however—the use of hyphenating maiden and married last names (by the wife and/or both), or each keeping their "own" names after marriage.

Sexual Metaphors and Labels

Sexual metaphors and labels is the final area of language and sexism explored in this section. Metaphors are intricately woven into our language. The metaphorical labels by which we refer to men and women are deeply rooted in, and strongly influence, our perceptions of women and men. There are very definite trends that characterize the metaphors we hear and sometimes use to refer to gender:

Women and Men as Food

A woman, or a man, may be called a "feast for the eyes," or it might be said that she or he looks "good enough to eat." Women are often compared to food in a way that views them as something to be enjoyed as good things—"tomato," "peach," "plum," "a peaches-and-cream complexion," "cookie," "sweetie-pie," "cream puff," or "cupcake." Using the same labels of "cream puff" or "fruit" for men has decidedly negative connotations. Men are occasionally labeled as "big cheese," "meathead," "hunk (of meat)," "cupcake" or "cookie," but they are generally not perceived as culinary delicacies (Nilsen, 1972, p. 260).

Women and Men as Animals

The food metaphors may seem obviously figurative and largely harmless, but animal metaphors are somewhat more descriptive. Ironically, we often refer to people as animals. Men are described by aggressive animal comparisons—"buck," "stud," "wolf," "tomcat." Women are typically defined as cute and harmless, or as pets—"kitten," "bunny," "lamb," or "chick." Stanley (1975) found animal metaphors to describe women as something to be hunted ("quail," "canvasback"), subordinated or domesticated ("filly," "sow," "dog"), feared ("bat"), or vicious ("minx"). We may use the generally neutral term "pig" to denigrate another, whether male or female, but in the absence of other information, the term is usually taken to mean a fat, undesirable female. The statement "he is a pig" may also refer to obesity, but more likely indicates general lack of cleanliness or bad manners. A hefty woman may be labeled a moose, but the nickname Moose is often given to males of impressive muscular strength and is far less demeaning. Calling a woman a dog is a common way of describing her as ugly, but calling a man a dog is entirely different. Certainly, we would be mistaken if we called a man a female dog or a female horse. The metaphors bitch and nag are negative terms reserved for women.

Women and Men as Inanimate Objects

Typically, metaphors for women as inanimate objects define women as passive objects on, or through which, men take action: "honey pot," "iron maiden," "baggage," or "ball and chain." Metaphors for men as inanimate objects, on the other hand, evoke images of independence and strength: "sturdy oak," "pillar," or "rock" (Stanley, 1975).

Metaphorical expressions come and go in the form of slang names. Feminist scholars have called attention to the negative impact of perpetuating gender stereotypes through the use of sexual metaphors and labels. The notion of "political correctness" heightened our awareness of the power of language and linguistic practices in America and extended the debate beyond the use of nonsexist language to establishing a greater sensitivity to the issues and practices that create inequalities in the public sphere.

Women and men alike struggle with the structural and contextual constraints that language places on us. The impact of acculturation as seen in ascribed gender roles, negative stereotyping, language inequities, and overall sociopolitical practices points to basic differences between men and women. Early research in gender and communication focused primarily on identifying how these differences were embodied in the communication patterns of women and men.

GENDER DIFFERENCES IN COMMUNICATION

The title of John Gray's book, *Men Are from Mars, Women Are from Venus,* captured interest almost immediately because of the striking dichotomy that it presented. The title alone provided a somewhat humorous perspective on the difficulties that men and women often face in interacting with one another—as though trying to communicate with an alien from another planet. In another popular book, *You Just Don't Understand: Women and Men in Conversation,* sociolinguist Deborah Tannen (1990a, p. 42) declares that "communication between men and women can be like cross cultural communication, prey to a clash of conversational styles." From her study of men's and women's talk, she identified differences between the typical *communication styles* of women and men. Many scholars (Kramarae, 1981; Treichler and Kramarae, 1983; Bate, 1988; Hall and Langellier, 1988; Rubin, Perse, and Barbato, 1988; Wood, 1993a), have shown that women and men typically engage in different styles of communication. An examination of these differing styles shows that men and women have different purposes, rules, and interpretations of talk.

Features of Women's Communication Style

For most women, communication is a primary way to establish and maintain relationships with others. They engage in conversation to share themselves and to learn about others (Johnson, 1996). Rubin, Perse, and Barbato (1988, p. 621) reported that women are "more likely to talk to others for pleasure, to express affection, to seek inclusion, and to relax." The relationship level of talk focuses on feelings and the relationship between communicators rather than on the content of messages. For women, talk is the essence of relationships (Wood, 1993a, 1993b; Wood and Inman, 1993). Women's speech, therefore, tends to display identifiable features that foster connections, support, closeness, and understanding.

The concern for establishing and maintaining relationships is reflected in a second feature of women's talk, equality between people, as being generally important in women's communication (Aries, 1987). Typical ways to communicate equality involve establishing common ground. Saying "I know what you mean, I've felt the same way," "I've had that happen to me before," or "I've been there myself many times" helps to build a sense of balanced investment in the interaction. Growing out of the quest for equality is a give-and-take mode of interaction in which communicators respond to, and build on, each other's ideas in the process of conversing (Hall and Langellier, 1988). Rather than simply taking turns expressing individual ideas, women build on what each other says in an interactive pattern.

A third feature in women's style of communication is showing support for others. To demonstrate support, women often express understanding and sympathy with a friend's situation or feelings. "Oh, you must feel terrible," "I really hear what you are saying," or "I think you did the right thing" show an understanding and support for how the other feels. In conversations between women, it is common to hear a number of questions that probe for greater understanding of feelings and perceptions surrounding the subject of talk (Beck, 1988; Tannen, 1990b). "Tell me more about what happened," "What are you going through?" "What do you think will happen next?" and "How will this affect your plans?" are the type of questions that help a listener understand a speaker's perspective. The focus is primarily on the feelings involved rather than the content of talk.

Conversational maintenance work is a fourth feature of women's communication style (Fishman, 1978; Beck, 1988). Conversational maintenance involves efforts to initiate or sustain conversation by inviting others to speak and by prompting them to elaborate. Women, for instance, ask a number of questions that initiate topics for others: "What have you been up to lately?" "Tell me about the new exhibit you saw," "How do you feel about the new charge-back policy at work?" This type of communication gets others involved in the conversation and keeps them involved in the interaction.

A fifth feature of women's communication, *responsiveness*, builds upon the conversational maintenance aspect of inclusivity (Beck, 1988; Tannen, 1990a, 1990b; Wood, 1993a). Responsiveness shows others that we care about them and makes them feel valued and included (Lakoff, 1975; Kemper, 1984). This type of communication helps to show an interest in what was said and encourages the other to elaborate. Women usually respond in some fashion to what others say. Women often prompt the other speaker to continue by maintaining eye contact, nodding, or prompting for more information through direct statements or questions: "That's interesting—tell me more," or "What do you mean by that?"

A sixth quality of women's communication is personal, concrete style (Campbell, 1973; Hall and Langellier, 1988; Tannen, 1990b). Women's conversation typically utilizes numerous details, personal disclosures, and anecdotes. Davidson and Duberman (1982) reported that women related twice as many personal accounts and three times as many relational accounts of communication with their female best friends than men and their friends. The detailed, concrete emphasis prevalent in women's talk also clarifies issues and feelings so that communicators are able to understand and identify with each other.

Perhaps one of the most widely explored features of women's speech is *tentativeness*. There are several ways that humans indicate tentativeness in their communication. One way is through *vocal properties* (such as statements ending in a rising intonation indicative of uncertainty or question) or linguistic constructions (such as verbal hedges, qualifiers, or tag questions). *Verbal hedges* are statements such as "I kind of feel you may be overreacting" or "Maybe we should not try that." *Qualifiers* are statements that qualify a claim, such as "I'm probably not a good person to ask about this, but I think we should . . ." The final way researchers have identified to keep talk provisional is to add a *tag question* to a statement in a way that invites another to respond: "That was fun, wasn't it?" "We could do well at that, don't you think?" Tentative communication allows the opportunity for others to respond and express their opinions.

There has been controversy about tentativeness in women's speech. R. Lakoff (1975) first noted that women use more hedges, qualifiers, and tag questions than men and suggested that these linguistic forms offer a way that "a speaker can avoid committing himself, and thereby avoid coming into conflict with the addressee" (p. 17). Lakoff and other scholars claimed that the tentative means of expression undermines the messages that women convey, making them appear uncertain, insecure, unstable, incompetent, and not to be taken seriously (Lakoff, 1975; McConnell-Ginet, 1983; Graddol and Swann, 1989). Other scholars (Edelsky, 1979; Bate, 1988; Penelope, 1990; Wood and Lenze, 1991) have different explanations for tentativeness in women's communication style. Dale Spender (1985), in particular, refuted Lakoff's conclusions. She points out that it is inappropriate to view tentativeness based on male communication styles as the standard. The distinctive validity of different speech communities should be recognized. Many researchers have concluded that interpretations of qualifiers, hedges, and tag questions must be made within the given context in which the communication occurs (O'Barr and Atkins, 1980; Bradley, 1981; Kramarae, 1982; Mulac and Lundell, 1986; Sayers and Sherblom, 1987; Ragan, 1989). The use of hedges, qualifiers, and tag questions is not necessarily a question of subordination. They serve as vehicles that facilitate open conversation and include others.

Features of Men's Communication Style

Masculine speech communities tend to regard talk as a way to exert control, preserve independence, and enhance status. Conversation is an arena for proving oneself and negotiating prestige. This leads to two general tendencies in men's communication. First, men often use talk to establish and defend their personal status and their ideas, by asserting themselves and/or by challenging others. Second, when they wish to comfort or support another, they typically do so by respecting the other's independence and avoiding communication they regard as condescending (Tannen, 1990b).

One feature of men's style of communication is the concern with establishing status and value. Men often speak to exhibit knowledge, skill, or ability that demonstrates their value to those they are interacting with. The tendency to avoid disclosing personal information that might make a man appear weak or vulnerable reflects this priority as well (Derlega and Chaiken, 1976; Lewis and McCarthy, 1988; Saurer and Eiseler, 1990). The tendency to give advice that Tannen reports is common in men's speech embodies both instrumental activity (knowledge, skill, or ability) and superiority. It does not acknowledge feelings. Between men, giving advice seems understood as a give-and-take, but it may be interpreted as unfeeling and condescending by women whose rules for communicating differ (Wood, 1997).

A second prominent feature of men's communication style is *instrumentality.* Men are socialized to do things, to achieve goals (Bellinger and Gleason, 1982). In conversation, this is often expressed through problem-solving efforts that focus on getting information, discovering facts, and suggesting solutions. Again, between men this is usually a comfortable orientation, since both speakers have typically been socialized to value instrumentality. However, conversations between women and men are often complicated by confusion over the central focus of the interaction. Women may be disconcerted by the apparent lack of regard for their feelings. When a woman discloses a problem to a man and he focuses on how he thinks the problem should be solved, the woman may feel that he is disregarding her emotions and concerns. He, on the other hand, may well be trying to support her in the way that he has learned to show support— by suggesting ways to solve the problem.

A third feature of men's communication style is *conversational dominance.* Research indicates that in most contexts, men not only hold their own, but dominate the conversation. Compared with girls and women, boys and men talk more frequently (Thorne and Henley, 1975; Eakins and Eakins, 1976) and for longer periods of time (Thorne and Henley, 1975; Eakins and Eakins, 1976; Kramarae, 1981; Aries, 1987). Further, men engage in other verbal behaviors that sustain conversation dominance and control. They may reroute conversations by using what another said as a jumping-off point for their own topic, or they may interrupt. Although both sexes interrupt, most research suggests that men do it more frequently (West and Zimmerman, 1983; Beck, 1988; Mulac, 1988).

A fourth feature is that men tend to express themselves in assertive ways. Compared with women, their language is typically more forceful, direct, and authoritative (Eakins and Eakins, 1978; Beck, 1988; Stewart, Cooper, and Friedley, 1990; Tannen, 1990a, 1990b). Research indicates that men use less tentative forms in their communication. Further research shows, however, that both sexes use tentative forms of expression at certain times and in a variety of contexts to convey affiliation and to facilitate interaction with others (O'Barr and Atkins, 1980; Holmes, 1990).

Fifth, compared with women, men communicate more abstractly. Men frequently use an abstract style in their communication with others. They speak in general terms rather than in the detailed, concrete style of women. Their communication tends to create distance from personal feelings (Schaef, 1981; Treichler and Kramarae, 1983). Public environments depend on communication that reflects theoretical, conceptual, and general thought. Abstract talk in private, more personal contexts, on the other hand, can make it difficult to share intimately.

Finally, men's communication style is not highly responsive to others (Beck, 1988; Wood, 1993a). Men, more than women, use verbalizations such as "umhmm," or "yeah," which are called "minimal response cues" (Parlee, 1979). Minimal response cues generally inhibit conversation with women, who demonstrate interest more enthusiastically, because they are perceived as indicating lack of involvement (Fishman, 1978; Stewart, Cooper, and Friedley, 1990). Men's conversations also often lack expressed sympathy, understanding, and self-disclosures (Saurer and Eisler, 1990). Men perceive revealing personal problems as risky and typically see sympathy as a sign of condescension. Women, on the other hand, count sympathy and disclosure as demonstrations of equality and support.

There are indeed distinct differences in communication styles between women and men. There seems to be a dichotomy of opposites at work: maintaining relationships versus preserving independence; conversational equality versus dominance; concrete versus abstract; responsive versus not highly responsive; tentative versus forceful. This chapter has explored a number of explanations for these differences, including culture with its underlying power structure which places men in a dominant role, as well as the constraints of language and linguistic practices that shape stereotypes and gendered role expectations. It is easy to focus on differences as negative forces or ascribe greater value to some features of communication over others. Women and men who wish to communicate effectively with each other, however, must be sensitive to the communication situations in which they are involved and respond appropriately.

An understanding of the communication differences between men and women is critical in making choices about how to interact with others in order to attain communication goals. Clearer insights into your own communication patterns and habits and those of others helps in identifying the most effective way to respond in any given situation. The scope of research on gender and communication alone would suggest that this is not easy. No one can be a successful communicator at all times. But each of us can be successful more of the time by increasing our communication competence regardless of our gender.

COMMUNICATION COMPETENCE

There are two fundamental aspects of becoming a more effective communicator: you accomplish your communication goal, and the others involved consider you a competent communicator. Attaining communication goals, on the most basic level, involves clearly identifying what you intend to communicate and anticipating how you come across to others. What do you intend to communicate? Do you communicate things unintentionally? To what extent do you plan out communication objectives? How well can you assess how you come across to others? Having the answers to these questions is important in attaining communication goals. *Communication competence* is connected with a determination of "appropriateness." People will judge you as competent if you behave in ways that are acceptable for the situation and the people in it. This involves developing a repertoire of skills that allow you to communicate in ways that others will judge situationally appropriate. The following four dimensions of competence reflect ways to help you be more successful in your communication more of the time.

Repertoire

Women and men develop patterns of communication throughout their lives that they are familiar and comfortable with. Within these patterns are communication behaviors that are unique to each person. One of the goals of communication competence is to have an expanded range of behaviors at one's disposal (Rubin, 1990). A highly competent individual has an extensive *repertoire* from which to choose when confronting various communication situations.

Selection

A repertoire of behaviors is only as good as the person's ability to analyze what a situation requires (Spitzberg and Cupach, 1984). The selection of specific communication styles and behaviors depends on an analysis of your goals, the other person's goals, and the situation.

Skill

To be competent, a person must be able to perform a behavior so that another person accepts it and responds positively (Rubin, 1982). The emphasis is not so much on polished or slick delivery of ideas, but on the ability to identify an appropriate goal (to initiate and sustain conversation) and behavior (ask questions that initiate topics and encourage elaboration).

Evaluation

The last part of this sequence is the ability to judge success. It is important to see if communication efforts have been successful in the way intended. This information should be used to continually adapt communication behaviors.

These four aspects are central to communication competence. People will be more successful in cross-gender communication if they: (1) develop a wider range of communication behaviors from which to choose; (2) know how to analyze a situation and select the most appropriate behaviors; (3) perform those behaviors with skill; and (4) carefully evaluate the results.

SUMMARY

The subject of women and men communicating is complex to say the least. This chapter provided a general overview of the key issues associated with understanding gender and communication. The importance of distinguishing sex as a classification based on genetic factors, and gender as a social and psychological construction, is an important start. Communication must also be understood as a complex process of sending and receiving messages to gain shared meaning. It is important to remember that the process is an ongoing exchange of symbols that has both content and relationship levels of meaning. And all communication is influenced by the context in which it takes place.

Our culture is the broadest context in which communication takes place. The way in which women and men interact is shaped by, and shapes, the social process. Feminist rhetorical movements have transformed social practices and helped change language usage to reflect a new understanding of women's roles in our culture. A greater awareness and sensitivity to language and sexism has come about through extensive studies on the impact of language use and specific linguistic practices. An examination of the differing communication styles of men and women shows that women and men have different purposes, rules, and interpretations of talk.

Having a solid insight into how women and men communicate is critical in making choices about how to interact with others. Achieving communication goals involves understanding your own communication style and behaviors as well as being able to assess what other people need and expect. Research on the communication patterns and habits typical of women and men helps in identifying the most effective way to respond to any given situation. While no one can be a successful communicator at all times, each of us can be successful more of the time by increasing our communication competence.

KEY TERMS

sex	man-linked terminology	vocal properties
gender	traditional terms	verbal hedges
androgynous	of address	qualifiers
communication	sexual metaphors	tag question
context	and labels	instrumentality
rhetoric	communication style	conversational
rhetorical movements	conversational mainte-	dominance
Sapir-Whorf hypothesis	nance	communication
linguistic determinism	responsiveness	competence
generic "he"	tentativeness	repertoire

DISCUSSION QUESTIONS

1. Which characteristics and behaviors do you exhibit that would be described as masculine and which would be described as feminine in our culture?

2. How often do you hear or use gender-biased language? What difference does it make to you? Has there ever been a situation where gender-biased language has had a significant impact on you?
3. If you decide to marry, how will you choose to be addressed? Why?
4. Does your personal communication style more closely match features of women's communication styles or men's? What influence does context have on your style?
5. The concept of communication competence would suggest that we need to identify our gender styles and be familiar with those of others to be more effective communicators. Identify one situation in which you would like to be a better communicator. What communication behaviors will you need to change? Why?

REFERENCES

Aries, E. (1987). "Gender and communication." In *Sex and gender*, P. Shaver and C. Hendrick (Eds.). Newbury Park, CA: Sage, pp. 149-176.

Arliss, L. P. (1991). *Gender communication*. Englewood Cliffs, NJ: Prentice-Hall.

Bate, B. (1988). *Communication and the sexes*. New York: Harper and Row.

Beck, A. T. (1988). *Love is never enough*. New York: Harper and Row.

Bellinger, D. C. and J. B. Gleason (1982). "Sex differences in parental directives to young children," *Sex Roles, 8:* 1123-1139.

Bem, S. (1993). *The lenses of gender: Transforming the debate on sexual inequality*. New Haven, CT: Yale University Press.

Berger, C. R. and J. J. Bradac (1982). *Language and social knowledge: Uncertainty in interpersonal relationships*. London: Edward Arnold.

Berger, C. R. and R. J. Calabrese (1975). "Some explorations in initial interaction and beyond, toward a developmental theory of interpersonal communication," *Human Communication Research, 1:* 99-112.

Blumer, H. (1969). *Symbolic interactionism: Perspective and method*. Englewood Cliffs, NJ: Prentice-Hall.

Bradley, P. H. (1981). "The folk-linguistics of women's speech: An empirical examination," *Communication Monographs, 48:* 73-90.

Campbell, K. K. (1973). "The rhetoric of women's liberation: An oxymoron," *Quarterly Journal of Speech, 9:* 74-86.

Campbell, K. K. (1989a). *Man cannot speak for her: I. A critical study of early feminists*. New York: Greenwood Press.

Campbell. K. K. (1989b). *Man cannot speak for her: II. Key texts of the early feminists*. New York: Greenwood Press.

Cassirer, E. (1978). *An essay on man*. New Haven, CT: Yale University Press.

Chase, S. (Ed.) (1991). *Defending the earth: A dialogue between Murray Bookclin and Dave Foreman*. Boston, MA: South End Press.

Cole, C. M., F. A. Hill, and L. J. Dayley (1983). "Do masculine pronouns used generically lead to thoughts of men?" *Sex Roles, 9:* 737-750.

Dance, F. E. X. and C. E. Larson (1976). *The functions of human communication*. New York: Holt, Rinehart and Winston.

Davidson, L. R. and L. Duberman (1982). "Friendship: Communication and interactional patterns in same-sex dyads," *Sex Roles, 8:* 809-822.

Derlega, V. J. and A. L. Chaiken (1976). "Norms affecting self disclosure in men and women." *Journal of Consulting and Clinical Psychology, 44:* 376-380.

DeVito, J. A. (1988). *Human communication: The basic course* (Fourth ed.). New York: Harper & Row.

Eakins, B. W. and R. G. Eakins (1976). "Verbal turn-taking and exchanges in faculty dialogue." In *The sociology of the languages of American women*, B. L. Dubois Crouch (Ed.). San Antonio, TX: Trinity University Press, pp. 53-62.

Eakins, B. W. and R. G. Eakins (1978). *Sex differences in human communication*. Boston: Houghton Mifflin.

Edelsky, C. (1979). "Question intonation and sex roles," *Language in Society, 8:* 15-32.

Faludi, S. (1991). *Backlash: The undeclared war against American women*. New York: Crown.

Fishman, P. M. (1978). "Interaction: The work women do," *Social Problems, 25:* 397-406.

Graddol, D. and J. Swann (1989). *Gender voices*. Cambridge, MA: Basil Blackwell.

Gray, J. (1992). *Men are from Mars, Women are from Venus*. New York: Harper-Collins.

Hall, D. and K. Langellier (1988). "Storytelling strategies in mother-daughter communication." In *Women communicating and studies of women's talk*, B. Bate and A. Taylor (Eds.). Norwood, NJ: Ablex, pp. 197-226.

Hamilton, L. C. (1988). "Using masculine generics: Does generic "he" increase male bias in the user's imagery?" *Sex Roles, 19:* 785-799.

Henley, N. (1973). "Power, sex, and nonverbal communication," *Berkley Journal of Sociology, 18:* 1-3.

Henley, N. M. (1989). "Molehill or mountain? What we know and don't know about sex bias and language." In *Gender and thought: Psychological perspectives*, M. Grawford and M. Gentry (Eds.). New York: Springer-Verlag, pp. 59-78.

Holmes, J. (1990). "Hedges and boosters in women's and men's speech," *Language and Communication, 10:* 185-205.

Ivy, D. K. and P. Backlund (1994). *Exploring gender speak*. New York: McGraw-Hill.

Johnson, F. (1996). "Friendships among women: Closeness in dialogue." In *Gendered relationships*, J. T. Wood (Ed.). Mountain View, CA: Mayfield, pp. 79-94.

Kemper, S. (1984). "When to speak like a lady," *Sex Roles, 10:* 435-443.

Kramarae, C. (1981). *Women and men speaking: Frameworks for analysis*. Rowley, MA: Newbury House.

Kramarae, C. (1982). "Gender: How she speaks." In *Attitudes toward language variation: Social and applied contexts*, E. Bouchard Ryan and H. Giles (Eds.). London: Edward Arnold, pp. 84-98.

Kramarae, C. (1983). "Women's talk in the ivory tower," *Communication Quarterly, 31:* 118-132.

Lakoff, R. (1975). *Language and woman's place.* New York: Harper & Row.

Lewis, E. T. and P. R. McCarthy (1988). "Perceptions of self-disclosure as a function of gender linked variables," *Sex Roles, 19:* 47-56.

MacKay, D. G. (1980). "Psychology, prescriptive grammar, and the pronoun problem," *American Psychologist, 35:* 444-449.

Maggio, R. (1988). *The nonsexist word finder: A dictionary of gender-free usage.* Boston: Beacon Press.

McConnell-Ginet, S. (1983). "Intonation in a man's world." In *Language, gender, and society,* B. Thorne, C. Kramarae, and N. Henley (Eds.). Rowley, MA: Newbury House, pp. 69-88.

Moulton, J., G. M. Robinson, and C. Elias (1978). "Sex bias in language use: 'Neutral' pronouns that aren't," *American Psychologist, 33:* 1032-1036.

Mulac, A. and T. L. Lundell (1986). "Linguistic contributors to the gender-linked language effect," *Journal of Language and Social Psychology, 5:* 81-101.

Mulac, A., J. M. Wieman, S. J. Widenmann, and T. W. Gibson (1988). "Male/female language differences and effects in same-sex and mixed-sex dyads: The gender-linked language effect," *Communication Monographs, 55:* 315-335.

Nilsen, A. P. (1972). "Sexism in English: A feminist view." In *Female studies VI,* N. Hoffman, C. Secor, and A. Tinsley (Eds.). Old Westbury, NY: The Feminist Press, pp. 102-109.

O'Barr, W. M. and B. K. Atkins (1980). "Women's language" or "powerless language?" In *Women and language in literature and society,* S. McConnell-Ginet, R. Borker, and N. Furman (Eds.). New York: Prager, pp. 93-110.

Parlee, M. B. (1979). "Conversational politics," *Psychology Today* (May), pp. 48-56.

Penelope, J. (1990). *Speaking freely: Unlearning the lies of the fathers' tongues.* New York: Pergamon Press.

Ragan, S. L. (1989). "Communication between the sexes: A consideration of sex differences in adult communication." In *Life-span communication: Normative processes,* J. F. Nussbaum (Ed.). Hillsdale, NJ: Lawrence Erlbaum Associates, pp. 179-193.

Reuther, R. R. (1975). *New woman/new earth: Sexist ideologies and human liberation.* New York: Seabury.

Rubin, R. B. (1982). "Assessing speaking and listening competence at the college level: The communication competency assessment instrument," *Communication Education, 31:* 19-32.

Rubin, R. B. (1990). "Perspectives on communication competence." Paper presented at the annual meeting of the International Communication Association, Dublin, Ireland.

Rubin, R. B., E. M. Perse, and C. A. Barbato (1988). "Conceptualization and measurement of interpersonal communication motives," *Human Communication Research, 14:* 602-628.

Saurer, M. K. and R. M. Eisler (1990). "The role of masculine gender roles stress in expressivity and social support network factors," *Sex Roles, 23:* 261-271.

Sayers, F. and J. Sherblom (1987). "Qualification in male language as influenced by age and gender of conversational partner," *Communication Research Reports, 4:* 88-92.

Schaef, A. (1981). *Women's reality: An emerging female system in the white male society.* Minneapolis: Winston Press.

Spender, D. (1984). "Defining reality: A powerful tool." In *Language and power,* C. Kramarae, M. Schultz, and W. O'Barr (Eds.). Beverly Hills, CA: Sage, pp. 195-205.

Spender, D. (1985). *Man made language* (Second edition). London: Routledge and Kegan Paul.

Spitzberg, B. H. and W. R. Cupach (1984). *Interpersonal communication competence.* Beverly Hills, CA: Sage.

Stanley, J. P. (1975). "Prescribed passivity: The language of sexism." In *Views on language,* R. Ordoubadian and W. Raffler-Engel (Eds.). Murfreesboro, TN: Inter-University Publications.

Stein, J. ed. (1979). *The Random House college dictionary,* Revised edition. New York: Random House, Inc.

Stewart, L. P., P. Cooper, and S. Friedley (1990). *Communication between the sexes: Sex differences, and sex role stereotypes* (Second edition). Scottsdale, AZ: Gorsuck Sarisbrick.

Tannen, D. (1990a). *You just don't understand: Women and men in conversation.* New York: William Morrow.

Tannen, D. (1990b). "Gender differences in conversational coherence: Physical alignment and topical cohesion." In *Conversational organization and its development* (Vol. 37), B. Dorval (Ed.). Norwood, NJ: Ablex, pp. 167-206.

Taylor, A., A. Meyer, T. Rosengrant, and B. T. Samples (1989). *Communicating* (Fifth edition). Englewood Cliffs, NJ: Prentice-Hall.

Thorne, B. and N. Henley (1975). *Language and sex: Difference and dominance.* Rowley, MA: Newbury House.

Thorne, B., C. Kramarae, and N. Henley (1983). "Language, gender, and society: Opening a second decade of research." In *Language, gender, and society,* Thorne, B., C. Kramarae, and N. Henley (Eds.). Rowley, MA: Newbury House, pp. 7-24.

Todd-Mancillas, W. R. (1981). "Masculine generics = sexist language: A review of literature and implication for speech communication professionals," *Communication Quarterly, 29:* 107-115.

Treichler, P. A. and C. Kramarae (1983). "Women's talk in the ivory tower," *Communication Quarterly, 31:* 118-132.

Wallis, C. (1989). "Onward women!" *Time,* December 4, pp. 80-89.

Watzlawick, P., J. Beavin, and D. D. Jackson (1967). *Pragmatics of human communication.* New York: W. W. Norton.

West, C. and D. H. Zimmerman (1983). "Small insults: A study of interruptions in cross-sex conversations between unacquainted persons." In *Language, gender, and society,* Thorne, B., C. Kramarae, and N. Henley (Eds.). Rowley, MA: Newbury House, pp. 102-117.

Wood, J. T. (1993a). "Engendered relationships: Interactions, caring, power, and responsibility in close relationships." In *Process in close relationships: Contexts of close relationships* (Vol. 3), S. Duck (Ed.). Beverly Hills, CA: Sage.

Wood, J. T. (1993b). "Engendered identities: Shaping voice and mind through gender." In *Intrapersonal communication: Different voices different minds,* D. Vocate (Ed.). Hillsdale, NJ: Lawrence Erlbaum.

Wood, J. T. (1997). *Gendered lives: Communication, gender, and culture.* Belmont, CA: Wadsworth.

Wood, J. T. and C. Inman (1993). "In a different mode: Recognizing male modes of closeness," *Journal of Applied Communication Research, 21:* 279-295.

Wood, J. T. and L. F. Lenze (1991). "Gender and the development of self: Inclusive pedagogy in interpersonal communication," *Women's Studies in Communication, 14:* 1-23.

Chapter 13

Philosophy and Women: Thinking About Women

Jean P. Rumsey

WHAT IS PHILOSOPHY AND WHY IS IT RELEVANT TO WOMEN'S STUDIES?

Let's begin with a dictionary definition: *Philosophy* is "the search, by logical reasoning, for understanding of the basic truths and principles of the universe, life and morals, and of human perception and understanding of these" (*Oxford American Dictionary*). Although Socrates, roughly 2500 years ago, argued that this search could never be ultimately successful due to the limitations of the human mind, many philosophers since his time believed that they had discovered and systematized these basic truths. This was particularly true of Western Enlightenment philosophers such as René Descartes, Benedict de Spinoza, and Immanuel Kant. A definition more appropriate in our modern world is that philosophy is "the love of wisdom." The first definition implies that some philosophers possess these basic truths, while the second calls only for philosophers to pursue wisdom, remaining humble about the limits of the human mind to know reality.

Philosophy can also be defined by its major fields: metaphysics, theory of knowledge, logic, ethics and social philosophy, and aesthetics. *Metaphysics* is the study of ultimate reality, physical and nonphysical—the reality that we can access by our senses, and the reality that may transcend the physical world. Closely related is the *theory of knowledge*, which deals with questions of in what ways and how much human minds can know. *Logic* and critical thinking investigate and set forth criteria governing ways through which the human mind pursues the truth, deductively and inductively. *Ethics* and social philosophy are also normative, examining questions of the good life, of how we should treat other beings who live with us on this planet, and how communities should be rightly governed. *Aesthetics* takes up questions of art and creativity, thus completing the traditional claim of philosophy to deal with the good, the true, and the beautiful.

Philosophy, then, deals with perennial questions that touch all our lives. As Kant put it: How should we live? What can we know? What can we hope? These are questions all of us must face, male and female, schooled and unschooled. So why should philosophy be included in a women's studies course?

There are three special reasons for its relevance. The first is that the women's movement, which enabled women's studies to invade heretofore male-dominated academies, also influenced the development of disciplines within them. This was especially true of philosophy, for the movement challenged basic assumptions about women's nature and place in this world. Women philosophers became less willing to shrug off passages by classic thinkers, such as this one by Rousseau, as historical oddments, having nothing to do with his philosophy per se:

> To be pleasing in his sight, to win his respect and love, to train him in childhood, to tend him in manhood, to counsel and console, to make his life pleasant and happy, these are the duties of woman for all time, and this is what she should be taught while she is young. (Rousseau, 1974, p. 328)

The second and third reasons are internal to the discipline. Philosophy had been a male-dominated field virtually until this century, with a long tradition of considering women essentially unfit for rational thinking. Because these philosophical conceptions about women can be seen to underlie popular conceptions of women's "nature" today, we need to become aware of them. For instance, Aristotle allowed that woman possesses some deliberative ability, but that "the male is by nature superior, and the female inferior; and the one rules, and the other is ruled" (Aristotle, 1941). Plato, on the other hand, held that women were not essentially inferior, and shocked his audience by saying that some women could become rulers in his Republic if they had the same training as men. However, elsewhere Plato repeatedly castigated women for being slaves to their desires and guided only by their emotions, and thus not being fully human. This is a view which the Enlightenment thinker Immanuel Kant forwarded in the last part of the eighteenth century: "[A woman's] education is not instruction, but guidance. She must know men rather than books. Honor is her greatest virtue, domesticity her merit." (Kant, 1904, p. 222). Elsewhere he explained what he took to be the difference between men's and women's mental processes:

Nothing of duty, nothing of compulsion, nothing of obligation . . . I hardly believe that the fair sex is capable of principles, and I hope by that not to offend . . . But in the place of it Providence has put in their breast kind and benevolent sensations, a fine feeling for propriety, and a complaisant soul. (Kant, 1964, p. 184)

Arthur Schopenhauer was more blunt, referring to women's "weaker reasoning power," which makes her a "mental myopic, in that her intuitive understanding sees very clearly what is close to her but has a very narrow field of business" (Schopenhauer, 1970, p. 82). Carol Gould quotes the following passage to show Schopenhauer's belief that women lack essential human properties: "[Woman] is in every respect backward, lacking in reason and reflection . . . a kind of middle step between the child and the man, who is the true human being . . . In the last resort, women exist solely for the propagation of the race" (cited in Mahowald, 1983, p. 432).

There were, of course exceptions, such as Mary Wollstonecraft (1971), who argued explicitly against Rousseau's views (see above) in *A Vindication of the Rights of Woman*. Though a contemporary of Kant, she did not buy into the *essentialist* conception of women then prevalent (the view that women were different from men by nature, not only by nurture). In her introduction she writes: "I shall first consider women in the grand light of human creatures, who, in common with men, are placed on this earth to unfold their faculties." She then asks her own sex to "excuse me, if I treat them like rational creatures, instead of flattering their fascinating graces, and viewing them as if they were in a state of perpetual childhood, unable to stand alone" (p. 17). She does admit that throughout history, women have been the weakest and most oppressed half of the species, an inferiority that men have increased "til women are almost sunk below the standard of rational creatures" (p. 48). Nonetheless, she concludes that truth, for both man and woman, must be the same, and that women must be enabled through education and reform of social practices to be the rational beings they are capable of becoming.

This stereotyping of women as nonrational, emotional beings has a long history, which is not yet concluded. In the fourth century A.D., Hypatia, an Egyptian philosopher, mathematician, and astronomer, respected teacher and leader of the Neoplatonic School in Alexandria, was dismembered by men jealously guarding their traditional beliefs and status. Her name was given to the first *feminist* philosophical journal, founded in 1983, whose purpose is to encourage and communicate many different kinds of philosophy from the perspective of women. This journal is now prosperous and respected, with a wide circulation, though articles published in its earlier issues were not considered on a par with mainstream journals for purposes of tenure and promotion. Even today the theme for the 1998 Convention of the Pacific Society for Women in Philosophy is "Why Are There No Great Women Philosophers?" (I am assuming the question is meant to be ironic, but am not sure, given the history of women in philosophy.)

The third reason why philosophy is relevant to women's studies is that today's feminist thinkers—women and men—are building new philosophies based on the experience of women. One such example is *Maternal Thinking* (1989), in which Sara Ruddick analyzes the moral experience of mothers and applies it to larger questions of conflict resolution. Past philosophers had found little of philosophical interest in what they considered an everyday biological experience, far from their own lives. For them the subject matter of philosophy was the thoughts and activities of males, conceived as *autonomous*, rational individuals. By "autonomous" is meant self-directing and independent, under the guidance of one's own reason.

An influential book published in 1983, *Discovering Reality*, took for its goal "making women's experience into a foundation for a more adequate and truly human [theory of knowledge], metaphysics, methodology and philosophy of science" (Harding and Hintikka, 1983). The editors, Sandra Harding and Merrill B. Hintikka, saw the task of feminist philosophers as twofold: the "deconstructive project"—critiquing established positions such as abstract individualism—and the "reconstructive project"—developing philosophical positions based on women's experience. Probably this reconstructive project has been most successful in ethics, where an ethic of care/affiliation has made great inroads into the traditional ethic of justice/autonomy (to be discussed later). Of course these two aspects of feminist philosophy are not always separable, as both the critiques and the constructions are based on women's experience.

More interestingly, "women's experience" is not all alike. In particular, women of color, women of different generations, and women having different sexual orientations may tend to view the world differently. While in the 1970s and 1980s, feminism was generally referred to as a singular noun, books and articles published in the 1990s often pluralize "feminism," as in Morwena Griffiths' (1995) *Feminisms and the Self*. Differing views can be classified into four basic types: *cultural feminism, liberal feminism, socialist feminism*, and *radical feminism* (following Alison Jaggar). Cultural feminists hold that women are essentially different from men, more emotional and spiritual, more tied to the earth. Liberal feminists hold to the view of Mary Wollstonecraft that were women given the same educational, social, and economic opportunities as males, they would be able to become complete human beings. Therefore this group of feminists is primarily concerned with equal rights and equality of opportunity. Socialist feminists take oppression as their touchstone, aware of the differences in power and resources that keep women and persons of color from developing to their full potential. Radical feminists are more difficult to categorize, but one example is Shulamith Firestone, who holds that women will always be disadvantaged unless the task of reproduction can be equally shared. Generally, essentialist and radical feminisms tend to be separatist, moving outside the existing patriarchal system, while liberal and socialist feminists tend to work for reform from within the system.

Despite these differences, some basic understandings are shared. Of these it can safely be said that they all agreed that philosophy is not simply a pure love of wisdom, or analysis of basic concepts, but that it is in a deep sense political, raising issues of power as well as those of knowledge. Second, feminist philosophers must base their philosophies on women's experience, rather than on the male-based assumptions handed down by the patriarchy, and that their task is both to critique these ideas and to articulate their own philosophical positions.

Because the following areas of philosophy are more central to contemporary feminist thought than others, and because of space limitations, I have chosen to discuss the following topics: (1) metaphysics, (2) theory of knowledge, and (3) ethics.

METAPHYSICS

What Is Reality Anyway?

Is everything in your experience equally real to you? Your brother, and the nightmare you had about him last night? The chair you are sitting on, and the atoms and molecules your chemistry teacher told you made up the chair? Your own soul, and your own body? *Ontology* is the branch of metaphysics that deals with the underlying assumptions we have about reality. Three basic views are as follows:

1. *Physicalism* (sometimes called materialism). The only things that exist are physical things, things we can perceive through the senses. This view is often held by modern scientists, though a Greek named Democritus had conceived of a physicalist atomic theory even before Plato's time, and other philosophers, such as Thomas Hobbes, set forth a physicalist theory in the seventeenth century.
2. *Dualism.* This is the view that two basic kinds of substance make up reality, physical and nonphysical. For Descartes this meant souls and God on one hand and bodies (human and other material substances)

on the other. As in Christian dualism, souls were thought to be immortal while bodies were perishable. Plato's view is also dualistic, but is more complex, with the nonmaterial Forms or Ideas said to be eternal realities. In comparison, the world that we live in, and that we think we know, is merely a changing set of imperfect reflections of these ideas—this love, that we take for real, this justice that we work for and will never achieve.

3. *Idealism/Constructivism.* Idealism is the view that the only thing that is real is nonphysical or mental. Bishop George Berkeley, an eighteenth-century philosopher, argued that "to be is to be perceived." This means that the desk you and I see exists only insofar as we perceive it; it has its existence in our minds only. We might object that surely the desk does not go out of existence when we leave the room; Bishop Berkeley would reply that it continues to exist because it exists in the mind of God, who perceives the entire world. A somewhat similar view is taken in certain Eastern religions, in particular Hinduism. This view is that all is *maya,* illusion; what we take for reality is simply appearance, ideas without substance. Without taking time to further explain these positions, let us briefly define constructivism. This is either the individual or the social construction of reality, in which "reality" is simply what is perceived by the individual or by the social group. Because in this position there is no true physical reality per se, apart from the way it is perceived, and perceptions vary from person to person and culture to culture, constructivism is considered a relativistic view.

In order for students to gain some insight into their own assumptions about what kinds of things are most real, Table 13.1 provides an ontological quiz. You should rank the items on a ten-point scale (ten being the most real and zero being not real at all) and then try to give reasons for their rankings. In the reasons you gave for assigning reality values to different categories, can you find any patterns? Though you may not have produced conclusive answers that define you as a dualist, physicalist, or idealist, you have been thinking about metaphysical questions, and that was the point of the exercise. Let's go on to examine selected philosophical arguments about these issues.

Deconstruction: Mind-Body Revision

The first task of the feminist project is to clear away mainstream conceptions of reality tracing back to Plato through Descartes. The first such concept is dualism, the view that the mind and body are very different kinds

TABLE 13.1. Some Metaphysical Questions

Using the following scale, rank these items from the most to the least real:

0	1	2	3	4	5	6	7	8	9	10
not at all real										most real

1. The chair I am sitting in	____	2. Atoms	____
3. My soul	____	4. My body	____
5. Ghosts	____	6. The number 7	____
7. Abraham Lincoln	____	8. God	____
9. My brother (assume I have one)	____	10. The nightmare I had about my brother (assume I had one last night)	____

of stuff, and that the body and its desires are inferior to the mind. Plato told us in the *Phaedo* that the philosopher's task throughout life was to prepare for death by ridding himself of all bodily desires. Thus his soul would not be impeded by his body in its progress toward immortality. This idea represents a view of the universe as constituted of dualistic oppositions: mind and body, reason and emotion, good and evil, eternal and temporal. These terms are value-laden, with only the first having positive value. To them we should add male and female, for males are identified with rationality, while women are identified with their bodies and with the emotions. Socrates directed that the women be taken away from his prison cell because of their weeping; as prisoners of their bodily existence, they were unable to understand that one should not fear death because the soul is immortal.

Descartes, continuing this tradition, proudly declares "I *am* my mind; I *have* a body." He saw the two as distinct, with the body having less reality and less relevance to himself than his mind, which was his essential self. In her article arguing against this view, "Woman as Body", Elizabeth V. Spelman (1996) connects Plato's denigration of the body with his *misogyny*—his contempt for women and the kinds of lives they lived. She argues that the mind-body distinction is a distorting lens through which to view our experience, which is never purely mental nor purely physical. In the experience of childbirth, for example, pain cannot be sharply separated into something only our bodies or only our minds undergo; it is an experience of a whole person. Similarly, it is not useful to try to distinguish the mental and physical components of pain and pleasure felt by an athlete competing in an event, for body and mind work together in this active experience. On the basis of her argument, Spelman urges us to rid philosophy of what she calls *somatophobia* (body-hating), and concludes that there is no foundation for the assumption that body and mind are distinct, much less that the body is to be valued less than the mind.

For the constructive part of her article she draws on the work of Adrienne Rich, who urges us to regard our physicality as "resource, rather than a destiny . . . we must touch the unity and resonance of our physicality, our bond with the natural order, the corporeal ground of our intelligence" (Bowie et al. 1996, p. 222). (Notice the allusion to Freud's statement, "Biology is destiny," which is another way of identifying women solely with their bodies.) In conclusion Spelman points out the connection of sexism with racism (for persons of color also are identified with their bodies, not their minds) and urges further research into this connection.

Religion: Beyond the Patriarchy?

Is there a power beyond the human, some kind of God or gods? And is it gendered, as in God the Father (patriarchy) or in Goddess religions? Traditional metaphysical questions concerned proof of the existence of a God or higher power, and whether finite human minds could know its nature. In this century, under the scrutiny of thinkers such as Mary Daly and Rosemary Radford Reuther, the role of religion in supporting women's oppression has been brought to the forefront. In Daly's view patriarchal elements in the Christian religion must be excised, freeing not only women but the Deity for full self-realization in the world. The very title of one of Daly's early works, *Gyn/Ecology*, shows the radical nature of her thinking. To combine the prefix for women with the word denoting the entire web of life is to deny the mind-body dualism in Christianity, and to identify woman with the physical in a holistic, earthbound religion. It is to place the sacred in the earth rather than in the heavens, and to make women rather than men its high priestesses.

Although the existence and nature of God/gods is an important metaphysical question, I need say little more here, as this volume includes a chapter on religion. However, it remains to be noted here that many women, especially cultural feminists, have turned to goddess religions, or to modern revivals of ancient witchcraft. Still others have embraced other religions, in particular Buddhism. It would seem that in many cases feminists have abandoned patriarchal religion without engaging in theological or metaphysical disputes, perhaps seeing themselves as opting for a new spirituality rather than the patriarchal religious beliefs on which they had been raised.

The Soul/Self—A Focal Metaphysical Question

Plato's conception of the soul was that the soul is imperishable and immortal. He argued that the body is visible, changeable, made up of different parts, and perishable (though he noted that the Egyptians had developed skills to postpone the body's decay). The soul, on the other hand, is invisible, incapable of being divided into parts, and thought to be unchangeable. *Platonic Ideas*, for which he had argued elsewhere, are invisible, incapable of being divided into parts, and are eternal; therefore because the soul is more like the Ideas than like the body, it is probably immortal.

In the eighteenth century René Descartes used some of the same arguments to demonstrate the immortality of the soul. Of course he had been taught as a child and in the Jesuit college he attended that the soul was immortal, but his philosophic dream was to prove the existence of God and the immortality of the soul through reason alone, without reliance on scriptural authority. (This "dream" of the autonomy of reason, and its separateness from his enculturation, has been much criticized by feminists and pragmatists alike.) He argued that the soul was so different from the body that it must be immortal, relying primarily on the arguments of indivisibility of the soul compared to the divisibility of the body, and the certainty of knowledge of the soul as opposed to the uncertainty of bodily knowledge.

In later philosophical discourse, the question of the immortality of the soul has become less important, being considered a matter of faith rather than reason. The concept "soul" began to give way to "self," and took on a more individualist and secular meaning through the emphasis on autonomy. The dominant conception of the self, exemplified in the late eighteenth century works of Immanual Kant, was that of an autonomous, independent being. By "autonomous," you will recall, is meant independent and self-regulating, under its own reason. In the nineteenth century, John Stuart Mill formulated the *principle of harm* to protect this self from interference by others. According to this principle the only valid reason for other persons, society, or government to interfere with any individual is that the individual is harming someone else; his or her own good is not a sufficient reason. This principle assumes that each of us possesses a sphere of action that concerns only ourself, which may even include suicide. Others may argue with us, remind us of life's joys and future pleasures, or urge us to seek psychiatric help, but they have no right to interfere with our act of self-destruction, *so long as we are not harming others.* But how often is this the case? How isolated are we from other selves? How many persons do you know who could commit suicide without harming anyone else?

Aristotle would disagree with this conception of the isolated, autonomous agent, for he held that humans were essentially social beings, interconnected from birth to death. And twentieth-century feminists have seriously questioned this conception of the isolated individual, substituting the *social* or *relational self* (the terminology varies but the meaning is essentially the same). In general terms, it is a self that is largely made up of its relationships to other selves, one in which a concern for others is fundamental. These relationships constitute the self and are internal to it. Caroline Whitbeck's (1983) early paper, "A Different Reality: Feminist Ontology," sets forth the concept of the social self as explicitly opposed to the existing paradigm. Whitbeck presents an ontology that "has as its core a conception of self-other *relation* that is significantly different from the self-other *opposition* that underlies much of so-called 'Western thought'." Whitbeck defines a person as "an historical being whose history is fundamentally a history of relationships to other people, developed in a practice of the (mutual) realization of people" (p. 77). She claims that many forms of this practice are considered women's work, unnoticed by the dominant culture: "Among those are the rearing of children, the education of children and adolescents, care of the dying, nursing of the sick and injured, and a variety of spiritual practices related to daily life" (p. 65).

Later, Lorraine Code draws specifically upon Whitbeck's work, but faults Whitbeck for giving maternal relations pride of place, suggesting that friendships provide a better model for the relational self. She endorses Whitbeck's general position, emphasizing its dynamic nature. Since personal relations and historical experiences, both one's own and those of one's community, constitute what each person is, the self must be continually evolving, a nexus of many other lifelines and experiences. It will continually shape the selves of others and be in turn shaped by its interactions with those others, being partially dependent and partially independent. Code (cited in Hanen and Nielson, 1987) stresses that one is always open to influence from others, and always has a capacity to influence others, for the self remains an open project throughout life. Bell hooks articulates a similar view from her own cultural perspective. Discarding an oppositional view of the self, she states, "I evoked the way of knowing I had learned from unschooled southern black folks. We learned that the self existed in relation, was dependent for its being on the lives and experiences of everyone, the self not as signifier of one 'I,' but the coming together of many I's." Hooks contends that the construction of the self in relation means that "we would know the voices that speak in and to us from the past," from our living and from our dead (hooks, 1989).

In this way the question of the immortality of the self, or soul, returns in a different form. For if each of us is a separate, autonomous being, why is it that we are so deeply affected by the deaths of others? And why, for so long a time, are our own selves held hostage to another's death? Let us examine testimonies of those who have survived the death of a loved one. A contemporary philosopher recounts the story of his daughter at age sixteen. They had talked together about death, expressing their anger and fears, and examining philosophical questions about death. The father reported that his daughter "maintained (or perhaps she only pretended to maintain) that her death would not be such a very bad thing for her—for she would be "out of it" once it took place. . . . She claimed that death would be worse for me, since I would be left behind to suffer its aftereffects." After her death, he confessed, for a while "I found it impossible to think coherently about anything" (Feldman, 1992). Similarly, the historian Gerda Lerner wrote of the difficulty of understanding that her husband had died—the way for a long time the knowledge of his death shimmered in her consciousness, now recognized, now denied (Lerner, 1985).

One way to read these stories is to say that the "selves" of the survivors are not complete, but are drawn toward the person who remains a part of them even in death. Intimate survivors are vulnerable to a loss that is not only without but within them. This implies that death is not final, for the person who dies remains a part of those selves with whom he or she was in life intimately related. Put more simply, on this view of the self, some parts or aspects of the dead survive in the living. This preservation of self in others is expressed by St. Augustine on the death of his closest friend: "I felt that my soul and his soul were one soul in two bodies; and therefore was my life a horror to me, because I would not live halved. And therefore perchance I feared to die, lest he whom I had much loved, should die wholly" (Dinnage, 1990). Ben Helfgott, the only survivor of a family that perished in the Holocaust, told Rosemary Dinnage that "As long as I think about them [my parents, sister, grandparents, aunts and uncles, friends and neighbors] I know they are alive—they are alive in *me*" (p. 291).

In this view, the soul or self does live on beyond death, in the soul/self of others with whom it was intertwined in life. One lives on through the memories of the persons one has known, loved, or perhaps hated—the others close to one, constituting the relational self. One need only reflect on one's own experiences to understand that these connections with others are not severed at the time of physical death. This conception of survival for a time is a modest one, falling far short of the conception of the soul as immortal. But unlike the physicalist conception of the soul, it does represent a conception of survival past one's physical death.

PROBLEMS OF KNOWLEDGE

Knowledge and Belief

Pilate's question, "What is truth?" has never been definitively answered, though it has been answered in different ways in different eras. Galileo lived in a time when the Church of Rome was considered the possessor of truth, about matters not only religious but scientific. He had plenty of time to contemplate that truth during his lifelong house arrest, after his scientific pursuits had brought him into conflict with the Church. We live in an age when some say that science presides over the truth, in the sense that scientific method, when properly followed, will yield the truth, and that we can point to bodies of knowledge in physics, biology, and other sciences. Others say that there is no such thing as "truth" per se, but only many different truths, relative to individuals and to cultures. Henry Thoreau answered Pilate's question in this way: "What everybody echoes as true today, may turn out to be falsehood tomorrow, mere smoke of opinion." Yet humans seem to be truth-seeking animals. How can we best go about this search?

Descartes formulated the problem in this way: "I have many beliefs, from many sources. Some are doubtless false and some are likely true. How can I distinguish the false from the true?" His method involved doubting the two accepted ways in which human beings acquired knowledge: through their senses (empiricism) and through logic and reason (rationalism). Charles Saunders Peirce categorized the way humans historically acquired beliefs as follows: (1) the method of tenacity—forming one's beliefs according to culture or personal relationships; (2) the method of authority— forming one's beliefs according to another person, an institution, or a state; (3) the method of intuition (a priori)—forming one's beliefs without any basis of experience; and (4) the method of science—using both sound reasoning and careful observation. He held, with many others, that the scientific method is objective in the sense that it is based on some real things which our own thinking does not cause. We can trust the scientific method because of its widespread success, and while we are not perfectly logical animals, we can trust that any scientist with sufficient background knowledge and normal senses will come to the same conclusion about a given matter that any similar scientist will. Peirce points out that clear scientific thinking should be selected for in evolution, because of its survival value; however, he notes that the hopefulness that comes from ignorance also has survival value, and may encourage in humans unrealistic, shortsighted thinking.

Turning to the general problems of knowing, we must ask what we mean when we say we know something. Do we mean, for instance, that we can never be proved wrong? If I say "I know my car is in parking lot H, because I left it there this morning," and it had been towed away because I forgot my tag, does that mean that I did not know it? Stating the question more formally, let us consider what criteria must be met to claim that I know something. This is generally represented as "S knows that P" [the

Subject knows that the Proposition is true]. Overall, the criteria are three: S must believe P, P must be true, and S must have justification for believing P. Let us examine these in turn.

S Must Believe P

If you know that your car is in the parking lot, then you believe it. You don't just have a hope, a desire, or a suspicion that the car is there. You have a positive belief. Imagine what a fool your friends would think you were if you said, "I know that my car is in the parking lot, but I do not believe it." They would think it very odd and rightly so. The bottom line is that if you claim to know something, you have to believe it. Of course sometimes we do dissociate belief from knowledge, as in "I know the President has been assassinated, but I don't believe it." But this is not literally true; we DO believe it, or else we would not be shocked. We believe it intellectually, but not emotionally. So "I know P" implies "I believe P."

Does it work the other way? Does "I believe P" imply "I know P?" Surely not. We have a good many beliefs of different kinds: seven is my lucky number; there is life in outer space; you really do get warts if you pick up a toad; you do not get warts if you pick up a toad, and so on. Some of these beliefs are false and most are unprovable, showing that "I believe P" does not imply "I know P." It only works the other way, for belief is only *psychological,* not *epistemic,* certainty. Epistemic certainty requires justification or evidence for the knowledge claim.

P Must Be True

That is, *P* must be true according to one of two accepted views: the correspondence or *coherence theories* of truth. According to the correspondence theory, the statement "a cat is eating a mouse on the steps of Founder's Hall" is true only if what is described in the statement is really happening in that very place. The state of affairs in the world corresponds one-on-one with that described in the proposition. It is an empiricist criterion which we can check out ourselves by our senses. It will work for simple detective cases, to determine who killed Jane Doe (physical evidence such as fingerprints on the weapon, DNA), but may not work to determine whether or not the killing was premeditated or was simply in self-defense. It is ineffectual in determining the truth of statements about, for instance, capitalism, for purely capitalistic states, unlike cats and murderers, do not exist in the real world.

The coherence theory holds that what is true is simply that statement or belief which is consistent with the overall network of our experience and beliefs, either in general or in a particular field, such as psychology or primatology. We accept a knowledge claim just because it coheres (hangs together) with our other beliefs, and leads to conclusions we can accept. Take an everyday example: you say you know that Sarah stole a $20 bill from your dresser. How can you say that since you did not see her do it? You did see her leaving the room just before you missed the money. You have been told that she got into serious trouble through shoplifting in high school, and you did see her returning that afternoon with a new CD. This is an example of thinking according to a coherence view, though the conclusion is only probably true. Your assumption that she shoplifted in high school may be false, told to you by someone who was jealous of Sarah. If the assumptions at the basis of a given body of knowledge are erroneous, then consistency with them will not produce truth. For instance, a paranoid's belief system is based on the assumption that everyone is out to get him. He will interpret all interactions with others consistently with that basic belief. His system is perfectly coherent, but may not be truth-producing.

Let us take a more complicated example from physics. For a long time the Newtonian model was dominant. But new data was discovered that did not fit in with that model, until the model was generally rejected in favor of Einsteinian physics. This process of testing accepted theories by new developments in the field is a primary way in which science progresses. The coherence theory is the dominant theory of truth in modern science, involving a recognition that the truth is not unchanging, but that scientists agree on evidence because it fits into their hypotheses, being consistent with dominant models in different fields, and adding up to a picture that holds together in terms of our present knowledge.

S Must Be Able to Present Justification for Believing P

A statement meets the criteria for knowledge—for epistemic rather than mere psychological certainty—if it is supported by good reasons. Two of the main sources of justification are sense experience and reason. These are in many cases taken to be self-evident: as in "a skunk just sprayed near here," two plus two is four, and X cannot be non-X. Much justification in ordinary life and academic disciplines is drawn from the works of others. Student papers, as well as papers in scholarly journals, credit the sources used to support their knowledge claims. In science, intersubjective testability—and in particular, the replication of experiments at different institutions—is a key element in justifying new theories. Finally, new claims to knowledge are justified on the grounds that these claims are consistent with what we already consider knowledge, in general or in a particular field.

Some Feminist Questions About This View of Knowledge

Is this conception of knowledge as justified true belief, as it purports to be, impartial and objective? The philosopher Lorraine Code (1991), in her book provocatively titled *What Can She Know?*, argues that it is not. The theory would be more adequate, she claims, if it examined the S—the knower—rather than focusing primarily on objective justification. For the knower, assumed to be an autonomous male, distanced from what he is studying, brings to his task many unexamined assumptions and biases. Her project is to unmask this theory's claims to occupy a neutral place outside the struggles central to people's lives, and to show that "Philosophical beliefs about knowledge and authority inform and are informed by social conceptions of what it is . . . to be a good knower and about how knowledge confers expertise . . . [which] extends far beyond the academy, with widespread social-political implications" (p. xi). On a simple level, her call to focus on the knower is recognizable to any critical thinker who is careful to notice whose lab was the source of benign new "information" about nicotine, or who spread the rumor about Sarah's shoplifting, but Code's criticisms run much more deeply. For instance, one chapter deals with what she calls the double standard for credibility as a witness. In the 1984 Grange inquiry into infant deaths from cardiac arrest at Toronto's Hospital for Sick Children, lawyers questioned doctors in terms of what they *knew*, but nurses in terms of their *experience;* in the investigation knowledge conferred authority whereas experience did not.

Even when women had obtained access to dominantly male fields they were less credible. Code reports that "In 1968 women graduate students in science at Yale were told that they were being trained to be the wives and research associates of their male fellow students" (p. 227). An essential part of knowledge, in Code's account, is acknowledgment by those privileged to recognize it. Some knowledge produced in noninstitutional settings, or in other "inferior" institutions, will go unrecognized, behind the mask of neutral objectivity, for "facts found and/or constructed by people in positions of power have a greater presumption of validity than knowledge claims advanced by occupants of 'underclass' positions" (p. 249). What is validated is not only particular knowledge claims, but the subjectivity of the knower, who is usually white, middle-class, and male.

The biologist Ruth Bleier (1988) also argues that the claim to neutrality of the theory of knowledge presented above is an empty claim. She says that while the set of idealized practices known as the scientific method is generally seen to protect science against "rampant subjectivities" and is thought to be the guarantor of the objectivity and validity of scientific knowledge, this is more myth than fact. Each step in the scientific method

is "profoundly affected by the values, opinions, biases, beliefs and interests of the scientist" (p. 3). These values and beliefs affect the questions
they ask, their assumptions, and the observations they make; "what they
see and fail to see; how they interpret their data; what they hope, want,
need and believe to be true" (p. 3). To support this generalization she gives
an example from primatology. With the exception of Japanese field workers, primatologists in the 1950s and 1960s simply could not see what
females were doing when they exhibited behaviors thought to be male—
dominance behavior, sexual aggressiveness and initiative, or female leadership of the troop. Efforts to explain these behaviors had to be put in the
Procrustean mold of male-centered explanatory systems (p. 3). This
androcentric bias is only one of many biases that pervade science, giving a
lie to the claim that science is value-free. Feminists such as Code and
Bleier are making the point that the pretensions of science and knowledge
to being value-free are dangerous. What we need to do is to become aware
of our own values and assumptions, as well as those of others. For as
Michel de Montaigne reminded us years ago, "though a man sitteth in the
seats of the godly, he still sitteth on his own behind."

ETHICS

What Is Ethics and Why Study Ethics?

You come into an ethics class having dealt with ethical questions for a
good part of your life. You have a set of values learned through socialization, by example or experience, and perhaps by reflection on what you
have been taught. Further, there seem to be no "facts" in ethics, and
therefore no experts in the subject. Given this, there are problems in
explaining why you should sign up for a class in ethics, other than that you
might need a three-credit class in the humanities. There is a second,
perhaps weaker, reason I sometimes offer: students who study ethics will be
able to make better choices, better moral decisions. But this reason is hard to
back up. Your grandmother or grandfather or kid brother may have a better
knowledge of ethical truths than your professor; for there are no experts
here, as there would be if you were studying chemistry or even history
(though historians, like ethicists, are given to sharp disagreements). So it
should be clear that each of you brings your own moral experience to an
ethics class (unlike, say, a Byzantine history class), to reflect on and perhaps
enlarge, as you learn more about how other thinkers—in your texts and in
your class—handle these questions. What is the good life? What is moral-

ity? Why should I be moral? These are questions all of us must answer for ourselves, through reflection and communication with others. Let us begin by examining the three basic types of moral theories.

Traditional moral theories fall into two basic types and a combination of the two: (1) *duty ethics*, those views that judge morality by standards of right and wrong (as in the Ten Commandments or the philosophy of Immanuel Kant); (2) *consequentialist ethics,* those views that judge morality by consequences of actions; and (3) *virtue ethics,* Aristotle's view, predating this distinction, incorporates elements of both. Although some actions, such as adultery, and some emotions, such as envy and malice, are wrong, the end or purpose of morality is happiness. Aristotle concerned himself mainly with two questions: What is the good life? What is a good person, and how can I live my life so as to become a good person? The answers to these two questions are interconnected, for the virtues developed in moral character enable a person to be happy. Furthermore, ethics and politics are closely related, for Aristotle held that it was not possible to become good in an immoral society.

Despite the differences between the Kantian and Utilitarian (Consequentialist) points of view, both views take actions, not character, as their main question. They ask, "How can we tell the difference between right and wrong?" Kantian and Utilitarian views both agree on the importance of sovereign principles, discoverable by reason, guiding the moral life, but those principles differ according to their reading of human nature. For Kant, the essential characteristic of human beings is reason, while the characteristic Utilitarians thought most important is their ability to enjoy pleasure and suffer pain.

For Kant, right and wrong actions are distinguished by whether they measure up to reason's standard of the universal law. When I ask whether a proposed action is right or wrong, I am asking "Could I live in a world where anyone in my circumstances could do this?" If, for instance, I wished to borrow money with no intention of paying it back, that action would be wrong, for trust would be eroded and banks depleted. A second test Kant proposed was whether one is using another without her/his consent. This is based on respect for human dignity, for humans are autonomous persons who should be authors of their own purposes, not used for the purposes of others.

The impartiality of Kant's view is also significant in Utilitarianism. Actions on this view are judged right if they produce (or are expected to produce) the greatest good for the greatest number, or the smallest amount of misery. This is a universal standard, applying to all affected by the action, with everyone's utility counting equally, as one. Utilitarians would probably agree with Kant's analysis of the deceptive effort to borrow money from the bank, for after all, the practice of lending money is socially useful. They would disagree with some results of the second test, in cases where deceiving a person would lead to a greater good. The Kantian holds that the suicide even of one suffering great pain is always wrong, because the agent is simply using his death as a means to escape pain, which violates human dignity. The Utilitarian may judge that one suicide is justified while another is not, according to the consequences for others affected by the act.

Both approaches have been strongly criticized in the twentieth century because of their impartiality and rigidity, which critics say deny the value of human relationships and their place in the good life. Take the following scenario: in 1975, a severe earthquake hit a small village in China. Ming Li, a resident of the village, returned to his home and, hearing the cries of his wife and child from underneath the rubble of their house, began to try to dig them out. But just then he heard the cries of their neighbor, the mayor, and went to his house to try to free the mayor. A good citizen, he realized that the mayor would be able to direct efforts to get the village back on its feet, whereas his wife and child would not. Ming Li would be a hero to a classic Utilitarian, whereas today's critics would think him morally insensitive. After all, they would ask, "even if the mayor could do a lot more good, would you want to live in a world like that, where your loved ones were of no more value than anyone else?"

In classical Utilitarianism, the moral agent is an abstract calculator, valuable only as an instrument for producing good or preventing evil in this world. In the Kantian view the moral agent has little discretion for using individual judgment. Certain actions are always wrong, such as lying, and there are no exceptions. But suppose you are sheltering Jews during World War II, and the Gestapo comes to your door asking whether you are hiding any Jews. Are you obligated to tell the Gestapo the truth? These questions and others like them have caused modifications in present-day Utilitarianism and in neo-Kantianism.

The most serious debate in contemporary ethics, however, is that between an ethic of justice and an ethic of care, generated by Lawrence Kohlberg and his former assistant, Carol Gilligan. As you may know, Lawrence Kohlberg, a prominent researcher in the field of moral development, devised a six-stage scheme by which to measure moral development. His research extended to subjects from eleven countries, over time, and he claimed that the regularities he found in this cross-cultural study would solve the relativity problem that had plagued philosophers for three thousand years. On the basis of his research, he argued that human moral development followed this invariant sequence: stages one and two are preconventional, motivated by self-interest and deference to authority. In the conventional stages three and four, the developing agents learn to seek the approval of others by conforming to stereotypical roles and norms, and acquire a minimal sense of duty—learning that this conformity contributes to social harmony. In the postconventional stages five and six, they associate morality with rights and principles that they understand to be universally valid. At the highest level they are able to make impartial, autonomous judgments between universal moral principles, Kohlberg's moral summit.

However, when Gilligan applied Kohlberg's developmental scale to females, she discovered that they did not perform well, rarely rising above the third stage on this scale. This seemed to indicate either that women are not capable of the same degree of moral development as men, or that something was wrong with the measuring device. Now it happened that Kohlberg's data base, though cross-cultural, had been made up entirely of males. Should that make any difference? Do males and females of the same species differ morally? Through her research, Gilligan found that they did, arguing in her famous metaphor that women have a different moral voice. Women err, according to Kohlberg's measuring device, by thinking contextually rather than formally and abstractly, and by choosing certain kinds of values over others.

For example, here is a well-known example of the hypothetical questions Kohlberg used, with typically gendered responses. Heinz's wife was near death from a rare form of cancer. One drug would save her, but it was new and expensive. Heinz went to everyone he knew to borrow the money, but could get together only half of what he needed. He told the druggist that his wife was dying and asked him to sell it more cheaply or to let him pay for it later. The druggist replied, "No, I discovered the drug and I intend to profit from it." Heinz got desperate and broke into the pharmacy to steal the drug. Should he have done that? Most male respondents took their thinking to the highest level: the sanctity of life and right to property are both important moral principles, but in the case of conflict, the former takes priority. Many females hoped to solve the problem through personal relations and face-to-face contact among the principals. Surely, they argued, Heinz could have arranged to have the pharmacist meet his wife and see how much she needed the medicine. Had they only met in person, they could have worked it out together, for the pharmacist could have been led to see that he would be responsible for her death. Those females who thought that theft was wrong objected not on principle but because if the theft were discovered, then Heinz would not be able to continue to care for his wife. This type of concrete, contextual reasoning was found to be characteristic of female thinking, unlike the increasingly abstract and impersonal reasoning Kohlberg had found as representing the highest stage of human moral development.

Such divergent reasoning led to the characterization of the two moral perspectives as "an ethic of justice" and "an ethic of care." The former is characterized by the values of autonomy, equal respect, justice, impartiality, and rights; the latter by compassion and care, self-sacrifice, relationship, and responsibility. The social world of males was conceived as a hierarchy, and that of females as a network. Gilligan (1982) urged that we should listen to, and learn from, women's voices, for "in the different voice of women lies the truth of an ethic of care, the tie between relationship and responsibility, and the origins of aggression in the failure of connection" (p. 65). A 1985 research conference, Women and Moral Theory, at Stony Brook, Long Island brought together a number of prominent philosophers with Gilligan to examine the implications of her research. Are these separate but equal theories? Is one more adequate than the other? Would it be moral progress to learn to see the world through both perspectives? Twelve years later, although these questions have not been satisfactorily answered, a vast literature on the topic attests to the fact that an ethic of care has entered the philosophic mainstream. Womanly habits of thinking about morality contextually rather than abstractly, of considering oneself as essentially affiliated with others rather than as an autonomous rights-bearer, and of thinking about responsibility rather than primarily about rights, have been instructive to philosophers, male and female, who are working to develop more adequate moral theories.

The emergence of an ethic based on women's experience has many features in common with feminist work in metaphysics and in theory of knowledge. Perhaps the most central is the demand that philosophy be grounded in the lived experience of all human beings, not only that of the privileged males who have presided over it in the Western tradition. Closely related is the distrust of abstract reasoning and universal principles. Lorraine Code's admonition that we must focus closely on the person who claims knowledge and the context from which that claim arose is a good example of this view. The rejection of hierarchical views of gender, class, race, and even species is another common element in different feminist philosophies. Mary Daly's *Gyn/Ecology* exemplifies this element, as does the influential movement called ecological feminism.

SUMMARY

Throughout all the areas of philosophy we have discussed—religion, the self, theory of knowledge, and moral theory—run three basic assumptions.

Perhaps most central is the demand that philosophy be grounded in the lived experience of women, not only that of the privileged males who have shaped the Western philosophic tradition, and that this experience is to be respected. Secondly, this experience has led women philosophers to distrust abstract reasoning and universal principles, and to question the dichotomies set forth in "malestream" philosophy: mind and body, reason and the emotions, eternal and temporal, male and female. The third assumption is that hierarchical views of gender, class, and race must be rejected, often in solidarity with other historically oppressed groups (as Elizabeth Spelman recommends). These assumptions make up a framework for feminist philosophy, from which have come powerful critiques of traditional views and compelling new theories in all fields of philosophy.

Still, within this framework great differences exist among liberal, cultural, socialist, and radical feminists, and between individual philosophers. Within it, women philosophers—and now some profeminist men—argue vigorously for the truth of their own views against those of others, using time-honored methods of philosophic inquiry. Although the framework itself is feminist, there is no one feminist philosophy as such, but only a diverse and growing number of feminist philosophers, working toward the wisdom that philosophers have always sought.

KEY TERMS

philosophy	liberal feminism	platonic ideas
metaphysics	socialist feminism	principle of harm
theory of knowledge	radical feminism	social/relational self
logic	ontology	coherence theory
ethics	physicalism	androcentric
aesthetics	dualism	duty ethics
essentialist	idealism/constructivism	consequentialist ethics
feminist	maya	virtue ethics
autonomous	misogyny	
cultural feminism	somatophobia	

DISCUSSION QUESTIONS

1 Are you a dualist? A physicalist? An idealist? Formulate an answer on the basis of the ontological quiz in this chapter, and your other reflections on the question. Then state the strongest objection to your position you can think of, and answer it as best you can.

2. On what basis does science claim to produce objective, impartial knowledge? On what basis do Code and Bleier argue that this claim is untrue? What is your view about this dispute? Give reasons.

3. What is the difference between an ethic of justice and an ethic of care? Which do you think is more adequate? In your own experience, do females and males view the world that differently? Take a position and give your reasons.

REFERENCES

Aristotle (1941). "Basic works of Aristotle." In *Politics,* Richard McKeon (Ed.). New York: Random House, pp. 950-952.

Bleier, Ruth (Ed.) (1988). *Feminist approaches to science.* New York: Pergamon Press.

Bowie, G. Lee, Michaels, Meredith W., and Solomon, Robert C. (1996). *Twenty questions: An introduction to philosophy,* Third edition. New York: Harcourt Brace and Company.

Code, Lorraine (1991). *What can she know?* Ithaca, NY: Cornell University Press.

Daly, Mary (1978). *Gyn/Ecology: The metaphysics of radical feminism.* Boston: Beacon Press.

Dinnage, Rosemary (1990). *The ruffian on the stair.* New York: Viking Press.

Feldman, Fred (1992). *Confrontations with the reaper.* Oxford: Oxford University Press.

Gilligan, Carol (1982). *In a different voice: Psychological theory and women's development.* Cambridge, MA: Harvard University Press.

Gould, Carol C. (Ed.) (1983). *Beyond domination.* Totowa, NJ: Rowman and Allanheld.

Griffiths, M. (1995). *Feminisms and the self.* New York: Routledge.

Hanen, Marsha and Kai Nielson (Eds.) (1987). *Science, morality and feminist theory.* Calgary: University of Calgary Press.

Harding, Sandra and Merrill Hintikka (1983). *Discovering reality.* Dordrecht: D. Reidel.

hooks, bell (1989). *Talking back.* Boston: South End Press.

Kant, Immanuel (1904). *The educational theory of Immanuel Kant.* Trans. Edward P. Buckner. Philadelphia: J. B. Lippincott Co.

Kant, Immanuel (1964). *Doctrine of virtue.* Trans. Mary J. Gregor. New York: Harper and Row.

Lerner, Gerda (1985). *A death of one's own.* Madison, WI: The University of Wisconsin Press.

Mahowala, Mary B. (Ed.) (1983). *Philosophy of woman.* Indianapolis, IN: Hacket Publishing Co.

Rousseau, Jean-Jacques (1974). *Emile, book V.* Trans. B. Foxley. New York: E. P. Dutton.

Ruddick, Sara (1989). *Maternal thinking.* Boston: Beacon Press.

Schopenhauer, Arthur (1970). *Essays and aphorisms.* New York: Penguin.

Spelman, Elizabeth (1996). "Woman as body." In *Twenty questions: An introduction to philosophy,* Third edition, Bowie, G. Lee, Meredith W. Michaels, and

Robert C. Solomon (Eds.). New York: Harcourt, Brace and Company, pp. 214-224.

Thoreau, Henry David (1981). *Walden and other writing by H. D. Thoreau,* Joseph Word Krutch (Ed.). New York: Bantam Press.

Whitbeck, Caroline (1983). "A different reality: Feminist ontology." In *Beyond domination*, Carol C. Gould (Ed.). Totowa, NJ: Rowman and Allanheld Publishers, pp. 64-88.

Wollstonecraft, Mary (1971). *A vindication of the rights of woman.* [Unabridged reproduction of the 1792 London edition.] New York: Source Book Press.

Chapter 14

Women and Religion: Recapturing Women's Spirituality

Evonne Jonas Kruger

INTRODUCTION

Women have always challenged the most basic tenets of the two major Western religions, *Judaism* and *Christianity*. In the past thirty years, they have been particularly successful in forcing *theologians*, those who study the nature of God and religious truth, and historians to rethink the enormous influence patriarchal societies have had upon religion, particularly the role of women. Both religions are *patriarchal*. As they evolved, God was generally perceived in masculine terms as father, king, lord, shepherd, judge, and so son; religious institutions were led by men up to the modern era; and women were assigned different, and frequently inferior, roles than men (Ruether, 1996).

The reasons why women began to more assertively challenge Judaism and Christianity are complex and interrelated, but the paramount influence has been the women's movement. First the women's movement conducted a broad and scholarly discussion of how patriarchalism shaped Western civilization. Second, it nurtured women's participation in discussions of religion and provided emotional support as they challenged fundamental theological and institutional beliefs held by men in positions of academic and religious power. Third, it focused on *women's ways of knowing* and experiencing the world. And fourth, the women's movement encouraged women to explore and create religious experiences and texts that were more personally relevant.

The latter two elements drew upon psychological literature that suggested women prefer to understand the world through the use of intuition and operate in the world by building networks and seeking connectiveness with others. Men, on the other hand, tend to prefer to understand the world through the use of rationality and logic, and operate in a more independent and competitive manner.

When women describe their spiritual experiences, they tend to use metaphors conveying the sense of moving down and inward in response to the *immanence*, or experienced nearness, of God. They speak about the still small voice from within, or being filled with the sense of God's presence. In comparison, men describe their spiritual experiences as moving upward and outward in response to the *transcendence* of God, or experience of God as being outside the human realm (Frankiel, 1990). Their metaphors include being high, being lifted up, and encountering God's radiant glory. Thus, patriarchal society has had a profound impact on the history of religious institutions, Western theology, and perceptions of spiritual experiences.

The Role of Feminist Scholarship

There have been three major responses by women scholars to the more patriarchal aspects of Judaism and Christianity (Plaskow, 1994). First, they are illustrating and reinterpreting patriarchal elements of texts, theories, and images, highlighting the muted voices of women and others such as the poor, who were marginalized by patriarchal religious institutions and societies. Second, they are conducting scholarly research demonstrating that specific texts, ideas, and symbols were not defined solely by men, but that women played significant roles and made important contributions that went unrecognized, were forgotten, or were deliberately suppressed. For example, working with data from the fields of anthropology, history, and religion, Meyers (1988) has conducted seminal research on ancient Israelite women.

Third, women are radically questioning and redefining theological concepts, creating what Plaskow (1994) terms theology from the feminist point of view. Gottlieb (1995), for example, has written a feminist theological and liturgical (worship) vision for Jewish women. Others have begun to fill in the silences concerning women in biblical texts by writing what Jews term *midrashim*, commentaries explaining the texts (Buchmann and Spiegel, 1994; Rosen, 1996). These midrashim (singular, midrash) provide women's perspectives on the texts, fill in the silent voices of women, and present a counterpoint to the *androcentric* (male centered) traditional interpretations.

In addition, women are continuing to work within religious institutions to increase the number of ordained women ministers and rabbis, purge masculine language and patriarchal concepts from prayer books and educational material, form women's prayer and study groups, develop more opportunities for women within lay leadership positions, and create unique rituals for women.

Within this evolving context, this chapter focuses on how women are (1) responding to the major patriarchal elements of Judaism and Christianity, and (2) using elements of ancient goddess-centered religions to enhance their spirituality.

WOMEN'S CRITIQUES AND NEW INTERPRETATIONS OF JUDAISM

Jewish women involved in Jewish women's studies, religious studies, and theology have been extremely active since the 1960s in criticizing and politically challenging Jewish institutions, theology, law, and religious practices. For example, by the late 1970s Jewish women's college courses included feminist theories of religion, women in the Hebrew Bible, women in Jewish and Christian traditions, and women and Judaism (Elwell and Levenson, 1982).

The most important area of concern for women criticizing Judaism has been the patriarchalism of the *Hebrew Bible*, termed the *Old Testament* by Christians, and its effect on Judaism, particularly the tendency of many Jews to understand God as the embodiment of masculine virtues. The second area of concern is the marginalization of women's stories, roles, and actions in the Hebrew Bible and postbiblical texts. The third area is the influence of Jewish law upon modern Judaism and how women reformulate existing, and create new, rituals and theology. Let us explore each of these three areas.

God

Jews define God primarily by using the Hebrew Bible or *Tanakh*, especially the first five books or *Torah*, and postbiblical rabbinical writings called the *Talmud*. In addition, a set of Jewish mystical writings, the *Kabbalah*, have influenced Jewish theology. The Bible and Talmud are patriarchal documents produced by a patriarchal society threatened by its neighbors' *polytheism*, the worship of many gods. Furthermore, they have been read, studied, and interpreted for nearly 2,000 years by people living within patriarchal societies who have incorporated their own biases into their interpretations.

A strong argument can be made that the biblical maleness of God is a reflection of the writers' culture. Plaskow (1994) suggests that God is not

(1) male, lord, or king; (2) outside, over, against, or manipulative of humans; or (3) dualistic. Rather, God is the "source and wellspring of life in its infinite diversity" who empowers humans to act creatively (p. 76).

Interestingly, there are several instances in the Bible where God is described using feminine metaphors and attributes. For example, the Hebrew word for compassion, *rahum*, one of the most important attributes of God, is from the word for womb. Metaphors of God include nursing mother (Jeremiah 49:15), mother eagle (Deuteronomy 32:11), mother bear (Hosea 13:8), and mother hen (Psalms 17:8; 36:7; 91:4).

Historically, however, it has been difficult for women to go beyond the God-He of the Bible. In response they have turned to postbiblical sources and rediscovered the feminine image of the *Shekinah*, a concept conveying God's immanence in the world, somewhat similar to the Christian concept of the Holy Spirit.

The word *Shekinah*, first used in rabbinic literature about 200 C.E. (Common Era), evolved from *mishkan*, the portable sanctuary used by the Israelites during the exodus from Egypt and *shakan*, the verb for "to dwell." The Israelites were commanded to construct the tent so that God's spirit, Shekinah, could dwell among "his" people. By 1000 C.E. the Kabbalah associated Shekinah with the feminine and most humanly accessible aspect of God. Shekinah dwelled in exile in our universe, waiting to be reunited with the highest and least humanly accessible aspect of God (Hoffman, 1995).

The Kabbalah concept of Shekinah has been merged with earlier concepts of Shekinah that incorporated traits shared by Near Eastern ancient goddesses. Shekinah now embodies both the positive and negative polarities of the feminine. She is the merciful, wise, compassionate, ever-loving mother, sister, mistress, bride, and old woman as well as judgment and death. She is identified with the earth, moon, night, sea, garden, and pools of water (Seghi, 1995). Many Jewish women, uncomfortable with a male God, now pray to Shekinah, God found mystically within. Debbie Friedman, a popular Jewish musician, sings about Shekinah "all around us." Gottlieb (1995) calls Shekinah "she who dwells within" us. Many observant women invoke Shekinah as they light candles ushering in the Jewish sabbath. Shekinah has become the image of the accessible, merciful, loving God.

Many Jewish women, however, recognize that God-She can be as limited as God-He. Falk (1989) rejects Shekinah as a viable image since she has never been considered equal to the male-centered vision. Falk recommends that immanence (Shekinah) should not be portrayed as secondary to transcendence (God-He). In her Jewish blessings Falk prefers to use nongendered metaphors such as rock of Israel, tree of life, and source of life.

A Jewish tradition supports Falk's argument for a genderless, or *gender-neutral God*. In Exodus, when Moses asked God who he should say sent him to Egypt to free the Hebrew slaves, God's reply was to say that "I am who I will become" sent Moses. A tradition of not naming God began with the Hebrew Bible, which was written without vowels. When it was read, the name of God was too sacred to be spoken. Many Jews still do not write or pronounce "God" in English or Hebrew, but prefer the term Ha Shem, "the name," and write "G-d." Furthermore, the second of the Ten Commandments states that Jews are to make no images of their God. As a result, there is no tradition of Jewish art depicting God as father, king, lord, shepherd, and so on. Thus many Jews argue that while the forces of patriarchalism within history have gendered God, there is sufficient biblical evidence and tradition indicating that God is beyond gender.

Both the Reform and Conservative Jewish traditions are responding to concerns about God's gender. Some congregations have developed prayer books that alternate male and female images. The Reform movement has recently produced "gender-sensitive" prayer books for both the special holy days and everyday use, which have removed all masculine descriptors of God in English and substituted non-gender-specific language such as Holy One or Redeemer.

Women in the Bible and Midrashim

Women's responses to the treatment of women in the Bible and post-biblical literature parallel their responses to the theology of God-He. They are criticizing texts, recovering and adding to texts through the midrashic process of writing their own interpretations, and are now developing a more complete understanding of women that synthesizes the dualistic approach encountered in the texts.

In the Hebrew Bible women are mentioned only when their lives intersect those of men. Beginning with Eve, through the matriarchs (Sarah, Rebecca, Leah, Rachel), or wives of the patriarchs (Abraham, Isaak, and Jacob), the women of Exodus, and the prophets Deborah and Yael, readers find little of substance about women. Even the two books named for women, Ruth and Esther, were written by men who were not interested in women's emotions, motives, and lives. Common biblical themes of women have been identified, however. For example, they are associated with enclosed places such as Sarah's tent, perhaps indicating the nurturing womb, and pools of water and wells, reflecting the fertility and life-giving nature of women as well as the significance of water in the desert.

Women are engaged in *depatriarchalizing* the Hebrew Bible, and are analyzing the masculine biases of its writers and interpreters. For example, since women were so marginalized in the text, many Jews believed they were subordinate to men in the eyes of God. Trible (1978), however, suggests the actual text of Genesis does not create Eve inferior to Adam in the Garden of Eden story. Women became subordinate to men only after the expulsion from the garden, after sin was committed. Frymer-Kensky (1994) notes there are biblical stories depicting women as having the same goals, abilities, strategies, and roles as men. She concludes the Hebrew Bible does not consider differences between men and women to be innate, but presents a unified vision of humankind based on the creation of both man and woman in God's image. Women and other socially marginal groups such as the poor, slaves, and foreigners are not negatively stereotyped. The Bible does stress distinctions between divine and human, holy and profane, pure and unpure, Israel and other nations, but male and female is not expressed as a category. Yet many women find depatriarchalization of texts and gleaning information from history, religious studies, and archaeology to be insufficient. Frymer-Kensky (1994) suggests that the basic construction of biblical stories leaves much for readers to both interpret and fill in.

The centuries-old technique of composing midrashim is now being used to fill in the silences about women and answer questions that have lain dormant and unnoticed by men (Rosen, 1996). Rabbis in the postbiblical era believed that every word in the Bible, particularly the Torah, was either dictated or inspired by God; therefore nothing was superfluous. They wrote midrashim that explained biblical ideas, nuances, and phrases. The word midrash comes from the Hebrew *lidrosh*, which means to search, ask, explain, or draw out. This literary form includes textual analysis, logical deduction, proofs by comparison with other texts, and adding to stories in order to explain how and why things happened. The early rabbis considered the composition of midrashim to be a form of revelation. Readers were free to believe or disbelieve the historical truth or spiritual relevance of any particular midrash, but were to consider its author inspired by God.

The famous story of *Lilith*, who is not named in the Bible, is found in the Midrash Rabbah on the Torah, edited from 200-800 C.E. Her story is of particular interest to feminists. The rabbis used Lilith to explain the two different creation stories found in Genesis. In the first story God created male and female in God's image. In the second story *Eve* is fashioned from Adam's rib. The midrash explained that the first creation was of Adam and his first wife Lilith. When Lilith would not assume a subordinate sexual position and Adam tried to overpower her, she incanted God's magic name and flew away. She then became a mythic queen of evil deeds who seduced men and threatened childbearing women and newborn infants.

(Even today some Jewish grandmothers tie a red ribbon or amulet on a crib to ward off Lilith's powers.)

After Lilith left, Adam petitioned God for another mate, and Eve was created from his rib, the early rabbis said, so that he would clearly be in control. Women's interpretations, however, argue that the Hebrew words for helpmate and partner do not signify Adam's dominance. Gottlieb (1995) has suggested that Lilith is the opposite, or dark side of the Shekinah. For modern women to achieve an harmonious whole, they must have a conscious awareness and acceptance of the opposites found within the feminine: active and passive, dark and light. Furthermore, if women can reconcile Lilith with Eve, they can imagine how the masculine and feminine can receive mutual respect and recognition in society (Seghi, 1995). Many women have written midrashim on Lilith in their quest to do so.

Writing midrashim can be spiritually gratifying and therapeutic as women attempt to answer questions relevant to their lives. These include the following: Why did Eve eat the fruit of the tree of knowledge of good and evil (Genesis 3)? What was Sarah's response when she learned that her husband Abraham had attempted to sacrifice their son Isaac (Genesis 22)? What actually occurred when Dinah was raped by Shekhem and afterward (Genesis 34)? Rosen (1996) summarized the uniqueness of midrashim by stating that "midrash in the end is theology, as well as questions, answers, details, reasons, fiction, truths—stories" (p. 28).

Reinterpretations and Creation of New Spiritual Opportunities

Jewish women are creating unique spiritual experiences in response to their feelings of exclusion and marginalization. They focus more on the role of biblical women during celebrations of Jewish holidays; have reclaimed an ancient Jewish women's holiday, Rosh Hodesh; and are creating new rituals.

One holiday that is being reinterpreted is Passover. Traditionally women spent weeks cooking and preparing for the spring festival commemorating the Jews' exodus from Egypt, and then sat through the Passover seder, or table service, where the patriarchal Haggadah (service) was read. Today they are writing women's Haggadahs, holding women's seders, and including stories and songs about exodus women in their family seders. Along with the stories of Moses, Pharaoh, and Aaron they include stories of the Jewish midwives Shifra and Puah, who would not kill the newborn Hebrews as ordered by Pharaoh; Moses's birthmother Yocheved; his sister and prophet Miriam; his adopted mother Bitiah, who was daughter of Pharoah; and Serach, who knew the location of Joseph's bones when the Hebrews left Egypt. Another holiday is Purim, celebrated in late winter to commemorate the Book of Esther in the Hebrew Bible. In the book, Esther, a Jew living in exile in Persia, marries King Ahasuerus. When a royal advisor, Haman, plots to have the Jews killed, Esther uses her influence with her husband to save her people. Although Esther's strength of character and decisive action have always been stressed, some women have reclaimed Vashti, the king's first wife. According to an ancient midrash, Vashti was deposed by the king when she refused to dance nude before his friends. Vashti is now viewed as a woman of character who said "no" to the king, not the vain and selfish woman described by the rabbis, who declined the king's offer because she felt her body was blemished.

The most significant holiday that Jewish women are reclaiming is *Rosh Hodesh*, the monthly celebration of the new moon. The history of celebrating the new moon goes back to pre-Israelite times when ancient goddesses were associated with the moon. Like many ancient religions, Judaism uses a lunar calendar. Rosh Hodesh, the monthly appearance of the new moon, is greeted with a special prayer to the creator of the natural cycle of the universe. In the eighth century C.E. women were given Rosh Hodesh as a holiday in reward for their devotion to God during the exodus. An early midrash tells that while Moses was on Mt. Sinai receiving the Ten Commandments from God, the men gave their gold to make a golden calf to worship, but the women refused, remaining faithful. During Rosh Hodesh women generally avoid hard labor and spend time in prayer. Today many women's spirituality and study groups meet on Rosh Hodesh. Part of its attractiveness has been its focus on nature. The cycles of the moon are paralleled by the cycles of a woman's body: the rise and fall of estrogen and fertility, and the appearance of the menstrual period. Later in this chapter we will again consider women's spiritual affinity for nature during a discussion of goddesses.

In addition to writing women's Haggadahs and midrashim, Jewish women also are creating new rituals. Gottlieb (1995), for example, has created women's ceremonies celebrating Shekina, Rosh Hodesh, the initiation of young girls into womanhood at the time of their first menstrual periods, menopause, and old age. Others are experimenting with prayers and rituals addressing divorce and sexual violation. Many Jewish congregations hold healing services that focus on the physical and emotional health of their members. Most Reform and Conservative congregations have women's groups who write and conduct women's services.

Women in Jewish Law and Leadership Positions

In ancient Israel Jewish women were excluded from most public aspects of Judaism, although there were women prophets and leaders. In

Exodus only males from the tribe of Levi were permitted to become priests. Women were considered ritually unclean, able to pollute sacred objects, spaces, and the relations between men and God because their bodies emitted blood during their menstrual periods (Kraemer, 1992). They were bound by Jewish law to observe three major sets of commandments. First, women were to bake challah, an egg bread, and keep kosher homes following a complex set of laws concerning prohibited and permitted foods and how permitted foods should be prepared and eaten. Second, women's lives and relationships were proscribed by the laws concerning *niddah* or intimacy. Among other things, women were to abstain from sex for the duration of their menstrual periods plus seven additional days. The third set of laws, *hadlik ner*, concerned the lighting of sabbath candles and preparations for, and observance of, the sabbath (Frankiel, 1990). Taken in their entirety, these laws, which many Orthodox, or more traditional Jewish women, still observe, defined women as wives and mothers and restricted their relationships with men other than their husbands and young sons.

Since the Torah exempted women from cultic obligations such as animal sacrifices, the rabbis argued they could not assume rabbinic roles. Other arguments against women rabbis included historical precedence and the religious separation of men and women based upon extensions of the laws concerning the ritual uncleanliness of women. Orthodox Jews still do not have women rabbis, women are not allowed to read from the Torah during services, they are separate from men during services, and women are not encouraged to study Torah together. Women have been ordained rabbis and invested as cantors in the Reform and Conservative movements of Judaism since the 1970s. Cantors conduct services by singing and chanting prayers and songs, and perform certain clerical duties.

WOMEN'S CRITIQUES AND NEW INTERPRETATIONS OF CHRISTIANITY

The critique of Christianity by Christian women is similar to that of Judaism by Jewish women because they are responding to the effects of 2000 years of theological, institutional, and societal patriarchalism. In fact, Christian women have had a more difficult time effectively communicating their concerns and influencing change within Christianity because Christian theology is more overtly patriarchal than Jewish theology, and there has been a greater frequency of misogyny, hatred of women, arising from elements of Christian theology. This section will focus on (1) women's concerns with the theological concepts of God, Christ, the Holy Spirit, Mary, and the origin of evil; and (2) the role of women within the Church.

God, Christ, and the Holy Spirit

Because Christians and Jews share a large body of texts and traditions through the Old Testament (the Hebrew Bible), Christian and Jewish women both confront the concept of God arising from the ancient Hebrews' experience of desert patriarchy (Reuther, 1996). Although God is predominantly referred to as male in the Old Testament and has been seen through patriarchal eyes as the ultimate lord and king, there still remains a strong Jewish theological belief, discussed above, that God is beyond gender. Within Christianity, however, the tradition and theology of a genderless God is less strong. First, the historical Jesus' identification as the *Son of God* introduced an overwhelmingly masculine metaphor. Jesus reinforced the image of *God the Father* by using the term *Abba,* an intimate word of love and respect for a male parent or parent figure, to refer to God.

Second, the theological identification of the risen *Christ* with the *historical Jesus* was used to reinforce the metaphor of Father and Son. The risen Christ arguably can be interpreted as beyond male and female, but the very name Jesus Christ melds the historical male Jesus with the Christ of the Godhead represented by the Trinity, the unity of God, Christ, and the Holy Spirit. Third, iconography and religious art have consistently portrayed God as the father/king. Nearly every Sunday school child has seen a picture of God as king sitting on a throne "up" in heaven or the Zeus-like God of the Sistine Chapel. These three facts have converged within a patriarchal tradition and patriarchal societies to create indelible images of the male God and Christ.

The *Holy Spirit* was identified by early Christians as the experienced presence of God. For example, Christians could become so "filled" with the Spirit that they frequently spoke in tongues (glossolalia), danced, or went into trances. The early Church often used female imagery drawn from the Jewish tradition of the female *Hokmah* or spirit of God and the concept of Shekinah to describe the Holy Spirit. Feminine imagery was gradually rejected, however, in favor of the masculine. The *doctrine of the Trinity,* which views God as the union of the masculine Father, Son, and Holy Spirit, solidified this view. To a degree, feminine imagery for the Spirit continued within the Church. For example, descriptions of the Spirit by mystics are quite similar to those found in the Jewish Kabbalah literature. As Reuther (1993) has observed, however, a female Spirit is still subordinate to the male God and Christ.

Like Jewish women, Christian women are responding to the gender of God by frequently changing from God-He to God-She to God. Referring to the tendency to move from God-Father to God-Mother, Reuther (1993) cautions that substituting the image of mother goddess for father god is insufficient. The modern Christian image of the loving and gracious parent God, whether mother or father, perpetuates the image of an adult parent-nonadult child relationship between God and humans in which humans remain God's dependent children, incapable of autonomy and the assumption of adult responsibilities.

God-He, God-She, God-Father, God-Mother, and God-Parent are all dualistic concepts, reinforcing a view of the world as composed of dualisms such as nature-spirit or holy-profane rather than as an organic, integrated creation. Reuther (1993) prefers more liberating language such as Redeemer, Source or Being, and Liberator. It has even been suggested that until Christians are able to agree upon gender-neutral God language that perhaps everyone should use four dots in place of "God" in writing and not speak the name "God" out loud (Ramshaw, 1990).

Mary

Very little is said about *Mary* in the New Testament (Macquarrie, 1990). It states that she was a young virgin who conceived by the Holy Spirit, became the mother of Jesus, and appeared at various times during his ministry and at his death. Most stories are found in the Gospel of Luke. Mary became a major figure in the early Church, where she was frequently symbolized as the church triumphant, ascended to heaven and seated at the right hand of Christ as "his" bride and called the Mother of God. Even today Mary is the most venerated image in Western culture (Gadon, 1989). The early church viewed Mary as the new Eve, a perfectly obedient female untouched by carnal sexuality, who reversed the disobedience of the first Eve, who introduced sin into the world. (This ignored Gospel accounts of Jesus' brother and sisters, presumably Mary's children.) Early views, which later became the doctrines of Mary's Assumption (1950) and Immaculate Conception (1854) reinforced this view. According to the doctrine of the Immaculate Conception, Mary was chosen to become the Mother of God even before her birth. God therefore preserved her from the taint of original sin at her conception. Thus Mary had neither the will nor the capacity to sin. The doctrine of Mary's Assumption states that since Mary was conceived without the taint of sin and lived a sinless life, she was spared the consequences of human sin: death. Pope Pius XII declared that Mary was assumed, or taken "up" body and soul to heaven when she was near death.

During the Middle Ages, particularly the twelfth and thirteenth centuries, the veneration of Mary took on cult trappings. Many of the greatest Gothic cathedrals built along pilgrimage routes, such as Chartres and Notre Dame, were dedicated to Mary. In Henry Adams' (1961 edition) famous autobiography written in 1907, a chapter titled "The Dynamo and the Virgin" compared the tremendous energy expended by men and women on behalf of Mary in the Middle Ages with the energy released by the Industrial Revolution.

Most Protestant women see Mary as the human mother of Jesus. Within Roman Catholicism, Eastern Orthodoxy, and some Episcopalian churches, however, responses to Mary vary. Many women identify with the young virginal Mother as mediatrix between them and the masculine Trinity; this role appears to be growing in importance. Others are critical of the Mariological (Mary) tradition because they believe it expresses the ideal of the feminine from the patriarchal perspective (Reuther, 1993). The image of Mary captured by the doctrines of the Immaculate Conception and Assumption perpetuate "sexuality as the cause of sin and mortality as the consequence of sin" (Reuther, 1993, p. 152). Feminists feel that Mary has been portrayed for too long as sexless, meek, obedient, self-effacing, and inferior to men. They prefer to focus on Mary's free choice to accept God's offer to be the mother of Jesus found in Luke rather than the agreement made without Mary's participation between God and Joseph in Matthew. Reuther (1993) interprets Luke's account as real cocreatorship between God and humanity. Radical feminists frequently reject the entire patriarchal tradition including the masculine Trinity and have elevated Mary to a status approaching goddess (Macquarrie, 1990).

Women in the New Testament and Early Church

As the church institutionalized patriarchalism, women turned to the Gospels for more positive messages concerning their lives and souls. In his words and actions Jesus expressed unique concern for women. For example, in the Mary and Martha story, Jesus defends Mary's right to study with the disciples (Luke 10). Parables such as the mustard seed (Luke 13; Matthew 13) and the widow's lost coin (Luke 15) depict women as equivalent to men before God and as relatively independent participants in society. Women in the parables relate to God not as father or creator, but as personal redeemer (Reuther, 1993). Throughout the Gospels, particularly Luke, Jesus interacts with, and directs his message to, marginalized members of society: women, the poor, slaves, and outcasts.

The Bible stories of *Mary Magdalene* are of particular interest to women. Mary Magdalene is mentioned several times as a disciple of Jesus, remaining faithful at the cross, and leading other women to the empty tomb. The difference between the views of Mary Magdalene held by men and women is illustrated by their interpretations of a passage in the Gospel of John where Jesus tells Mary not to touch him when he appears after his resurrection. Historically, men interpreted this as indicating Jesus' abhorrence of a woman's touch. Reuther (1996) provides a woman's interpretation that Mary's attempt to embrace Jesus reflected the fact was she was accustomed to touching him. Jesus therefore had to warn her that his risen body was filled with dangerous spiritual power.

Reuther (1996) notes that the New Testament states that Mary Magdalene was healed of "seven demons," possibly epilepsy. The early Church fathers combined this passage with several others about unnamed women in the Gospels and portrayed Mary Magdalene as a prostitute and weeping sinner, presumably in order to eradicate the tradition of women disciples and Church leaders. Like the Virgin Mary, Mary Magdalene was widely represented in Christian art during the Middle Ages. Her image was that of a prostitute, whereas Mary was depicted as chaste. Thus the polarized image of women as either virgins or whores was perpetuated and reinforced. Since human women were not spotless virgins, they were considered little better than whores, enticing men to submit to carnal sin. Due to the sinful nature of women, men were advised to either practice celibacy or engage in sex only for the goal of procreating children within marriage (Gadon, 1989).

Many Christian women are now reclaiming the lost tradition of Mary Magdalene as a disciple of Jesus, and are reconstructing early Church history. Fiorenza (1990), for example, has reinterpreted Romans, Chapter 16 to demonstrate that women were early Church missionaries, apostles, and co-workers with Paul. Several women were greeted by Paul and identified as co-workers. Phoebe must have had a central role as a missionary based on his recommendation of her to the Romans. Fiorenze (1983) argues that in Paul's letters to Corinth he affirmed the "equality and charismatic giftedness of women and men in the Christian community" (p. 235). The *Acts of Paul and Thecla* is another example where Paul commissioned a woman to preach. Cloke (1995), Torjessen (1993), and Kraemer (1992) provide scholarly histories of women's leadership in the early Church.

Although women served in leadership roles in the early Church, the Church fathers did not consider them to be representative of the capabilities of other women who were not leaders. Instead they were considered so superior to other women that they were in a separate category, or as one Church father said of one such woman, "this female man of God" (Cloke, 1995). Regardless of their many contributions to the early Church, they could not change the views of the Church fathers about women (Cloke, 1995).

Eve and the Origin of Evil

The reason why the Church fathers did not view women as equal to men was primarily rooted in their *theology of sin*. In Genesis God tells Adam and Eve not to eat the fruit of the Tree of Knowledge of Good and Evil. The snake tempts Eve to eat and she tempts Adam. As a result they are aware of their nakedness, frequently interpreted by the Church fathers as a result of sinful carnal lust. In punishment for their sin God casts them out of the Garden and announces that men must toil to bring forth food from the earth and women must suffer in childbirth. Early Christianity interpreted the Fall and expulsion from Paradise as indicating the inability of humans to avoid evil impulses and thus their need to be redeemed from sin by the atoning death of a divine savior (Reuther, 1996). (Jews, on the other hand, believe sin originated when the Hebrews deliberately chose to reject God by worshipping the golden calf; humans can avoid sin; and sex was created by God.)

The early Church used the New Testament Epistles to buttress its interpretation of Genesis. For example, I Timothy (2:9-14) states that Eve was created second and sinned first. A passage in I Corinthians (6:12-7:39) concerning sex and marriage was similarly used to justify subjugating women. In an interesting interpretation, however, West (1990) suggests that St. Paul was not offering his own opinion, but was quoting that of his correspondent, whose sexual ideals and practices arguing against marriage and sex he did not endorse. His correspondent's position was frequently taken by members of the early Church, called spiritualists, who felt sex was so sinful that it should be rejected. West's interpretation is that Paul supported marriage and even divorce under certain circumstances.

From these interpretations the early Church fathers developed the theological position that the subordination of women was God's will because women were not only more sinful than men, they were created inferior. According the Reuther, the Church fathers did not deny women's souls could be redeemed, but they believed the female was the opposite of the divine. In order to avoid the worst forms of sin found in sexual activity sex was renounced and chastity was encouraged. Thomas Aquinas even used the Aristotelian belief that the male was the perfect expression of the human species and the female was an accident to argue that Christ had to be male and women were not even made in God's image (Lloyd, 1996). Their only function was to be mothers of sons. By the fourth century the Church hierarchy relegated marriage to a position below that of celibacy, and celibate women were sent to convents where they could not tempt male religious (monks and priests).

Women in the Reformation

The *Reformation,* the separation of Protestant churches from the Roman Catholic Church in the sixteenth century, only slightly modified the patriarchalism of the church. Martin Luther, a Reformation leader, encouraged married clergy based on his interpretation of Genesis that God created men and women for marriage. His message, spread by the Reformation, was that sexuality was a God-ordained good. This clashed with the position of the Roman Catholic Church that clerical celibacy and male monasticism were the ideal states; sex was sinful and marriage was only for those with incurable lust. However, the Reformation's reevaluation of sexuality and marriage only partially liberated women (Torjessen, 1993). Women were to marry in order to provide assistance and emotional support to their husbands; they remained clearly subordinate, reflecting the natural social hierarchy ordained by God. A woman could be saved and experience grace equal to a man, but she was created to serve him as wife, mother of his children, manager of his household, and provider of emotional support.

Women's Leadership in the Church

The major argument supporting women clergy has been Acts 2:17-18, where men and women equally receive the gifts of the Spirit (Reuther, 1993). Arguments against women clergy include (1) biblical authority, usually using passages of Paul; (2) the social inferiority of women that precluded them from preaching in large meetings; and (3) social convention and historical tradition (Zikmund, 1981).

Although there is evidence of women church leaders in the early Church, by the Middle Ages women were religiously empowered and permitted positions of leadership only within the confines of the cloister, where McLaughlin (1990) argues their spirituality was a source of "wholeness, meaning, power, and authority" (p. 100). The Reformation eliminated cloisters from Protestantism, but it did not alter the role of women within the church. It was not until the seventeenth century that women began to serve as preachers in English Baptist and Quaker congregations. The Quakers continued the tradition of women clergy in America.

By the mid-nineteenth century American women were religious leaders in the Pentecostal and Holiness movements. In 1852 the Congregational Church ordained its first woman, Antoinette Brown, a friend of the early feminist Quaker minister Lucretia Mott. Earlier, Mother Ann Lee founded the Shakers on the principle of sexual equality and a theology of God as both male and female, father and mother. Mary Baker Eddy founded the Church of Christ, Scientist (Christian Science) espousing her belief that the feminine was the principle of spiritual perfection. While African Methodist churches have had a long tradition of women clergy, white Methodists and Presbyterians only ordained women beginning in the 1950s. The Episcopal and Lutheran churches in the United States began ordaining women in the 1970s; the Church of England approved women's ordination in 1992. The Roman Catholic Church and Greek Orthodox Church still refuse to ordain women, frequently using the argument that since Jesus, a male, founded the Church, only males can aspire to his image. However, within most Protestant denominations women have achieved equality in both clerical and lay leadership positions.

Feminist Christian Theology

Christian women are developing a theological voice and are active in major divinity schools (e.g., Rosemary Radford Ruether) and universities (e.g., Elisabeth Schussler Fiorenza and Ross Shephard Kraemer). They continue to depatriarchalize texts, conduct scholarly research on women's contributions, and fight for more inclusive theological language. They address the traditional topics of theology previously defined by men, such as God, Christology, Mariology, sin, redemption, repentance, eschatology (the end of the world), ecumenism (relationship between different religions), and social justice, but add new perspectives drawn from their spiritual lives and experiences as women. Women have helped identify new areas of theological discussion about the ecological healing of the world and gender relationships. Central to women's theology is their vision of "a world of connection and relationship (not dualism, division, or hierarchy), a world in which pluralism and diversity (not monolithic unity) are celebrated as contributing to the richness of the whole" (Plaskow and Christ, 1989, p. 269).

WOMEN'S SEARCH FOR THE GODDESS

As women address Western religions' patriarchalism, many are exploring the worship of ancient *goddesses,* in the Near East, the Greco-Roman empire, and throughout the world. Their interest in Goddess worship has been prompted by several considerations. First, in order to depatriachalize texts women need to understand both their ancient languages and cultural milieus. The Hebrew Bible reflects the Hebrews' attempt to establish a patriarchal religion while surrounded by polytheism. For example, the Canaanites worshipped powerful goddesses such as Asherah and Astarte, who had cults among the Hebrews. Christianity spread throughout the Roman Empire when Greek and Roman Goddess worship was almost universal. Second, as women study ancient goddesses they are attracted to many basic concepts: the immanence of the divine, a positive view of sexuality, an holistic approach to the body, and the earth's sacredness. Third, some Jewish and Christian women have used concepts from Goddess religions to enrich their theologies. Fourth, some radical feminists have rejected patriarchal theologies and histories and have turned to images of the divine in the form of the Goddess as an alternative. They call themselves witches, Druids, Goddess worshipers, or just pagans.

The Attractiveness of the Goddess

What perspective do ancient goddesses add to Western spirituality that causes so many women to be attracted to them? There are three major reasons: (1) they were earth centered; (2) they were body affirming; and (3) they were holistic in their approaches to life. Let us examine each of these.

The goddesses were *earth centered* yet cosmic. Goddess rituals and celebrations were connected to solstices and equinoxes, full moons and new moons. At the same time, the earth was perceived to be alive, a concept that has reemerged with James Lovelock's (1979) *"Gaia hypothesis"* that the earth is a living organism. All of the earth was perceived as sacred, to be respected, not dominated, communicated with, not tamed. Native American, African, and Polynesian Goddess accounts and rituals particularly focused on the sacred earth (Stone, 1990). Because the goddesses were so closely tied to nature, their worship resulted in a deeper understanding of the cycle of birth, aging, and death and the acceptance of change and transformation in life (Stone, 1990).

Women who worshiped goddesses were close to nature and the cosmos, and used their intuition and frequently the metaphysical in their roles as priestesses and healing shamans. They practiced divination through Tarot, I Ching, astrology, runes, dreams, trances, omens, and other intangible ways of accessing information. The logic of the cosmos was understood to be the connection of past, present, and future. Women accepted experiences of divine guidance and intervention as integral parts of their lives. The spider's web frequently symbolized the connection of life and all things. Noble (1991) interprets connectedness by saying, "nothing we do is without consequence in the larger scheme of things. Each of our lives matters" (p. 73). Yet each human is only a tiny part of the greater whole.

Goddesses were *body affirming*, not body denying. Frequently depicted as pregnant or giving birth, with large, abundant breasts, goddesses were worshiped as life-giving sacred forces. They were earth goddesses, containing all the life-giving forces of the universe. It has been hypothesized that menstruation led to the primacy of Goddess worship because women could bleed every month and not die (Eller, 1993). Yet even postmenopausal goddesses were worshiped. They were crones, full of wisdom because they no longer lost their sacred blood every month, but retained it. Menstruation was sacred and menstruating women were perceived as especially creative and powerful. In fact, the Hindu Sanskrit word *ritu,* the root for "ritual," means "menses." During their menstrual periods, women in ancient times gathered in menstrual huts to relax, commune with one another, and become emotionally replenished while their bodies were cleansed. Only later under patriarchy were they banished to huts as unclean (Eller, 1993). The Jewish laws concerning women discussed previously in effect did this.

Sex was a prevalent theme in Goddess worship, frequently incorporated as the sacred marriage with a male consort. Gods and consorts were present in Goddess worship, although they were subordinate. Lyrical poetry such as the Inanna hymns of the ancient Near East describe personal, passionate sexual encounters from the woman's perspective. (The Inanna hymns are strikingly similar to the Hebrew Bible's Song of Songs.) Women shamans and priestesses were portrayed as sexual, chanting, singing, dancing, healing, birthing, playing instruments, weaving, planting, and otherwise connected to the earth (Noble, 1991).

Goddess religions were *holistic*, not *dualistic*. Before the goddesses were suppressed, life was perceived holistically. There was equality between women and men, animals and plants, rocks and rivers, earth and its atmosphere. Goddesses incorporated all aspects of life: rational and irrational, life-giving and life-taking, nurturing and destructive, capacity for good and evil, order and chaos. The Goddess was the unification of Eve and Lilith. Experienced as immanent, not transcendent, goddesses were found within women, men, and nature, not outside, over, and above their creations. Goddess religions and societies were relatively peaceful and egalitarian, although woman-centered. They did not disempower or subordinate men (Eller, 1993). The goddesses symbolize the richness of ancient wisdom (Stone, 1990).

The Fall of the Goddesses

Goddesses were not only found in the Far East and Greco-Roman Empire, but throughout the world (Stone, 1978, 1990). Famous artifacts such as the Venus of Willendorf (30000-25000 B.C.E.) and the Maltese Goddess (3600-3000 B.C.E.) bear witness to the extensiveness of Goddess worship before recorded time.

How did goddesses die and patriarchalism triumph within Judaism and Christianity? About 4400-4300 B.C.E., 3400-3200 B.C.E. and 3000-2900 B.C.E. nomadic peoples from the Asiatic and European north overran the Goddess cultures of southeastern Europe, the Near East, and India. They brought gods of thunder and war, sky gods who ruled from the heavens, not from the earth, and an accompanying patriarchal social system. Later, Europeans conquered the native Goddess-worshipping cultures of the Americas in a similar manner.

It took patriarchy nearly 2,500 years beginning in the third millennium B.C.E. to be fully established and suppress the *matriarchal cultures*. Its progress can be followed in a series of rituals and religious myths explaining how first the goddesses required the assistance of lesser gods, and then became subservient to them, until finally the gods usurped their roles. The myths include forced marriages of goddesses to powerful gods, the transformation of goddesses to minor or even evil goddesses, the transfer of their powers to their male consorts, the appearance of father gods, and their murder by gods. The expulsion of Adam and Eve from the Garden might have been a myth of a particular patriarchal takeover (Noble, 1991).

Monotheism, in which one male omniscient being rules both heaven and earth, dealt the final death blow to the goddesses. There was no longer any room for other gods and goddesses. Evolved by the ancient Hebrews less than 4,000 years ago, monotheism is relatively recent compared to polytheism. The Roman Emperor Constantine declared the exclusive authority of one universal male (Christian) god in Western culture only about 1,700 years ago.

Monotheism brought a radical paradigm shift that included dualistic categories of being, new relationships between men and women, and different views of life and death (Gadon, 1989). Its truths included: (1) a male deity created the world; (2) this god gave humans the right to dominate nature; and (3) because God was a male, men had the right to dominate women (Gadon, 1989).

When monotheism suppressed the goddesses, many theological elements were incorporated into Judaism and Christianity. Others emerged in new forms. Still others were used selectively to subordinate women. An example of adaptation is the incorporation of three Canaanite seasonal Goddess-centered festivals into Judaism when the Hebrews conquered Canaan: the Festival of Unleavened Bread became Passover; the early summer Weeks of Pentecost became Shavuot, the celebration of God's covenant with the Hebrews; the fall Festival of the Ingathering (Exodus 23:16) became the festival of Sukkot, celebrating the dwelling in huts in the wilderness.

The snake is an example of the negative transformation of a symbol associated with goddesses. Because the shedding of its skin was perceived as a life-renewing activity similar to women's menstruation, the snake was associated with goddesses. Christianity coupled the snake with the evil impulses of women and their need to be subordinated and punished. Christianity also appropriated Goddess festivals such as the winter solstice when the Goddess gave birth to the divine child represented by the sun. It was natural that Christmas, occurring a few days after the winter solstice, would be selected for the birthday of God's divine Son. Similarly, Easter was selected as the first Sunday after the full moon following the vernal equinox, another sacred goddess day. Some believe that Easter was named after the Anglo Saxon goddess Eostre (Gadon, 1989).

Christian men took the irrational, chaotic, intuitive, and destructive elements from the holistic goddesses and associated them with the feminine. When the old European (pre-Christian) goddesses were suppressed, elements emerged in cults of the Black Virgin and women healers who continued to worship goddesses and nature (Gadon, 1989). It has been estimated that a large number of the millions of women who were burned as witches by Christians were those who worshiped nature and goddesses (Eller, 1993). Many European cathedrals built to venerate Mary were located on ground associated with goddesses. Within the Americas, the Native Americans accepted Christianity, but they frequently retained elements of Goddess worship. For example, worship of the Virgin of Guadalupe contains elements of the original Aztec goddess Tonantzin (Carmody and Carmody, 1993).

In conclusion, Gadon (1989) discusses why women are searching for the Goddess, an amalgamation of all of the earth goddesses, as we enter the twenty-first century. The Goddess is the ultimate symbol of female empowerment. She serves as a catalyst for an earth-centered spirituality that is perceived by many as more meaningful than Christianity or Judaism. The Goddess is used as a metaphor for the earth as a living organism, Mother Gaia. She is recognized as the archetype for feminine consciousness, a mentor by those following the holistic healing paradigm, and inspiration for women artists. Lastly, the Goddess is a model for what Gadon (1989) terms the resacralizing of women's bodies and the mystery of human sexuality. For many women the Goddess is not an ancient belief structure, but a living, life-sustaining force.

CONCLUSION

Women have forced Western religions to confront the full impact of patriarchy on both theology and religious institutions. Jewish, Christian, and pagan women are actively creating authentic spiritual experiences that meet their needs as women in a *postpatriarchal* society. They are redefining their concepts of God and how God has acted historically and acts in the present. For some, God is still He, for others God is She, and for many God is now God. Women are affirming their experiences of the immanence of the divine, whether it is called Shekina, Mary, or the Goddess. Similarly, they are affirming their sexuality and relationship to, and responsibility for, the earth. Rewriting history through scholarly endeavors, they are reclaiming their past achievements as religious leaders. Finally, they continue to study and reinterpret ancient texts as they creatively amplify the lost voices of their ancestors.

KEY TERMS

Judaism	Kabbalah	Mary
Christianity	polytheism	Mary Magdalene
theologians	Shekinah	theology of sin
patriarchal	gender-neutral God	Reformation
women's way of knowing	depatriarchalizing	goddesses
immanence	Lilith	earth centered
transcendence	Eve	Gaia hypothesis
midrash(im)	Rosh Hodesh	body-affirming
androcentric	Son of God	holistic
Hebrew Bible	God the Father	dualistic
Old Testament	Christ	matriarchal cultures
Tanakh	historical Jesus	monotheism
Torah	Holy Spirit	
Talmud	Doctrine of the Trinity	

DISCUSSION QUESTIONS

1. What have been the historical and theological impacts of patriarchalism upon Judaism? Upon Christianity?
2. Discuss the concepts of immanence and transcendence.
3. Compare the role of Lilith in Judaism with that of Mary Magdalene in Christianity.
4. How are Jewish women responding to the more patriarchal elements of Judaism?

5. Discuss the concept of a genderless God within Judaism and Christianity.
6. Compare the role of Shekinah within Judaism with that of Mary within Christianity.
7. How are Christian women responding to the more patriarchal elements of Christianity?
8. Why are some women so attracted to Goddess worship?

REFERENCES

Adams, H. (1961). *The education of Henry Adams.* Cambridge, MA: Houghton Mifflin.

Buchmann, D. and C. Spiegel (Eds.). (1994). *Out of the Garden.* New York: Fawcett Columbine.

Carmody, D. L. and J. T. Carmody (1993). *Native American religions.* New York: Paulist Press.

Cloke, G. (1995). *"This female man of God": Women and spiritual power in the patristic age, AD 350-450.* London: Routledge.

Eller, C. (1993). *Living in the lap of the Goddess.* New York: Crossroad.

Elwell, E. S. L. and E. Levenson (Eds.) (1982). *The Jewish women's studies guide.* Fresh Meadows, NY: Biblio Press.

Falk, M. (1989). "Notes on composing new blessings." In *Weaving the visions,* J. Plaskow and P. Christ (Eds.). San Francisco: Harper, pp. 128-138.

Fiorenza, E. S. (1983). *In memory of her: A feminist theological reconstruction of Christian origins.* New York: Crossroad.

Fiorenza, E. S. (1990). "Missionaries, apostles, co-workers: Romans 16 and the reconstruction of women's early Christian history." In *Feminist theology: A reader,* A. Loades (Ed.). Louisville, KY: Westminister John Knox Press, pp. 57-71.

Frankiel, T. (1990). *The voice of Sarah.* New York: Biblio Press.

Frymer-Kensky, T. (1994). "The bible and women's studies." In *Feminist perspectives on Jewish studies,* L. Davidman and S. Tenenbaum (Eds.). New Haven, CT: Yale University Press, pp. 16-39.

Gadon, E. W. (1989). *The once & future Goddess.* San Francisco: Harper.

Gottlieb, L. (1995). *She who dwells within.* San Francisco: Harper.

Hoffman, E. (1995). "The Tree of Life and the 'City of the Just.' " In *Opening the inner gates,* E. Hoffman (Ed.). Boston: Shambhala, pp. 5-19.

Kraemer, R. S. (1992). *Her share of the blessings.* New York: Oxford University Press.

Lloyd, G. (1996). "Augustine and Aquinas." In *Feminist theology: A reader,* A. Loades (Ed.). Louisville, KY: Westminister John Knox press, pp. 90-98.

Lovelock. J. E. (1979). *Gaia, a new look at life on earth.* London: Oxford University Press.

Macquarrie, J. (1990). *Mary for all Christians.* Grand Rapids, MI: Eerdmans.

McLaughlin, E. (1990). "Women, power, and the pursuit of holiness in medieval Christianity." In *Feminist theology: A reader*, A. Loades (Ed.). Louisville, KY: Westminister John Knox Press, pp. 99-122.

Meyers, C. (1988). *Discovering Eve*. New York: Oxford University Press.

Noble, Vicki. (1991). *Shakti woman*. San Francisco: Harper San Francisco.

Plaskow, J. (1994). "Jewish theology in feminist perspective." In *Feminist perspectives on Jewish studies*, L. Davidman and S. Tenenbaum (Eds.). New Haven, CT: Yale University Press, pp. 62-84.

Plaskow, J. and C. Christ (Eds.). (1989). "Transforming the world." In *New patterns in feminist spirituality*, J. Plaskow and C. Christ (Eds.). San Francisco: Harper San Francisco, pp. 269-273.

Ramshaw, G. (1990). "The gender of God." In *Feminist theology: A reader*, A. Loades (Ed.). Louisville, KY: Westminister John Knox Press, pp. 168-180.

Reuther, R. B. (1990). "The liberation of Christology from patriarchy." In *Feminist theology: A reader*, A. Loades (Ed.). Louisville, KY: Westminister John Knox Press, pp. 138-147.

Reuther, R. B. (1993). *Sexism & God-talk*. Boston: Beacon Press.

Reuther, R. B. (1996). *Womanguides*. Boston: Beacon Press.

Rosen, N. (1996). *Biblical women unbound*. Philadelphia: Jewish Publication Society.

Seghi, L. F. (1995). "Glimpsing the moon: The feminine principle in kabbalah." In *Opening the inner gates*, E. Hoffman (Ed.). Boston: Shambhala. pp. 133-159.

Stone, M. (1978). *When God was a woman*. New York: Harcourt Brace Jovanovich.

Stone, M. (1990). *Ancient mirrors of womanhood*. Boston: Beacon Press.

Torjessen, K. J. (1993). *When women were priests*. San Francisco: Harper San Francisco.

Trible, P. (1978). *God and the rhetoric of sexuality, overtures to biblical theology*. Philadelphia, PA: Fortress.

West, A. (1990). "Sex and salvation: A Christian feminist Bible study on I Corinthians 6.12-7.39." In *Feminist theology: A reader*, A. Loades (Ed.). Louisville, KY: Westminister John Knox Press, pp. 72-80.

Zikmund, B. B. (1981). "The struggle for the right to preach." In *Women & religion in America, Vol. I*, R. R. Ruether and R. S. Keller (Eds.). San Francisco: Harper & Row, pp. 193-241.

Chapter 15

Women in Literature:
Women's Writing, Writing About Women

Kathryn Graham

TRADITION AND CHANGE
IN WOMEN'S LITERATURE

The sense of a tradition in women's writing, the "communality and self-awareness" that the word tradition implies, does not appear in Anglo-American women's literature until the *Victorian period,* which lasted from the birth of Queen Victoria in 1837 until her death in 1901. In the United States, very few books by women appeared in the eighteenth century, and though the majority of eighteenth-century novels in England were female-authored, apparently very little direct influence was exerted by these early novelists on the women novelists born after 1800 (Showalter, 1977). Even the work of Jane Austen (1775-1817) had little influence on nineteenth-century women novelists. Mary Wollstonecraft (1759-1797), whose *A Vindication of the Rights of Women* (1792) is seen as the first manifesto of women's rights, was not widely read in the nineteenth century because of her scandalous life (Showalter, 1977).

The British Tradition

Elaine Showalter, whose 1977 study *A Literature of Their Own: British Women Novelists from Brontë to Lessing* is the definitive work on the female literary tradition, points to the 1840s as the real beginning of that tradition in England. Only then did the job of novelist become a recognizable profession for women. As in other literary subcultures, such as African American or Canadian, the first phase of women's writing, the *feminine phase,* is a rather long period of *imitation* of the dominant tradition. Showalter calls these novelists, born between 1800 and 1820 and publishing from the 1840s until 1880, the *feminine novelists*. These women, such as the Brontë sisters, Elizabeth Gaskell, and George Eliot, specialized in *domestic realism*, novels about the home, the community, religion, educa-tion, and society (Showalter, 1977). According to Inga-Stina Ewbank (1966) the focus of these novels is the woman as an influence on others within her domestic and social circle. The typical woman novelist of the 1840s used the novel to demonstrate woman's proper sphere. Ironically, the very act of writing for a woman was deemed a violation of woman's role in Victorian society. Women were expected to live out their lives in service to the family; working outside the home was seen as unwomanly behavior. Hence, many feminine novelists adopted male *pseudonyms* or false names: Mary Ann Evans became George Eliot; Charlotte, Emily, and Anne Brontë became Currer, Ellis, and Acton Bell.

As Showalter (1977) explains:

> One of the many indications that this generation saw the will to write as a vocation in direct conflict with their status as women is the appearance of male pseudonyms. Like Eve's fig leaf, the male pseudonym signals the loss of innocence. In its radical understand-ing of the role-playing required by women's effort to participate in the mainstream of literary culture, the pseudonym is a strong marker of the historical shift. (p. 17)

Examples of "feminine" novels include *Jane Eyre* (1847), *Wuthering Heights* (1847), *Mary Barton* (1848), and *Middlemarch* (1872), just to name a few.

The death of George Eliot in 1880 marked the beginning of the second phase of women's literary tradition, the *protest phase*, lasting until 1920 when women won the vote. The women novelists born between 1820 and 1840, Showalter calls the *feminist novelists*. Protesting the standards and values of the patriarchy, advocating women's rights and values, and demanding autonomy, this second generation of women novelists consoli-dated the gains of the feminine novelists, but were not as original nor as dedicated (Showalter, 1977). Among the feminist novelists were, for example, Sarah Grand, Charlotte Yonge, Eliza Lynn Linton, and Margaret Oliphant.

Of particular interest during this phase was the emergence of the *Ama-zon Utopia*, which depicted a country of all women totally isolated from the male world. Some feminist writers, such as Florence Dixie (*Gloriana*, 1890) and "Ellis Ethelmer" (*Woman Free*, 1893) in England, and Charlotte Perkins Gilman (*Herland*, 1915) in the United States, created worlds gov-erned by women, virgin births, and feminist revolutions (Showalter,

1977). But while they offer interesting and provocative visions of matriarchal societies, they do not suggest solutions to the problems of the patriarchy. Sheila Rowbotham explains, "The dominated can tell stories, they can fantasize, they can create Utopia, but they cannot devise the means of getting there" (Showalter, 1977, p. 58). Nevertheless, the feminist writers had a strong sense of sisterhood and missionary fervor as they penned their stories in support of their "suffering sisters" (Showalter, 1977). About her novel, *From Man to Man* (1926), Olive Schreiner wrote, "I feel that if only one lonely and struggling woman read it and found strength and comfort from it one would not feel one had lived quite in vain" (cited in Showalter, 1977, p. 183).

By the turn of the century the building momentum of the women's movement and the attendant rise of consciousness provided fertile ground for the feminist writers. Olive Schreiner, Mona Caird, and Elizabeth Robins, for example, were developing theories about woman and her relationship to marriage, family, class, work, and production. Members of the Women Writers Suffrage League were theorizing about women's literature and drawing connections between women's socioeconomic position and the female characters and images of women's fiction. Also, the militant suffrage movement was forcing women writers to take a stand on women's rights and thus confront their own feelings of self-hatred and inhibition (Showalter, 1977). Ultimately, however, the feminists retreated from their vision. Many of the novels conclude in images of withdrawal and look forward to a higher female truth (Showalter, 1977).

The third generation of women writers, the *female novelists*, were those born between 1880 and 1900. This group, which most notably includes Virginia Woolf, Dorothy Richardson, and Katherine Mansfield, began publishing in the 1920s during the suffrage movement and after World War I. Gone in this last phase of development are the imitation of the first phase and the protest of the second. The final stage of development in a subculture's literature is characterized by autonomy and *self-discovery*, an introspection that does not rely on opposition, and a search for identity (Showalter, 1977).

In women's literature this last stage begins in the 1920s and extends to the present, including a new stage of self-awareness in the 1960s. Showalter (1977) calls this the female phase because these writers, in their courageous self-exploration and innovations of language and form to reflect the new reality of modernism, created a deliberate female aesthetic. Virginia Woolf is, perhaps, the most important writer of the early female phase. Doris Lessing's work represents the new awareness of the 1960s. Her 1962 novel, *The Golden Notebook*, is a landmark female-phase novel.

It is important to note, however, that any singling out of female-phase novelists is somewhat arbitrary given the vast number of women novelists in this last phase, many of whom are still producing.

The American Tradition

Though the pattern is somewhat different for American women writers, they, too, produced their earliest significant work in the nineteenth century. But the homogeneity of the English tradition is obviously lacking in the American tradition, given the multicultural nature of our society. Twenty years after *A Literature of Their Own* was begun, Showalter (1991) tells of the difficulty in defining an American women's literary tradition:

> when we add to the current debate about what, precisely, the word "American" means the arguments within feminist criticism about class, race, identity and so forth, it becomes clear that writing about American women's literature in the 1990s raises much more complicated problems . . . than did writing about English women's literature . . . in the 1970s. (p. 4)

Nevertheless, Showalter's book, *Sister's Choice: Tradition and Change in American Women's Writing* (1991), provides useful and insightful, if not comprehensive, information about women's writing in the United States. While she makes no attempt in this book to categorize the writing according to the phases of imitation, protest, and self-discovery, both books show that American women's writing has gone/is going through the same phases of development.

The imitative phase in the American tradition is both an imitation of men's writing and, perhaps more important, an imitation of English writing as well. The American women writers' literary identity developed in response to European and English criticism of American culture (Showalter, 1977).

Thus, American feminine novels of the nineteenth century, like their counterparts in England, usually end in marriage, rarely following women characters beyond motherhood. The emphasis in both countries was the domestic sphere. Woman's special and only perceived power in the society lay in the home, and her management and moral surveillance of the home were elevated to cult status. Novels such as Susan Warner's *The Wide, Wide World* (1851) and Harriet Beecher Stowe's *Uncle Tom's Cabin* (1852) depict this special women's culture and its dominant ideology, which venerates motherhood and other female relationships (Showalter,

1991). Women authors believed that if each woman became a worthy representative of domestic values, then women collectively could make a peaceful revolution, changing others by changing themselves (Baym, 1978). Women writers advocated motherly behavior as a subtle critique of patriarchal institutions such as slavery. The gentle, nurturing, educating nature of mothers was offered as a way to ameliorate social problems and make our world a better place (Showalter, 1991). This belief in the moral superiority of women and the home as women's special sphere was shared by feminine—and, indeed, male—novelists on both sides of the Atlantic. But American heroines moved out of the home earlier than did their British sisters.

By the end of the Civil War (1865) women writers could no longer believe in the redemptive powers of domesticity (Baym, 1978), and women's literature entered the phase of protest in the United States. No longer content to stay in the home, women characters assumed male roles and embraced the work ethic that in England was largely confined to males. Showalter (1991) cites the example of *Dora, the American Amazon* (1864) who disguises herself as a man and breaks through rebel territory to deliver information to the Union. And, while English women writers were preoccupied with the problem of women's vocations beyond the boundaries of the home, American women writers assumed that women should work outside the home. A character in *Little Women* (1868) states, for example, "Young ladies in America love independence as much as their ancestors did, and are admired and respected for supporting themselves" (cited in Showalter, 1991, p. 3). Another Alcott character, Christie Devon, in the feminist novel *Work* (1873) works at many jobs and becomes a feminist leader who speaks out for women working. Alcott's own father spoke at women's suffrage conferences about the abilities of women, using his daughter as an example of what American women could accomplish (Showalter, 1991). American women's novels in the last three decades of the nineteenth century were decidedly feminist.

One of the most significant feminist works at the turn of the century, "The Yellow Wallpaper" (1891) by Charlotte Perkins Gilman, is a chilling indictment of patriarchal institutions that treat women as children and rob them of the exercise of their intellectual faculties. Gilman also wrote *Herland* (1915), an Amazon utopian novel mentioned earlier, which argues the superior nature of a society peopled only by women.

One of the most important American women's novels of the nineteenth century and, indeed, "the first aesthetically successful novel to have been written by an American woman" (Showalter, 1991, p. 65) appeared at the very end of the century. The publication of *The Awakening* by Kate Chopin in 1899 marks the beginning of the female phase in American women's literature. Innovative in form and theme, it is characterized by that turning inward, that self-exploration which signals the advent of a conscious female aesthetic. Because of its daring foray into sexual and personal freedom and its withering critique of marriage, *The Awakening* was condemned in its day and lost for many years, unheard of by many generations (Showalter, 1991). Today, however, it is seen as a turning point in women's literature. Other early twentieth-century women writers who contributed significantly to a female aesthetic were Edith Wharton (1862-1937), Willa Cather (1873-1947), and Zora Neale Hurston (1901-1960).

The twentieth century has seen the full development of that female aesthetic and the development of a wide range of literature as well. In their recently published second edition of *The Norton Anthology of Literature by Women* Gilbert and Gubar (1996) have changed their subtitle from the 1985 edition, "The Tradition in English," to "The Traditions in English" to reflect the diversity of women writers covered by the second edition. As they explain in the preface:

> Not only have we included a host of writers who extend our coverage of English, Scottish, Welsh, Irish, Canadian, Australian, Indian, African, Euro-American, Native American, African American, Jewish American, and Asian American authors, but also the anthology now contains new writers from India, Nigeria, Ghana, Botswana, Ireland, and the Caribbean as well as newly emerging voices in Chicano literature. (p. xxxi)

Only history can reveal which writers will endure the test of time, but because of the recovery efforts of scholars like Gilbert and Gubar and the work of many other feminist scholars, it will be a true test, not determined by the arbitrary nature of "canon."

CANON

Many of the women writers we have been discussing are familiar names to us and we know their stories. Some of these stories, such as *Jane Eyre* and *Uncle Tom's Cabin,* have become a part of our cherished heritage, their characters and plots woven into the mythic fabric of our culture. However, there are many women writers whose names we do not know, whose books were widely read but have since gone out of print or have only recently been resurrected by scholars, such as Kate Chopin and her novel, *The Awakening.* The reason why so many of these women writers are lost to us, why their work has disappeared, is that it has not become a part of the *canon*. The canon is that body of literature deemed worthy of study by the literary establishment which, historically, has been composed of white upper- and upper-middle-class men. Until about thirty years ago, the commonly accepted notion about the canon was that only works which met certain objective standards of form and aesthetic value were judged worthy to be canonized. Feminist literary critics in the 1960s were the first to challenge that notion by pointing out that these so-called "objective" judgements were political (Warhol and Herndl, 1991). Hence, the battle over canon was launched and has been raging ever since. Recently, however, feminist critics and others have begun to reject the whole idea of canon since any attempt at objectivity is seen as futile in a world where race, class, gender, age, sexual orientation, and many other variables shape and influence our judgments and interpretations. As Nina Baym (1978), a feminist critic, asks, who is to say that a whaling ship is a more viable symbol of American strength and community than a quilting circle?

THE DEVELOPMENT OF FEMINIST LITERARY CRITICISM

In describing the development of feminist literary criticism, Gilbert and Gubar (1985) identify that early challenge to canon as the first of four overlapping stages, a stage they call the *critique*. During the 1960s and 1970s feminist critics began to explore the devaluation of women characters portrayed by male authors in terms of their own fears and fantasies. In her landmark study of 1970, *Sexual Politics*, Kate Millett demonstrates that critics must take into account the larger cultural context of literature. In another study, *The Lay of the Land* (1976), Annette Kolodny shows how male metaphors exploit and marginalize women.

The feminist critique led to the *recovery stage,* in which lost or neglected female writers and their work were resurrected or reclaimed. Feminist scholars began to study the commonality of women and their work and focused on female literary careers and studies of particular writers and their work. Ellen Moers published *Literary Women* in 1976, and in 1977 the extremely influential study by Elaine Showalter, *A Literature of Their Own,* appeared. Other feminist scholars were examining female creativity, linguistics, and language. Patricia Meyers Spacks's *The Female Imagination* (1975) and Gilbert and Gubar's *The Madwoman in the Attic* (1979a) revolutionized the way we look at women's writing and gave us a new appreciation for female creativity.

This shift from critique to recovery was a shift in focus from male-authored texts or *androtexts* to female-authored texts or *gynotexts*. Elaine Showalter (1981) coined these terms and the term *gynocritics,* meaning the study of "the history, styles, themes, genres, and structures of writing by women; the psychodynamics of female creativity; the trajectory of the individual or collective female career; and the evolution and laws of a female literary tradition" (p. 248).

The work of Gilbert and Gubar and Showalter initiated the third stage of feminist literary criticism: *reconceptualization* of literary history. The fact of female literary commonality showed the existence of an alternative literary history, which provided a new context for already established works and a tradition in which out-of-print texts could be placed (Showalter, 1977). Feminists raised questions about our inherited perceptions of the past as well as the criteria that shape our notions of literary excellence. They called for a revision of the canon and the principles of evaluation that determine greatness. Nina Auerbach's *Communities of Women* (1978) and Gilbert and Gubar's *Shakespeare's Sisters* (1979b) represent the reconceptualization stage.

The final stage of feminist literary criticism is *reassessment,* which has mothered forth a new body of scholarship on gender and creativity. Many commonly accepted ideas about literature are being reevaluated, neglected and forgotten authors and forms are being studied, and women's works that are already established are now being read in the context of a female literary tradition.

Examples of reassessment scholarship include Judith Fetterley's *The Resisting Reader* (1975) and Mary Hiatt's *The Way Women Write* (1977). In 1985 W.W. Norton and Company published its first anthology of *Literature by Women* (Gilbert and Gruber, 1985), a significant breakthrough in canonization.

The four stages of development in feminist literary criticism are not discrete as they overlap and intersect repeatedly. Moreover, they should be viewed as an ongoing process since the recovery of neglected or forgotten women's writing is not finished, and feminist critics across the disciplines continue to contribute new insights and knowledge in the accumulation of scholarship about women and their work.

CONTEMPORARY FEMINIST LITERARY CRITICISM

Today, some thirty years after the early critique stage, feminist literary criticism has indeed grown up. Remarkable for its range of thought and its accommodation of a number of different feminist positions, it is usually defined in terms of geographical brands of feminist literary theory: American, British, and French. Showalter (1979) distinguishes the first two in the following way: *American feminist criticism* has been largely confined to the academy, in English departments and women's studies programs. American feminist critics are preoccupied with the impact of feminist literary ideas on the classroom, the curriculum, and the canon. In Great Britain, however, the bases for feminist criticism have been outside the universities, in radical politics, journalism, and publishing. *British feminist criticism* focuses on the connection between gender and class, popular culture, and feminist critique as Marxist literary theory.

Despite these differences, however, the British and American schools are usually linked together as Anglo-American feminist criticism because they share as their focus the history of women as readers and writers.

French feminist criticism, on the other hand, focuses on the definitions, representations, or repressions of the feminine in art, psychoanalysis, language, and metaphysics (Showalter, 1979). The theoretical base of the French feminists is the work of Jacques Lacan, psychoanalyst; Jacques Derrida, deconstructionist philosopher; and Roland Barthes, structuralist critic. Studying these theorists led French feminists such as Helene Cixous ("The Laugh of the Medusa," 1975) and Julia Kristeva (*Desire in Language,* 1977), to their preoccupation with language and the development of the theory called *l'ecriture feminine,* which means "writing in the feminine." According to Showalter (1985),

> l'ecriture feminine is not necessarily written *by* women; it is an avant-garde writing style . . . However, the most radical French feminist theorists also believe that l'ecriture feminine is connected to the rhythms of the female body and to sexual pleasure *jouissance,* and that women have an advantage in producing this radically disruptive and subversive kind of writing. They urge the woman writer to ally herself with everything in the culture which is muted, silenced, or unrepresented, in order to subvert the existing systems that repress feminine difference. (p. 9)

American feminists are somewhat skeptical as to whether the revolutionary nature of French feminist criticism can have any real revolutionary social impact (Showalter, 1985). But the influence of French theory is a powerful one in critical debate.

Perhaps the single most important issue in feminist literary criticism is the concept of *essentialism.* The French feminists believe that the "realm of the body . . . is . . . somewhat immune ('impregnable') to social and gender conditioning ('rhetorics, regulation, codes') and able to issue forth a pure essence of the feminine" (Barry, 1995, p. 128). Most feminists, however, argue that femininity is socially constructed as a result of our conditioning and the influence of cultural images. They fear that to argue as the French do that femininity is something women just mysteriously possess is to undermine the position of women in the culture. How can women be anything they want to be if they are locked into femininity by birth? The Freudian notion "anatomy is destiny" assumes more credence with the essentialist position. Hence antiessentialism has come to dominate critical theory as we approach the millennium (Barry, 1995).

Another key concept that exerts tremendous influence in critical circles is the concept of *semiotics*, whose major spokesperson is French philosopher, linguist, and psychoanalyst Julia Kristeva. She argues that:

> the pale of sexual difference is the semiotic which is the time of mother/child bonding, a moment of birth erotics, melodies and maternal rhythms, all of which precede the symbolic—the paternal zone. The meeting point of the semiotic and the symbolic in art and literature is in moments of "jouissance" or pleasure. In *Desire in Language* (1977) Kristeva suggests that the symbolic represses the maternal drives, the semiotic, but that these erupt into language in the form of puns and verbal slips. (Humm, 1992, p. 211)

The critical response to l'ecriture feminine, and in particular to the notion of semiotics, is helpfully articulated by Peter Barry (1995), who writes:

> For some feminists this visionary 'semiotic' female world and language evoked by Cixous and Kristeva is a vital theatre of possibilities, the value of which is to entertain the imagining of alternatives to the world which we now have, and which women in particular now have. For others, it fatally hands over the world of the rational to men and reserves for women a traditionally emotive, intuitive, transrational and 'privatized' arena. Not surprisingly, therefore, the language question is one of the most contentious areas of feminist critique. (p. 130)

Despite the Anglo-American rejection of the notion of l'ecriture feminine because of its essentalist nature, feminist literary theory, both at home and abroad, has been strongly influenced by the French feminists. Semiotics has become a valuable tool for literary critics regardless of their critical orientation.

A final comment on contemporary feminist literary theory must recognize the contribution of such groups as African-Americans and lesbians, who in the 1970s and 1980s accused mainstream feminists of excluding their voices and experiences from the dialogue of critical debate. Barbara Smith (1977), for example, and Bonnie Zimmerman (1981) attacked feminist theorists who, in speaking about women and women's writing, assume that there is a common female identity that is essentially white, middle class, and heterosexual. Mainstream feminists, they argued, had replicated the evils of patriarchy in their politics of exclusion. Barbara Smith called for a "thorough articulation of the Black feminist aesthetic" (p. 197). Zimmerman hoped for an expanded "understanding of the lesbian literary tradition and a lesbian aesthetic" (p. 219).

Largely due to their pioneering efforts, feminist literary critics today carefully qualify their use of the word "women" and speak in terms of "feminisms" rather than "feminism." As Naomi Schor has said:

> It is in the interprenetration of different national traditions, the crossing of lesbian, black, marxist, and mainstream feminists, in short in the multiplication of all differences—national, racial, sexual, and class—that the future of feminist literary theory and criticism should lie, and not in the perpetuation of myths of segregation and national superiority. (cited in Showalter, 1991, p. 6)

TOWARD A FEMINIST THEORY OF READING

In 1978, with the publication of her book *The Resisting Reader*, Judith Fetterley was among the first to articulate a feminist theory of reading. Examining several American classics written by men, such as Washington Irving's *Rip Van Winkle* and F. Scott Fitzgerald's *The Great Gatsby*, Fetterley shows how the literature of our culture, our curricula, our canon, since it represents the perception of its male authors, valorizes male experience and excludes female experience, providing, instead, males' perceptions of female experience. And if this isn't bad enough, it insists that male perception and male experience are universal while at the same time describing universality in male terms. As a result, the female reader has to participate in something from which she is excluded. She must identify against herself.

Fetterley goes on to quote Elaine Showalter's powerful piece:

> Women are estranged from their own experience and unable to perceive its shape and authenticity . . . they are expected to identify as readers with masculine experience and perspective, which is presented as the human one . . . . Since they have no faith in the validity of their own perceptions and experiences, rarely seeing them confirmed in literature, or accepted in criticism, can we wonder that women students are so often timid, cautious, and insecure when we exhort them to "think for themselves?" (pp. xxi-xxii)

It is the task then of feminist critics and, indeed, women readers in general to become *resisting readers*, who, by refusing to assent, begin to dispel the male thinking that has shaped our perceptions. As resisting readers we must begin to ask questions about the social acts of construction in the text, as Jean Ferguson Carr (1991) suggests: "Who speaks the shaping words? Who gets to frame or to challenge the terms? Who is left silent?" (p. 575).

As resisting readers we need to approach literature with a new consciousness and thereby come away from it with a new understanding. A new understanding will change the effect literature has on us and pave the way for cultural change.

Fetterley quotes Adrienne Rich's (1972) famous and enormously influential essay, "When We Dead Awaken: Writing as Re-Vision":

> Re-vision—the act of looking back, of seeing with fresh eyes, of entering an old text from a new critical direction—is for us more than a chapter in cultural history: it is an act of survival. Until we can understand the assumptions in which we are drenched we cannot know ourselves. And this drive to self-knowledge, for women, is more than a search for identity; it is part of her refusal of the self-destructiveness of male-dominated society. A radical critique of literature, feminist in its impulse, should take the work first of all as a clue to how we live, how we have been living, how we have been led to imagine ourselves, how our language has trapped as well as liberated us; and how we can begin to see—and therefore live—afresh. (p. xix)

KEY TERMS

Victorian period	self-discovery phase	reassessment stage
imitation phase	(female)	American feminist
(feminine)	canon	criticism
feminine novelists	critique stage	British feminist criticism
domestic realism	recovery stage	French feminist criticism
pseudonyms	androtexts	l'ecriture feminine
protest phase (feminist)	gynotexts	jouissance
feminist novelists	gynocritics	essentialism
Amazon Utopia	reconceptualization	semiotics
female novelists	stage	resisting readers

DISCUSSION QUESTIONS

1. Describe the three phases of women's literary tradition.
2. Explain the evolution of feminist literary criticism.

3. How do you distinguish among the American, British, and French schools of feminist literary criticism?
4. What can women do to become resisting readers?

REFERENCES

Auerbach, N. (1978). *Communities of women: An idea in fiction.* Cambridge, MA: Harvard University Press.

Barry, P. (1995). *Beginning theory: An introduction to literary and cultural theory.* Manchester, UK: Manchester University Press.

Baym, N. (1978). *Women's fiction: A guide to novels by and about women, 1820-1870.* Ithaca, New York: Cornell University Press.

Carr, J. F. (1991). "Afterword: Images of writing/writing images." In *Images of women in literature,* Fifth edition, M. A. Ferguson (Ed.). Boston: Houghton Mifflin Company.

Ewbank, I. S. (1966). *Their proper sphere: A study of the Brontë sisters as early-Victorian female novelists.* London: Edward Arnold.

Fetterley, J. (1978). *The resisting reader: A feminist approach to American fiction.* Bloomington, IN: Indiana University Press.

Gilbert, S. M. and S. Gubar (1979a). *The madwoman in the attic: The woman writer and the nineteenth-century literary imagination.* New Haven, CT: Yale University Press.

Gilbert, S. M. and S. Gubar (1979b). *Shakespeare's sisters.* Bloomington, IN: Indiana University Press.

Gilbert, S. M. and S. Gubar (1985). *The Norton anthology of literature by women: The tradition in English.* New York: W. W. Norton and Company.

Gilbert, S. M. and S. Gubar (1996). *The Norton anthology of literature by women: The traditions in English.* New York: W. W. Norton and Company.

Hiatt, M. (1977). *The way women write.* New York: Teachers College Press.

Humm, M. (1992). *Modern feminisms: Political, literary, cultural.* New York: Columbia University Press.

Kolodny, A. (1976). *The lay of the land: Metaphor as experience and history in American life and letters.* Chapel Hill, NC: University of North Carolina Press.

Millett, K. (1970). *Sexual politics.* London: Virago.

Moers, E. (1976). *Literary women.* Garden City, NY: Doubleday.

Rich, A. (1972). "When we dead awaken: Writing as re-vision." In *On lies, secrets and silence,* A. Rich. New York: W. W. Norton and Company.

Showalter, E. (1977). *A literature of their own: British women novelists from Brontë to Lessing.* Princeton, NJ: Princeton University Press.

Showalter, E. (1979). "Toward a feminist poetics." In *The new feminist criticism: Essays on women, literature, and theory,* E. Showalter (Ed.). New York: Pantheon Books.

Showalter, E. (1981). "Feminist criticism in the wilderness." In *The new feminist criticism: Essays on women, literature, and theory,* E. Showalter (Ed.). New York: Pantheon Books.

Showalter, E. (1985). *The new feminist criticism: Essays on women, literature, and theory*. New York: Pantheon Books.

Showalter, E. (1991). *Sister's choice: Tradition and change in American women's writing*. New York: Oxford University Press.

Smith, B. (1977). "Toward a black feminist criticism." In *The new feminist criticism: Essays on women, literature, and theory*, E. Showalter (Ed.). New York: Pantheon Books.

Spacks, P. M. (1975). *The female imagination*. New York: Knopf.

Warhol, R. R. and D. P. Herndl (1991). *Feminisms: An anthology of literary theory and criticism*. New Brunswick, NJ: Rutgers University Press.

Wollstonecraft, Mary (1792). (reprint, 1989). *A vindication of the rights of women*. Buffalo, NY: Prometheus Books.

Zimmerman, B. (1981). "What has never been: An overview of lesbian feminist criticism." In *The new feminist criticism: Essays on women, literature, and theory*, E. Showalter (Ed.). New York: Pantheon Books.

Chapter 16

Women and Art: Uncovering the Heritage and Building New Directions

April Katz

A reader browsing through standard art history texts written before the late 1980s would have to conclude there were few—if any—women artists in 5,000 years of human history. As Dickinson (1995) notes Gardner's *Art Through the Ages* (published in 1975) mentioned 5,000 men and four women; Janson's *History of Art* (published in 1985) included 3,000 male artists and no female artists. This lack of success for women in the field cannot convincingly be explained by a gendered difference in ability. Rather, sociocultural forces have impeded women artists' development and lowered their status (Nochlin, 1971).

As the feminist movement of the 1970s began to affect the art world, interest in uncovering women artists from the past grew. Undergraduate art history texts now include at least some women artists. For example, Janson's 1995 edition now has 38 women and 3,000 men. The most significant contribution of feminist art historians, however, has been their research into gender issues within the discipline. The study of women artists both affirms women's artistic potential and aids in a critical examination of the art history field. The following brief history of Western women artists examines these women's accomplishments in light of their cultures. The subsequent section on feminist artists examines their unique contributions to contemporary art.

THE MEDIEVAL PERIOD

In contrast to our own times, during the medieval period women who entered convents had the greatest opportunity for intellectual and artistic development as well as financial security. While most of the artwork coming from this period is anonymous, some was signed. A number of images from illuminated manuscripts of the ninth through twelfth centuries were signed by women artists, including Claricia, Guda, Ende, and Hitda. Claricia's signature accompanies a humorous portrait of herself, swinging from an "O" to form the tail of the initial "Q." The abbess Hildegard von Bingen (1098-1179) was a visionary mystic, artist, musical composer, and political and religious leader. The nuns in her convent recorded her writings along with thirty-two images depicting her revelations, in a manuscript known as the *Scivias*. Another significant abbess, Herrade of Landsberg, wrote and illustrated *Hortus Deliciarum (The Garden of Delights)* to educate the nuns in her convent during the twelfth century.

THE RENAISSANCE PERIOD

The Renaissance, a period marked by a rebirth of *Classicism* (a style based on ancient Greek and Roman art in which balance, proportion, and rational order are emphasized) and a celebration of individualism, also was the time in which the glorification of art celebrities began. Names such as Leonardo and Michelangelo were widely recognized, and these men's lives and achievements were chronicled. However, women artists faced increased obstacles in their careers. There was decreased support for convents and limited access to the guilds that provided necessary art training. Studying the nude, especially from antique sculpture, became increasingly important for artists, but was not considered appropriate for women. Male artists studied and worked in urban art centers, yet these were considered too dangerous for women on their own. In addition, women were pressured to follow the strictly defined societal roles of wife and mother. Finally, a new hierarchical evaluation of art evolved during the Renaissance. It elevated painting to the highest levels of creativity, while it relegated traditional "feminine" arts, such as embroidery, to lower levels.

In spite of these limitations, quite a few women were successful artists. Many received training and support from their artist fathers. This was true for Sofonisba Anguissola (1535-1625). Her father, a widower, chose to educate his six daughters as well as his one son. Sofonisba, the eldest, received professional encouragement from Michelangelo and lived and worked primarily as a portrait painter in the court of Phillip II of Spain for almost twenty years. In the progressive city of Bologna, whose university had matriculated women since the thirteenth century, women were encouraged to participate in all of the humanities. Lavinia Fontana (1552-1614), whose father was a painter, became an official painter to the papal court, and a medal was created in her honor.

THE BAROQUE PERIOD

The seventeenth-century *Baroque* style emphasized emotional expression through dynamic compositions and dramatic lighting. Elisabetta Sirani (1638-1665) was a prolific painter who died at age twenty-six. More than 150 extant works have been attributed to her. While she was still alive, her father, also a painter, began to claim her works as his own. Her response was to paint in public to prove the authenticity of her works and demonstrate her ability. Her 1663 *Virgin and Child* was featured on a 1994 Christmas stamp issued by the United States Postal Service (see Figure 16.1).

One of the most well-known woman painters from this period was Artemesia Gentileschi (1593-1652) daughter of the famed painter Orazio Gentileschi. Unfortunately his studio assistant, who served as Artemesia's teacher, raped her, and she went through an arduous public trial. During her long career she made many dynamic paintings of powerful women, including Mary Magdalene, Esther, Cleopatra, the apocryphal story of Judith, and her own self-portrait.

DUTCH AND FLEMISH ART IN THE RENAISSANCE AND BAROQUE

In Northern Europe the development of a middle class, increased commerce, and improved literacy affected the position of art in that society and indirectly provided more opportunities for women artists. After the sixteenth century Reformation, art was produced for the decoration of middle class homes and not for churches. Artists in Protestant countries such as the Netherlands no longer relied on church commissions but were able to sell their paintings in a free market. The prohibition against religious images led to an increase of allegorical works and broader development of still life, landscape, and *genre* (scenes of everyday life) as subjects.

Artists such as Clara Peeters (1594-1657) and Maria van Oosterwyck (1630-1693) created *vanitas* paintings, moralizing representations in the form of still lifes. Depictions of natural objects such as flowers and fruit conveyed the transience of life. These works were highly naturalistic, with great attention paid to the surface textures and play of light on the objects depicted. Judith Leyster (1609-1660) is best known for her genre paintings that depict women and men actively involved in their daily activities. Many of her works have been mistakenly attributed to male artists of her time, particularly her teacher, Frans Hals. When one famous painting was attributed to Hals, it was considered a masterpiece. However, after estab-

FIGURE 16.1. *Virgin and Child* (1663), oil on canvas, 34″ x 27½″, by Elisabetta Sirani (1638-1665). Reprinted with permission from The National Museum of Women in the Arts/The Holladay Collection.

lishing that Leyster had created it, reviewers described it as weak and feminine (Greer, 1979; Chadwick, 1990).

Accompanying the increase in exploration and colonization during this period in Dutch history, the classification, cultivation, and illustration of newly-discovered plants were popular pursuits. A remarkable woman of this period whose work reflects these cultural influences was Maria Sibylla Merian (1647-1717). Her father was an engraver of flower illustrations, and her stepfather was a flower painter. When she was twenty-two she published her first volume of engravings, *The Wonderful Transformation of Caterpillars and Their Singular Plant Nourishment*. In 1699 she went to a Dutch colony in South America with her daughter to study insects, plants, animals, and even native customs. The sixty plates in her resulting volume, *Metamorphosis Insectorum Surinamsium*, reflect the important role she played as a scientific investigator and the aesthetic contributions she made to botanical illustration (see Figure 16.2).

The flower paintings of Rachel Ruysch (1666-1750) show her interest in vanitas and the study of natural forms, particularly flowers. Her father, a professor of anatomy and botany, and her mother, an intellectual, encouraged her artistic development by arranging for her apprenticeship to a respected flower painter. Although Ruysch raised ten children, she maintained her membership in the painting guild, was a court painter, and sold her paintings for more money than those of her famous contemporary, Rembrandt. Her floral compositions, with their swirling diagonal arrangements and dramatic lighting, reflect the Baroque style.

EIGHTEENTH CENTURY

During the eighteenth century, the art world became more structured as academies were formed to teach and promote the arts. Although women were allowed in the academies as an honor, many membership privileges were withheld from them. Women members were often prevented from attending drawing classes, teaching, holding office, or competing for prizes in exhibitions. Although the Academie Royale in Paris had seven women members in 1682, it was almost forty years before another woman was granted membership. In 1706 the policy was reversed, and new women members were prohibited. In spite of this rule, women were admitted occasionally. In 1753, to reconcile the difference between the rules and the existence of four women members, the academy established a new limit of four women. The English Royal Academy, founded in 1768, had only two women members, Mary Moser and Angelica Kauffman, until the twentieth century.

FIGURE 16.2. Plate 12 from *Dissertation in Insect Generations and Metamorphosis in Surinam* (1719), bound volume of seventy-two hand-colored engravings, Second Edition, by Maria Sibylla Merian (1647-1717). Reprinted with permission from The National Museum of Women in the Arts/The Holladay Collection.

Despite these limitations, there are records of many women artists actively working during this century. The works of many eighteenth-century women artists have been used during the twentieth century to demonstrate that work by women artists is light, sentimental, and frivolous. These qualities, however, reflect the then popular *Rococo* style (characterized by ornate, asymmetric, and curvilinear ornamentation with pastel colors) and the stylistic expectations of artists' aristocratic patrons. During this century, women in the upper classes, particularly in France and England, began to enjoy increased influence socially and intellectually as leaders of salons and as patrons of the arts.

Rosalba Carriera (1675-1752), the eldest of three daughters, helped her mother make lace when she was young. As that industry declined, Carriera began painting portrait miniatures on ivory. She was best known for her lifelike pastel portraits such as the one she made of King Louis XV. Her pastels combined controlled detail and looser, more spontaneous passages and helped to popularize the medium. The Academie Royale, in recognition of the quality of her pastels, invited Carriera to become a member. Her patrons included members of the aristocracy in Denmark, England, Italy, and Poland.

One of the most successful women artists of this period was Marie Louise Elizabeth Vigee-Lebrun (1755-1842). Before the age of twenty she was a successful portraitist of the Parisian aristocracy, and by twenty-five she was working for Queen Marie Antoinette, who supported her entrance into the Academie Royale. The stylistic variations found in her portraits reveal the cultural forces that influenced women artists of her time. She depicted members of the aristocracy in a flattering and formal manner, friends in a more relaxed and inventive style, and herself in a stylized, ladylike way. During the course of her career she completed almost 800 paintings.

Adelaide Labille-Guiard (1747-1803) was admitted into the French Academy in 1783, simultaneously with Vigee-Lebrun. She painted portraits of the academicians to win their favor and gain acceptance into the academy. Once her career was established, she became an important teacher of young female artists and a spokesperson for their rights. She painted *Self-Portrait with Students* (1785) after the academy established a quota of four women members. This work symbolically elevated her students' reputations and indicated her importance as a teacher.

When it became apparent that the Swiss artist Angelica Kauffman (1741-1807) was exceptionally skilled, her artist-father stopped his own painting to manage her career, and they traveled throughout Europe seeking commissions. In Italy, where she was accepted into the academy, she encountered *Neoclassicism*. This style was based on classical Greek and

Roman themes with a visual emphasis on balance, proportion, and harmony. By this time the art world had developed a hierarchy of value in which history painting was the most prestigious subject matter. Kauffman refused to focus exclusively on portraiture and adopted the neoclassical principles of stagelike space, idealized figures, and calm compositions in her history paintings. In 1766 she went to England, where she helped to found the Royal Academy and maintained an international array of clients. Her reputation, immense during her lifetime, was made evident upon her death, when she was honored with a grand funeral procession in Rome in which representatives from French, Italian, and Portugese art academies marched. Her funeral was based on a similar ritual commemorating the famous Renaissance artist, Raphael.

NINETEENTH CENTURY

Dramatic social changes stemming from the industrial revolution marked this century, in which the bourgeoisie became the dominant social class. The social spheres considered appropriate for members of each gender were clearly differentiated during this, the Victorian Era. In contrast to the previous century, nineteenth-century women's very restricted place was seen to be in the home, and new standards of appropriate domestic behavior were widely disseminated. Women were idealized as virtuous and moral, providers of beauty, and necessary for the establishment and maintenance of domestic order. In Western Europe and the United States, however, reform movements fought for equality for women. Women raised by families involved in these movements were given a broader range of options in their lives.

During this century, *Romanticism* advanced the concept of "artist" as a male creative genius who was antisocial, eccentric, and a loner. On the other hand, a "woman artist" was one who showed good taste and delicacy, was skilled at repetitive and mindless activities, and was involved in the minor arts. While late-nineteenth-century Victorian art historians recognized the increasing number of professional women artists, they spoke of them belonging, as in the rest of Victorian life, to a separate and lesser sphere (Chadwick, 1990).

By the middle of the century, lower wages made it difficult for one parent to support a family. The Civil War in the United States and the Napoleonic Wars in Europe decreased the numbers of male workers; increasingly, large numbers of unmarried women needed to support themselves. The abolitionist movement politicized many women, and an active women's rights movement was established. Women seeking to develop professional art skills began demanding the right to work with nude models and to gain access to the most highly respected art academies in England, France, and the United States. Separate art schools, life drawing classes, and art associations for women were instituted. However, by the time women began to be admitted into the established academies and life drawing classes on a regular basis, this type of work and training had become outdated.

Many nineteenth-century women artists nevertheless overcame social obstacles and had successful careers. Sarah Miriam Peale (1800-1885) was more easily able to support herself as a painter due to her decision to remain single. She studied painting from her father and her well-known uncle, the artist Charles Wilson Peale. (Charles's strong belief in women's equality is evident in the names he chose for four of his daughters: Sophonisba Anguisciola, Angelica Kauffmann, Rosalba Carriera and Sybilla Miriam Peale.) Sarah was an important portrait painter in Baltimore and later in St. Louis. During her career of more than fifty years, she successfully competed with men for commissions and painted the portraits of such famous people as Daniel Webster, the Marquis de Lafayette and Senator Thomas Hart Benton. Unfortunately, many of her works have been lost or attributed to other artists.

Lilly Martin Spencer (1822-1902) was one of the most renowned genre painters in the United States during this time. Her parents, who came to the United States with the intention of living in a utopian community, were involved in the abolitionist, women's rights, and temperance movements. They provided all their children with a thorough education at home. When, at a young age, Lilly expressed interest in art, her father accompanied her to Cincinnati to help her pursue this goal. She married Benjamin Rush Spencer, with whom she had thirteen children, seven of whom lived. Her husband, recognizing her abilities, handled their domestic needs and managed the business aspects of her career. As the family's sole wage earner, Spencer satisfied the public's taste for sentimental domestic scenes.

The French artist Rosa Bonheur (1822-1899) learned from her reformist father that women and artists are superior beings who have a responsibility to elevate society, an attitude that led to her lifelong dedication to work. She chose not to marry but remained in a devoted relationship with Natalie Micas, her companion of forty years. Since Bonheur's realistic, energetic images of animals were based on observation of her own menagerie of animals and those at slaughterhouses and animal markets, she depended on the greater mobility pants offered, compared to standard women's fashions. However, at this time women were not allowed to wear pants without special permission from the French police, which Bonheur applied for and received. Activists in the Victorian movements for women's and animals' rights were concerned about issues of power and free will. *The Horse Fair*, her most famous work and one of the best-known paintings of the century, attracted critical attention when it was exhibited in France, England, and the United States. Queen Victoria arranged for a private viewing of the work at Buckingham Palace. Later in life, Bonheur was the first woman artist to receive the French Cross of the Legion of Honor.

In the nineteenth century, American neoclassical sculptors travelled to Italy for its fine marble, skilled artisans (who could translate clay models into stone), low cost of living, and the many classical sculptures available to them for study. Harriet Hosmer (1820-1908), the most famous woman sculptor of the century, was the first of a group of American women sculptors to travel to Italy. Her unorthodox upbringing included abundant physical activity and a permissive and liberal education that fostered an independent attitude. Hosmer, in her sculpture *Zenobia in Chains*, depicted a defeated and chained queen from the third century who nevertheless remains bold and dignified.

The most unusual of the women neoclassical sculptors, from a cultural perspective, was Edmonia Lewis (ca. 1843-1909). Her mother was a Chippewa Indian and her father was African-American. Overcoming many obstacles early in her life, she was able to go to Italy with funds both from sales of her work and from supportive patrons. Lewis is best known for her naturalistic sculptures, such as *Forever Free*, which convey the pain and suffering of enslaved African Americans. Although considered stylistically conservative by the end of the century, women neoclassical sculptors had successful careers, and their works remain on public display throughout the United States.

Throughout the century, painters became increasingly interested in working outside, directly from nature, in a looser, more spontaneous style that focused on the effects of light. Continuing from these earlier efforts, *Impressionism*, which began in the 1870s, used loose brushwork and brilliant color to capture momentary effects of light and atmosphere. Due to the influence of photography, invented earlier in the century, Impressionists frequently cropped their subjects in an attempt to enhance the sense of a fleeting moment.

Contemporary feminist critics have supplemented this standard formal description of Impressionism with an in-depth social investigation. They point to the fact that women artists had easier access to the Impressionists' preferred subjects of genre and the landscape, as opposed to nudes. Male Impressionists often painted scenes of public life. Women Impressionists, however, had to focus on their experiences in the domestic world, since public spaces were not considered appropriate for women. Feminist examination of the paintings of women and children by Impressionists Mary Cassatt and Berthe Morisot reveals much about the gender-separated culture they lived in (Chadwick, 1990).

Mary Cassatt (1844-1926) moved to Europe for further study after four years of what she considered "constrictive" training at the Pennsylvania Academy of Fine Arts. By 1873 she had a studio in Paris and was exhibiting and selling her work. Her parents and sister came to live with her in 1877. As an unmarried daughter, over the years, she was the one who had to nurse all three through long, fatal illnesses. Although family obligations limited her production, Cassatt had a very successful career as a painter and innovative printmaker, helped to promote the Impressionists in the United States, served as consultant for a number of important art collectors in the States, and was politically active as a suffragist.

Her work was realistic, with a solid foundation of drawing, and included brilliant color, unusual angles, cropped compositions, candid poses, and decorative pattern. She is best known for images of women and children, often drawn from family members. Cassatt's depiction of women, from childhood to adolescence and to old age, served as a visual analysis and critique of their socialization. For instance, in *Mother and Child,* painted in 1905, a mother holds a hand mirror up for her young daughter, seated on her lap. Both are reflected in a larger mirror behind the seated pair. While the mirrors formally serve to extend our view and the space, they convey the socialization of women as subject to other people's observation (Chadwick, 1990).

Berthe Morisot (1841-1895) and her sister, like other young girls of the time, were given drawing lessons as part of their upper-class education. The teacher, alarmed at the girls' proficiency, warned their parents that it would be catastrophic for them, as women, to be artists. The Morisots, however, remained supportive of their daughters' interest in art. Although her sister stopped painting when she married, Berthe painted all her life. As one of the founding members of the Impressionists, Morisot had the advantage of regular interaction with many of the leading Impressionists, including Edouard Manet, who was her husband's brother. Like Cassatt, Morisot's primary subjects were women and children in domestic spaces.

EARLY TWENTIETH CENTURY

The dramatic changes that occurred in every aspect of twentieth-century life were paralleled by rapid stylistic changes in its art. The new century was marked by such technological advances as electric power, automobiles and airplanes, telephones, and new building materials such as reinforced concrete. Movies, radio, genetics, the theory of relativity, the discovery of radioactive materials, and psychoanalysis all appeared around 1900. Photography had become fairly common, exerting a powerful influence on art. The concept of reality was greatly influenced by all these dramatic cultural and technological changes. While the Impressionists visually represented light's impact on our perception of a subject, later artists, particularly Cézanne and the Cubists, showed that the observer's particular viewpoint affects perception.

Twentieth-century *Modernism* includes a broad range of art movements in which formal manipulation of both media and visual elements is the primary objective, while realistic representation of the visual world is not considered important. Within Modernism, *Expressionist* styles focus on the manipulation of these elements to convey a personal or subjective response to the world. Women artists have been involved in all of the major modern art movements of the twentieth century. The degree of recognition they received, however, was consistently less than that for men. They continued to face more obstacles than their male colleagues.

The Expressionist Suzanne Valadon (1867-1938) used the pure, brilliant color, pattern, and flat compositions of the Impressionists, but included outlines and broader paint application. Valadon was the illegitimate daughter of a laundress. Forced to support herself from the age of ten, she was modeling for artists by the 1880s. As an uninhibited model with numerous lovers, Valadon was positioned outside bourgeois notions of the feminine. This marginal status explains her ability to paint nudes, an unusual subject for women artists of her time. Her women seem to be engaged in purposeful thoughts and activities, unconcerned with the viewer. Valadon's portrayal of the relationship between a mother and daughter in *The Abandoned Doll* from 1921 (see Figure 16.3) conveys a theme similar to Cassatt's 1905 *Mother and Child.* Here, a mother sits reassuringly by her young, naked, adolescent daughter, who curiously regards herself in the mirror while her doll, or childhood, lies abandoned on the floor.

Paula Modersohn-Becker (1876-1907) was a prolific Expressionist painter who lived and worked in a rural art colony in Worpswede, Germany. Regular solitary trips to Paris helped her escape the confinement she felt in her marriage and the stylistic conservatism of the colony. Modersohn-Becker used simplified forms, warm earth tones, and cropping to transform her images of rural German women into monumental icons of motherhood and fertility. She died at age thirty-one, three weeks after her daughter was born.

Throughout her career, Käthe Kollwitz (1867-1945) created drawings, prints, and sculptures that movingly expressed the pain of poverty, war, death, and economic hardship. Her etching from 1900, *The Downtrodden,*

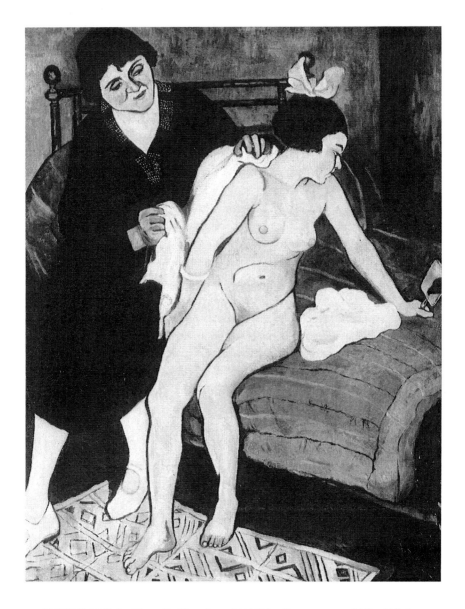

FIGURE 16.3. *La Poupée Abandonné* (1921), oil on canvas, 51″ x 32″, by Suzanne Valadon (1865-1938). Reprinted with permission from The National Museum of Women in the Arts/The Holladay Collection.

shows Kollwitz's characteristic manipulation of tone to draw our attention to her figures' expressive faces and hands. From the dark background a pale, grim woman's face stares down at the pasty white face of her dead child. The mother's gnarled hands hold the child's face, while the father hands her a rosary and covers his own face in grief. Kollwitz was the first woman to be elected to the Prussian Academy of the Arts, and became director of its graphic arts division, but was later forced out by the Nazis.

Sonia Delaunay (1885-1979) was born to a wealthy Russian family who supported her study of art. Her marriage to the painter Robert Delaunay in 1910 led to a lifelong partnership of mutually acknowledged collaboration. Although her first one-person exhibition was in 1908, she did not exhibit her own paintings again until 1953, following her husband's death. Instead, she applied the abstract ideas they had developed together to the applied arts of tapestry, books, furniture, textiles, and fashion design. In so doing, she helped to extend the avant-garde concepts of abstraction beyond the fine art world and brought functional design ideas to the fine arts.

The utopian ideologies associated with postrevolutionary Russia enabled the greatest egalitarian participation by women in the development of the arts that had occurred in any Western society. Women *Constructivists* (artists working in the Russian style of nonobjective art) such as Liubov Popova (1889-1924) and Varvara Stepanova (1894-1958) applied these theoretical positions professionally to their theater, textile, and industrial designs.

Georgia O'Keeffe's (1887-1986) paintings of flowers, cow skulls, and desert landscapes are among the most universally recognized works by any American artist. There is ample documentation of her strong work ethic, independent spirit, training, influences, and the promotion of her work by her husband and art dealer, the photographer Alfred Stieglitz. Her paintings involve abstraction through simplification of form and the use of bright, pure color. The similarity of the organic, sensual forms of her large-scale flowers to women's vulvae was recognized by Freudians in the 1920s and feminists in the 1970s. O'Keeffe resented the emphasis critics placed on the feminine quality of her work, and stressed her interest in the beautiful formal qualities of her subjects, instead.

Modernist optimism over the promise of technology ended with World War I. The scope of the devastation wrought by this new age of technological military might was horrifying. *Dada*, the ensuing nihilistic art movement, reflected the disillusionment and lack of meaning evident in postwar society. Hannah Höch (1889-1978) exhibited photomontages of newspaper and magazine photographs, illustrations, and text with other Berlin Dadaists in the postwar years. Challenging the political status quo, her collages such as *Cut with the Kitchen Knife* juxtaposed absurd combinations of figures and machines with dramatic shifts of scale and viewpoint to challenge our sense of reality and order.

Many of the visual qualities associated with Dada were adopted by the *Surrealists*, whose works expressed the bizarre and often illogical workings of the unconscious. Most of the mature works of the women Surrealists were made after they severed their ties to the movement and to the male Surrealists with whom they were intimately involved. Feminists note the marginal status women had in the movement. Their criticism shows this marginalization was partially based on the fundamental Surrealist objectification of woman as a symbol of the unconscious and as man's muse and inspiration (Chadwick, 1985). This position is in direct conflict with an artist's need to be an active subject who freely expresses herself. The misogynist attitudes of the male Surrealists were also evident in their frequent depiction of mutilated women's bodies, often headless, dismembered, or pierced.

In spite of these attitudes, Whitney Chadwick points to the benefits Surrealism offered women artists. "In recognizing her intuitive connection with the magic realm of existence that governed creation, Surrealism offered the woman artist a self-image that united her roles as woman and creator. . . ." (Chadwick, 1985 p. 182). Remedios Varo (1913-1963) and Leonora Carrington (b. 1917) created mythical images based on women's experiences of creativity. Varo's painting *Harmony*, like many of her works, shows an androgynous creator involved with an alchemical fusion of natural and mathematical elements in a spiritual setting.

Several of the women Surrealists made paintings that conveyed negative feelings about the experience of procreation and motherhood. *Maternity*, by Dorothea Tanning (b. 1910), depicts a barefoot mother with torn clothes and distended belly, holding her child in a menacing and barren landscape. Frida Kahlo (1910-1954) explored this theme repeatedly in works such as *My Birth* and *Henry Ford Hospital*. The first depicts Kahlo's adult head as she emerges in birth from between her mother's legs, and the second expresses her pain following one of her miscarriages.

LATER TWENTIETH CENTURY

World events in the 1930s and 1940s helped establish New York City as the capital of the Western art world by the 1950s. The New York art world benefitted from the large numbers of artists and intellectuals fleeing war and fascist control in Europe. Under their influence, the first internationally recognized American art style, *Abstract Expressionism*, developed. In these very large, energetic, spontaneous, and nonobjective paintings, the mark or gesture of the individual artist was extremely important. The macho attitudes of the artists (and their exuberant style) reflected the United States's new position of international leadership and increasing prosperity following World War II.

Although women involved in Abstract Expressionism made significant contributions and had successful careers, their work was overshadowed by the phenomenal publicity and commercial success of their husbands. Artists Lee Krasner and Elaine de Kooning were less recognized and given fewer exhibition opportunities than their husbands, Jackson Pollock and Willem de Kooning, the stars of the movement. During the 1950s women were expected to be homemakers; women artists were not perceived as committed professionals.

Helen Frankenthaler (b. 1928), a second generation Abstract Expressionist, was a Color Field painter. Her innovative process of allowing poured paint to stain the raw canvas influenced other artists and was highly praised by critics. Her paintings contain large, fluid, organic shapes that resonate with color and light. Alma Thomas (1892-1978), an African-American artist who taught art in the public schools of Washington, DC, for thirty-five years, did not enjoy national recognition until the end of her life, when she was given one-person shows at the Whitney Museum and Corcoran Gallery. Her color fields are composed of bright, mosaic-like shapes of color derived from her appreciation of nature.

In reaction to the self-absorption of Abstract Expressionism, 1960s *Minimalism* adopted a clean, systemic approach to abstraction that hid all traces of the artist's hand and expression. The quiet, unified grids of Agnes Martin (b. 1912) offer visual fields that, like the surfaces of waterfalls, encourage meditation. Her classical, ordered approach is a revolt against the expressive theatrics of the Abstract Expressionists and results in paintings with a pure and spiritual presence. She has been recognized as one of the most significant painters in the movement. Bridget Riley (b. 1931) was one of the founders of *Op Art*, a hard-edged, slick, abstract style that explored optical illusions. In Riley's patterned paintings, the elements undergo precise modulations that create the illusion of movement.

FEMINIST ART

Lack of information regarding women artists, limited professional opportunities, and the art world's ingrained biases against women artists contributed to their peripheral position. In 1970, 60 percent of students in American art schools were women, and 50 percent of the artists in the United

States were women. Yet, in that same year, only 11 percent of university art professors were women; only 2 percent of the studio faculty were women; ten of the major commercial galleries in New York City had exhibitions for 190 male artists and only 18 women artists; only 6 percent of the Whitney Museum's 1969 Annual Exhibition of important contemporary artists were women; and only 18 percent of the commercial galleries in the country showed works by women (Olin and Brawer, 1989).

In reaction to these statistics, feminist activists organized public protests to fight women's exclusion from exhibitions. Women-only galleries, such as A.I.R. (Artists in Residence) and SOHO 20 in New York City, Artemisia in Chicago, The Woman's Building in Los Angeles, and MUSE Gallery in Philadelphia provided venues for women to exhibit their work. Also in the 1970s, books about women artists began to be published, and feminist art journals such as *Chrysalis*, *womanart*, and *Heresies* were founded. Professional associations for women artists established at this time helped provide women with a network of support.

Judy Chicago and Miriam Schapiro originated a completely new model for artists' education in the Feminist Art Program at the California Institute of the Arts in the early 1970s. Students researched women artists, writings, and feminist theory; relied on consciousness-raising to link personal experience to political issues; made work in which content, often autobiographical, was the focus; asserted women's sexuality and power through body imagery; appropriated popular imagery; used craft-related media and techniques; created performances and rituals; produced collaborative pieces; and frequently employed collage techniques.

While the aforementioned strategies helped to increase opportunities for women artists, the statistics, as of 1995, are still bleak. According to one source, in 1995 more than 50 percent of professional artists in this country were women, and at least 50 percent of the art students were women. Despite some improvements, only 28 percent of art faculty were women, and women artists still earned significantly less than men. Women artists made up only 14.5 percent of invitational exhibitions. Yet in blind, juried exhibitions, when the artists' identities were unknown, 48 percent of the included artists were women (Dickinson, 1995).

Numerous artists react to gender bias through their art. Mary Beth Edelson honored women artists in her 1972 piece, *Some Living American Women Artists*. Edelson replaced the men pictured in Leonardo da Vinci's *Last Supper* with contemporary American women artists. Georgia O'Keeffe is shown in Christ's position at the center of the table. Over sixty additional women artists' portraits serve as a frame for this women's celebration dinner.

Judy Chicago, in her 1970s installation *The Dinner Party*, also responded by celebrating women's accomplishments. This work is composed of a triangular table, forty-eight feet on each side, and includes thirty-nine place settings that correspond to specific historic or mythic women. Each woman's place is identified with a fabric runner created with techniques, materials, and symbols significant for her life and times. Each setting also has a ceramic plate painted with an abstract butterfly-labia symbol. On the plates representing Georgia O'Keeffe and Virginia Woolf, the last two in the chronology, the ceramic labia actually project above the surface of the plates, conveying liberation and transformation. The names of 999 significant women from throughout history are written on the ceramic floor. Some of the women honored at the table include goddesses such as Kali, a Hindu goddess of death, and Ishtar, the Great Goddess of ancient Mesopotamia; writers such as Emily Dickinson, Sappho, and Virginia Woolf; political leaders such as Queen Elizabeth I. and Hatshepsut; and healers such as Margaret Sanger and Elizabeth Blackwell. The installation required extensive historical and technical research, included help by hundreds of people, and required over five years to complete. More than 75,000 people viewed it in the Brooklyn Museum, and it has been displayed in other locations internationally.

The highly publicized *The Dinner Party* has provoked vehement debate within the art world, the feminist community, and the general population. The revised history of Western culture and the sexual imagery presented in the installation met with conservative resistance. Modernist art critics, faced with Chicago's bold challenge to their ideals about the nonreferential purity of art, ridiculed her work. While *The Dinner Party* has been affirming to thousands of women, it has generated considerable controversy among feminists. The central vulvar imagery—employed by Chicago as a symbol for women's consciousness of their own bodies, sexual pleasure, and power—has been condemned as an *essentialist* or falsely universal view of women as biologically determined. *Poststructural* feminists who attempt to deconstruct assumptions about universal truths criticize her approach. Some feminists applaud collaborative art making and the use of craft processes and media as effective methods to combat the art hierarchy. However, there was a very clear power structure for those working on *The Dinner Party*. It was not true collaboration; this was Judy Chicago's creation. Chicago's emphasis on the achievements of "great," primarily white, women and her desire to create a monumental masterpiece for women were criticized for not challenging the fundamental hierarchical values of the art world and society in general. *The Dinner Party*, as a significant icon of Feminist art, continues to generate debate, discussion, and imitation.

With the recognition that our cultural assumptions are not all true or essential came the desire by a number of feminist artists to expose the gender biases of our society. Sylvia Sleigh's painting *The Turkish Bath* (1973) embodies this concern. The painting depicts six nude contemporary male art critics, posed in a relaxed group. This work critiques the Western tradition of paintings of nude women exemplified by Ingres' *The Turkish Bath* (1820). Ingres's painting portrays almost two dozen nude women reclining in varied sensual positions—passive objects intended to give pleasure and power to the presumed male observer (Berger, 1977). The discomfort viewers have upon seeing Sleigh's painting of nude men in similar poses helps to expose the gender inequity inherent in conventional nudes. Traditionally, artists depicted nude women in the glossy manner associated with advertising: rounded, alluring, smooth, and without blemish or unique personal traits. However, since Sleigh's depiction of the six men was individualized, the men were less objectified than Ingres's women were. Sleigh's work suggests the value of approaching the naked model as an individual rather than as a generic nude.

The debate between essentialists and poststructuralists shows that positive, nonobjectified representation of women's bodies is difficult. A particularly challenging work that directly addressed this dilemma was Linda Benglis's 1974 ad in the national magazine *Artforum*. The ad contained a photograph of Benglis in a pinup position with a dildo rising from her crotch. The image's combination of masculine-feminine and passive-aggressive qualities destroyed the usual allure associated with beautiful women in advertisements.

Lorna Simpson combines photographic imagery with text to encourage the critical examination of perception. Simpson, an African American who began her career as a documentary photographer, questioned the objectivity implied in that genre. Her work focuses attention on the ways stereotypical language describing race and gender negates individual identity. *You're Fine* includes a color photograph showing the back view of a black woman, wearing a nondescript white slip, reclining in a pose reminiscent of the traditional female nude. To the left of the photograph are twelve plastic plaques, stacked one above the other. Each plaque is engraved with a medically oriented word or phrase, such as "PHYSICAL EXAM," "CHEST X-RAY," "REFLEXES," "URINE," and "HEIGHT." To the right of the photograph are two plaques engraved with the words "SECRETARIAL POSITION," while ceramic letters above and below the photo state "YOU'RE FINE" and "YOU'RE HIRED." The text adds many levels of meaning beyond the feminist critique of the privileged male gaze. The concept of a public, institutional gaze—which has the right to control and objectify—and issues of class subjugation and racial discrimination are elements of Simpson's works.

Cindy Sherman also uses photography to examine identity. Using herself as the model, she transforms her identity so significantly through makeup, costumes, sets, lighting, and camera angle that these works cannot be considered self-portraits. Instead, her subjects are socially defined women's roles. During the late 1970s, Sherman made black and white photographs of herself that resembled stills from B movies. In the nearly eighty images from this series, she critically examined media stereotypes of women. For her later art-historical portrait series, she recreated famous painted portraits with color photographs of herself. Most recently she has included mannequins, masks, doll parts, and artificial limbs with images of herself in photographs based on pornographic pictures and horror films. These latest, often violent works, extend her concern with gender into examination of abuse and women's objectification.

Inquiry into homosexuality challenges prevailing notions of gender identity. Lesbian artists' marginalized position enables them to offer alternative images of women that serve to deconstruct the dominant culture's gender biases. Lesbian art from the 1970s and early 1980s, influenced by feminist concerns about women's objectification and by the antipornography movement, tended to be asexual or to hide sexuality in coded abstraction. Hollis Sigler's 1978 drawing *Let Me Love You in Fleshy Colors* shows a warm, domestic space in which two people are embracing. Their gender is not apparent, however, as was typical of work from that time. Harmony Hammond's abstract sculptures from this period were made of armatures wrapped with cloth and covered with various combinations of rubber, acrylic, wax, and charcoal. See Figure 16.4 for an example. These soft yet massive forms were intended to convey the sensuality and sexuality found in Wittig's lesbian novels *Les Guerilleres* and *The Lesbian Body.*

Tee Corinne's *The Cunt Coloring Book* (1975) was much more explicit than other lesbian art from the period because its distribution was limited to lesbians. The line drawings from this actual coloring book—based on observation of her friends—celebrated eroticism, and echoed other women artists' exploration of the female form during that time. By embracing a word that had been used pejoratively, Corinne and other feminists empowered themselves. Many lesbian artists from the late 1980s and 1990s rebelled against the censoring elements of the antipornography movement and embraced their sexuality and the role of fantasy. Deborah Bright, in her series *Dream Girls,* pastes photographs of herself as a butch

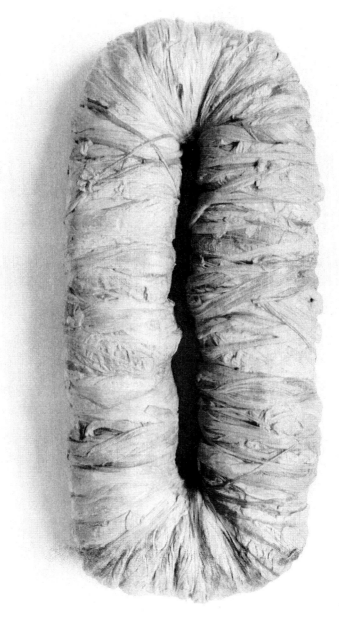

FIGURE 16.4. *Adelphi* (1979), cloth, foam, gesso, rubber, rhoplex, wood, 30½″ x 68½″ x 13″, by Harmony Hammond (b. 1934). Reprinted with permission from The National Museum of Women in the Arts/Gift of Lily Tomlin.

into stills from Hollywood movies. These images transform the narrative by making lesbian presence real and by challenging heterosexist assumptions.

Kiss and Tell, a collective of three lesbian artists from Canada, created an interactive photographic installation called *Drawing the Line* (1988). It included 100 photographs of lesbian sexuality, for which two of the collective members modeled and the third photographed. The photographs were arranged around the walls of the gallery, moving from tender, sensual images to those with increasing passion, and ending with sadomasochistic depictions. Women viewers were asked to write their responses on the walls, while men could respond in a book placed near the end of the exhibit. Viewer response to each image varied considerably. The exhibit raised questions about the difference between pornography and eroticism, power and trust, pleasure and pain, objectivity versus subjectivity, and sexual activity versus sexual representation.

Numerous women interested in spiritual concerns create works that include Goddess-based imagery as a different means of confronting gender inequity. Cultures that celebrated goddesses often affirmed women by providing a full and varied range of woman-oriented symbols. Through study of examples such as the numerous Eurasian Mother Earth figures carved in stone between 25000 and 5000 B.C., the matriarchal Minoan civilization on Crete in 3000 B.C., the Goddess temples of Malta, the goddesses of ancient Egypt, Greece, and Rome, and the varied images of Mary, we can understand that gender roles are not fixed but change over time. "The Great Goddess" issue of *Heresies* so clearly addressed women's needs that within four months of its publication in 1978, the entire edition of 4,000 sold out and a reprint was required.

In addition to her work honoring contemporary women, Mary Beth Edelson has created a large body of work celebrating the Goddess. During private rituals that she photographed and later made drawings of, Edelson pictured herself as the Goddess in a series called *Woman Rising*. These images show woman as powerful, sexual, and energetic. Her public *performance art* usually occurs within an installation of her design and involves other participants and viewers. Two of Edelson's public performances, *Your 5,000 Years Are Up!* and *Memorials to 9,000,000 Women Burned as Witches in the Christian Era*, focused on the problems women have experienced under the patriarchy and their ability to overcome them. Through these works she endeavors to provide empowering symbols for herself and other women.

Nancy Spero and Betsy Damon also looked to the past to find affirming Goddess symbols for women in their work. Spero, whose scroll-like paper pieces are made with collage, hand-stamped prints, and paint, often juxta-poses images of goddesses from a variety of cultures with active contem-porary women. These nonhierarchical, cinematic arrangements of figures, combined with text, place woman in the role of protagonist. For her 1977 New York City street performance, *The 7,000-Year-Old Woman*, Damon modeled her costume after the ancient, many-breasted figure of Artemis of Ephesus. In this ritualistic public performance, Damon wore hundreds of small, multicolored bags of flour as an archetypal symbol of women.

Ana Mendieta symbolically became Mother Earth in her private perfor-mances. In almost 200 works from the *Silhouetta Series*, she physically fused the shape of her body with the landscape using a variety of pro-cesses, and then photographed the results. The series included carving her silhouette into a hillside, blasting her form into a huge tree trunk with gunpowder, filling a carved-out earthen silhouette with flowers, and mod-eling her form with clay and mud.

Feminist spirituality often incorporates a belief in the interconnected-ness of life. Ecofeminism combines feminist beliefs with ecological con-cerns. Many artists have been involved in this movement and have used their work to affirm nature's importance. Michelle Stuart literally and symbolically incorporates the land into her work. In her pieces from the 1970s and 1980s she marked muslin-backed paper with earth and rocks from particular sites. The resultant earth-colored and textured large scrolls and books poetically symbolize those locations. Her ritualized rubbing and pounding of earth and stone into the paper allude to women's traditional activities such as grinding corn in a metate. In later works Stuart added photographic images of simple tools to her earthen paper pieces to more directly symbolize human interaction with the land.

Beginning in the late 1960s *earth artists* tried to counter the increasing commercialism of the art world by making work that was inseparable from the site for which it was designed. Nancy Holt is an earth artist who explores the larger implications of the geography of a specific site in her sculptures. A good example is *Sun Tunnels*, comprising four concrete pipes that are eighteen feet long and nine feet in diameter. The pipes, lying in Utah's Great Basin Desert, are arranged in an X configuration. The tunnels frame the rising and setting of the sun at the summer and winter solstices. The top halves of the tunnels are drilled with holes in the arrangement of constellations seen at the site. The variation in hole size corresponds to the magnitude of each hole's related star. During the day and on bright nights, the constellations appear as spots of light that move across the inner surface of the tunnels. *Sun Tunnels* frames the desert's vastness. The structure's ability to mark the shift from day to night and to reflect the change of seasons, as well as its similarity in function and scale to ancient observatories such as Stonehenge, result in a blend of scientific and romantic associations that enhances viewers' appreciation of that particular site and the environment in general.

An increasing number of artists are not content merely to sensitize their audiences to the environment; they want their work to effect change. Linda Hull—with the help of biologists and zoologists—designs and locates her sculpture primarily for the benefit of animals. For instance, in response to the fact that power lines were killing large numbers of birds of prey in Midwest prairies, Hull created a series called *Raptor Roost*. These tall, aesthetically pleasing sculptural *assemblages* provide a safe perch for eagles, owls, and hawks. In another series she created floating sculptures that provide a haven for waterfowl.

Mierle Laderman Ukeles transformed her early feminist awareness of the time-consuming maintenance activities she performed as wife and mother into performance pieces. This theme evolved into work that focused viewer attention on the maintenance systems of urban areas, primarily New York City, producer of 26,000 tons of garbage a day. As the unsalaried artist-in-residence for New York City's Department of Sanitation, she makes work that pays tribute to sanitation workers and increases viewer awareness of the department's work. The year-and-a-half long performance piece, *Touch Sanitation*, involved her attempt to shake the hand of the 8,500 sanitation workers in appreciation for their labor. *Flow City*, designed in 1983 as part of an upgrade of New York City's Marine Transfer Station, will provide a public observation area of the waste system; construction of a ramp from recycled materials; information about the environment and waste management; and views of the nearby Hudson River. Ukele's work raises consciousness about environmental concerns and directly integrates art into life.

Another area of feminist concern centers on modernist attempts to maintain a hierarchical separation between abstraction and decoration. Cubist-derived, modernist abstraction, linked to the "high" or fine arts tradition, has been described as male, virile, and spiritually and morally significant. Decoration, associated with the "low" arts or crafts, has been trivialized as woman's work, inferior, and merely beautiful, without transcendent qualities.

The *Pattern and Decoration* movement that began in the mid-1970s directly challenged the hierarchy of fine arts over crafts, Western over Third World art, and painting over weaving. The men and women in this movement sewed and painted on fabric with patterns appropriated from areas as diverse as Mexico, Turkey, and China to present a multicultural view of art and to challenge gender and ethnic biases. Joyce Kozloff and Miriam Schapiro were significant artists within this movement. Kozloff's works have a richness of color, variety of shape, and intricacy of pattern and line that purposely reflect Third World ceramic, architectural, and fiber folk art patterns. Although her early works involved paintings on canvas, in the mid-1980s she began making permanent ceramic tile installations for public spaces such as train stations and airports. Schapiro integrates fabric work by anonymous artists—including found embroidered handkerchiefs, samplers, and quilts—with printed fabric and paint into patchworked and painted pieces she calls "femmages." This name refers to women's traditional activities of sewing and quilting that parallel modernist collage. Her work honors and validates the accomplishments of women, who despite the demands and anonymity of their domestic roles created beautiful works of art.

Related to this concern with the decorative arts is an interest in the relative importance assigned to various art media. In the traditional art hierarchy, painting was considered the highest art form, followed by sculpture. Fiber, ceramics, and other craft media were considered relatively insignificant. Many feminist artists confronted this bias by adopting either nontraditional, nonart materials or craft media for their work. One of the most influential of these artists was Eva Hesse, who died of a brain tumor when she was only thirty-four years old. A 1972 memorial exhibition at the Guggenheim Museum contained examples of her visceral, vulnerable, limp, and erotic abstract forms, made with such materials as latex, fiberglass, string, and wire mesh.

Barbara Chase-Riboud is an African-American artist and author whose travels to Rome, Africa, and Asia influenced her sculptural forms and choice of media. In a series of sculptures created during the 1970s, complex organic bronze forms seem supported by a skirt of silk cords. The massiveness, strength, and hardness of the bronze forms contrast markedly with the soft, undulating, and supportive lower forms. While the fundamental concept of joining hard and soft materials was partially derived from African masks, her intent was to convey a new unity by combining dichotomies traditionally associated with masculine and feminine qualities and the "high" and "low" arts.

Another African-American artist whose choice of media challenged the traditional art hierarchy is Faith Ringgold. In the early 1970s Ringgold created lightweight fabric sculptures of figures and masks for performances that were more accessible to a wider audience than her paintings had been. The new works were easily transported, incorporated some of the African crafts processes she was teaching in her community, and allowed her to collaborate with her mother, a fashion designer and dress-maker. Most recently she has been making painted and dyed storybook quilts with a narrative content that conveys her sense of the African-American experience.

During the 1970s, many women painters embraced naturalism in opposition to the nonobjective styles of Abstract Expressionism and Minimalism. A significant number of these artists chose images that focused on the content of women's lives. Audrey Flack, initially an Abstract Expressionist, became an early and significant *Photorealist*. Her painting *Marilyn (Vanitas)* recalls the realism and symbolism of Dutch and Flemish vanitas. This still life includes photos of Marilyn Monroe, fruit, a rose, perfume, jewelry, and makeup. The fragile, temporary nature of beauty is implied by an hourglass, a calendar, a burning candle, and a stopwatch. Janet Fish, another Photorealist, is best known for highly rendered paintings of glasses filled with water and placed on mirrors. In these light-filled compositions, transparencies and reflections fracture the forms, creating an energetic and evenly distributed overall composition. Her works picture beauty within domestic spaces.

Finally, some feminist artists overtly attempt to affect audience awareness of political issues and create social change. An anonymous group of feminist artists known as the Guerrilla Girls has been actively fighting sexism and racism in the art world since 1985. The Museum of Modern Art's 1985 *An International Survey of Painting and Sculpture*, considered a showcase of the most important contemporary art, included only thirteen women out of the 169 artists chosen. In response, the newly formed Guerrilla Girls plastered the city with posters listing galleries, museums, and critics who gave little or no attention to women artists. One of their most notable posters includes a reproduction of Ingres's *Odalisque*, a nude woman seen reclining from the back. The Guerrilla Girls put a gorilla mask on her and included this text: "Do women have to be naked to get into the Metropolitan Museum? Less than 5 percent of the artists in the Modern Art Section are women, but 85 percent of the nudes are female." As the self-appointed "conscience of the art world," they continue to research art world statistics, create and distribute posters, billboards, and magazine ads, and give lectures that alert people to the inequities they find. To protect their individual careers as artists, these "guerrilla" artists work anonymously, wearing gorilla masks to avoid the repercussions they would face if identified.

May Stevens has created several painting series during her career that reflect the feminist belief that the personal is political. In the *Big Daddy* series (named after Big Daddy in the Tennessee Williams play *Cat on a*

Hot Tin Roof), she depicted men with phallic, missile-shaped heads symbolizing the abuse of power associated with patriarchal society. The men, based in part on her father, were surrounded by such symbols of abusive power as Ku Klux Klan and army uniforms, bulldogs, and weapons. In her later series, *Ordinary/Extraordinary,* she juxtaposes images of her mother with images of Rosa Luxembourg, an early twentieth-century German socialist leader and theorist who was jailed and later murdered. Stevens's mother, a poor working-class woman, was committed to a state mental hospital for most of her adult life. In these rich, painterly works Stevens combines images from both lives with text from Luxembourg's private letters, speeches, and political pamphlets. This series encourages reexamination of the forces that shape women's lives.

Suzanne Lacy is an artist who, since the 1970s, has made collaborative performance pieces with artists and nonartists, intending to raise the awareness of the general public about women's issues. *Three Weeks in May* was a very well publicized and complex combination of events. Actual rapes reported to the Los Angeles Police Department during a three-week period in 1977 were publicly recorded on a map daily. Additional public and private performances, rituals, and exhibitions were held; government, business, religious, and social service organizations helped publicize planned events, educate the public about rape, and create support structures for victims; and radio and television media provided extensive coverage of all related events.

Barbara Kruger, another artist whose works encourage the viewer to question social norms, combines appropriated photographic images with text. One typical work is a black-and-white photographic side view of a seated woman who appears to be pinned in a subservient position. Placed over the figure in bold letters are the words, "We have received orders not to move." Kruger's images encourage questions. Who gave the orders? What group does "we" represent? Why can't "we" move? Text used in other works also implies feminist concerns. "We won't play nature to your culture" questions the essentialist notion of women as inherently more intuitive and natural, and men as more rational and cultured. In another work Kruger combines the phrase, "Your gaze hits the side of my face" with a side view of a stone sculpture of a woman's head, referring to the objectification of women. Kruger's works also question values within the art world with such texts as, "When I hear the word CULTURE I take out my checkbook" and "You invest in the Divinity of the Masterpiece."

Feminist art is seen by some as one of many short-lived modern styles. Others view it as a movement with a radical social agenda which some consider utopian and naive. It is most useful, however, to consider the lasting impact feminist artists, critics, and art historians have had on the Western world of art. Feminist art emphasized content, social criticism, and personal narratives at a time when Modernist formalism was the norm. Stylistic eclecticism and the appropriation of imagery further challenged the Modernist ideal of formalist purity and the isolated artist-genius. Finally, the embracing of craft-related media and techniques, decoration, collaboration, and performance directly confronted long-established art hierarchies.

These visual qualities and concepts are all associated with *Postmodernism*, an eclectic approach in the visual arts that began in the 1980s. An international movement, now influential throughout the humanities, it rejects the hierarchical values of Modernism in favor of a blend of styles from far more varied historical and geographical sources. This far-reaching ideological shift, with its questioning of established existing fundamental assumptions and its demand for greater inclusiveness, may best reflect feminist art's influence and serve as its greatest legacy.

KEY TERMS

Classicism	Expressionism	performance art
Baroque	Constructivism	poststructuralism
genre	Dada	earth art
vanitas	Surrealism	assemblage
Rococo	Abstract Expressionism	Pattern and Decoration
Neoclassicism	Minimalism	Photorealism
Romanticism	Op Art	Postmodernism
Impressionism	feminist art	
Modernism	essentialism	

DISCUSSION QUESTIONS

1. Discuss four indicators of gender inequity in the twentieth-century art world.
2. Name two women, from two different centuries, whose life styles were an exception for their era. How did this difference enable them to succeed professionally?
3. Name a woman artist whose primary concern was to raise people's awareness of social problems. How did the media and images used enhance the message?
4. Discuss two women artists whose works show an interest in the natural world. Choose one from the twentieth century and one from an earlier century.

5. Compare and contrast two women artists who use nontraditional media.
6. Choose any work of art and critique it from a 1970s feminist viewpoint. Now assume a poststructuralist stance and critique the same work.

REFERENCES

Berger, John (1977). *Ways of seeing.* New York: Penguin Books.

Chadwick, Whitney (1985). *Women and the surrealist movement.* Boston: Little, Brown and Co.

Chadwick, Whitney (1990). *Women, art, and society.* London: Thames and Hudson.

Dickinson, Eleanor (1995). *Statistics: Gender discrimination in the art field.* Sponsored and distributed by National Artists Equity Association, Women's Caucus for Art, the Coalition of Women's Art Organizations, and California Lawyers for the Arts.

Greer, Germaine (1979). *The obstacle race.* New York: Farrar Straus Giroux.

Nochlin, Linda (1971). "Why have there been no great women artists?" In *Art and sexual politics*, Thomas Hess and Elizabeth Baker (Eds.). New York: Macmillan Publishing Co., pp. 1-39.

Olin, Ferris and Catherine Brawer (1989). "Career markers." In *Making their mark: Women artists move into the mainstream, 1970-85*, Nancy Grubb (Ed.). New York: Abbeville Press, pp. 203-230.

Index

Page numbers followed by the letter "t" indicate tables; those followed by the letter "f" indicate figures.

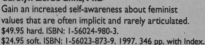